Make Your Safety Training Stick

Improve Retention and Get Better Results

Make Your Safety Training Stick

◆

Improve Retention and Get Better Results

Linda M. Tapp

American Society of Safety Professionals, 520 N. Northwest Highway, Park Ridge, IL 60068
Copyright © 2022 by American Society of Safety Professionals
All rights reserved. Published 2022.

American Society of Safety Professionals, ASSP, and the ASSP shield are registered trademarks of the American Society of Safety Professionals.

Limits of Liability/Disclaimer of Warranty
While the publisher and authors have used their best efforts in preparing this book, they make no representations or warranties with respect to the accuracy or completeness of the contents of this book, and specifically disclaim any implied warranties of merchantability or fitness for a particular purpose. The information is provided with the understanding that the authors are not hereby engaged in rendering legal or other professional services. If legal advice or other professional assistance is required, the services of a qualified professional should be sought.

Managing Editor: Rick Blanchette, ASSP
Editor: Cathy Lombardi
Text design and composition: Cathy Lombardi
Cover design: Janet Chen

ISBN-13: 978-0-939874-39-2 (print)
ISBN-13: 978-0-939874-40-8 (e-book)

Printed in the United States of America

30 29 28 27 26 25 24 23 22   1 2 3 4 5 6 7 8

Library of Congress Cataloging-in-Publication Data

Names: Tapp, Linda M., 1965- author.
Title: Make your safety training stick : improve retention and get better results / Linda M. Tapp.
Description: Park Ridge, IL : American Society of Safety Professionals, [2022] | Includes bibliographical references and index. | Summary: "The content in Make Your Safety Training Stick can help anyone delivering safety training take a giant leap forward in their ability to create and present great safety training programs that show real results. Safety professionals or anyone responsible for creating and delivering safety training can greatly improve their classes by applying learning science to their training programs. Topics include background information and techniques to help improve training class, research-based methods for increasing retention, benefits of applying concepts from the field of gamification to training initiatives, instructions for various safety training games, and online learning and image-based safety training topics"-- Provided by publisher.
Identifiers: LCCN 2022009322 (print) | LCCN 2022009323 (ebook) | ISBN 9780939874392 (trade paperback) | ISBN 9780939874408 (ebook)
Subjects: LCSH: Safety education, Industrial. | Industrial safety.
Classification: LCC T55.2 .T37 2022 (print) | LCC T55.2 (ebook) | DDC 658.3/82--dc23/eng/20220328
LC record available at https://lccn.loc.gov/2022009322
LC ebook record available at https://lccn.loc.gov/2022009323

Contents

Preface   xiii
List of Activities   xvii

Part 1: Beyond the Basics
Chapter 1 Training Alone Is Not Enough   3
- Retention and Transfer   3
- Memory Formation   4
- Categories of Learning   5
- Measuring Retention and Transfer   7
- The Learning Pyramid   9
- Trainee Attention   11

Chapter 2 Why Safety Training Is Different   17
- Safety Training Is Required by Standards   19
- Safety Training Is Repeated   22
- Training Diverse Audiences   24
- Highly Technical and Site-specific Training   25
- Practice Opportunities   25
- Proving Training Effectiveness   26

Chapter 3 Challenges and Methods of Knowledge Transfer   41
- The Training Transfer Problem   41
- Perception Barriers   42
- Near versus Far Transfer   43
- Four Factors Contributing to Poor Transfer   44
- Trainer Credibility   45
- Forgetting is Normal   45
- Primacy and Recency   46
- Mental Models   48
- Cognition   50
- The Nine Events of Learning   51
- Levers of Transfer Effectiveness   53

Chapter 4 Will They Remember?   57
- Three Deterrents to Remembering   57
- The Learning Culture   59
- Kirkpatrick Training Evaluations   63

Chapter 5 Accelerated Learning Principles   69
- Accelerated Learning versus Traditional Learning   70
- A Positive Affective State   71
- Stress and Learning   72
- The Importance of Fun   72
- Collaboration   73
- Activity-centered Learning   74

Chapter 6 Introduction to Instructional Design   79
- Instructional Design Systems   80
- Learning Theories   82
- Externally Created Training   87
- Andragogy   91

Chapter 7 Facilitation and Motivation   95
- Facilitation   95
- Emotions   100
- Training Environment   101
- Motivation   103
- Self-determination Theory   105
- Organizational Culture   107
- Peer Support   108
- Motivation to Pay Attention   109

Part 2: Make It Stick

Chapter 8 Preclass and Postclass Communication   117
- Preclass Communication   117
- Flipped Classrooms   118
- The Transtheoretical Model   119
- Communication of Objectives   120
- Influencers and Subject Matter Experts   121
- Management Support   122

- Advanced Organizers   122
- Postclass Communication   124
- Evaluations   124
- Organizational Goals   124
- Consistency   125
- Five-minute Refreshers   125
- Experts and Coaches   126
- Posttraining Follow-up   127
- On-the-job Support   128
- Job Aids   129
- Removing Constraints   129
- Publicize Success   131
- The Pygmalion Effect   131
- Reinforcement   132

Chapter 9   Making It Real   135
- Experiential Learning Activities   135
- Simulations   136
- Virtual Reality   137
- Augmented Reality   139
- Stories   140
- Adaptive Expertise   143
- Error-exposure Training   143
- Tabletop Exercises   148

Chapter 10   Repetition, Spacing, Retrieval Practice, and Interleaving   153
- Definitions   154
- Repetition   155
- Spacing   155
- Retrieval Practice   159
- Forgetting   162
- Interleaving   162

Chapter 11   Retrieval Methods   171
- Free Recall   172
- Desirable Difficulty   174
- The Value of Evaluation   175

- Retrieval Practice Options and Activities   176
- Covert Retrieval Practice   178
- Agendas   178

Chapter 12 Microlearning and Chunking   181
- Challenges and Benefits of Microlearning   181
- Microlearning Defined   183
- The Adaptability of Microlearning   183
- Three Elements of Microlearning   184
- Three Types of Engagement   185
- Six Types of Microlearning   185
- Designing Microlearning Programs   187
- Technology Reinforces Microlearning   188
- Microlearning Implementation   189
- Microlearning and Gamification   190
- Short Sims   191
- Chunking   191
- Cognitive Load   192

Chapter 13 Predicting Results and Testing   199
- Predicting Results   199
- Pause–Predict–Ponder   200
- Using Prediction in Safety Training   201
- Curiosity as a Training Tool   202
- Tests as Learning Events   203
- Forward Testing Effect   204

Chapter 14 Productive Failure   209
- Build Mental Models   209
- Vary Conditions of Practice   210
- The Benefit of Being Wrong   210
- Challenging Tests   211
- Stories of Failure   212
- Failure in Gamification   213
- Confidence Ratings   213

Chapter 15 Teamwork and Collaboration   217
- Benefits of Teams   217
- Forming Teams   218
- Problem Behaviors   221
- Collaboration   223
- Connectedness   223
- Toolbox Training   225
- Teamwork Activities   225

Chapter 16 Games, Gamification, and Technology   229
- Why Games Work   229
- Facilitation of Games   230
- Technology and Gamification   231
- Game Versatility   232
- Game Effectiveness   233
- Practical Information for All Games   233
- Fun and Games   234
- Serious Games   235
- Games as Evaluations   236
- Failure in Games   236
- Types of Players   238

Part 3: Applications and Activities
Chapter 17 Choosing the Right Activity   245
- Is it Appropriate?   245
- Cultural Differences   247
- Locus of Control   247
- Training Design and Outcomes   248
- Humor and Fun   249
- Game Mechanics   250
- Personas   250

Chapter 18 Error-Based Examples and Activities   257
- Ask the Experts   257
- Safety Sort Activities   260

- A Hazard Hunt   262
- Serious Error-based Games   263

Chapter 19 Sequencing Activities   267
- Sequencing Activities and Accelerated Learning   267
- Creating Sequencing Activities   268
- Debriefing Sequencing Activities   270
- Applying Variations to the Activity   271

Chapter 20 Sorting Activities   275
- How to Use Sorting Activities   275
- Sample Sorting Activities   277
- Sorting by Probable Cause   279

Chapter 21 Repetition and Retrieval Activities   283
- Getting Started   283
- Repetition through Pre- and Postclass Communication   285
- Flash Cards   286
- Free Recall   288
- Clickers and Feedback   292

Chapter 22 Summarizing Activities   297
- Summary Quizzes   297
- Creative Activities   297
- Sample Summarizing Activities   298

Part 4: Special Considerations

Chapter 23 Retention Techniques for Online Learning   313
- Distractions   314
- Testing   314
- Social Learning   315
- Digital Assistants   315
- Some Disadvantages of Online Training   316
- Learning Theory and Online Training   316
- Using Interactive Activities   319
- Infographics   321
- Grab Their Attention   322

- Video   323
- QR Codes   324
- Drag and Drop   325
- Other Considerations   328

Chapter 24 Image-Based Safety Training for Increased Retention   333
- Visual Aids   333
- Images Reinforce Learning   335
- Six Types of Drawings   336
- Infographics   342
- Illiteracy and Non-Native Speakers   343
- Sample Image-based Safety Training Activities   344
- Hazard Hunt   346

Chapter 25 Self-Learning and Retention Techniques for the Reader   359
- Microlearning   359
- Directness   360
- Retrieval Techniques   361
- Make it Public   362
- Feedback   363
- Experimentation   363

Index   367

Preface

While speaking with thousands of safety professionals around the world, one common frustration often surfaces. When delivering safety training, which often covers life-and-death information, safety professionals are unable to get and keep the attention of those attending their classes. All too often, training is attended by trainees looking only to meet compliance requirements. Further, trainees often seem to remember very little about the rules, policies, and safety procedures included in the training. Training like this is a waste of time, not only for the individual delivering the training but for those in attendance as well. The lack of safety training retention is an often-overlooked problem and, unfortunately, it can also lead to serious accidents and fatalities.

Many years ago, I was faced with the challenge of presenting a three-day safety leadership class to a group of chemical plant supervisors who were not excited about spending three full days in a class learning about soft skills. I decided to try to make this training experience less painful for them—and myself—by building in many class activities throughout the course. In fact, I facilitated learning activities approximately every ten to fifteen minutes in an attempt to keep the trainees engaged and paying attention. Much to my surprise, it worked! At first, the supervisors were not thrilled about having to get up, move around, discuss safety with their peers, and overall be active participants in their own learning. But, after the first day, several supervisors in attendance commented on how much they appreciated the chance to be involved, especially since they were expecting to sit and listen to a lecture, view endless PowerPoint slides, and watch off-the-shelf safety videos they had seen many times before. Due to the success of this class, I began adding interactive activities into all of my safety training classes, and soon I was spending even more time teaching other safety professionals how and why to do the same.

Who Should Read This Book

Safety professionals or anyone responsible for creating and delivering safety training can greatly improve their classes by applying learning science to their training programs. By planning for increased retention and opportunities to increase the transfer of knowledge to the workplace, individuals delivering safety training can help their training programs serve the purposes for which they were intended. This book provides the background and guidance to do just that. Most people delivering safety training have not been fortunate enough to study instructional design or adult learning theory in much depth. The content in this book can help anyone delivering safety training take a giant leap forward in their ability to create and present great safety training programs that show real results.

How To Read This Book

While the temptation might be to jump directly to the chapters focused on sample interactive games and activities, I suggest that time be spent reviewing why each of these games and activities work, based on learning science supported by dozens of research studies. This is important because you will undoubtedly want to make modifications to the sample activities presented so that the activities align closely with the topics you are presenting. In order to make sure your planned changes will not negatively affect the activity as designed, reading through the chapters in Part 1 and Part 2 is recommended before jumping in and adopting (or changing) the activities as described in Part 3 and Part 4.

Part 1 of this book, Beyond the Basics, includes background information and techniques to help improve any safety training class and highlights many of the challenges associated with training, providing suggestions for overcoming these challenges. Part 2, Make It Stick, goes deeper into research-based methods for increasing retention and introduces the benefits of applying concepts from the field of gamification to training initiatives. Part 3, Applications and Activities, provides detailed instructions for various safety training games that align with the ideas and principles covered in Part 2. Part 4, Special Considerations, delves into online learning and image-based safety training topics. Techniques for safety professionals to use themselves when trying to learn, remember, and apply new information can also be found here.

Finally, since this book is about how to increase attention, retention, and transfer of content, it makes sense to provide readers with specific activities to help them retain key information for each chapter. A great deal of information is included in these twenty-five chapters, including more than fifty methods to help increase learning and retention. To support any reader interested in remembering this information so that it can be more easily recalled when needed (e.g., transferred), a retention activity is provided in each chapter. These activities are optional but, if undertaken, will provide a way for readers to learn and apply the techniques described in *Make Your Safety Training Stick*.

List of Activities

The following is an alphabetical list of the activities and games found in *Make Your Safety Training Stick*.

1-2-3 (page 98)
Advanced Organizers (pages 122–123)
Agendas (page 178)
A–Z Race (pages 237–238, 301–303)
Braindump (pages 172–173, 289)
Covert Retrieval Practice (page 178)
Drag and Drop Activities (page 325)
Dunning-Kruger Effect Activity (page 62)
Fall Protection Safety Sequence (page 269)
Feynman Technique Activity (pages 62–63)
Free Recall (pages 172–173, 289–292, 330)
Hazard Hunt (pages 262, 319, 346–348)
Infographic Training Activities (pages 298–301, 322, 342)
Jeopardy Flashcard Activity (page 287)
Lone Ranger (page 277)
Make Your Mark (page 352)
Making Connections Activity (page 201)
Match Game (pages 278–279)
Metaphors/Analogies (pages 99–100)
Mind Maps (pages 78, 307–309, 365)
Movie Reviewer (page 273)
Nine Events of Learning Sequencing Activity (pp. 272–273)
One Big Thing (page 98)
Pause–Predict–Ponder (page 200)
Pictogram Partners (page 350)
Pin the Pain (pages 350–352)
Probable Cause Sorting Activity (pages 279–280)
QR Codes (page 110)
Questions (pages 176–177)

Quiz Creator (pages 227, 306–307)
Red Light/Green Light (page 98)
Safety Bingo (pages 290–292)
Safety Consultant for a Minute (page 226)
Safety Flash (pages 277–278)
Safety Lotería (pages 177–178, 344)
Safety Sort Activities (pages 275–281)
Scaffolding Sort Activity (page 276)
Seek and Find Activities (pages 325–326)
Sherlock (Safety) Holmes (page 309)
Shopping for Safety (pages 303–304)
Snowball Fight/Ask in the Airplane (pages 284–285)
Summary Group Grids (pages 305–306)
TABB Exercise (page 98)
Ten-cent Summary (pages 304–305)
Timeline (page 307)
Training Tutor (pages 177, 225–226)
What Happens Next? (pages 146–147, 200, 258)
While You Were Out (page 277)
Word Cloud (pages 202, 306)

Part 1

◆

Beyond the Basics

Chapter 1
Training Alone Is Not Enough

Safety training is a key part of most environmental health and safety programs. Training is often created and delivered because it is required by standards. Anyone who has come in contact with or even attended safety training, or training on any topic, knows that training alone is not enough to produce positive outcomes. There are many reasons why safety training alone may not be sufficient. These reasons may include lack of trainee motivation, unsupportive environments, lack of time and resources, and even lack of skilled trainers. All of these obstacles and more are described in the following chapters. More importantly, the solutions to overcome these hurdles are within reach and are also provided in this book. Techniques such as trainee involvement, improved training design, and better evaluations can easily be added to existing safety training programs and can make a big difference in the effectiveness of the safety training that is delivered.

Retention and Transfer

To be considered effective, safety training needs to serve its intended purpose (assuming the purpose is to have a positive effect on workplace safety and not just to meet the requirement of a standard), which is to prevent workplace accidents and injuries. *Training* can be defined as "the provision that is aimed at creating intentional learning processes that contribute to improving the performance of workers in their present job" (Esqueda 2008). Retention is commonly used to refer to how much something is remembered. One official definition states "the continued possession, use, or control of something," or "the fact of keeping something in one's memory." *Retention* is the storage of knowledge and skills in long-term memory so that trainees can retrieve (remember) the information when needed and apply it outside of the training environment.

The term transfer is closely related to retention but is slightly different. *Transfer* refers to how the knowledge and skills are put to use when needed or expected on the job. Transfer is a "magical link between classroom performance and something which is supposed to happen in the real world" (Swinney 1989). Another definition of transfer is "the effective and continuing application in the job environment of the skills and knowledge gained in a training context" (Baldwin and Ford 1988). Training retention is important because, without first retaining information, there would be no transfer, which is the ultimate goal. Instead of simply sharing information with trainees, safety trainers need to plan for and include ways to make safety training better in a deliberate effort to increase retention and transfer. Training should not be thought of as a standalone event but always as part of the bigger picture. Increased retention and transfer can make a real difference in helping safety drive performance and therefore meet organizational goals. The ultimate goal of training is not just to impart the information to trainees, or to meet a regulatory requirement, but to ensure the training has a true effect back in the workplace and ultimately on the overall goals and mission of the company or organization.

Memory Formation

Just as a training initiative is not a standalone event, neither is *memory formation*. It involves multiple processes that can be simplistically stated as (1) receive the information, (2) filter the information, (3) store the information, and (4) recall the information.

Receiving information refers to the process of hearing and learning new information in a training situation. In order for safety trainees to hear and learn new information, they must first pay attention; so getting trainee attention is one of the first priorities for a safety trainer. The importance of trainee attention is discussed later in this chapter. A facet of accelerated learning (discussed in detail in Chapter 5) is to get and keep the attention of the trainees. If trainees are not paying attention, there is no way the information can be retained and ultimately applied later on the job.

The filter stage refers to a trainee's unconscious or conscious choice whether or not to pay attention and make any attempt to remember the information he or she is hearing. How does the brain consciously or unconsciously make this decision? Two factors, emotional significance and relationship to information already known, are responsible for whether the new information makes it through the trainee's filter. The brain will have an easier time deciding how to store new information if there is a strong emotional link or a link to an existing memory (Russell 1999). Emotional links can be encouraged through trainers' actions, such as storytelling and making training as realistic as possible (both covered in Chapter 9). A trainer can help trainees connect the new information to what they already know through the use of debriefing and exercises (see Chapter 7) and evaluations (see Chapter 4).

In the context of training, the third stage—store the information—refers to safety trainees putting the new information into their long-term memory and creating a way to access it. When information is first learned, it is stored in short-term memory; the next step is to move it to long-term memory. The safety trainer can help trainees decide to store the new information in long-term memory by helping them see that something is worth remembering. Once the brain decides the information is worth remembering, it has to decide where to put it. Mental models, discussed in Chapter 3, can help or hamper the ability to learn something new when attempting to change behavior.

Finally, recalling the information refers to the ability to remember what was learned. When anyone tries to remember something previously learned, the brain attempts to look up the location of the memory with clues from the context and the request. The more clues that are available, the more easily a memory is recalled (Russell 1999). A few of the influences that determine whether a memory is recalled include primacy, recency, uniqueness, emotion and motivation, culture, visualization, chunking, and practice. These topics are discussed in Chapters 3, 5, 7, 4, 25, 12, and 10, respectively.

Categories of Learning

When a safety professional purposefully begins to create and deliver training, it is helpful to have an understanding of the two general categories of learning: surface learning and deep learning (Hollins 2017). *Surface learning* is what usually occurs in many traditional safety training classes and simply refers to gathering knowledge and facts and memorization. When trainees are expected to sit and listen to a lecture and then demonstrate knowledge by taking a multiple-choice quiz, this is most likely surface learning. On the other hand, *deep learning* involves deeper understanding and refers to the ability to see meaning. When a trainee has a deeper understanding and can see the meaning behind the standards, diagrams, technical terms, and policies that are presented during a training class, the training content will not only be more useful but will be remembered longer. Since trainees are unlikely to be sitting in a training class or in front of a computer at the moment they need to rely on the information learned in a training session, the ability to retain invaluable safety information and recall it later is paramount. Although it is expected and desired that trainees remember information when it is needed most, it is up to the safety trainer to deliver information in such a way that makes deep learning possible. In order to do this, it is important to understand the basics of instructional design (see Chapter 6) along with other ways trainers can help increase retention.

In addition to the two types of learning, safety professionals should also understand the two types of transfer. The first type of transfer is called *near transfer*. This occurs when a trainee learns something specific, such as how to work on a particular piece of machinery, and then goes back to work and is able to operate that particular piece of machinery or tool. Many people learn this way at home. If an individual needs to perform a specific home repair, a quick search online is bound to provide information that can be quickly learned and immediately applied. If that same repair were needed a year later, the individual would probably need to watch the instructional learning video again. Near transfer learning has its purpose but can cause problems in the workplace. If an employee moves to a new workstation or changes jobs where there are different but similar machines, the original training will be obsolete if the original experience involved only near transfer.

The other kind of transfer is called *far transfer*, and this applies to trainees learning theoretical principles or general information and procedures. These theoretical principles and general information and procedures are called declarative knowledge. When safety trainers present a class on lockout-tagout principles, they are often not presenting information on how to lock out and tag a particular piece of machinery but on the principles of energy control in general. Once trainees know the basic principles of lockout-tagout, they will be able to apply those principles and follow the proper and safe procedure no matter what type of equipment they are working on as long as it's a similar hazard. Although not always possible, or necessary for that matter, it can be beneficial to work toward presenting opportunities for far transfer.

Regardless of the type of learning and transfer that has taken place as a result of safety training, a plan to maintain that information is imperative.

Whether or not knowledge is maintained is not only controlled or determined by the design and delivery of the training class materials but by the involvement of trainers, trainees, direct supervisors, and management as well. The trainer or safety professional needs to make sure the design of the training is going to improve performance and meet the overall objectives and goals of the company. This is tied to instructional design, which is covered in detail in Chapter 6. The trainee has the responsibility to take what is learned in class and apply it back on the job. The supervisor or manager must make sure everyone involved is willing to support the trainee who is attempting to use these new skills and knowledge. For example, if a new hire attends safety training and learns the importance of separating incompatible chemicals, then returns to the job site and finds coworkers and supervisors are not following those safety procedures, the trainee is not going to have the support he or she needs to transfer that new learning to the workplace, and it will not stick. Further information on the responsibilities of the trainee, direct supervisor, and management are tied to the culture of an organization and are discussed in Chapter 4.

Measuring Retention and Transfer

Training retention and transfer rates are extremely difficult to measure. One popular estimate is that 10 percent of training is remembered (Georgenson 1982). Another study that looked at self-reports from thousands of trainees across a variety of companies estimated that the transfer rate was 40 percent (Burke et al. 2006). Another study showed results as high as 50 percent (Saks 2002). Whatever the correct retention percentage is, these levels are unacceptable when it comes to occupational health and safety.

It's important to pay attention to these rates, but it's more important to look at the amount of transfer. Without useful application of the training, it is simply a waste of time. When measuring the results of a training class, it is best to evaluate them using the formula: results = learning x transfer. A learning event, such as a training class, might get great evaluations, say an average of 95 based on trainee feedback and/or a high average grade on a final quiz, but if the transfer back to the job is zero, the overall results equal zero. No matter how good a training class is, if trainees cannot remember the information and apply it on the job, the training is worthless.

Training that has no effect is called *scrap training*, which means it was time and money wasted. In 2018, companies spent an average of $1,299 annually per employee on training, and individual trainees spent an average of 34 hours a year on formal learning—that's more than 4 full-time workdays (Association for Talent Development 2019). If training is not created and delivered in a way that enables trainees to remember what they learned, the money spent on training every year goes to waste. The pressure to show a return on investment (ROI) for training expenditures is never-ending, so scrap learning for any topic is problematic, but for occupational safety training, it can be disastrous. For many companies, return on investment is the most important metric, and measuring the ROI for training is notoriously difficult (Kong 2019), especially because it is so difficult to show a correlation between improved safety performance and the training investment. These difficulties are discussed further in Chapter 2.

If very little of the current safety training is remembered and used, then the ROI for most safety training is very low. So there is increased pressure to justify health and safety investments (Goldenhar et al. 2001). If much of the safety training that is delivered were not required by some type of standard, would it still be created and delivered, requiring workers to spend so much time away from work when minimal results can be shown? Probably not. Research suggests moderately and highly engaging training methods are, on average, more time consuming and possibly more expensive in the short term, but they are potentially less costly and more effective in the long term (Burke et al. 2006). Many of the techniques presented in this book offer safety professionals methods for providing greater learning engagement opportunities that are not necessarily more costly or more time consuming. In fact, many of the ideas for implementation discussed in the following chapters are inexpensive or free.

Like ROI and measures of retention, measuring the amount of training transferred back to the job also poses difficulties, but there are ways to do it. A variety of studies have attempted to measure the amount of training transfer, and the results have not been good. Generally, estimates of the amount of training transferred are extremely low, and some studies have shown transfer failure may be as high as 90 percent for some training courses (Foxon 1993). Some common measurement techniques include surveys of the trainees' supervisors, surveys of the trainees themselves, interviews with trainees or managers, and observations of the trainees back on the job. Many of the reports that are produced in a safety department can also identify improvement in trainee behavior. For example, if injury data shows the most common type of workplace injuries in a facility are small lacerations, and training was delivered on how to prevent hand injuries, the same injury data could be looked at 6 months or a year after training delivery to determine if any change had occurred.

Another gauge would be to look at inspection reports. If missing machine guards were a common inspection finding, inspection reports from several months or longer after the machine guarding safety training occurred could help determine if trainees actually used the new information on the job. While both of these types of analyses show promise for the measurement of transfer, it is difficult to isolate the cause of the improvements and therefore equally difficult to measure the true amount of transfer that occurred.

The Learning Pyramid

Many people have seen the learning pyramid at one time or another. It appears in various forms, but in general, it appears something like the pyramid shown in Figure 1.1.

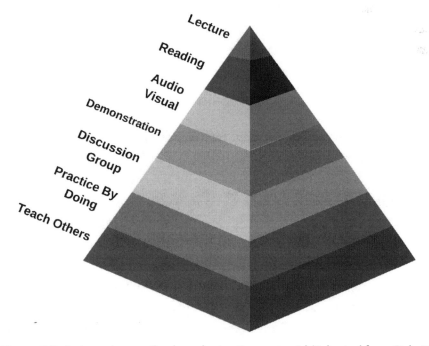

Figure 1.1 ✦ Learning methods and retention pyramid (Adapted from Dale 1946)

Statements such as "10 percent is remembered if XYZ is done" or ". . . percent is remembered if this delivery method is used" are commonly stated and restated, but this popularly shared information isn't based on research (Thalheimer 2018). Most people agree that the learning pyramid looks basically like this, but actual percentages of learning or retention based on each type of delivery have not been proven. The pyramid can provide a general guide on effectiveness of delivery methods or retention rates and can be used as a general predictor of the relative effectiveness of different delivery methods, but that is all it is—a general predictor—and one of many factors to consider.

Regardless of actual percentage, retention of training material varies with the training method. Numerous studies have shown that lecture as a training delivery method results in the lowest amount of retention when compared to other instructional methods. For example, one study found that retention after 3 days is 10 percent from lecture and 20 percent from demonstration (Moore 2005).

The top of the pyramid illustrates that "lecture" as a delivery method provides the least amount of retention, and unfortunately, this is often where safety training starts and stops. At the bottom, "teaching others" is shown to be the delivery method that provides the greatest amount of retention. Regardless of the actual percentages associated with retention of each of these delivery methods, lecture undoubtedly provides the least amount of memory retention (Hollins 2017) and will not be as effective in providing meaningful training as the methods shown toward the bottom of the pyramid. The pyramid shows the many options available for delivery of safety training. It also shows how training can move along a continuum from the most passive, information-based methods to more interactive and engaging methods. There is ample evidence in the training literature that active approaches to learning are superior to less active approaches (Frese and Zapf 1994).

The most engaging methods of safety training are, on average, approximately three times more effective than the least engaging methods in promoting knowledge and skill acquisition, and the most engaging methods of safety training are, on average, most effective in reducing negative outcomes, such as accidents. The greater effectiveness of more engaging, hands-on training in reducing negative outcomes and increasing knowledge acquisition lends support to researchers and practitioners advocating for the design and implementation of learner-centered, participatory approaches to worker safety and health training (Burke et al. 2006). The interactive training activities provided throughout this book, and in particular, those found in Chapters 18–22 are designed to increase engagement and hopefully have the desired effect of reducing workplace accidents.

Trainee Attention

If safety trainers are asked to name their biggest challenges, the answers usually involve getting and keeping trainee attention. In today's world there are more distractions than ever before. It's a safe bet that most trainees have their mobile phones with them, possibly even on the desk or table in front them throughout the training class, and this one little piece technology alone can make it very difficult to stay focused.

No matter how hard a safety trainer tries to select or create a safety training program that will be best for all trainees, there is no one-size-fits-all model that's guaranteed to capture the attention of every learner in the room. Although the idea of preferred learning styles has been debunked by numerous studies (Furey 2020), different trainees prefer to participate and learn in different ways. Because of this, it's important to incorporate several different methods of presenting information in a safety training class. Diversifying these methods will not only ensure that trainees stay involved, it will also increase the likelihood that trainees will connect with and pay attention to new learning content.

Studies have shown that attention is extremely important in motivating action. *Immersion* is the term that describes a neurological state produced when someone is attentive to an experience that also generates emotional resonance (Zak 2020). Other studies have been done to determine what motivates someone to act in a particular way, and these studies have shown that an experience provokes action when two networks activate in the brain. The first network causes people to pay attention to the experience. Attention is metabolically costly, and the brain is stingy with its resources, so attention must be earned. The second brain network necessary to establish value generates emotional resonance with the experience and is associated with the release of oxytoxin. This network tags the experience as important and causes the brain to store the information in a way that makes it easily accessible. Experiences that tap into emotions lead to both a higher likelihood of immediate actions and easier recall weeks or months later (Zak 2020).

Safety training activities designed to get and maintain attention and be emotionally significant can lead to immersion. These experiences will more likely be stored in long-term memory and will also be easier to recall in the future. There are wearables on the market that can determine the activity of the nerves surrounding the heart to see how much immersion is occurring, but these are not realistic tools for most safety trainers. Safety trainers will have to rely on other methods of observation and evaluation to determine how engaged safety trainees are during particular training experiences. Evaluation methods are discussed in Chapter 4.

Stories are one way to create an emotional response that leads to immersion, and storytelling as a way to increase retention is discussed in greater detail in Chapter 9. Studies have shown that when using stories the amount of immersion is greatest at the arc of the story, so if a 20-minute story is used in a safety training presentation, trainees are likely to pay more attention at the height of the story and pay less attention at the beginning and the end, which means trainee attention may fade off (Zak 2020). One way to reverse the problems that occur with this type of immersion and the trailing off of attention is to build in opportunities for trainee participation. Interactive activities and training materials used during learning are key parts of making safety training stick, as discussed in various chapters throughout this book.

Another reason trainees may not pay attention is because they don't believe the training applies to them. Perhaps they have thirty years of experience and think they know everything. Perhaps they think the safety training topic is on a procedure, skill, or situation they would never realistically face in their day-to-day job. Even young trainees could think they don't need to pay attention if they sat through the same class several years in a row. If trainees are not paying attention, they are never going to remember the information for very long after the class is finished. The safety trainer is responsible for helping trainees see why the information is important and how it applies to them. This can be done through a planned debriefing exercise.

Debriefing, an essential part of all training activities, is discussed along with accelerated learning principles in Chapter 7. In addition to failing to convince trainees that the materials are applicable to their day-to-day job, trainees often fail to transfer the new information to the workplace if they do not feel it is relevant, and in reality, often it may not be. In a world of compliance training and mandated topics, trainees may be presented with material that does not apply to their job.

For example, OSHA's electrical safety standard (1910.332) requires that anyone exposed to parts of electric circuits operating at 50 volts or more to ground be trained in electrical safety. This includes people that are not electricians but still meet those requirements. Company maintenance people, such as painters, would need to attend this training if they occasionally need to paint in areas that have electric circuits operating at 50 volts or more. Although painters face a risk of electric shock in these situations, without the trainer helping them to understand why it is important, they may think this type of training is unnecessary and will not see the importance of attending and actively participating. Without seeing a clear reason for being in the training class, the painters may have a difficult time focusing and realizing how they can apply the information in their daily work.

Trainees will also have trouble paying attention enough to remember the content of safety training classes if they are bombarded with too much information. Particularly in training classes mandated by an outside body, the trainer may have little control over the amount of material that must be presented to the trainees in a short amount of time. Good instructional design, as discussed in Chapter 6, and breaking down information into chunks, as described in Chapter 12, are good places to start in helping to reduce the chance of information overload that can occur in these situations.

Trainees also forget because of learning interference. Interference is discussed more in Chapter 4. For example, if a new hire attends an 8-hour training class on chemical safety on Monday and then on Tuesday attends another 8-hour class on forklift safety and on day three attends another safety class on security procedures, the information covered on day one may interfere with the information covered on day three. Sometimes different topics can work well together and sometimes they can make learning more challenging. For example, presenting chemical safety on day one and general lab safety on day two could have a beneficial effect since those topics are somewhat related.

Although training is often the first type of corrective action suggested when something goes wrong, training may not be the answer. If an absence of training is truly the cause of whatever happened, training by itself, especially in its traditional form, is not enough. Safety training, as many have experienced, is often quite different from what an effective learning transfer experience looks like. A plan to increase retention is critical and cannot be left to luck. "Training is expensive to design and deliver; it should be the last, not the first, intervention. Even if training is mandated, it should be accompanied by improved work procedures, feedback systems, or other interventions" (Broad 2007).

Review and Retention Activity

This learning and retention activity is structured as a fill-in-the-blank activity at the end of learning. Fill-in-the-blank quizzes as a learning and retention technique are described in Chapter 11 on retrieval methods.

1. Training is meant to create _____ learning processes that contribute to improving the performance of workers in their present job.

2. _____ is commonly referred to as how much something is remembered.

3. _____ refers to how knowledge and skills are put to use when needed or expected on the job.

4. _____ learning is more likely to be remembered longer because it involves deeper understanding and the ability to see meaning.

5. When measuring the results of a training class, it is best to evaluate it using the following formula: _____

6. _____, as a delivery method, generally provides the least amount of retention.

7. One of the biggest challenges of safety trainers when delivering content is getting and keeping _____ of trainees.

8. A facilitated discussion that occurs after a training activity to help learners make sense of what occurred and how it applies to them is called _____.

Activity Answers

1. intentional
2. retention
3. transfer
4. deep
5. results = learning x transfer
6. lecture
7. attention
8. debriefing

References

Association for Talent Development (ATD). 2019. "State of the Industry" report. Alexandria, VA: ATD Press.

Baldwin, T. T., and J. K. Ford. 1988. "Transfer of Training: a review and directions for future research." *Personnel Psychology*, 41(1):63–105.

Broad, Mary L. 2007. *Beyond Transfer of Training: Engaging Systems to Improve Performance*. San Francisco, CA: Pfeiffer.

Burke, M. J., S. A. Sarpy, K. Smith-Crowe, S. Chan-Serafin, R. O. Salvador, and G. Islam. 2006. "Relative Effectiveness of Worker Safety and Health Training Methods." *American Journal of Public Health*, 96(2):315–324.

Dale, E. 1946. *Audiovisual Methods in Teaching*. New York: Dryden.

Esqueda, O. J. 2008. *International Encyclopedia of Adult Education*, Vol. 11. Leona M. English, ed. Basinstoke, New York: Palgrave Macmillan.

Foxon, M. 1993. "A process approach to the transfer of training, Part 1." *Australian Journal of Educational Technology*, 9(2):130–143.

Frese M., and D. Zapf. 1994. "Action as the core of work psychology: a German approach." In H. C. Triandis, M. D. Dunnette, and L. M. Hough, eds., *Handbook of Industrial and Organizational Psychology*, pp. 271–340. Palo Alto, CA: Consulting Psychologists Press.

Furey, W. 2020. 'The Stubborn Myth of "Learning Styles."' *Education Next*. April 7, 2020. https://www.educationnext.org/stubborn-myth-learning-styles-state-teacher.

Georgenson, D. 1982. "The Problem of Transfer Calls for Partnership." *Training and Development Journal*, 36(10):75–78.

Goldenhar, L. M., A. D. LaMontagne, T. Katz, C. Heaney, and P. Landsbergis. 2001. "The Intervention Research Process in Occupational Safety and Health: An Overview from the National Occupational Research Agenda Intervention Effectiveness Research Team." *Journal of Occupational and Environmental Medicine*, 43:616–622. doi: 10.1097/00043764-200107000-00008.

Hollins, P. 2017. *The Science of Accelerated Learning: Advanced Strategies for Quicker Comprehension, Greater Retention, and Systematic Expertise*. Scotts Valley, CA: CreateSpace Independent Publishing Platform.

Kong, J. 2019. "Why is it difficult to measure the ROI of a training program." The International Institute for Innovative Instruction Blog, February

13, 2019. https://fuse.franklin.edu/cgi/viewcontent.cgi?article=1072&context=i4blog.

Moore, K. D. 2005. *Effective Instructional Strategies: From Theory to Practice*. Thousand Oaks, CA: Sage.

Russell, L. 1999. *The Accelerated Learning Fieldbook*. Jossey-Bass. San Francisco, CA: Pfeiffer.

Saks, A. 2002. "So What Is a Good Transfer of Training Estimate? A reply to Fitzpatrick." *Industrial Organizational Psychologist*, 39(3):29–30.

Swinney, John M. 1989. "Who's Gonna Turn the Crank OR Implementing Training or Performance Improvement Projects." *Performance and Instruction*, 28(1):3337.

Thalheimer, Will. 2018. "Debunk This: People Remember 10 Percent of What They Read." Association for Talent Development. May 4, 2018. https://www.td.org/insights/debunk-this-people-remember-10-percent-of-what-they-read.

Work-Learning Research. 2015. "Mythical Retention Data—The Corrupted Cone." Work-Learning Research Blog. https://www.worklearning.com/2015/01/05/mythical-retention-data-the-corrupted-cone.

Zak, P. J. 2020. "At Attention." *TD Magazine*, September 2020:43–47.

Chapter 2
Why Safety Training Is Different

Before reading this chapter, complete the Review and Retention Activity on page 37.

The key to successful employee development is the retention of newfound knowledge that can be immediately applied to on-the-job performance (Taylor 2017). While this is a true statement for any training delivered to the workforce, it is especially important for safety training. According to the Association for Talent Development, the three most frequent types of training delivered in 2019 include manager and supervisory training (14%), mandatory and compliance training (13%), and interpersonal skills (10%). The other training areas consist of job- or industry-specific training and new employee orientation (Ho 2019). Additionally, approximately 25 percent of an employee's total formal training time is allotted to safety-related topics (Waehrer and Miller 2009). Therefore, it is probable that mandatory and compliance training, such as that which is dedicated to safety, is experienced by most of the workforce at some time during the year.

Safety training can be delivered through a variety of mediums. Most people have attended safety training delivered in the traditional lecture format. Unfortunately, dry, boring safety training lectures are what give much of safety training a bad name. Safety training may also be delivered online (especially now with so many people working from home), on the job, through self-study, and through hands-on activities.

In contrast to supervisory and leadership training, as well as training on interpersonal skills, the same type of negative consequences will not result if the safety training information is not retained. If the information presented in a sales training class is quickly forgotten, the consequences might be lack of sales and ultimately loss of a job. If the information presented in a computer skills or software class is forgotten, the consequences may be the loss of the ability to get work done and coding errors. If information presented to attendees in a class on communication skills is not remembered, the negative effect may result in misunderstandings. All of these examples of poor performance due to lack of retention would not be positive, but they do not begin to compare to the types of negative consequences that can occur if safety training information is not remembered. Consider the following:

- Poor retention of training on how to use fall protection equipment resulted in falls from heights.
- Back injuries occurred after a lecture on safe lifting that did not involve active involvement of trainees.
- Electric shocks occurred because employees were asked to work around live electrical equipment after attending training they did not think applied to them.
- Chemical burns occurred because trainees did not remember the correct type of PPE to use when cleaning up a spill.
- Employees became unconscious when working inside confined spaces because they did not remember how to read an oxygen level meter properly.
- A piece of heavy machinery failed because a safety check was not completed, although it was covered in training, and the employee passed the quiz at the end of class.

"Incident investigation, empirical research, and industry reports consistently identify training-related deficits as key contributors to catastrophic safety events across a wide range of industries" (Skogdalen 2011). Research conducted by Waehrer and Miller suggests "Safety training has real safety effects on days-away-from-work incidents, especially in smaller firms" (Waehrer and Miller 2009).

In addition to the financial impact of scrap safety training, discussed in Chapter 1, the biggest and most detrimental costs associated with poor safety training stem from a lack of productivity, which includes mistakes that must be corrected and costs associated with both minor and major accidents. To achieve productivity goals with a minimum number of accidents (preferably zero), better training is needed on the safe use of equipment and tools and on safe work practices to minimize injuries, but this training is only going to help achieve those goals if designed and delivered in a way that is most effective for the trainees.

Safety Training Is Required by Standards

The Occupational Safety and Health Administration (OSHA) is charged with enforcing standards developed under the Occupational Safety and Health Act of 1970 in an effort to ensure safe and healthy working conditions. These standards include many requirements for training. (For a quick reference, see the list of OSHA standards that require training at the end of this chapter). Depending on the industry, various types of training are required by different rules and regulations. In addition to Federal OSHA, safety training may be mandated by states, countries, or specific industries. Internally, specific safety training also may be mandated within a corporation.

Many OSHA standards include explicit safety and health training requirements to ensure workers have the required skills and knowledge to do their work safely. For example, OSHA's 1910.1030 standard on bloodborne pathogens requires employees to receive bloodborne pathogen training at the time of initial assignment (and at least annually thereafter). OSHA believes training is the central part of every employer safety and health program, protecting workers from injuries and illnesses. The document published by OSHA titled "Training Requirements in OSHA Standards" states that it is "a good idea to keep a record of all safety and health training" since one of the first questions an incident investigator will ask is "Did the employee receive adequate training to do the job?" Although OSHA expressed the best of intentions with this statement, the fact that training was delivered is not enough—it doesn't tell us that trainees were trained appropriately and are likely to use that training when needed. Trainees may have attended a training class but paid little or no attention throughout the class, so the fact that a trainee *received* training says little about the type of training received or how much of the training was retained and therefore was able to be transferred back on the job. If a trainee is not able to remember any of the training information and/or is not able to transfer it back to the job, it may not be the fault of the trainee; instead, the fault may be poor training design and/or delivery.

The training requirements in OSHA's standards are a good start toward ensuring that training is being provided when required, but implementing other suggestions found throughout this book, based on learning and development research, will increase the likelihood that potentially life-saving safety training is meeting the goal of reducing injuries and accidents. OSHA has many different types of educational material available in a variety of languages that can be used to complement safety training. These materials are in the form of brochures, fact sheets, posters, small laminated cards, newsletters, and more. These materials should not be used as the primary method of providing information to trainees and are not considered safety training. It is better to use this type of information as reinforcement after a trainee has completed a training program. Chapter 8 discusses methods for reinforcement in greater detail.

OSHA training requirements are specific to different types of hazards since there is no one set of general safety training principles that can apply to the variety of hazards found in the many different types of workplaces. Specific training requirements often include the exact content that must be covered, how often and when the training must be conducted, how long it must last, how it must be documented, the qualifications a trainer must have, and how the material must be delivered.

An example of very specific requirements required by OSHA can be found in the *Hazardous Waste Operations and Emergency Response* (HAZWOPER) regulations that have been around since 1990 and require several levels of training based on the hazards faced. HAZWOPER is also different in a good way from the other standards listed here since it points out the benefits of learning from past experiences and using those as a way to improve safety training. In Chapter 9, "Make it Real," the importance of using realistic situations and stories is discussed further, but section 1910.120(e)(4) of the OSHA HAZWOPER standard gets it right.

The American National Standards Institute has two standards related to safety training. The first, Z490.1, is titled *Criteria For Accepted Practices In Safety, Health And Environmental Training*, and a second similar standard, Z490.2, developed to work in conjunction with the first, provides additional guidance on safety training delivered as e-learning. The idea behind the ANSI standards is to create criteria for good environmental health and safety training. Safety trainers can learn a lot from these standards and improve their training so it provides value as intended. The standards help safety trainers to understand best practices for developing, delivering, evaluating, and keeping records/documentation of safety training.

According to the ANSI standard for safety, health and environmental training (ANSI/ASSP Z490.1), "the trainer shall have some measure of subject-matter expertise as well as an expertise in training delivery." For many topics, it is not uncommon that a full-time company trainer delivers the actual training without any actual experience in the topic being presented. While this may work for workplace issues such as communication skills or sales skills, it is much harder to do with credibility when delivering safety and health information. The ANSI standard affirms as much.

A major part of the ANSI standard relates closely to the content of Chapter 6 and to the development of environmental health and safety training. The standard spells out the need for elements such as a needs assessment, learning objectives, appropriate content, evaluation methods, and a plan for continuous improvement. These important topics are covered throughout this book in various chapters. The standard also requires that training is delivered by competent trainers in an appropriate training environment. When it comes to safety training, the actual environment where training is delivered may be more challenging than for other types of training. If safety training must be delivered to a construction project team, and all of the trainees are on site all day, every day, modifications will most likely need to be made.

The importance of training class evaluation is discussed in Chapter 4. The ANSI standard for safety, health, and environmental training includes provisions for evaluating the program itself, the training process, and the training results. Section 4.5 of the ANSI standard states "the training provider shall develop a strategy for evaluating the trainees' achievement of the learning objective(s)." Section 6.0 of the standard, in particular Section 6.2.3, goes much deeper into evaluation with similar guidance as provided in Chapter 4, which focuses on the evaluation of the content based on the successful application of it by the trainee (i.e., the transfer back to the workplace). The end goal is that trainees use the information presented to them in a training class, and by focusing on evaluating the effects of the training after the training has been completed, a trainer can understand the true value of the training that was presented.

An additional positive benefit of mandatory compliance training was shown by some studies to result in slightly better outcomes than voluntary training (Salas et al. 2012). Additionally, some companies also receive worker's compensation premiums or other insurance discounts for instituting prevention initiatives, including safety training programs. Another positive is that training transfer rates are higher for technical courses than training on soft skills. In technical training classes, trainees typically must apply what they learned immediately upon returning to work, and this makes transfer easier (Pollock and Jefferson 2012). These factors can work to make a safety trainer's job easier to a point, but additional steps are still needed to make safety training truly effective.

Also somewhat beneficial is the fact that some types of compliance training, such as safety courses, often have strict disciplinary procedures as part of the company's safety program. A company may have a rule stating that anyone overriding a machine guard will be immediately fired. If a worker has previously attended a training class on machine guarding and not only learned machine guarding safety rules and techniques but also learned about related disciplinary procedures, there is a high likelihood the trainee will follow what he or she learned in class. Not all types of training have this type of *stick* to ensure training is applied on the job, and although a *stick* such as the threat of discipline is not necessarily the best way to get safety trainees to pay attention during a training class and use what they learn during their day-to-day work, it can provide an added incentive for safety trainees to transfer the information back to the job.

Unlike other types of training, such as sales training, safety training generally isn't seen as something that contributes to the bottom line. If 100 salespeople were trained on a new sales technique, it would be easy to measure the impact in real dollars. Although a dollar amount could be put on the amount saved or added to the bottom line by a particular type of safety training class, this is rarely done, most likely because it is so difficult to do. Without this *proof*, safety training may only be conducted at a company because it is required, and this is not a good mindset for those attending a training class or those delivering it.

Safety Training Is Repeated

The nature of many safety training courses has led to requirements (or at least recommendations) for annual *refresher* training. If training content were remembered for a longer period of time, would refresher training even be needed? If the original training is not remembered the first time around, why would the second time be any different? Simply hearing something twice does not automatically ensure it will be remembered longer. Trainees may arrive at a refresher class already knowing a good amount of the content and may see refresher training as a waste of time, and not only the trainees but their supervisors as well.

The following are a few examples of OSHA-required refresher training:

- *Occupational Noise Exposure* (1910.95[k][2]), requires that the noise exposure training program be repeated annually for every employee included in the hearing conservation program.
- *Hazardous Waste Operations and Emergency Response* (1910.120[e][8]) requires 8 hours of refresher training annually.
- *Respiratory Protection* (1910.134) training is required every year and (1910.134[k][5][ii]) requires training be provided when there are "inadequacies in the employee's knowledge or use of the respirator that indicate that the employee has not retained the requisite understanding or skill; or (iii) Any other situation arises in which retraining appears necessary to ensure safe respirator use."
- *Bloodborne Pathogens* (1910.130[g][2][ii]) requires annual training.
- Various standards related to individual chemicals, including vinyl chloride (1910.1017), inorganic arsenic (1910.1018), lead (1910.1025), cadmium (1910.1027), benzene (1910.1028), acrylonitrile (1910.1045), ethylene oxide (1910.1047), formaldehyde (1910.1048), methylenedianiline (1910.1053), and 1,3-Butadiene (1910.1051), all require annual training.

Note: This list is not all-inclusive of standards (federal, state, or otherwise) that require annual or refresher training.

Although these standards are well intentioned, several aspects of the requirements warrant further discussion. The HAZWOPER standard requires 8 hours of refresher training. Where does this 8-hour requirement come from? What if the training could be covered effectively in 6 hours? Like initial HAZWOPER training, which is to be 24 hours, there doesn't seem to be an explanation for the required length of class. If a trainer only needs to spend 20 hours to get key information across, the other 4 hours are a waste of everyone's time. Having trainees experience 4 hours of filler content will leave them with bad expectations of future training classes, which can lead to low motivation and lack of attention. Unfortunately, a safety trainer's hands may be tied in this regard.

The respiratory protection standard requires retraining when the employee is found to be incorrectly wearing a respirator. This type of requirement for retraining is similar to sending an employee to be retrained as a punishment for not following safety procedures. While the employee can certainly benefit from interventions to improve his performance, sending him back to a class, where he didn't learn the information the first time, or using retraining as a punishment to encourage workers to follow safety procedures in the future, is a waste of time and money (but in this case will enable the company to meet the requirements of the standard).

Training Diverse Audiences

Safety training is often delivered to a particular group based on job title or work area. This could mean that everyone working in maintenance would be required to attend some type of electrical safety training, for example. Administrative assistants, upper management, and actual electricians could all end up sitting in on a basic electrical safety class. Additionally, the attendees may have vastly different levels of education, experience, and training. Terminology and abbreviations very familiar to an electrician may require added explanation for others. When this type of explanation is occurring, more knowledgeable trainees will likely tune out while the less knowledgeable may also be tuning out but for a different reason.

In some industries, it is not uncommon that employees who work side by side every day speak two or more languages. Training these groups can be particularly tricky since translating training materials or providing a translator is not always possible. Additionally, the cultures of these diverse groups may affect the type of training activities that will be successful. All of these differences require extra attention when preparing safety training.

Although it is difficult to find statistics on the number of accidents that are the result of poor or missing training, research has linked the increased number of accidents in the Hispanic workforce to a lack of training materials in Spanish (OSHA n.d.). People learn best when the training material is presented to them in their native language. Otherwise, their brain must first convert it to their own language and then go through the process of trying to learn it (Hale 2014). It is estimated that language barriers are a contributing factor in 25 percent of workplace accidents (De Jesus-Rivas et al. 2016). Since 2011, foreign-born Hispanic workers experienced almost double the amount of fatalities as native-born Hispanic workers (BLS 2022). Foreign-born workers are generally less proficient in English than native-born laborers (Fernández-Esquer et al. 2014). While OSHA cannot force any company to provide training in a language other than English, OSHA compliance officers do check whether training is provided in a language trainees can understand, and employers who fail to properly train their employees are subject to citations and penalties (Hale 2014).

Highly Technical and Site-Specific Training

Safety training also often involves highly technical terminology and can be very site specific. An off-the-shelf training program, such as one available for learning new software or communication skills, will not always work for safety training. Showing a generic safety training program can sometimes be as bad as not showing anything at all. For example, showing a safety training video about warehouse safety that takes place in a large sprawling warehouse full of self-driven automatic robotic forklifts would not be very effective for a small shop with one loading dock and one forklift driver. Off-the-shelf chemical safety training that mentions flammable storage but does not name the specific flammables used by the trainees or the specific flammable storage locations used in the work area will not be very meaningful and therefore be quickly forgotten. A statement such as "all flammables must be stored in approved flammable storage units" means nothing to trainees without specific details that make the information meaningful and important to them.

Off-the-shelf safety training may contain information presented out of context, and when this happens, it is even more difficult for trainees to make a connection to what they already know and experience. It is important, as a trainer, to remember to show how the specific training class fits into the overall picture; specifically, what cues in the workplace would trigger the need for that specific training. Follow-up communications and reinforcement can help firm up these connections. Posttraining interventions that create opportunities for transfer are discussed in Chapter 8.

Practice Opportunities

Many times, the best training classes try to include some type of practice opportunity so trainees can make the connection between what is being learned and how it will be applied on the job. This is a great way to move content from surface to deeper learning. For example, if trainees attend a class on negotiation skills, it can be a valuable experience to have the trainees practice what they are learning with others in the class. Mistakes can be made in a safe environment, and as will be discussed in Chapter 14, productive failure is a great learning tool. Unfortunately, much of what is taught in safety training classes cannot be practiced in the real world without adding unnecessary risk to the training class or exposing employees to hazardous conditions. In arc flash training, for example, should trainees really be expected to experience an arc flash? For something as simple as fire extinguisher training, a real fire can be started in a controlled setting and trainees can practice putting out the fire. This is a great way to add hands-on practice, but it is not always possible. Trainees that put out a real fire in a controlled environment will have gained the basic skill of using a fire extinguisher, but any fire they are likely to face in the workplace will undoubtedly be different. Presenting training in a way that enables the trainee to transfer that skill to any situation is the goal.

Consider the way safety training is normally delivered. Then consider if it's possible to deliver a realistic practice scenario safely. With some effort and added expense it may be possible, but it is not as easy to add these types of practice opportunities as opposed to sticking with other types of low-risk training classes.

When training includes skills and knowledge that are only necessary in emergency situations, one can hope this type of training never needs to be recalled and used. However, when it isn't necessary to remember and use the information, it is much more difficult to do so when needed. Without the opportunity to practice what was learned in a training class immediately after the class, the rate of learning decay is faster. When trainees learn something that can be used in their day-to-day job and feel motivated to use their new knowledge and skills, having enough opportunities to apply their new knowledge is crucial to training transfer (Burke et al. 2006). Simulations using technology, such as virtual reality headsets, or low-tech simulations, such as tabletop drills, can be effective in providing close-to-real-life practice situations. These learning opportunities are discussed in Chapter 9, "Making It Real."

Proving Training Effectiveness

Proving the benefits of safety training is another challenge that is experienced in other training areas. It is hard to prove whether positive results seen after training are due to the training or due to other inputs or even a combination of both. Many studies have shown that training interventions can lead to positive effects on safety knowledge, adoption of safe behaviors and practices, and safety and health outcomes. However, the qualitative reviews are speculative as to the specific factors that enhance the relative effectiveness of safety and health training interventions in reducing or preventing worker injury or illness (Burke et al. 2006).

Measuring the transfer of learning material to the actual job tasks is difficult for a variety of reasons. If training involved motor skills, it is easy to see if the training is being applied back on the job. When training is focused on instructions for safe behaviors, it is more difficult to identify whether the training is what caused these behaviors to change and be transferred to the workplace. It can be very difficult to separate out other causes of new workplace behavior. Is there a new supervisor who enforces safety rules and regulations? Is there peer pressure to work safely, perhaps due to the presence of a safety promotion or incentive program? Is the new behavior the direct result of the safety training class the trainee attended? Because it is so difficult to determine whether transfer has truly occurred, it is recommended that training transfer be viewed as a process.

Since much of safety training is required by standards, trainees probably have been exposed to similar training before, even if this is their first time attending training on that topic at a particular company or by a particular trainer. Safety training is also different because individual trainees often have deeply ingrained attitudes, beliefs, and values toward safety as compared to other types of training topics (Krauss et al. 2014). If previous training used passive techniques, such as lectures, trainees may fail to show any interest in attending and learning from subsequent training classes on the same topic. In this case, training design factors and preclass communication techniques described in chapters 6 and 8 should be added to the existing safety training refresher program. In addition to preexisting beliefs, preexisting and past behaviors with respect to safety procedures can have an impact on whether or not safety training classes are taken seriously; all of these need to be considered during training design. Imagine trainees are asked to learn about a computer panel on a piece of machinery. They are unlikely to have preexisting beliefs about the use of a computer panel, so the trainer is able to approach the topic with a clean slate and does not need to worry as much about preconceived notions.

An individual's culture may also play a significant role in their training experience. Cultural background and its effects on training have been well documented. For example, if one's culture has created trainees who are hesitant to speak up and question a trainer, the end result would be much more serious if the behavior occurred in a safety training class. If this behavior happened in a sales training class, the trainees might not be as successful in their sales work, but unlike a trainee in a safety training class, their level of participation is not going to result in a potential injury (Hu-Chan 2014).

Finally, safety training has a bad reputation (Association for Talent Development 2017). So many trainees have had to endure poor and meaningless safety training for so long that their mental state and commitment before a class even begins is not where it should be for an optimal experience. Further, management may have the same viewpoints as trainees, and without management support of the training session, no matter how good or well planned it is, trainees will be less likely to pay attention and be actively involved. A "get it over with" attitude is not uncommon, and this is not helpful to safety trainers trying to provide the best learning environment possible so life-saving safety information gets remembered and used when needed. It will take repeated delivery of excellent training for viewpoints, followed by behavior, to finally change.

Safety training serves as an integral role within most safety management systems and creates a foundation for strong individual, team, and organizational safety performance as well as symbolizing the importance of safety across a company (Khanzode et al. 2012). Considering the serious negative consequences, both financial and involving the trainees' ability to work in a safe manner, it is of utmost importance for safety trainers to provide training that sticks. The many special challenges faced by safety professionals as described in this chapter can be overcome with the right knowledge, support, and plans.

OSHA Standards that Require Training

GENERAL INDUSTRY

    29 CFR 1910

    Subpart E – Exit Routes and Emergency Planning
    1910.38   Emergency action plans
    1910.39   Fire prevention plans

    Subpart F – Powered Platforms, Manlifts, and Vehicle-Mounted Work Platforms
    1910.66   Powered platforms for building maintenance

    Subpart G – Occupational Health and Environmental Control
    1910.95   Occupational noise exposure

Subpart H – Hazardous Materials
1910.106   Flammable liquids
1910.109   Explosive and blasting agents
1910.110   Storage and handling of liquefied petroleum gases
1910.111   Storage and handling of anhydrous ammonia
1910.119   Process safety management of highly hazardous chemicals
1910.120   Hazardous waste operations and emergency response

Subpart I – Personal Protective Equipment
1910.132   General requirements
1910.134   Respiratory protection

Subpart J – General Environmental Controls
1910.142   Temporary labor camps
1910.145   Specifications for accident prevention signs and tags
1910.146   Permit required confined spaces
1910.147   The control of hazardous energy (lockout/tagout)

Subpart K – Medical Services and First Aid
1910.151   Medical services and first aid

Subpart L – Fire Protection
1910.155   Fire protection
1910.156   Fire brigades
1910.157   Portable fire extinguishers
1910.158   Standpipe and hose systems
1910.160   Fixed extinguishing systems
1910.164   Fire detection systems
1910.165   Employee alarm systems

Subpart N – Materials Handling and Storage
1910.177   Servicing of multi-piece and single-piece rim wheels
1910.178   Powered industrial trucks
1910.179   Overhead and gantry cranes
1910.180   Crawler locomotive and truck cranes

Subpart O – Machinery and Machine Guarding
1910.217   Mechanical power presses
1910.218   Forging machines

Subpart Q – Welding, Cutting, and Brazing
1910.252   General requirements
1910.253   Oxygen-fuel gas welding and cutting
1910.254   Arc welding and cutting
1910.255   Resistance welding

Subpart R – Special Industries
1910.261   Pulp, paper, and paperboard mills
1910.264   Laundry machinery and operating rules
1910.266   Logging
1910.268   Telecommunications
1910.269   Electric power generation, transmission, and distribution
1910.272   Grain handling facilities

Subpart S – Electrical Safety-Related Work Practices
1910.332   Training

Subpart T – Commercial Diving Operations
1910.410   Qualifications of dive team

Subpart Z – Toxic and Hazardous Substances
1910.1001   Asbestos
1910.1003   13 Carcinogens (4-Nitrobiphenyl, etc)
1910.1017   Vinyl chloride
1910.1018   Inorganic arsenic
1910.1025   Lead
1910.1026   Chromium (VI)
1910.1027   Cadmium
1910.1028   Benzene
1910.1029   Coke oven emissions
1910.1030   Bloodborne pathogens
1910.1043   Cotton dust
1910.1044   1, 2-Dibromo-3-Chloropropane
1910.1045   Acrylonitrile (vinyl cyanide)
1910.1047   Ethylene oxide
1910.1048   Formaldehyde
1910.1050   Methylenedianiline
1910.1051   1,3-Butadiene
1910.1052   Methylene chloride
1910.1096   Ionizing radiation

1910.1200   Hazard communication
1910.1450   Occupational exposure to hazardous chemicals in laboratories

MARITIME
29 CFR Part 1915 – Shipyard Employment
Subpart A – General Provisions
1915.6   Commercial diving operations
1915.7   Competent person
1915.9   Compliance duties owed to each employee

Subpart B – Confined and Enclosed Spaces and Other Dangerous Atmospheres in Shipyard Employment
1915.12   Precautions and the order of testing before entering confined and enclosed spaces and other dangerous atmospheres
1915.13   Cleaning and other cold work
1915.14   Hot work
1915.15   Maintenance of safe conditions

Subpart C – Surface Preparation and Preservation
1915.35   Painting
1915.36   Flammable liquids

Subpart D – Welding, Cutting and Heating
1915.53   Welding, cutting and heating in way of preservative coatings
1915.54   Welding, cutting and heating of hollow metal containers and structures not covered by 1915.12
1915.55   Gas welding and cutting
1915.56   Arc welding and cutting
1915.57   Uses of fissionable material

Subpart E – Scaffolds, Ladders and Other Working Surfaces
1915.71   Scaffolds or staging

Subpart F – General Working Conditions
1915.89   Control of hazardous energy (lockout/tags-plus)

Subpart G – Gear and Equipment for Rigging and Materials Handling
1915.112   Ropes, chains and slings
1915.116   Use of gear
1915.117   Qualifications of operators

Subpart H – Tools and Related Equipment
1915.135 Powder actuated fastening tools
1915.136 Internal combustion engines, other than ships' equipment

Subpart I – Personal Protective Equipment (PPE)
1915.152 General requirements
1915.154 Respiratory protection
1915.159 Personal fall arrest systems (PFAS)
1915.160 Positioning device systems

Subpart K – Portable, Unfired Pressure Vessels, Drums and Containers, Other Than Ship's Equipment
1915.172 Portable air receivers and other unfired pressure vessels

Subpart P – Fire Protection in Shipyard Employment
1915.508 Training

Subpart Z – Toxic and Hazardous Substances
1915.1001 Asbestos
1915.1003 13 Carcinogens (4-Nitrobiphenyl, etc)
1915.1017 Vinyl chloride
1915.1018 Inorganic arsenic
1915.1025 Lead
1915.1027 Cadmium
1915.1028 Benzene
1915.1030 Bloodborne pathogens
1915.1044 1,2-Dibromo-3-Chloropropane
1915.1045 Acrylonitrile
1915.1047 Ethylene oxide
1915.1048 Formaldehyde
1915.1050 Methylenedianiline
1915.1200 Hazard communication
1915.1450 Occupational exposure to hazardous chemicals in laboratories

29 CFR Part 1917 – Marine Terminals
Subpart A – General Provisions
1917.1 Scope and applicability

Subpart B – Marine Terminal Operations
1917.23 Hazardous atmospheres and substances

1917.25	Fumigants, pesticides, insecticides, and hazardous preservatives
1917.27	Personnel
1917.28	Hazard communication
1917.30	Emergency action plans

Subpart C – Cargo Handling Gear and Equipment
1917.44	General rules applicable to vehicles

Subpart D – Specialized Terminals
1917.73	Terminal facilities handling menhaden and similar species of fish

Subpart G – Related Terminal Operations and Equipment
1917.152	Welding, cutting and heating (hot work)

29 CFR Part 1918 – Safety and Health Regulations for Longshoring
Subpart A – Scope and Definitions
1918.1	Scope and application

Subpart H – Handling Cargo
1918.85	Containerized cargo operations

Subpart I – General Working Conditions
1918.93	Hazardous atmospheres and substances
1918.94	Ventilation and atmospheric conditions
1918.97	First aid and lifesaving facilities
1918.98	Qualifications of machinery operators and supervisory training

CONSTRUCTION

29 CFR 1910
Subpart B – Adoption and Extension of Established Federal Standards
1910.12	Construction work

29 CFR 1926
Subpart C – General Safety and Health Provisions
1926.20	General safety and health provisions
1926.21	Safety training and education
1926.32	Definitions
1926.35	Employee emergency action plans

Subpart D – Occupational Health and Environmental Controls
1926.50   Medical services and first aid
1926.52   Occupational noise exposure
1926.53   Ionizing radiation
1926.54   Nonionizing radiation
1926.55   Gases, vapors, fumes, dusts, and mists
1926.57   Ventilation
1926.59   Hazard communication
1910.1200   Hazard communication
1926.60   Methylenedianiline
1926.61   Retention of DOT markings, placards, and labels
1926.62   Lead in construction
1926.64   Process safety management of highly hazardous chemicals
1926.65   Hazardous waste operations and emergency response

Subpart E – Personal Protective and Life Saving Equipment
1926.102   Eye and face protection
1926.103   Respiratory protection
1910.134   Respiratory protection

Subpart F – Fire Protection and Prevention
1926.150   Fire protection
1926.155   Definitions applicable to this subpart

Subpart G – Signs, Signals, and Barricades
1926.200   Accident prevention signs and tags
1926.201   Signaling
1926.202   Barricades

Subpart I – Tools – Hand and Power
1926.300   General requirements
1926.302   Power-operated hand tools

Subpart J – Welding and Cutting
1926.350   Gas welding and cutting
1926.351   Arc welding and cutting
1926.352   Fire prevention

Subpart K – Electrical
1926.416   General requirements

Subpart L – Scaffolds
1926.450   Scope, application and definitions applicable to this subpart
1926.451   General requirements
1926.454   Training requirements

Subpart M – Fall Protection
1926.503   Training requirements

Subpart O – Motor Vehicles, Mechanized Equipment, and Marine Operations
1926.602   Material handling equipment
1910.178   Powered industrial trucks

Subpart R – Steel Erection
1926.760   Fall protection
1926.761   Training

Subpart S – Underground Construction, Caissons, Cofferdams and Compressed Air
1926.800   Underground construction
1926.803   Compressed air

Subpart U – Blasting and the Use of Explosives
1926.901   Blaster qualifications

Subpart V – Power Transmission and Distribution
1926.955   Overhead lines

Subpart X – Stairways and Ladders
1926.1060 Training requirements

Subpart Y – Diving
1926.1076 Qualifications of dive team

Subpart Z – Toxic and Hazardous Substances
1926.1101 Asbestos
1926.1126 Chromium (VI)
1926.1127 Cadmium

Subpart AA – Confined Spaces in Construction
1926.1207 Training
1926.1211 Rescue and emergency services

Subpart CC – Cranes and Derricks in Construction
1926.1401   Definitions
19261404   Assembly/Disassembly – general requirements
1926.1408   Power line safety (up to 350 kV) – equipment operations
1926.1419   Signals – general requirements
1926.1423   Fall protection
1926.1424   Work area control
1926.1425   Keeping clear of the load
1926.1427   Operator qualification and certification
1926.1428   Signal person qualifications
1926.1430   Training
1926.1436   Derricks
1926.1438   Overhead & gantry cranes
1926.1441   Equipment with a rated hoisting/lifting capacity of 2,000 pounds or less

AGRICULTURE

29 CFR 1928

Subpart C – Roll-over Protective Structures
1928.51   Roll-over protective structures (ROPS) for tractors used in agricultural operations
1928.57   Guarding of farm field equipment, farmstead equipment, and cotton gins

Subpart M – Occupational Health
1928.1027   Cadmium

FEDERAL EMPLOYEE PROGRAMS

29 CFR 1960

Subpart B – Administration
1960.7   Financial management

Subpart D – Inspection and Abatement
1960.25   Qualifications of safety and health inspectors and agency inspections

Subpart E – General Services Administration and Other Federal Agencies
1960.34   General provisions

Subpart F – Occupational Safety and Health Committees
1960.39 Agency responsibilities

Subpart H – Training
1960.54 Training of top management officials
1960.55 Training of supervisors
196056 Training of safety and health specialists
196057 Training of safety and health inspectors

Subpart K – Field Federal Safety and Health Councils
1960.85 Role of the Secretary

Review and Retention Activity

This learning and retention activity is based on the idea that predicting an answer can lead trainees to add meaning and make connections to content and is discussed further in Chapter 13, "Predicting Results and Testing."

Before reading this chapter, list three ways you think safety training may be different than other nonsafety-related types of training.

1. _____

2. _____

3. _____

References

ANSI/ASSP Z490.1. 2016. *Criteria for Accepted Practices in Safety, Health and Environmental Training.* Park Ridge, IL: American Society of Safety Professionals.

ANSI/ASSP Z490.2. 2019. *Accepted Practices for E-Learning in Safety, Health and Environmental Training.* Park Ridge, IL: American Society of Safety Professionals.

Association for Talent Development (ATD). 2017. *Using the Power of Stories in Compliance and Technical Training.* Alexandria, VA: ATD Press. https://www.td.org/videos/using-the-power-of-stories-in-compliance-and-technical-training.

Bureau of Labor Statistics (BLS). 2022. Census of Fatal Occupational Injuries. January 27, 2022. https://www.bls.gov/iif/.

Burke, M. J., S. A. Sarpy, K. Smith-Crowe, S. Chan-Serafin, R. O. Salvador, and G. Islam. 2006. "Relative effectiveness of worker safety and health training methods." *American Journal of Public Health*, 96(2):315–324.

De Jesus-Rivas, M., H. A. Conlon, and C. Burns. 2016. "The Impact of Language and Culture Diversity in Occupational Safety." *Workplace Health & Safety*, 64(1):24–27. doi: 10.1177/2165079915607872.

Fernández-Esquer, Maria Eugenia, Natalie Fernández-Espada, John A. Atkinson, and Cecilia F. Montano. 2014. "The Influence of Demographics and Working Conditions on Self-Reported Injuries among Latino Day Laborers." *International Journal of Occupational and Environmental Health*, 21(1):5–13. doi: 10.1179/2049396714y.0000000083.

Hale, Ti. 2014. "Training in Native Language Makes Workplaces Safer." The Society for Human Resource Management. January 24, 2014. https://www.shrm.org/resourcesandtools/hr-topics/risk-management/pages/training-native-language-workplace-safe.aspx.

Ho, M. 2019. "Learning by the Numbers." *TD Magazine.* December 2, 2019. https://www.td.org/magazines/td-magazine/learning-by-the-numbers.

Hu-Chan, M. 2014. "Lost in Translation? Sidestep the Perils of Presenting to a Global Audience." *TD Magazine.* December 19, 2014. https://www.td.org/insights/lost-in-translation-sidestep-the-perils-of-presenting-to-a-global-audience.

Khanzode, V., J. Maiti, and P. K. Ray. 2012. "Occupational Injury and accident research: A comprehensive review." *Safety Science*, 50(5):1355–1367.

Krauss, A., T. Casey, and P. Y. Chen. 2014. "Making Safety Training Stick." In S. Leka and R. R. Sinclair, eds., *Contemporary Occupational Health Psychology: Global Perspectives on Research and Practice*, Volume 3. Chichester: Wiley-Blackwell. doi: 10.1002/9781118713860.ch12.

Occupational Safety and Health Administration (OSHA). n.d. "Hispanic Outreach." Accessed October 2020, 4AD. https://www.osha.gov/OshDoc/data_Hispanic/hispanic_outreach.html.

———. 1989. OSHA 29 CFR 1910.120. *Hazardous Waste Operations and Emergency Response*. Washington, DC: US Department of Labor.

———. 2016. "Training Requirements in OSHA Standards." Washington, DC: US Department of Labor. https://www.osha.gov/Publications/osha2254.pdf.

Pollock, R., and A. Jefferson. 2012. *Ensuring Learning Transfer*. Alexandria, VA: American Society for Training and Development (ASTD) Press.

Salas, E., S. I. Tannenbaum, K. Kraiger, and K. A. Smith-Jentsch. 2012. "The Science of Training and Development in Organizations: What matters in Practice." *Pyschological Science in Public Interest*, 13(2):74–101. doi: 10.1177/1529100612436661.

Skogdalen, J. E., I. B. Utne, and J. E. Vinnem. 2011. "Developing safety indicators for preventing offshore oil and gas deepwater drilling blowouts." *Safety Science*, 49(8):1187–1199.

Taylor, T. 2017. "The Key to Workforce Performance? Retention of Corporate Training." *HR Dive*. February 21, 2017. https://www.hrdive.com/news/the-key-to-workforce-performance-retention-of-corporate-training/436581.

Waehrer, G., and T. Miller. 2009. "Does Safety Training Reduce Work Injury in the United States?" *The Ergonomics Open Journal*, 2:26–39.

Chapter 3
Challenges and Methods of Knowledge Transfer

The effectiveness of safety training has not been studied in great detail, but general training effectiveness strategies have been and can be applied to safety training. Like other subject areas, such as psychology, motivation, and leadership, whose lessons are frequently applied to safety operations, the research around training and learning in general can be applied to occupational safety training efforts (Krauss et al. 2014).

A number of challenges exist that affect the extent to which safety training class content is transferred and used back on the job during normal (and unexpected) work duties. The employer's commitment to promoting training and posttraining activities and reinforcement can affect the success of the safety training efforts. However, many attendees return to jobs in a location that makes posttraining activities and follow-up difficult. In a fast-paced environment with little downtime for reinforcement, it is simply not easy to provide posttraining follow-up to most of the workforce receiving safety training.

The Training Transfer Problem

If training transfer, as defined in Chapter 1, is a trainee's ability to use learned skills and knowledge once back on the job as well as to maintain this knowledge and skill level over time, then the *training transfer problem* refers to situations where completed safety training fails to be used in the workplace. The amount of training that fails to be transferred immediately after the training has occurred has been shown to be anywhere from 60 percent (Fitzpatrick 2001) to 90 percent (Cromwell and Kolb 2004). It is widely known that as time goes on even more learning is forgotten.

Perception Barriers

Barriers to training transfer related to perception exist in most organizations, and these barriers represent substantial impediments to change. Perception barriers can refer to the perceptions of executives and the perceptions of trainers. In both cases, these groups believe that lack of reinforcement on the job is a major reason why trainees don't apply what they learned to their jobs (Broad and Newstrom 1995).

Barriers to successful transfer of training on the job can occur before training, during training, and after training. Examples of barriers that occur before training include an unsupportive organizational culture and pressure from coworkers. Examples of barriers that may occur during the training include the trainee's perception that the training class is impractical or unnecessary, the trainee's unwillingness to change the way he or she does things, and interference from the trainee's work environment. If the trainee is frequently paged or constantly hears workplace communications going on over intercoms, or if the trainee's mobile phone is routinely flooded with text messages demanding his or her attention, that is a major environmental barrier. Examples of interference that can happen after the training is completed include lack of reinforcement on the job, an unsupportive culture, being apart from the supportive environment of the trainer and training class, and pressure from coworkers to do things the old way. While all of these types of barriers can occur before, during, and after a training class, the most problematic time is after a training class. An organization cannot wait until after the training class is completed to address the problem of training transfer (Broad and Newstrom 1995). Instituting many of the procedures and suggestions found throughout this book will help to remove or at least decrease these barriers. Removing the barriers is one step toward providing an environment where trainees are more likely to retain safety information and transfer it back to the job.

One study asked trainers what they believed to be the biggest barriers to learning transfer. In order from the greatest barrier to the lowest barrier, their answers were as follows (Broad 2007):

- Lack of reinforcement on the job
- Interference from immediate work environments
- Unsupportive organizational cultures
- Trainees' perception of impractical training programs
- Trainees' perception of irrelevant training content
- Trainees' discomfort with change and associated effort
- Separation from inspiration or support of the trainer
- Trainees' perception of poorly designed or delivered training
- Pressure from peers to resist changes

Most safety trainers would agree that these barriers exist in their own workplaces as well, not only for workers receiving safety training but also for themselves after attending any type of training. For example, if a safety trainer attended an offsite training class on how to give constructive feedback or deliver difficult conversations, not having a trainer's guidance and coaching when back at work may make it very difficult to apply these new skills. Similarly, a trainee that attends a training class on the importance of good housekeeping and then returns to a work area that is continually messy may also have a difficult time applying what he or she learned.

Managers are usually viewed as responsible for removing many of these barriers. "Managers hold the most significant keys to resolving the problems of transfer of training while trainers hold the primary responsibility for any problems concerning training if it is impractical, irrelevant, or poorly designed and delivered. Several other major barriers are partially with trainees themselves and at least three may be perceptual. These include trainees' perceptions that the training is impractical, irrelevant or poorly designed or delivered and their own attitudes regarding the personal cost associated with change" (Broad 2007).

Near versus Far Transfer

Another challenge associated with training transfer is encountered with the concept of near versus far transfer. *Near transfer* is the extent to which individuals apply what was learned to situations very similar to those in which they were trained. The success of this type of transfer depends heavily on the identical elements approach, which strives to make the training experience closely approximate the task demands of the job itself. *Far transfer*, by contrast, is the extent to which trainees apply the training to novel or different situations than the ones in which they were trained. The success of far transfer often depends on how well trainees can apply general principles acquired during training to unique problems (Laker 1990). Safety trainers can do a lot to help trainees draw upon what they learned if training materials are presented in a way that motivates trainees to use the information to tackle new situations in their workplace. Chapter 9, titled "Making it Real," is based on the idea that realistic training environments do much more for attracting and keeping attention than those that are not believable or realistic.

Four Factors Contributing to Poor Transfer

In addition to the barriers already described, over 100 different factors can cause poor training transfer (Foxon 1993). These factors have been grouped into four distinct categories and are listed below:

1. *Organizational climate factors*
   Organizational factors include things such as unsupportive environments, demands of the job, lack of opportunity to apply the training, and the failure to provide the resources necessary to use the training. Some of these issues are within the control of the safety trainer—providing resources that will help the trainee apply the training after the class is completed, for example. Others may be more difficult to address.
2. *Training design factors*
   Training design factors include things such as course material that is either too difficult, too easy, or irrelevant. There is a variety of mandated compliance training that some trainees may not feel applies to their day-to-day jobs. As a result, they will not pay attention to the content being presented.
3. *Individual learner characteristics*
   Individual learner characteristics refer to the trainees' motivations to utilize the training; this motivation is related to whether the trainees think the course material is useful for them personally.
4. *Training delivery factors*
   Training delivery factors refer to the way the training material is presented, such as the method, the media, and the delivery style. If

the training content is great but is presented in a boring, monotone voice in a lecture format during a training class that includes 100 PowerPoint slides, the trainees probably will not pay attention and thus will not be able to transfer the information back to the job.

Trainer Credibility

Related to number 4 in the above list, another factor that can negatively affect training is having a trainer who is not credible. ANSI training standards recommend safety trainers have some level of expertise in the content that's being presented. If a trainer from a company's training department has no background in safety and health, yet is expected to train a group of workers on safety and health issues, the credibility of the trainer may be a problem in this instance.

Forgetting Is Normal

It's difficult to talk about the challenge of remembering information without mentioning the Ebbinghaus forgetting curve. Herman Ebbinghaus was a scientist in the 19th century who came up with some ideas about how people remember and how much they forget that are still talked about today. Ebbinghaus approached the problem in a very unusual way by using himself as the sole subject of his research to see how much he could remember after various periods of time. His findings led him to develop what is known as the Ebbinghaus forgetting curve, which shows how new information is lost from memory over a short period of time. He found that after he relearned what he had previously memorized, his memory was stronger, and after a third refresher, it was even stronger. The Ebbinghaus curve suggests relevant information is lost over time when there is no attempt to retain it. Although Hermann Ebbinghaus conducted his research in 1880, his experiments were successfully duplicated by Murre and Dros in 2015 (Murre and Dros 2015). These studies led to further research into the spacing effect, which is described in greater detail in Chapter 10.

Multiple studies have found that the rate of decay is lessened if (1) a memory is strong and powerful, (2) the memory has personal significance to the learner, and (3) the information is reviewed often. What does this mean for safety professionals? At a minimum, trainers must come up with

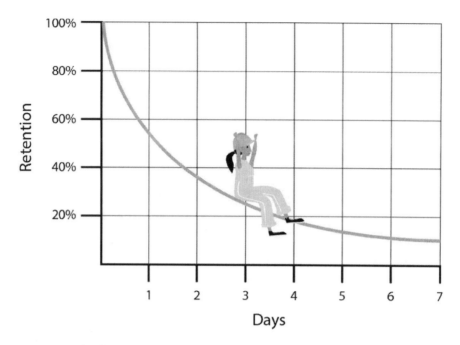

Figure 3.1 ✦ The Ebbinghaus forgetting curve (Based on Murre and Dros 2015)

ways to make the training personally significant and provide opportunities for reinforcement. Figure 3.1 shows how a rate of retention curve might look when learning is affected by repetition over time as described by Ebbinghaus.

Primacy and Recency

Primacy and recency are two ideas a safety trainer can consider when attempting to combat training design factors that may inhibit transfer. The ability to remember information presented early in a training class is known as the *primacy effect*. Some studies suggest information presented early is stored in long-term memory, and as the rest of the content is presented, the mind has a chance to process the information from the first point of contact (Greene et al. 2000). The *recency effect* states that information presented last is remembered more clearly than information that was heard first. With the recency effect, items are stored as short-term or working memories. Since this information is experienced last, there is no time for recall since this information is not moved into long-term memory. The information heard last might be better remembered in the short term, but without any additional repetition, information stored in short-term memory will decay as time goes on and it gets pushed out by new information.

However, it is important to remember that when information in the short-term memory is recalled, it can then be moved from short-term memory into long-term memory. The primacy–recency effect also states that people remember least the information presented just past the middle of a learning session (Sousa 2017).

Figure 3.2 shows how the primacy–recency effect influences retention during a 40-minute learning episode (Buzan 1991). The times are approximate and averages. Two periods of greater retention are shown, one being at the start of a class and the second at the end. These represent the ideas of primacy and recency. In between is an area called the downtime where retention is at its lowest. This is not a time when no retention takes place, but represents a time when it is most difficult for retention to occur (Sousa 2017).

Safety trainers can use the primacy–recency effect to increase trainee retention by using the following suggestions:

1. Present new information first. New information is more likely to be remembered long term. If an important update is to be included in a refresher class, it would be wise to cover it first before reviewing information the trainees have already seen before.
2. Plan for practice opportunities or review during the downtime. The downtime, as shown in the graph in Figure 3.2, refers to the time in the middle. Interactive safety training games and activities are a great

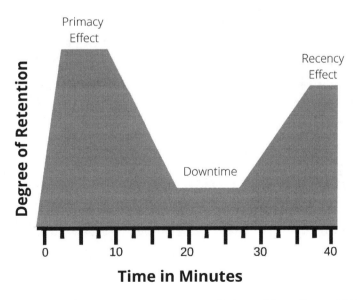

Figure 3.2 ✦ Primacy–recency curve (Adapted from Sousa 2017)

way to help trainees practice new skills and review content. Games and activities have the added benefit of helping to maintain attention and involvement at a time when trainees may be beginning to lose focus.
3. Plan to wrap up the training class with reinforcement just before ending since this is the second most powerful learning position. A safety trainer can do this by using one of the summarizing activities described in Chapter 22.

As shown in Figure 3.2, the downtime is much shorter in duration than the primacy and recency segment added together. In the 40-minute class, for example, the downtime is approximately 25 percent of the lesson time. If the class stretches out to 80 minutes, the downtime increases to 38 percent of the total time (Sousa 2017). As seen on the graph, as the length of time increases, the percentage of downtime gets increasingly longer as well. Simply put, as more and more information is entering the brain, it can't be sorted and stored in long-term memory fast enough before new information comes in. Basically, it's like the brain getting cluttered with random information without time to store it where it belongs. The brain likes to chunk information so it can be more easily recalled in the future; this process is disturbed when there is an overabundance of information. When this backup occurs and new information is not moved into long-term memory, retention will decrease.

Alternatively, in a very short class, such as one that is only 20 minutes long, the downtime is reduced to 2 minutes, or only 10 percent of the total time. It would seem apparent then that shorter classes would be more effective in increasing long-term retention. All of the numbers relating to Figure 3.2 are averages; the important thing to remember is more retention occurs when lessons are shorter and more meaningful (Sousa 2017). The idea of making lessons shorter and more meaningful is integral to microlearning, which is discussed in detail in Chapter 12.

Mental Models

When any new pieces of information enter the brain, the brain attempts to organize them in a way that makes sense. Otherwise, there would be an unbelievable amount of unrelated information all mixed together in our minds. To organize this information, our brains utilize mental models. By understanding more about mental models, safety trainers can use them to their advantage when designing better safety training classes. *Mental models* are "deeply ingrained assumptions, generalizations, or even pictures and images that influence how we understand the world and how we take action" (Senge 2006). Mental models affect what people see, and in turn, what they see affects how they act. If one trainee has a different mental model than a second trainee, the two trainees may perceive the intended message of a safety training class differently, even though they sat through the same class.

Imagine there is a group of new employees and they're getting ready to attend their first training session. They have never met the trainer, and they do not know anything about the training class (other than attendance is mandatory), but they will already have some ideas about what the trainer and the class will be like. Even though their ideas and assumptions might be incorrect, they will nevertheless have these ideas—before the training class even begins. These ideas and assumptions about the trainer and the training class can be considered the mental model this group of employees holds.

"Forming mental models is the essential manner in which the brain learns from the past and then directly influences the present and shapes future actions" (Siegel 1999). The individual trainees in the new employee group will likely each have different mental models, and these models depend on many things. If trainees have been to any safety training class before, they will have an idea about what the safety training class will look like and sound like, while someone who has never attended any type of safety training class will have a totally different mental model. A trainer who has never met the trainees in his or her safety training class is already viewed a certain way by the trainees. Before a trainer even mentions one word or puts up one slide, the trainees have expectations, and these can affect how they will react to the safety training class and content. Unfortunately, many safety training classes are boring and may be seen as irrelevant by the attendees. If this is the situation with the trainees who are about to listen to a trainer talk for an hour or more, the trainer is already facing a challenge that will be difficult to overcome.

A person's mental models will influence what they pay attention to and will define how they approach different situations. Although it may not always be possible, it is helpful if the safety trainer has some idea about the mental models of the trainees in the class. If the trainer can identify how much the audience knows about the topic already and how they feel about it, this will help the trainer create a message that's most appealing to that audience. If the training class is presented to a group the safety professional works with every day and/or has worked with for many years, the trainer most likely has some idea about the trainees' experience and attitudes toward training. If the trainees are new to the organization or the trainer is not familiar with the trainees, a little bit of research is appropriate. This can bring some clarity to the mental models existing in that group. At a minimum, the trainer should know what type of experience the trainees have and acquire any knowledge the department supervisors might have about the trainees' willingness to participate in a safety training class. Once this information is known, a decision can be made about what material to include and focus on and even what order the information should be presented in. Whenever possible, the training class should be customized to the specific audience (Weinschenk 2018).

Cognition

Cognition is a word that appears frequently when reading about adult learning and training. It basically means the process of thinking. When it comes to *safety training cognition*, it refers to how the information in a trainee's head is held together, processed, and more importantly, how it is remembered.

A lot of the research on learning will break down the acquisition of knowledge into two different types. The first type is *declarative knowledge*, which really focuses on what is known and includes things like facts and concepts. The second type of knowledge is called *procedural knowledge*—what people do. Much of what is provided in safety training falls under the category of procedural knowledge, although safety training is usually a mix of both types. For example, consider a forklift safety training class. A forklift operator needs to know how to turn on a forklift and which controls to use to safely lift a load. These are examples of declarative knowledge. Forklift operators also must know how far in advance to slow down at an intersection and how far to swing out before making a turn. These are examples of procedural knowledge.

If it is so easy to forget what we learn, why do most people remember how to ride a bicycle many years later? "There is evidence that procedural skills such as riding a bicycle are stored in a different way from declarative knowledge such as knowing how to do a certain mathematical calculation. This difference between *knowing how* and *knowing that* may also have different implications for long-term memory. Procedural skills such as the ever-remembered bicycling, are much less acceptable to being forgotten than knowledge that requires explicit recall to retrieve" (Young 2019).

Knowing this information can actually benefit the design of safety training programs. A dominant learning theory suggests most skills are learned by proceeding through stages and may start out as declarative but end up being procedural as they are practiced more and more (Taie 2014). Imagine the first time a safety professional delivers safety training: he or she is consciously thinking about the necessary steps to facilitate an activity in a training class. Knowing how to do this is one type of knowledge. After a trainer has been facilitating training classes for years, the trainer will not have to think through all of the aspects of facilitating; it will come more naturally. This is an example of learning that moves from declarative to procedural. Since it's known that procedural knowledge is stored longer than declarative knowledge, a trainer can consider trying to get the trainees focused on skills over knowledge. For example, if a safety class is focused on fall protection, having trainees put on a fall protection harness over and over again will likely move the knowledge from declarative—what trainees know they should do and in what order—to procedural—where the act becomes second nature.

The Nine Events of Learning

Robert Gagné was a psychologist and one of the first people to study the science of instruction. He is famous for his Nine Events of Learning (also called the Nine Conditions of Learning) that follow (Gagné 2011):

1. Gain attention
2. State objective
3. Recall prior learning
4. Present stimulus
5. Guide learning (show examples, coaching)
6. Practice
7. Feedback
8. Assessment
9. Transfer

Attention is the most significant bottleneck in the whole learning process (Pollock et al. 2015), and it's further discussed in Chapter 7. Trainers must find a way not only to get the attention of trainees but also to keep it throughout a training class. In Gagné's nine steps, *gain attention* is in the number one position for an important reason. Without getting the attention of trainees, nothing else is going to progress. It can be simple to get trainee attention and does not necessarily require much effort or elaborate planning. To get trainee attention, the trainer can ask a simple question, give a short quiz, or introduce any type of class-related activity.

The second step in Gagné's nine events is *state the objective*. Instead of reading off a list of formal training objectives, the trainer simply needs to explain to the trainees why they should care about the content. Trainees need to know why they're sitting there and spending their time on the safety training material, and it's the trainer's job to make that very clear.

The third step, *recall prior learning*, serves to take advantage of an important way adults learn. Learning builds on prior learning, and the more connections trainees can make with what they already know, the more they will be able to learn and retain the new information.

The fourth step, as stated in Gagné's list, is to *present the stimulus*. The stimulus relates to the training content itself. Following Gagné's steps, no material would be presented until after a trainer has gotten the attention of trainees, ensured they understand what's in it for them, and found a way to tie the new information to what trainees already know. Only then is it possible to present the training class content. When presenting the content, there are many instructional strategies that can be used to make this more effective, and these are discussed throughout this book.

The fifth step is stated as *guide learning*. A trainer's job is to use methods that will help trainees get this information stored in their long-term memory. This is especially important if the information is going to be transferred back to the job. A variety of safety training activities can serve this purpose and are discussed in Chapters 21–26.

The sixth step in Gagné's list is *practice*. It is very difficult to learn anything when there is no opportunity for practice. The old phrase "practice makes perfect" is not necessarily true; however, it is important that the practice a trainee undertakes is correct practice. Many of the activities described in Chapter 5 on making training real provide opportunities for trainees to practice what they've learned in a safe environment. Practice is not particularly valuable without the next step—feedback.

Feedback is the seventh step. If there is no feedback when a trainee tries something new, there will be no opportunity to learn from mistakes or to reinforce what is correct. Feedback takes place not only in the training environment but also when the trainee is back on the job.

The eighth step is *assessment*, which refers to testing—making sure trainees have actually learned what they were supposed to learn. Chapters 8 and 13 describe ways testing can be used most effectively; in particular, trainers should not simply provide multiple-choice questions, but should provide the trainees with better opportunities to recall information that is stored in memory.

The ninth step, *transfer*, refers to the trainer's responsibility to help the trainee find ways to remember the training content as well as use it back on the job. Things such as job aids, workflow learning opportunities, coaching programs, mentors, technology-based support, and action plans are all examples of ways trainers can help set up the trainee for success (Gagné 2011).

Levers of Transfer Effectiveness

While Gagné looked at the nine events of learning, with the last of the events being transfer, researcher Dr. Weinbauer-Heidel focuses her research on that ninth step. She has studied the field extensively and come up with the 12 Levers of Transfer Effectiveness. These 12 levers can be found and are described in various ways throughout different chapters of this book. To summarize, Dr. Weinbauer-Heidel found that the 12 levers could be broken down into three different types:

1. The trainees themselves
2. The training design
3. The organization

The *trainees themselves* are one type of lever. Their part in learning transfer includes their motivation for transfer, self-efficacy, and transfer volition. Trainees are ultimately in control of whether or not the training will be applied. Some trainees may believe they have no control over what happens to them, so regardless of the training or if they use it, whatever will happen will happen. In general, trainees will be highly motivated to do what is necessary to implement the training, but others may not be as dedicated.

The second type of lever is *training design*. The training design includes clarity, relevance, practice opportunities, and the plan for transfer. Different facets of training design are discussed in detail in Chapter 6 on instructional design. Since most safety professionals probably have very little experience with instructional design, working to improve the design of their training programs is important since it will increase retention and transfer.

The *organization* is the third type of lever and includes opportunities for application, personal transfer capacity, support from supervisors, support from peers, and transfer expectations within the organization (Weinbauer-Heidel and Ibeschitz-Manderbach 2018). These elements are discussed further in Chapter 4.

Even with the best training in the world, if a trainee does not want to remember and apply the training, there is little the safety trainer can do. To ensure a trainee is willing to make the effort to transfer learning, the safety trainer should make sure the trainee understands why this safety training information should be followed. Making sure trainees know why the training is important is essential in almost all areas of occupational safety and health. Luckily, for most areas of safety training, this explanation is easy. Trainees can be told how they will personally avoid injury, or worse, and therefore can continue to provide for their families. The safety trainer is supplying the necessary information that will allow trainees to work safely, but ultimately it is up to them to follow through.

It is also important to make sure the completed training does not go unnoticed. What type of recognition does the trainee receive for having attended and successfully completed a training class? Do the department supervisor and/or manager and/or coworkers know the trainee has even gained this new information or attended a refresher class? As stated elsewhere in this book, training classes are not one-time events. It is important to pay attention to training before, during, and after, and the involvement of supervisors and managers is central to a successful program. In fact, they are more important than many people recognize in affecting the decision a trainee makes to use new skills back at work. Supervisors and managers need to know what was covered in the training and how the trainee is expected to use the new knowledge at his or her job. This means that supervisors and managers need to be more in the loop and promise their support. Finally, rewards, consequences, and systems should be in place to support the transfer and application of the new information.

Although there are many challenges, including poor transfer environments, the natural tendency to forget, the difficulty of getting trainee attention, and the inability to control a trainee's desire to learn, the learning science research has provided a variety of solutions safety professionals can use to address them. With extra attention placed on the best design and delivery options for trainees, safety trainers can make a big difference in the effectiveness and value of occupational safety and health training.

Review and Retention Activity

This learning and retention activity is based on the concept that focusing only on one idea makes it easier for learners to remember and act on it. The One Big Thing activity is discussed further in Chapter 7, "Facilitation and Motivation."

Describe the One Big Thing learned after reading this chapter, that if implemented immediately, would make an impact on the effectiveness and value of the safety training delivered.

_____

_____

_____

References

Broad, Mary L. 2007. *Beyond Transfer of Training: Engaging Systems to Improve Performance.* San Francisco, CA: Pfeiffer.

Broad, Mary L., and J. W. Newstrom. 1995. *Transfer of Training: Action-Packed Strategies to Ensure High Payoff from Training Investments.* Reading, MA: Addison-Wesley Publishing Company.

Buzan, T. 1991. *Use Both Sides of Your Brain.* New York, NY: Dutton.

Cromwell, S. E., and J. A. Kolb. 2004. "An examination of work-environment support factors affecting transfer of supervisory skills training to the workplace." *Human Resource Development Quarterly,* 15(4):449–471.

Fitzpatrick, R. 2001. "The strange case of transfer of training estimate." *Industrial Organizational Psychology,* 39(2):18–19.

Foxon, M. 1993. "A process approach to the transfer of training, Part 1." *Australian Journal of Educational Technology,* 9(2):130–143.

Gagné, R. M. 2011. *Principles of Instructional Design.* Belmont, CA: Wadsworth.

Greene, A. J., C. Prepscius, and W. B. Levy. 2000. "Primacy versus recency in a quantitative model: activity is the critical distinction." *Learning and Memory,* 7:48–57.

Krauss, A., T. Casey, and P. Y. Chen. 2014. "Making Safety Training Stick." In S. Leka and R. R. Sinclair, eds., *Contemporary Occupational Health Psychology: Global Perspectives on Research and Practice,* Volume 3. Chichester: Wiley-Blackwell. doi: 10.1002/9781118713860.ch12.

Laker, D. R. 1990. "Dual dimensionality of training transfer." *Human Resource Development Quarterly*, 1:209–223. doi: 10.1002/hrdq.3920010303.

Murre, Jaap M. J., and Joeri Dros. 2015. "Replication and Analysis of Ebbinghaus' Forgetting Curve." Dante R. Chialvo, ed. *Plos one*, 10(7):e0120644. doi: 10.1371/journal.pone.0120644.

Pollock, R. V. H., A. Jefferson, and C. W. Wick. 2015. *The Six Disciplines of Breakthrough Learning: How to Turn Training and Development into Business Results.* Hoboken, NJ: John Wiley & Sons.

Senge, P. M. 2006. *The Fifth Discipline: The Art and Practice of the Learning Organization.* New York: Currency Doubleday.

Siegel, D. J. 1999. *The Developing Mind: Toward a Neurobiology of Interpersonal Experience.* New York: Guilford Press.

Sousa, D. A. 2017. *How the Brain Learns.* Thousand Oaks, CA: Corwin, A Sage Publishing Company.

Taie, M. 2014. "Skill Acquisition Theory and Its Important Concepts in SLA Theory and Practice in Language Studies." *Theory and Practice in Language Studies*, 4(9):1971–76. doi: 10.4304/tpls.4.9.1971-1976.

Weinbauer-Heidel, Ina, and M. Ibeschitz-Manderbach. 2018. *What Makes Training Really Work: 12 Levers of Transfer Effectiveness.* Hamburg, Germany: tredition GmbH.

Weinschenk, S. 2018. *100 Things Every Presenter Needs To Know About People.* Independently published. Edgar, WI: The Team W Inc.

Young, S. H. 2019. *Ultralearning: Master Hard Skills, Outsmart the Competition, and Accelerate Your Career.* New York City: Harper Business.

Chapter 4
Will They Remember?

Although it is difficult to predict whether trainees will remember safety training days, weeks, or months after a training class has been completed, a safety professional can at least help ensure training programs are designed and delivered in a way that makes retention possible. To do this, it is first important to understand why trainees may not retain learning.

Three Deterrents to Remembering

Researchers have found there are three main reasons why people forget much of what they learn. The first reason is *decay*, which refers to the amount of information that is slowly lost over time. This is often known as the Ebbinghaus effect and is discussed in Chapter 3. The second reason is *interference*, which occurs when new information replaces old information. The third reason is that people do not remember what they learned because *cues are forgotten*. Once these three deterrents are understood, strategies can be devised to help counteract them. These three reasons all focus on why an individual trainee may not remember, but they do not address the effects trainers, the organization, coworkers, or management have on the learning outcome. All of these groups can influence whether or not a trainee will remember class content.

Before looking at strategies an organization can employ to foster learning retention, the three main reasons individuals may not remember deserve further consideration.

Decay is often represented by the Ebbinghaus forgetting curve, which is a theory of forgetting that explains how what we experience is slowly forgotten over time. If people think about their own training experiences, they probably remember some things and have completely forgotten others, so it can't simply be the case that less information will be remembered when a longer amount of time has passed. Ebbinghaus found that vivid and meaningful things were remembered, and things that were not very meaningful were forgotten. Therefore, one way to predict if training will be retained is to determine whether the training experiences emotionally resonate with trainees, since these experiences more likely will be easily remembered.

The second theory is that learners experience interference. When new information is learned, old information that is already stored will be replaced. The idea of interference says that "memories that are similar but distinct can compete with one another" (Young 2019) when it comes to learning new information. There are two types of interference. The first is *proactive interference* that happens when information learned in the past makes it more difficult to learn new information. For example, if a series of codes must be entered into a machine in order to get it to work, and a similar machine is brought in with new codes, the new codes would be difficult to remember. The second type of interference is called *retroactive interference* and occurs when learning new information erases or suppresses old information learned in the past. For example, when attempting to learn a new language, retroactive interference often occurs. If French is being studied for the first time, and Spanish was learned years ago, the new French words and phrases may replace the Spanish vocabulary.

The third assumption about why we forget has to do with forgotten cues. *Retrieval cues* are prompts that help access a memory and can include images, certain words or phrases, sounds, emotions, and more. This idea is based on the premise that we never forget anything we have learned, instead we are just unable to access it. What may happen in this case is that "one of the links in the chain of retrieving the information has been severed (perhaps by decay or interference) and therefore the entire memory has become inaccessible" (Young 2019). The forgotten cues theory suggests that if the queue to that memory is restored the information will be remembered. This suggests it is easier to relearn information than it is to learn it initially.

Forgetting information is the default for everyone inside or outside of the training room. Without taking steps to create a different outcome, trainees will forget information that is presented to them. If a trainer reviews training that is about to be presented, or was recently delivered, and sees there is nothing in place to overcome these obstacles to learning, the trainer can predict that the trainee will have a difficult time remembering.

To combat decay, the trainer should build in ways to make the training vivid and personally meaningful. Chapter 9 on making safety training real provides ways to do just that.

The Learning Culture

A *company's learning culture* is another indicator of whether or not trainees will remember essential safety information (Bates and Khasawneh 2005). The learning culture can be created by the company's management, coworkers, direct supervisors, and even by the trainer.

As discussed in Chapter 7, there is a link between an unsupportive organizational climate and the lack of learning transferred to the job (Mosel 1957). Studies have concluded that training will only transfer to the extent that supervisors support and practice the same behaviors the staff is taught in the training environment. Safety professionals have long known that without a supervisor in place who backs up safety procedures and policies, it's unlikely workers at all levels will support those same policies. If trainees learn one thing in a safety training class and then go out to the work site and learn something else by watching coworkers and management do things a different way, the training is not going to be transferred effectively. If the organizational culture supports not only training but also the application of the training content, there will be a greater amount of transfer (Foxon 1993). As discussed in Chapter 6 on instructional design, it is important to match the learning objectives to the overall goals and values of a company.

When this connection exists, it can increase management support. If the company's goals and values do not meet or match the training content, partial transfer or even failure of the information to transfer will be the result (Gradous 1991). Trainees may leave a training class with every intention of applying what they learned back on the job, but a variety of environmental factors may begin to undermine their motivation almost immediately, inhibiting transfer (Foxon 1993). Even with the best of intentions and a supportive environment, trainees may return to the job, having missed a day or more of work, and immediately focus on catching up so they are not behind. The information learned in the training class will become a distant memory. Alternatively, what occurs during the course, as well as immediately after, may increase trainee motivation to apply what they learned. If the training focused on increasing the confidence level of the trainees by allowing a lot of time to practice and hone in on the usefulness of the skills they were learning, and if the trainees leave with a good idea of when and how to use the information back on the job, the return to the workplace and the application of the learned material will be much different (Foxon 1993). Instead of relying on chance and hoping for the best, trainers must use strategies to improve the odds in favor of transfer and maintenance of training information. If a trainer works on strengthening the supports that will be necessary back on the job, as well as minimizing the factors that may inhibit the trainees from using that information, the likelihood of training transfer is greater.

In *Beyond Transfer of Training* (Broad 2007), six different factors that support performance are presented as ways a trainer can take action to improve the training culture. If a trainer builds these six factors into a class plan, it may be easier or more likely for the trainees to perform as expected after a training class. The six factors include:

1. *Clear performance expectations*
   Trainees need to have a very clear idea of what is expected of them back on the job. If they are expected to follow the new safety procedures they just learned in a safety training class 100 percent of the time, that needs to be clearly spelled out and not just assumed.
2. *Timely and relevant feedback*
   One form of feedback is an end-of-class evaluation, but there are a variety of other feedback methods that can be very helpful to trainee efforts to perform as expected. Feedback that is timely and specific is important so the trainees can successfully transfer new knowledge in a way that has the greatest connection to the safety class content. Workplace observations are one good way to do this. If trainees have a chance to practice their new knowledge during the training class, receiving feedback immediately after their efforts are successful (or not) is an important part of helping the trainees successfully apply it later.
3. *Appropriate consequences*
   Consequences can include things like recognition, rewards, and incentives but can also include consequences for lack of performance. Consequences for an individual not following safety rules can vary greatly by company, but whatever the consequences are, they need to be clearly communicated to the trainees, and preferably, this communication needs to take place before the training class is completed.
4. *Individual capability*
   In order for trainees to use what they learned, each trainee needs to have the necessary physical, mental, and emotional capabilities to perform the job. Consider that a trainee has just attended a training class on emergency first aid. If the trainee is physically, mentally, or

emotionally unable to perform those skills, there is no chance the skills learned in that training class will be used.

5. *Requisite knowledge and skills*
   In order to perform as expected back on the job, trainees need to have the knowledge, skills, and attitudes that are a result of past experiences and training, and they need support from others.
6. *Required time and resources*
   Trainees should be provided with the appropriate tools and information and the necessary time to apply their new skills, and should be given opportunities to use what they learned.

Based on these factors, there are key predictors safety trainers can use to establish the likelihood that trainees will remember safety training content. A trainer can ask the following questions to determine if trainees are likely to remember the content.

Q. Was a training needs analysis completed?

A training needs analysis has been shown to be a significant factor in training transfer. Providing a training plan is crucial for the subsequent application of the content (Goldstein 1993). If adequate planning is not undertaken before a training class is created and delivered, there is less of a chance the content will be remembered. Part of a training needs analysis includes looking at what is needed for the company to meet organizational goals as well as meet the needs of the trainees. Without determining this ahead of time, there will be no way to accurately analyze the value of the training provided.

Q. Was there enough learning?

Another technique to consider is overlearning—in the case of safety training, this could be referred to as overtraining. Time constraints may not make this possible in many companies, but the concept is worth considering. Research has shown that additional practice beyond what is required to perform adequately can increase the length of time memories are stored. For an individual, *overlearning* means continuing to practice after a skill is done correctly. Performance does not improve past this point, but the overlearning can extend the durability of the skill (Young 2019). Consider, for example, annual training on the correct use of fire extinguishers. The trainee is likely able to use a fire extinguisher effectively and for its intended purpose, but when allowed to practice the skill over and over, although it is already mastered, the trainee can achieve longer retention.

Another aspect of overlearning is advanced practice. In *advanced practice*, trainees learn higher level and more difficult skills that are above the core parts or lower levels of a skill set. When this occurs, the lower-level skills are overlearned. Some studies suggest that this type of advanced practice can decrease forgetting.

Q. Is the amount of content appropriate for the allotted time?

Spacing (discussed in Chapter 11), microlearning (discussed in Chapter 14), and preclass communication (discussed in Chapter 8) can be used to avoid cramming.

Q. Are trainees able to ask good questions?

"The Dunning-Kruger effect occurs when someone with inadequate understanding of a subject nonetheless believes he or she possesses more knowledge about the subject than the people who actually do" (Young 2019). When someone lacks knowledge about a subject, they also tend to lack the capacity to assess their own abilities. It is true that the more one learns about a subject, the more questions arise. The reverse also seems to be true, and when fewer questions are asked, less is likely known about the subject. A trainer can turn this idea into an activity by asking trainees to work alone or together to come up with a list of questions about the topic. The better the trainees understand the topic, the more questions they will be able to come up with. If a team comes up with only a few questions, the trainer can see this as an indicator that the level of desired understanding is not there.

Q. Can trainees explain the training content to a child?

Richard Feynman, a Nobel Prize-winning physicist, created something called the Feynman Technique as a way to learn something. This technique includes four basic steps:

1. Pick a concept and write it out as if explaining it to a child (no technical words or jargon).
2. Identify areas where there was trouble explaining the concept. This is where there are gaps in knowledge. The learner needs to go back and find the missing information, study it, and then try to relay that information to an eight year old.
3. Organize notes into a story. The learner compiles his or her notes into a story that is, again, simple and easy to understand. If there are still confusing parts, the summary story needs to be rewritten.

4. Tell someone else about it. A good way to see if the material is really understood is to explain it to someone else.

A safety trainer can also use the ideas behind the Feynman Technique as a safety training activity. Before a safety training class, the trainer can make a list of the main ideas that will be covered. These ideas should be written on a flip chart or whiteboard or be included on a slide. After the content has been covered, the trainer should ask the trainees which topic they would have the most trouble explaining to someone else. Once each trainee has identified one of the items, they should be put into teams with other trainees who had the same answer. Once trainees are in these groups, tell them to come up with a simple story explaining that concept to an eight year old. Alternatively, the trainer can tell them to imagine they are sitting around the dinner table that night and need to explain the idea or procedure to their family. The teams should use whatever learning materials they have access to, including the internet and coworkers, in order to gain a better personal understanding. After a designated amount of time, the trainer should ask each team to briefly tell its story/explanation to the rest of the class. If the teams still have difficulty explaining the concept, there is more work to be done. If time allows, the steps of the Feynman Technique should be started again.

Q. Does the organizational learning culture support learning transfer?

An organization's learning culture can predict the climate of learning transfer (Bates and Khasawneh 2005). If a trainee works in an environment where training is seen as something that has to be done in order to comply with standards, and nothing more, the chances are high that the learning won't be retained or used on the job.

Q. Will training be evaluated at all levels?

It's important to provide summary information on evaluations in order to understand the different ways measurement works. The most popular training evaluation model is known as the Kirkpatrick model.

Kirkpatrick Training Evaluations

The *Kirkpatrick model* shows four levels of training evaluation. Level 1 is the simplest and most commonly used type of evaluation, but unfortunately, this type of evaluation tells us very little about the actual content and retention. Level 1 evaluations are often known as "smile sheets" since they simply tend to ask learners if they liked the training class and if the instructor or presenter did a good job. Although level 1 evaluations are designed to evaluate reactions, it is worth considering whether a learner's positive feedback at this level translates to his or her desire to pay more attention to the content. If a trainee at the basic level likes the instructor, likes the content, and finds it easy to understand, he or she may be more likely to pay attention and not tune out. Getting and keeping trainee attention is an important first step in increasing retention, which is key to having the information actually applied on the job.

Level 2 of the Kirkpatrick evaluation model looks at how much learning occurred. This type of evaluation is also frequently done as part of safety training classes. Most people view the amount of learning that occurred as directly correlating with how well a trainee does on some type of postclass learning evaluation. Some Occupational Safety and Health Administration (OSHA) standards require testing to assess trainee knowledge at the end of a training class. These types of quizzes and exams are designed not only to meet a standard but also to assess whether a trainee learned the required content. For a variety of reasons, someone passing this type of quiz or evaluation may or may not have adequately learned the information, but level 2 evaluations are used to assess this the best they can. If a trainee takes the same exact final exam year after year, and after attending the same training class, he or she will probably do well. Additionally, if a training exam is designed with multiple-choice questions, and the exam is fairly simple to complete overall, a passing result on the exam may still not represent accurate information about the trainee's knowledge. Also, as discussed in Chapter 10 on repetition and spacing, if the trainee learns the class information through repetition and is immediately tested on that information, there is a greater chance the trainee will do well on a test given at the end of the class. However, if the trainee is tested on the same information a few days or weeks after the training class has been completed, he or she will likely not remember much of the information at all.

Level 3 of the Kirpatrick evaluation model starts to get at the heart of learning retention and transfer. When conducting a level 3 evaluation, a trainer assesses if the information taught in the training class actually changed learner behavior. Watching how trainees have changed what they do in their day-to-day jobs reveals whether the training class had the desired effect. For example, in a safety training class on safe housekeeping procedures, trainees may be instructed to immediately clean up all spills and mark the area with a safety cone. If observations were done later to determine if trainees are now doing these things when they did not do them before, this would be an example of a level 3 evaluation.

If a training class reviewed a particular set of safety procedures, a trainer or department supervisor can observe the trainees back on the job to see if those new procedures are actually being followed. Observing workplace behaviors (i.e., doing level 3 evaluations) is a good way to see if the trainees not only remembered what they learned in the training class but also are applying the new information and skills on the job.

Finally, level 4 of a training evaluation assesses the overall impact of the training on an organization. This evaluation level is less likely to be conducted but is the most important factor to look at when trying to prove there was any type of return on the training investment. Looking at such things as costs associated with accidents or property damage that may be lowered as a result of the training is one way of using a level 4 evaluation. If a major cost of injuries at a particular workplace were due to excessive back injuries, and safe lifting procedures had been implemented in the previous year, the trainer and company management can see if those costs decreased. Although it is difficult to tie the results directly to a particular cause, taking a look at this data and attempting to make the connection is a good start.

If various levels of evaluation are frequently done within a company, it may be possible to predict the outcome for similar types of training classes with similar methods of delivery. If a standard, off-the-shelf training video is shown every year to a group of trainees, and level 4 evaluations always confirm that trainees use the training information on the job, it would be expected that similar training classes would have the same effect. In another example, a group of trainees is evaluated after completing a training class on housekeeping. The level 1 evaluations show that trainees think the video is fine but nothing exceptional; the level 2 evaluations are very high with all trainees scoring almost a perfect score on the final exam; and the level 3 evaluations, based on workplace observations, show that trainees are taking extra steps to follow good housekeeping procedures. After reviewing all three evaluations, a trainer could expect that a similar result would occur for other safety training topics designed and delivered in the same way.

However, if showing a group of trainees a generic video on how important housekeeping is for safety, and the level 3 evaluations show the training class and video made little change in the housekeeping behaviors, a trainer would know he or she needs to think twice about using similar training methods in the future. It could be expected that the information is not going to be retained or transferred back on the job. If evaluations from other safety training programs are predicting classes delivered with the same types of materials, and in the same way, are not going to help trainees use important safety training information, it is time to reevaluate the current safety training plan and make adjustments where necessary.

To win the safety training retention game, trainers have to battle against the inevitable human tendency to forget. There are ways to predict whether trainees will remember vital information, and trainers need to use a planned training strategy to counter the most common reasons why information is forgotten.

Review and Retention Activity

This learning and retention activity is based on the Feynman Technique discussed in this chapter.

Select one of the topics presented in this chapter and apply the steps of the Feynman Technique to the material.

1. The Feynman Technique suggests four steps for learning new material. The first step is to write out the concept as if it were being presented to a child. Complete step one now.

   _____

   _____

   _____

2. The second step in the Feynman Technique is to identify areas where there was trouble explaining the concept. After completing the first step, have any of these troublesome areas become apparent? If so, return to the chapter and find the missing information, study it, and then try to complete step one again.

   _____

   _____

   _____

3. Third, organize notes taken while reading about the topic in this chapter into a story that is simple and easy to understand.

_____

_____

_____

_____

4. Finally, explain the topic in this chapter to someone else.

References

Bates, R., and S. Khasawneh. 2005. "Organizational learning culture, learning transfer climate and perceived innovation in Jordanian organizations." *International Journal of Training and Development*, 9:96–109.

Broad, Mary L. 2007. *Beyond Transfer of Training: Engaging Systems to Improve Performance*. San Francisco, CA: Pfeiffer.

Foxon, M. 1993. "A process approach to the transfer of training, Part 1." *Australian Journal of Educational Technology*, 9(2):130–143. www.ascilite.org.au/ajet/ajet9/foxon.html.

Goldstein, I. L. 1993. *Training in Organizations: Needs Assessment, Development, and Evaluation*, 3rd ed. Pacific Grove, CA: Brooks/Cole Publishing Company.

Göschlberger, B. 2016. "A Platform for Social Microlearning." *Adaptive and Adaptable Learning*. Proceedings of the 11th European Conference on Technology Enhanced Learning (EC-TEL), Lyon, France, September 13–16, 2016.

Gradous, D. 1991. "The Development and Validation of a Transfer-of-Training System. Project Number Forty-Five." St. Paul, MN: Minnesota University, Dept. of Vocational and Technical Education.

Mosel, J. D. 1957. "Why training programs fail to carry over." *Personnel*, 34(3):56–64.

Young, S. H. 2019. *Ultralearning: Master Hard Skills, Outsmart the Competition, and Accelerate Your Career*. New York City: Harper Business.

Chapter 5
Accelerated Learning Principles

Accelerated learning, taken literally, means changing behaviors at increasing speed. It is believed to have started in the 1960s when psychiatrist Georgi Lozanov developed the theory of suggestology. *Suggestology* was described as the interweaving of various techniques in order to get the left brain, generally thought to be responsible for analytical thought, and the right brain, generally thought to be more creative, to work together to help people learn faster and better.

"Accelerated learning is multi-sensory, brain-compatible teaching and learning methodology. It uses information from brain research to ensure that less time is wasted than in more traditional learning processes. Accelerated learning involves both the packaging of the content and the condition of the learners so that students can absorb and retain material faster through overcoming traditional barriers to learning. Accelerated learning is a multidimensional approach in which the learner is the focal point of the experience. The learners are in control of the learning" (McKeown 1995). Learning is not the passive storage of information but the active creation of knowledge. Training needs to be created by the trainees and not necessarily given to them. When trainees learn, they are creating new meanings, associations, and neural networks within their existing self. One thing good safety training always tries to accomplish is getting the trainee to understand how the training applies to him or her in a realistic way. Getting and keeping trainee attention, providing opportunities for interaction, and helping trainees see how the training personally applies to them and their work, can all be accomplished with the use of accelerated learning principles.

Accelerated learning is different from traditional learning in many ways. Figure 5.1 highlights these differences.

Accelerated Learning vs. Traditional Learning

ACCELERATED LEARNING	TRADITIONAL LEARNING
• nonlinear • systemic • knowing how • informal • flexible • unconscious • intuitive and applicable knowledge • "want to" learning • fun • effortless • emotional • active	• linear • knowing about • formal/structured • conscious • memorized facts • "have to" learning • hard work • emotion free • passive

Figure 5.1 ✦ Accelerated learning versus traditional learning

Accelerated Learning versus Traditional Learning

One of the best ways to think about the difference between accelerated learning and traditional learning is that, in an accelerated safety training class, the safety trainer acts as a facilitator of learning and is not responsible for putting information into the trainees' heads. Instead, the safety trainer provides material to the trainees in an interactive way so they can control their own learning.

There are many benefits of accelerated learning. The individual trainee can learn more and can learn faster, and most importantly, will remember information longer. Accelerated learning also leads to better transfer of the training content back on the job (Russell 1999). Trainers also benefit from accelerated learning because trainees are usually more enthusiastic about being in a training class based on these principles. Once trainees are used to learning this way, they know the time they spend in the classroom or in front of the computer will be well spent, and they may even have fun.

One idea from accelerated learning that is easy for safety trainers to implement is that learning should involve the whole mind and body. This means having activities that require trainees to move around and involve their senses and their emotions. Whenever possible, training should also include auditory aspects, visual aspects, and the intellectual parts of learning.

Accelerated training is focused on the results and not the methods. If a safety trainer is simply told to "train on electrical safety," for example, that leaves a lot of options for exactly how to get that task accomplished. If the safety trainer is told to "show this video and read the operating procedures" to a group of trainees, that is much more of a challenge, and it may be impossible to get trainees to remember anything. If the goal is to have a group of knowledgeable and highly skilled electricians at the end of the training session who remember the content long after the class is over, then having the flexibility to focus on the outcome, and not the methods, will provide a better outcome for everyone.

A Positive Affective State

Positive emotions are also very important in enhancing learning. If someone is sitting in a lecture for hours, they probably won't have positive emotions for very long. Activities can help increase positive emotions. If someone is stressed or bored or angry, learning will be inhibited. If learning is positive, relaxed, and engaging, learning will be increased. Activities can help to keep the trainee engaged. To implement accelerated learning principles, trainers should strive for trainees to have a positive affective state. This basically means encouraging positive and not negative emotions. It is very difficult to learn and absorb anything when in a bad mood. The use of fun can be a great way to add positive emotions to a training class. Other ways include creating a learning environment that is as comfortable and welcoming as possible. Most children in school are told to sit still, to sit up straight and not fidget, but research has found that fidgeting can be good. Some trainers go as far as putting small toys that promote fidgeting on the tables where trainees will sit to encourage fidgeting. Although seating and training-room location might not be controllable, trainers can tell trainees that it's fine if they need to get up and move around during class. For longer training classes, it's especially good to add movement as much as possible.

When using interactive safety training activities, trainees will have the opportunity to move around if teams are assigned and composed of individuals seated in different areas of the room. Trainees may at first complain about having to pick up their things and move, but the move will benefit everyone.

Having plenty of opportunities for people to get up and out of their seats and move around can increase the learning process, keep the attendees more involved, and help chase away boredom. Getting people physically active and planning ways for trainees to use as many senses as possible will help awaken the body and improve circulation, and this will have a positive impact on learning.

The part of the human brain involved with movement is the motor cortex, and it is located right next to the area used for problem solving. If training is designed in a way that restricts bodily movement, the brain is also restricted from functioning at its best. Learning is hampered when we separate the body from the mind. Many people find it difficult to concentrate when their bodies are not doing something physical, such as fidgeting. The people in training classes who are constantly doodling, twirling their pens, or bouncing their legs up and down are examples of people who probably learn better when they are active. The trainees do not need to be active 100 percent of the time, but when periods of activity are interspersed with periods of passive learning, retention will increase.

Stress and Learning

Safety trainers can also take simple steps to create a learning environment that reduces stress and creates positive feelings. A trainer should never create an environment that causes stress. A trainer may cause stress by singling out people and possibly embarrassing them, even if this were never the intention. Additionally, if trainees are sitting in a dingy, dirty training room where they can hear the company intercom endlessly paging them, they are not going to be relaxed enough to learn well.

The Importance of Fun

One of the key facets of accelerated learning is having fun. Some people might say that fun has no place in safety training, but used appropriately, it can help ensure trainees pay more attention and remember more of the important safety information that is shared. It is important to note that all training class fun is not created equal, and fun, deliberately added, should still be related to the class objectives. Everything in an accelerated learning class is focused on the results and not the materials or activities themselves.

The importance of positive emotions in a training class is discussed in Chapter 7 on facilitation and motivation. Laughter and humor are easy ways to encourage positive emotions. Additionally, laughter alleviates tension and can transcend any negative emotions a trainee may have. Humor can aid in memorization and rapport building among trainees and with the trainer. In almost every instance, trainees will respond positively.

Although the whole idea of learning styles has been debunked, (Quinn 2018) most experts believe different individuals have different learning preferences. This does not mean that individuals learn better with one method; instead, they *prefer* to learn one way as opposed to another. Many trainees are quite capable of learning by reading a text, listening to a lecture, or watching a video, but may still prefer one of these methods to another. A safety training class based on accelerated learning principles will consist of a combination of various types of learning methods.

Collaboration

Accelerated learning also relies on group learning rather than individual learning. Trainees often learn more and learn better when learning from their peers (Meier 2000). Collaboration among learners greatly enhances learning. For this reason, many training activities presented in this book involve the use of teams. Good learning is social, and trainees learn much more by learning from peers. Most people probably learned in environments that fostered a great amount of individual competition. When trainees work together in teams, learning can be greatly enhanced. The use of team-based interactive activities is very effective in getting trainees involved in their own learning and the learning of others.

It's important to discuss effectiveness of learning in a book about learning retention. For any material to be remembered and put to use when needed, a trainee first needs to pay attention and interact with it enough to have the option of remembering it later on. Trainers should design in opportunities for the attendees to collaborate with one another and be social, which will help to increase retention. When trainees work together, they will use more of their total brain, and learning will increase. An easy way to add teamwork in a training class is to divide training classes into teams and then have the teams work on a problem, exercise, or training game together to find the solution.

Activity-Centered Learning

Accelerated learning is often thought of as activity-centered learning since the introduction of training games and activities into a training class will bring along with it many of the basic principles of accelerated learning. An added bonus is that activity-centered learning can be designed in a fraction of the time it takes to design a presentation-centered training class. Most safety trainers spend a great deal of time making PowerPoint presentations, handouts, and copies of related materials like sections of OSHA standards. When trainers realize people learn much more and much faster from experiences combined with feedback, accelerated training can begin to save safety professionals a lot of time. Trainers may not be able to eliminate the PowerPoint format entirely, but when accelerated learning is introduced, the written materials will not be the focal point or the most important part of a training class. PowerPoint slides can help to initiate, guide, and support the activities and experiences used in the class.

Central to increasing training retention is finding a way to connect the new information to what trainees already know. Trainers should encourage trainees to think about how they will use the new information they are learning when they are back on the job. Being able to visualize how and why the new material is useful is a key part of retention.

Several different types of group activities can be used for this purpose. Trainees can be given problem-posing and information-accessing exercises that get them to think, make connections, and create meaning for themselves. It is very important in safety training for trainers to help trainees learn to take the information presented to them and customize it for their specific needs. For example, in a hazard communication training class, a trainer would not just review a sample safety data sheet, but would also (1) have the trainees locate the safety data sheet for a product they actually use in their daily work, (2) ask them to determine which types of personal protective equipment would be required when using that chemical, and (3) ask them where they would find that personal protective equipment. Safety trainers should strive for total learner involvement (i.e., having the trainees totally and actively involved, taking full responsibility for their own learning).

Accelerated learning also focuses on providing content visually as well as verbally. Our nervous system is more of an image processor than a word processor, so any time we can take concepts and make them visual, the brain is more likely to learn. When trying to teach someone to ride a bike, it would be almost impossible if the instruction could only be provided verbally. Even if the goal were not to teach an individual how to ride a bike, but to explain how anyone rides a bike, it would be very, very difficult to do so without the use of visual aids. Activities are great ways to turn the safety concepts trainers must teach into actual images that will help the trainee learn more and faster. For this reason, and many more, image-based safety training is very important in communicating important safety information to trainees. Greater detail can be found in Chapter 24, titled "Image-based Safety Training."

Since accelerated learning principles state that a variety of learning methods and all of the trainees' senses should be accessed in order to provide a better learning experience, it is relatively easy for safety trainers to incorporate small changes into training programs as a way to benefit from these principles. The following list provides ideas based on the principles of accelerated learning on how to do this:

- Break down materials into smaller pieces or chunks. Chapter 12 provides details on how microlearning and chunking can positively affect learning retention.
- Ask trainees to act out how something works, such as having them perform a lockout-tagout (LOTO) procedure.
- Ask trainees to simulate how a structure or function in the human body works. In a respiratory protection class, teams could be given some basic tools and gadgets and asked to show why particles of different sizes deposit in different parts of the respiratory system.
- Ask trainees to act out a communication process. An example would be to ask them to role-play giving feedback to a coworker when an unsafe act was committed.
- Have trainees create large pictograms. This can easily be used with any safety and health topic.
- Provide a new experience and then, after reflecting on it, lead a discussion about it. Trainers can ask the trainees to try a new procedure and then report back to the class at a future training class.
- Have trainees complete a project that requires physical activity. The trainees could be asked to go out into the workplace and perform an activity related to the class and then return.
- Lead an active learning exercise, such as a learning game. Games such as crossword puzzles and BINGO can be great learning tools for any

safety and health topic as long as they are intellectually challenging enough.
- Lead a field trip out into the plant. Afterwards, have attendees write, draw, or talk about what they learned. Trainers can ask trainees to inspect the workplace for a particular type of hazard.
- Have trainees interview people outside the class. Have trainees complete interviews of coworkers on a particular safety topic and report back at the next class.
- Ask trainees to talk about what they are learning. This will work for any safety training class.
- Encourage trainees to talk about an experience such as a close call. This is especially effective if someone had a close call (or actual incident) they can share with the class.
- Ask trainees to "think out loud" when performing a hands-on learning activity. This would require they verbally explain what they are doing while they are doing it.
- Have teams of trainees read something and then paraphrase it for the class. This can be very effective when it is important to go over the actual wording of an OSHA standard.
- Tell stories that have the learning concepts imbedded in the material. Original stories or stories heard from others are okay as long as they relate to the topic being taught.
- Pair trainees up and have them tell each other what they just learned and how they are going to apply it. This works well for any topic area.
- Request that trainees work together to create a rap, rhyme, or auditory mnemonic out of the material they are learning. This also works well for any topic area but remember to have the class work in teams.
- Include vivid presentation graphics. Use photos of the actual workplace instead of generic images whenever possible.
- Use picturesque language, such as metaphors and analogies. Think of something that is directly related to the training that will help trainees remember.
- Bring 3-D objects into the safety training class. If they are too big or heavy (like a forklift, for example) have the class travel to the object or bring a model into class.
- When using stories, paint a vivid picture using specific details. As noted earlier, stories can be original or created. Either way, it's

important to make sure details are described clearly. Painting a clear picture captures the attention of trainees.
- Have the class go into the plant to do observations and then report back to the class. Digital cameras can be provided if trainees do not have their own mobile phones with cameras to use.
- Include colorful decorations and peripherals around the training room. Boring training rooms often lead to boring classes—try to liven up the room. This suggestion might seem most unusual for safety training classes, but there is a way to do this that will not result in trainees rolling their eyes. When decorating a training room, use colorful and/or humorous safety posters. When trainees' minds begin to wander—and they inevitably will at some point—they can wander to the decorations in the room. When they do, safety messages will be reinforced.
- Incorporate mental exercises, such as visualization, into the class. Ask the class to close their eyes and imagine themselves doing something they just learned about.
- Provide a variety of interactive class activities, including problem-solving exercises.
- Provide the details of an external event or experience and ask the class to analyze it.
- Provide a topic and objectives to a group of trainees and ask them to create and present a learning activity.
- Ask trainees to distill information. One way to do that is to break the class into teams and ask each team to provide a one-sentence summary of one segment of the class. This works best for multitopic/segment classes where multiple teams can each be assigned a separate section to distill.
- Have trainees create their own quiz questions. Teams can work together to create quizzes for other teams.

Whatever learning tools work to increase and enhance learning can be called accelerated learning methods. Many safety professionals spend a good amount of their work week training others. Accelerated learning principles can help safety professionals spend less time creating training and can help trainees learn faster (and remember more), so accelerated learning applied to safety training can be a win-win situation for everyone.

Review and Retention Activity

This learning and retention activity is based on the principles of accelerated learning discussed in this chapter.

On a large piece of paper, draw a colorful mind map that shows the main parts of this chapter. A mind map is a nonlinear visual representation of a central theme and connected ideas and concepts, represented by images and text, where branches off of the main central idea are used to show relationships to the main idea and other branches. Chapter 22 includes an example mind map for reference.

When creating a mind map for this activity, add branches to each point that include examples of where that point applies in safety training. Additionally, add a small sketch to illustrate each key point. Finally, look over the completed mind map and draw connections between related points.

References

McKeon, K. J. 1995. "What is this thing called accelerated learning?" *Training & Development.* June 1995, 49(6):64.

Meier, D. 2000. *The Accelerated Learning Handbook a Creative Guide to Designing and Delivering Faster, More Effective Training Programs.* New York: McGraw-Hill.

Quinn, C. N. 2018. *Millennials, Goldfish & Other Training Misconceptions: Debunking Learning Myths and Superstitions.* Alexandria, VA: ATD Press.

Russell, L. 1999. *The Accelerated Learning Fieldbook.* Jossey-Bass. San Francisco, CA: Pfeiffer.

Chapter 6
Introduction to Instructional Design

The first time any safety professional hears about instructional design is likely to be the first time they try to gain an understanding of the science behind training (or maybe, it's when reading this chapter). Instructional design is in itself a career, but one most safety trainers are unlikely to find familiar. To put it simply, the whole idea behind instructional design is to create a path toward achieving a particular goal and is an approach to creating instruction or learning experiences. The whole idea of instructional design comes from the notion that training is most effective when it provides learners with a clear statement of what they must be able to do as a result of the training and how their performance will be evaluated. Sounds simple right? Throwing in a video to meet a regulatory requirement for training is not instructional design. *Instructional design* is purposeful and is the process of creating training to get to a certain place using different methods of facilitation. Safety professionals delivering safety training are more likely to be subject matter experts (SMEs) than instructional design professionals. It's probable that SMEs do not "sign up" to be trainers, but they may (or may not) find that they really enjoy this role. SMEs learning a bit about instructional design can make training more enjoyable not just for trainees but also for themselves since no one likes to waste time, money, or energy on something that has limited effectiveness.

Safety professionals are often familiar with system safety, which is a way of applying engineering and management principles, criteria, and techniques to optimize safety. System safety is a way of managing risks that considers the work environment as a system. Just like system safety, it is helpful to think of instructional design as a system—there are inputs and outputs and most likely indirect as well as direct relationships between different aspects of the design. Without considering instructional design, the goal of delivering a safety training course can be met, but little else will be achieved.

Instructional Design Systems

It may seem like the consideration of instructional design principles is going to add too much time and effort to an already long list of job responsibilities, but done correctly, the use of instructional design principles will make safety training efforts more efficient by being more effective and will help trainees remember key information longer. There are a variety of popular instructional design systems to consider. Two of the more popular are ADDIE (Analyze, Design, Develop, Implement, Evaluate) and SAM (Successive Approximation Model). They are similar systems, but the general idea is they are exactly that—systems. Once a system is in place, designing future training programs will go more quickly and be more efficient. A good instructional design system will work because it will produce observable, measurable, and replicable elements. When it comes to the all-important Holy Grail of training, measuring return on investment, instructional system design can play a major role in helping the trainer be able to do that.

Instructional design is important in planning for trainee retention of safety training materials because of the basic process training flows through when these systems are in place. In the ADDIE model, there is a five-step cycle, shown in Figure 6.1.

Figure 6.1 ✦ ADDIE method of instructional design (Adapted from Sink 2014)

The graph, and the letters ADDIE, refer to: analysis, design, development, implementation, and evaluation, which then feed back into analysis again. If evaluation shows that trainees are not remembering information or using it on the job as expected, that information feeds back up into the analysis stage, which then allows the trainer to redesign or tweak the development before the next time the training program is delivered.

The first step in the ADDIE model is *analysis*, and this is important as it relates to retention of the training material. When an instructional designer or safety professional decides to create a safety training program, training analysis will make it clear whether or not training is the answer. If training is not quite sticking, then it is possible that training was not the solution to the problem to begin with. A safety professional can create and deliver an exceptional safety training program and then wonder why there's no change in the workplace. The lack of change will not be because the information didn't stick but because training was likely not what was needed. A thorough analysis will help direct the trainer to the appropriate solution.

The second step in the ADDIE model is *design*, and this step can be essential in creating safety training that will be remembered after the class is completed and applied in the workplace. Central to the design process is coming up with goals and objectives that will be tied directly to the evaluation, so it's important to spend some time in this area.

The next stage in the ADDIE model is *development*. In this stage, all of the safety training materials will be produced, and pilot testing should be conducted. Pilot testing is often overlooked, but it can be a critical step in making sure that no time or money is wasted. If a safety trainer waits until after the first training class to see how well the safety training program works and then gets negative feedback or information, a lot of time and money has already been wasted. During the development phase, the training materials are prepared and should be reviewed by the subject matter expert, if that is not the safety trainer. The training materials include any interactive activities that will be used in the program. There are several chapters in this book that talk about the importance of adding in participatory learning, and example activities are provided throughout this book. In the development phase, a trainer can see what can be added in and how it will tie into the overall objectives.

The fourth stage in the ADDIE model is *implementation*. Implementation is when the program is actually delivered. The actual delivery of a training class may be all that is done in many safety training programs; if this is the case, the training is lacking. By using all of the steps of ADDIE, a safety trainer can greatly improve the effectiveness of the training material.

The fifth stage is *evaluation*, and although it is listed last, it actually continues to occur through all of the other stages in the ADDIE process. When a training program is finished, supervisors can be contacted to see if the goals of the training have been met. Additionally, evaluations that have been completed by the trainees and other stakeholders can be reviewed and acted upon.

The Successive Approximation Model, better known as SAM, is a simplified version of ADDIE and is designed to gain feedback and create working models faster than those created in the ADDIE process. Many talent development professionals prefer one system over the other. Regardless of which instructional design system is selected, ADDIE or SAM, both will increase the chance that training programs created will align with training class objectives and company goals.

Learning Theories

One of the major figures in adult learning, Robert Gagné, mentioned in Chapter 3, described learning theory as a set of processes that provide "conceptual structures involved in the process of taking in information and getting it transformed so that it is stored in long-term memory and later recalled as an observable human performance" (Gagné 2011). Safety professionals may question why they should know about learning theories. Having knowledge of adult learning theories will allow safety professionals to consider different strategies, tactics, and learning environments that support the different types of theories. Once familiar with different types of learning theories, training materials can be designed in a way that aligns with the different ways that adults learn. If safety trainers are questioned about a particular training delivery format, they will be able to explain how it relates to a particular learning theory. Knowing different learning theories will also help safety professionals understand how decisions they make with respect to training class design and delivery can influence knowledge acquisition, retention, and how learning is successfully transferred back on the job.

Three main theories of instructional design include constructivism, cognitivism, and behaviorism. A basic introduction to each follows.

Constructivism

Constructivist theories state that the trainee is in control of his or her own learning. Constructivists focus on how learners internalize what they have learned. The theory explains that learners construct knowledge from assimilation and accommodation. What this means for safety professionals is that, when trainees attempt to assimilate new training content, they are incorporating it into what they already know. *Assimilation* may occur when a trainee's new experiences are aligned with internal beliefs of the world. The opposite of assimilation is *accommodation*, and this occurs when a new experience contradicts what a safety trainee already believes. If a safety trainer is able to get a trainee to experience accommodation, then the trainee is going to reconsider how he or she thinks about a particular situation or experience. Accommodation is the mechanism by which failure leads to learning. In Chapter 14, the importance of failing in learning as it relates to retention is explained in greater detail.

When a trainer is designing safety training classes based on constructivism, they are designing experiences that are discovery oriented. Learning activities such as Safety Consultant for a Minute, described in Chapter 15, provide multiple chances to experiment. Training activities based on constructivist theory will provide many chances for trainees to encounter what happens in their day-to-day jobs, including all of the issues and uncertainties that may arise. Constructivists also believe that how people learn is influenced by their cultural settings. The importance of culture is covered in greater detail in Chapter 7.

To incorporate constructivist theories when designing safety training, safety professionals should keep the following in mind:

- Learners should be held responsible for their own learning. This is also mentioned as an important part of accelerated learning principles as explained in Chapter 5.
- Learning activities should be included that will provide the trainees with a variety of experiences.
- A trainer should be more of a facilitator and guide the learners in their own learning.
- Trainers using constructivist theories would not be reading from slides or only delivering a lecture.
- Constructivist-based safety training should also have real-world relevance, as most safety training should.

- Interactive safety training activities should provide plenty of opportunities for trainees to work together.

As mentioned in Chapter 5, one facet of accelerated learning is to have trainees learn from one another, and this is a constructivist's perspective. In fact, many of the suggested ways to incorporate constructivist theory are closely related to the principles of accelerated learning.

Finally, constructivist safety training activities should allow for a variety of outcomes from each activity. All of these outcomes will not be positive; some may include failure as well. One way to achieve different outcomes is through the use of safety training games. See Chapter 16 on gamification and retention and the sample games described in Chapters 19–22.

Cognitivism

Cognitivists believe that the learner observes behavioral patterns and then focuses on how to learn. *Cognitive theories* pinpoint what is happening to learning internally (Sink 2014). Cognitivism focuses on the thought process behind the behavior and the idea that learning occurs primarily through exposure to logically presented information. Much of the information presented in safety training can benefit from focusing on the thought processes behind specific acts because the real world, where the safety training needs to be applied, can be highly variable. Being able to think through why a particular action may or may not be the best step to take is critical in a work environment where there are risks and safety should be optimal. For example, in a hazardous waste clean-up class, it would be impossible to present trainees with every possible scenario they may potentially face if they are called upon to clean up a hazardous waste spill. Since cognitivism focuses on how to learn, trainers using cognitivism in their training materials would include things like problem-solving exercises, thinking, information processing, and concept formation. Especially important is finding ways to help the trainees connect new information to prior knowledge. As discussed in Chapter 3, building upon what we already know is important to learning retention.

Safety trainers wanting to use cognitive theories when creating safety training classes may consider the following suggestions:

- Carefully organize training information. The information should be presented clearly in chunks, with well-designed instructions and order.
- Assimilate new content into existing knowledge.

- Use real-life stories and plenty of examples whenever possible.
- Plan to help the trainees strengthen any new information they are learning and put it into their long-term memory by providing plenty of opportunities for practice followed by feedback.
- Provide summary information.
- Use testing and evaluations as ways for the trainees to apply what they learned when they're back on the job.
- Include a variety of methods to get and keep the attention of trainees.
- Always make sure trainees understand the benefits of being in the class, learning the material, and applying it on the job (i.e., "What's in it for me?").
- Add opportunities for movement and activities as discussed in Chapter 5 on accelerated learning.

Behaviorism

Behaviorism has to do with the study of measurable and observable behaviors that are repeated until they are automatic. Most basic high school or college psychology classes discuss B. F. Skinner, his dog experiments, and operant conditioning, which explain the causes of actions and consequences. If trainers remember this idea from high school or college psychology class, they know that behaviors can be directed by looking at the relationships between stimuli and responses. In the training world, behaviorists look at training as a way to encourage learning with the reinforcement of desired responses. Safety training that's based on behaviorism considers how to shape trainees' behaviors through reinforcement.

B. F. Skinner applied his findings from the laboratory to something called programmed learning. In *programmed learning*, the information to be presented is divided into small steps. In each small step presented, only one idea or new concept is introduced, and material previously introduced is reviewed. When each step is presented, the trainees then respond appropriately, gaining immediate feedback. The idea here is that, as the trainees move through the various steps and get immediate feedback on their answers or actions for each step, the behavior will be gradually shaped until the learning objective is achieved. Much like concepts taught in behavioral safety, behaviorism focuses on observable behaviors.

Behaviorism is concerned with what can be observed and not the thought processes behind why someone does or does not do something. Behaviorists focus on what the trainees need to know. Techniques to get trainees to learn only what they need to know include things like identification and memorization. Although not preferred, the behaviorist approach has some value in areas of safety training where understanding the meaning of a sign, for example, can be learned through pure memorization. Let's say that trainees need to know that a particular sound means a forklift is backing up. The sound is heard and the trainee stops walking and identifies where the forklift is and gets out of the way. That is an observable behavior. The trainee can identify the sound and behave accordingly. That is behaviorism.

Behaviorist theory can also be used for skill building. It can be used while the trainee remembers a skill and practices, while receiving feedback from the trainer, followed by additional practice. In safety training, this can be used at a surface level with safe lifting. The trainer demonstrates how to safely lift a box, instructs the trainees how to do it, watches them perform the skill, corrects them along the way, and then allows them to practice. This is an example of a behavioral skill that can be observed. In reality, many training programs on back safety go deeper into how the back works so that safe lifting techniques make more sense. Instead of just following a set of instructions, understanding why the steps to safe lifting are correct can help trainees to make deeper connections and understand the material more clearly.

The following are a few ways that safety trainers can include the basics of behaviorism in safety training classes.

- Provide objectives for every safety training class.
- Implement criterion reference testing. Criterion reference testing is designed so that a trainee's behavior is measured against predetermined criteria, including a passing score. For example, in an exam for tower crane operators, the test taker must successfully be able to demonstrate a variety of operations, such as shift inspections, movement of hooks and chains, and operation of the crane on a zigzag corridor.
- Test training classes and activities on a small sampling of a class before fully implementing them.
- Chunk contents based on the learning objectives. For example, for every objective, there should be a separate smaller learning module.
- Create measurable learning outcomes.
- Use tangible rewards and informative feedback.
- Guide trainees in mastering a set of predictable skills and behaviors.

Constructivism, cognitivism, and/or behaviorism theories can be selected as a basis for a training class design based on the learning content to be delivered. The behavioral approach can be good when trainees have no prior knowledge. The cognitive approach can be used when trainees will be expected to solve problems in unfamiliar situations (a common occurrence in safety training). The constructivist approach works when trainees need to deal with problems that are not well designed and call for reflection (Ertmer and Newby 2013). The three basic theories of instructional design can be used together when necessary and can work well together.

Externally Created Training

When creating safety training programs, it is important to tie instructional design principles, including the different learning theories, into the training content. If the safety training program were purchased, and the safety professional simply told to implement it as is, the safety trainer can still evaluate the program and modify or add to it to fit the needs of a particular training class. Hopefully, and especially if the purchased training materials were from a reputable training provider, instructional design principles were already used in the development. When reviewing safety training class materials prepared by an outside company or by someone else, the safety trainer should ask the following:

- Is the information presented clearly and simply? Is there limited use of technical jargon?
- Are glossaries or other learning aids provided for technical terms?
- Has the overall goal of the training program been identified?
- Are there appropriate and well-defined learning objectives?
- Is the goal of the training broken down into chunks or separate topics?
- Are assessments provided that accurately measure the amount of learning that occurred?
- Have the learning needs of the trainees been considered based on trainees' backgrounds, education levels, and preferences?
- Have trainees' specific needs been taken into account?
- Do the trainees know what is expected of them in the training program?
- Do training materials provide exactly what the trainees need? (Nothing more and nothing less.)

- Will it be possible to evaluate whether the trainees learned what they needed to as a result of the training program?
- Does the training program match the goals and meet the needs of the company?

Delivery Method

One of the key decisions to be made with respect to instructional design is the method of delivery. Since the Covid-19 pandemic, more and more training is being delivered online, either over a platform like Zoom or through an established e-learning platform. Chapter 23 discusses retention techniques for online delivery.

Needs Analysis

A needs analysis, discussed earlier in the chapter, is ideally completed before every training class. This analysis would reveal who the trainees are, where they are located, their background, and their particular skills and experience. Knowing all this can provide direction to a safety trainer, suggesting what delivery medium to use. A basic procedure for conducting a training needs analysis is shown in Figure 6.2.

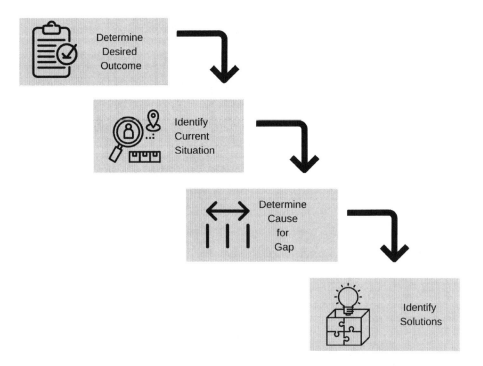

Figure 6.2 ✦ Needs analysis procedure (Source: Rossett 1987)

If a safety trainer is asked to create and/or deliver safety training, the first step is to identify the desired outcome. Safety training is not always the answer, in particular for things like bad attitudes or failure to follow the rules. If the outcome is to increase knowledge of safety procedures or provide training on skills necessary to perform a job safely, the needs assessment can move to the next step.

When it has been determined that training can help improve the situation, the trainer needs to gather information on the current status of the problem. This can be done through review of inspection and accident reports, workplace observations, informal interviews with the workers expected to attend the training, and interviews with supervisors.

Determining causes is something most safety professionals do fairly often but probably not in the context of safety training. Asking a series of "Why" questions can help identify why the gap exists between the current situation and the desired outcome. Once the causes are identified, the training can be designed and delivered to address the causes.

When the needs analysis has been completed and the best method of delivery has been determined, knowing the company's goals and objectives can solidify the decision. For example, if a company wants every single employee trained on a new company policy across six locations around the world, but has a limited budget, online learning will likely be the best solution. If the goal were to train all mechanics in one facility on the use of a new tool, an in-person, hands-on class would probably work better.

Options for training delivery are listed below, although new technology may offer exciting options in the future:

- Online learning (web-based training, computer-based training, simulator-based training, and training via mobile devices)
- Classroom training (often called instructor-led training)
- Performance aids (including job aids and chatbots)
- Games, simulations, and experiential learning (including training class activities and tabletop exercises)
- Self-directed learning (self-paced learning using a variety of media)
- On-the-job training (training that happens during a normal work day)

Mixed delivery methods are another option and are very effective in increasing retention of training material. An example of a mixed delivery model for safety training would be a training program that included preclass reading on a technical topic, followed by in-class or on-the-job training on the same topic. In this example, the in-person portion would focus on hands-on activities. After the class has been completed, reinforcement could be provided through a series of texts created as microlearning modules. In this case, a variety of different delivery methods are combined for comprehensive coverage and maximum effectiveness.

After the delivery method has been chosen, additional design considerations need to be made. Begin with objectives. These do not have to be boring and simply written to make training records look more complete, but when written well, they can be a guide for the trainees to understand what is expected of them and what they must do to master the content. Objectives can also help ensure that unnecessary training material is not included and presented to the trainees. If a piece of training content does not match up to an objective, it should not be included. Breaking down a training course into objectives also helps trainers to organize the information in their course so it can be presented in a logical way that makes sense to the trainees. Sometimes when trainers are so familiar with the content, it can be easy to forget how a trainee will experience the information for the first time. If the training content is broken down into separate topics that all tie to different objectives, and the session ends up with 20 objectives, the trainer realizes there is way too much content to be covered in the training class and several classes may be needed.

The objectives also provide a piece of precourse communication to supervisors and trainees. More on the importance of preclass communication can be found in Chapter 8. Finally, the objectives directly tie back to the class evaluations, and evaluations can be central to demonstrating return on investment. Return on investment and evaluations are discussed further in Chapters 1 and 13, respectively.

After objectives are determined and explicitly written, it's time to plan how to meet each one. A subject matter expert acting as an instructional designer, which is the case with most safety professionals, has many choices when deciding what to include:

- Preclass activities, including trainee and supervisor communication (see Chapter 8)
- Postclass activities/follow-up, including personal action plans, future training, recall activities, reminders, posttests, assignments, and exercises (see Chapter 8).

- Effective introduction techniques, including ways to get attention, guidance for recall of past related training, expectation setting, and plans to help the trainees be comfortable and ready to learn (see Chapters 3, 5, and 7)
- Pretests, in-process tests, and posttests (see Chapter 13)
- Handouts, including the best format
- Activities, including structured questions, brainstorming, case studies, debate prompts, demonstrations, discussion, games, job aids, walk-abouts, lecture, quizzes, readings, and simulations (for examples, see Chapters 18–25)

When planning content delivery and activities, it's suggested that trainers use a variety of techniques. The goal is to increase learning and retention of information. When an experience engages multiple senses it's more likely to be remembered later. The more senses through which information is experienced, the more places in memory it is stored, and the more likely it will be remembered later (ATD Research 2017).

Andragogy

Another very influential individual in the field of adult learning is Malcolm Knowles. He developed the idea of andragogy, which is the theory of adult learning (Knowles et al. 1998). Malcolm Knowles was the first person to recognize that adults learn differently than children, so learning techniques that adults remember from attending grade school will not be the same techniques that work when providing information and training to an adult workforce. His *theory of andragogy* is based on his belief that five main principles are involved in the way adults learn.

1. *Self-concept of the learner*
   Self-concept of a learner means that as people get older they want to be able to direct what they learn and when they learn it. Having no control over their learning can cause resentment in older learners. Some of the theories mentioned earlier in this chapter describe the importance of having learners be responsible for their own learning, and this relates to the self-concept of the learner.
2. *Higher experience of the learner*
   An important part of learning for adults, and the trainees that safety professionals will have in their training classes, is that they have

already accumulated a lot of experience and knowledge before they even set foot in a training class. Unlike children, who may be exposed to a topic for the very first time when they hear it from their teacher, the trainees in safety training classes presumably will not be hearing something for the first time. Safety trainers should always try to connect any new material to what the trainee already knows; this will help to create a relevant training experience ("what's in it for me"). Guiding trainees toward changing their beliefs and accepting new information is pivotal to having an important and meaningful safety training class. If it's possible, safety trainers should allow the trainees in their class to assess what they already know and skip to what is new information and what is relevant to them. There's nothing worse for a trainee than having to sit through a class just to satisfy attendance when the information is already well known. Many experienced workers may feel they could teach the class because they have so much background in the area. Safety trainers always need to find ways to make the class information new and relevant, even if the trainees have been exposed to it many times before.

3. *Readiness to learn*
Readiness to learn refers to adults' desires to be able to do what they need to do. It's important to keep this in mind when designing training classes. Trainees will be more likely to pay attention and learn something when trainers make it clear that they are working toward and contributing to a particular goal. Further, adult trainees will be eager to learn something new when they know they can apply it to the real world.

4. *Orientation to learning*
Orientation to learning refers to trainees' needs to learn what will help them immediately. Instead of learning particular subjects, such as many people do in college and in earlier studies or training, an orientation for learning is more of a concern for adults. It is more important for adult trainees to study or learn something that will help them solve a current problem rather than to gain a broader understanding about particular subjects.

5. *Motivation to learn*
As trainees become adults, their motivation to pay attention and learn something new is increasingly driven by internal factors. For example, if there is a new person on a construction site who has never had to do a particular kind of work, that person will be more moti-

vated to learn the new job. When trainees are more familiar with a job and have been working on the construction site for a longer period of time, it's likely they are not very motivated to learn something new. However, if specific training promises a payoff, trainees will be more highly motivated to learn. For instance, if there is a new piece of equipment on the factory floor and anyone who knows how to use that piece of equipment will be eligible to work on it or be promoted or get a raise, that would generate enough internal motivation to prompt trainees to learn. For more on motivation, see Chapter 7.

Review and Retention Activity

The poster shown in Figure 6.3 is reinforcement in the form of retrieval practice. This learning and retention activity is described in Chapter 10, "Repetition, Spacing, Retrieval Practice, and Interleaving."

Review the poster and attempt to fill in the missing information. This act of retrieving information from memory will help the information be retained longer.

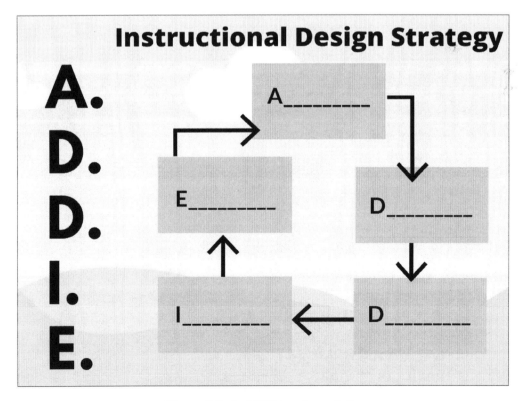

Figure 6.3 ✦ ADDIE poster activity

References

Association for Talent Development (ATD). 2017. "The Science of Learning: Key Strategies for Designing and Delivering Training." Alexandria, VA: ATD Press.

Gagné, R. M. 2011. *Principles of Instructional Design*. Belmont, CA: Wadsworth.

Ertmer, P. A., and T. J. Newby. 2013. "Behaviorism, Cognitivism, Constructivism: Comparing Critical Features from an Instructional Design Perspective." *Performance Improvement Quarterly*, 26(2):43–71.

Knowles, Malcolm S., Elwood F. Holton, and Richard A. Swanson. 1998. *The Adult Learner: The Definitive Classic in Adult Education and Human Resource Development*. 5th ed. Houston, TX: Gulf Publishing Company.

Rossett, A. 1987. *Training Needs Assessment*. Englewood Cliffs, NJ: Educational Technology Publications.

Sink, D. 2014. "Design Models and Learning Theories for Adults." *ASTD Handbook: The Definitive Reference for Training and Development*. E. Beich, ed. Alexandria, VA: American Society for Training and Development (ASTD) Press.

Chapter 7
Facilitation and Motivation

The way a safety trainer facilitates a training session and the motivation of the learner have a lot to do with how much of the training content gets remembered.

Facilitation

Facilitation is a learned skill and is extremely important in the delivery of good safety training. A good facilitator will work to get trainees very involved in their own learning and will use activities such as questioning techniques, brainstorming, small group discussions, and teamwork as ways to get trainees to share ideas. Often, safety trainers are simply told to deliver training without having any background in facilitation techniques. While successful safety careers have traditionally focused on technical knowledge, soft skills, such as facilitation techniques, are of equal importance.

The main purpose of a facilitator, as opposed to a trainer, is to guide trainees through training material by promoting discussions, leading activities, and administering end-of-class evaluations. Trainers delivering safety content without safety expertise may fall into the facilitator category. For many reading this book, the job of facilitator is also part of the safety trainer role.

In Chapter 3, the differences between working memory (also called short-term memory) and long-term memory were discussed. According to Taylor and Marienau, "Facilitation that encourages active engagement and involves conscious association and categorization early on can lead to more meaningful and longer-lasting learning" (Taylor and Marienau 2016). In Chapter 5 on accelerated learning principles, active learning was listed as important in helping trainees to remember longer. Simply making learning interactive by adding in an activity is not going to increase learning unless that activity is facilitated well.

Debriefing

A key aspect of facilitation is debriefing. *Debriefing* involves discussing an interactive learning activity after it has been completed in order to help trainees understand what they just learned and experienced, as well as help them make connections to how the experience will help them back on the job. If a training activity is used, and the class simply moves on when the activity is over with no discussion, most of the value of the activity is lost. A safety training activity is only as good as the debrief that follows when it encourages people to reflect and reinforce the learning (Matthews 2012). Unfortunately, this step is often skipped. Debriefing is probably left out for no reason other than lack of awareness by safety trainers about what it is or why it's important.

Trainers can begin a debriefing exercise by asking a few questions. After an activity or lecture, trainees can be asked, "What did you learn?" Once they have responded with a few points, trainers should ask the follow-up question—"So What?" Trainers should ask trainees why these points are important. Trainers should conclude by asking "And now . . . ?" With this last question, trainers are persuading trainees to commit to acting in a new way in the future or applying a new skill or the information they just learned.

Action Planning

One of the main purposes of debriefing is reinforcement. One type of reinforcement to consider is *action planning*. Some of the suggested debriefing activities later in this chapter suggest some sort of action planning. Having trainees identify the need to have a plan in place to use their new knowledge and then having them actually work on this plan is very important. This is probably not how they have been experiencing training before, so the reaction trainers may get from trainees might be one of disbelief or confusion. While action planning toward the end of a training class is a good idea, it is better suited for soft skills such as safety supervisor, leadership, or communication skills training. An action plan for something compliance based, like machine guarding, is likely to be very short indeed.

Emma Weber, an expert in learning transfer, suggests that action planning follow an *ACTION conversation model*, with ACTION representing an acronym for the stages of the learning transfer conversation. According to Weber, "A" represents *accountability*, which gives the trainee responsibility for his or her own learning transfer. "C" stands for *calibration*, which determines where the trainee is now and where he or she wants to be. "T" stands for *target*, which is where the trainee hopes to be. "I" stands for *information* and refers to what is currently going on and what people, places, or things might be standing in the way. "O" stands for *option* and reflects the various approaches the trainee has for the learning transfer. "N" stands for *next steps* and serves to formalize how the trainee is committed to the necessary steps to move forward. Getting trainees to identify and plan how they will use the information and skills is critical in ensuring transfer back to the job (Weber 2018).

Let's look at an example of a group of safety supervisors who are using the ACTION conversation model for providing feedback on unsafe behaviors. Most of these supervisors have never been in this position before and have never had any formal communications training. They are skeptical about using the new skills presented to them in providing feedback on unsafe behaviors, but since many unsafe conditions are going unchecked and uncorrected, it is imperative that trainees understand the importance of the skill they are being asked to learn. Starting with the "A" for accountability, the trainees need to take ownership for learning the necessary skills and putting them in place in the workplace. They need to understand they are responsible for putting their action plan into place and that there will be follow-up to check on their success and any additional support they may need. "C" for calibration, asks the supervisors to identify where they see themselves now. If a successful safety supervisor should be providing appropriate feedback whenever they see an unsafe activity 100 percent of the time, they can determine where their current actions lie with respect to that goal. "T" is the level of behavior they are shooting for, and it should align with the overall goal of the training program. "I" for information, is the determination, through data gathering, of what is currently going on and what might be a barrier to fixing it. In this hypothetical situation, information could include collecting reports of unsafe behaviors that continue regardless of trainees being corrected, noting when those behaviors occur, and figuring out why the existing feedback doesn't work. "O" for option, spells out the various options the trainees could take. What are the choices the trainees will be able to draw from? Finally, the trainees must commit to taking action toward getting where they want to go. "N" stands for the next steps they will take toward reaching their goals.

Debriefing can take the form of guided questions or can be in the form of a formal activity. Suggestions follow for debriefing any training activity. Some of these techniques may be better suited for certain training activities and not suited for others.

Sample Debriefing Activities

Red Light/Green Light

Ask trainees to draw two columns on a piece of paper, or the trainer can draw two columns on a flip chart or whiteboard. On one side of the page, a green light should be drawn, and on the other, a red light. The trainer should ask trainees to brainstorm what they will start or continue to do as a result of the training, and these results should be written under the green light. The trainees should next be asked what they will stop doing, and those ideas should be written under the red light.

1-2-3

At the end of an exercise or lecture, trainees should be asked to think of one thing they still have a question about, two things they feel extremely confident about, and three ways they will use the new information back on the job. This will not only help trainers to see where additional clarification is needed or where confusion exists, but also will help trainers recognize where trainees feel confident, which further helps them make the commitment to apply what they learned back on the job.

One Big Thing

At the end of a training class, trainees should be asked to name the One Big Thing they learned, the one thing they could start doing as soon as they are back on the job that would make a big difference for their safety and the safety of others. By focusing on only one idea, it will be easier for a trainee to remember and act on it.

TABB Exercise

One way to encourage commitment is with a TABB exercise. This is also a good activity to use when wrapping up a class. To use the TABB exercise, each trainee is given a piece of paper with the letters T, A, B, and B across the top. These letters stand for takeaways, actions, barriers, and benefits. Trainees should be asked to write appropriate responses under each of the columns and then hand them in to the trainer at the end of class. After reviewing them, trainers can identify where future training classes may need to be adjusted, as well as where the trainee may need additional help in removing any barriers that will stop him or her from applying the safety training. If the same barriers are identified by many trainees there is a bigger issue overall that the safety trainer can begin to address.

In debriefing exercises, trainees are able to identify the most important information they learned and why it matters. Debriefing also helps trainees remember the new information and act on it by applying it to their real-life situation. Debriefing can be thought of as action-focused reflection and is regarded as the key to knowledge acquisition and transfer of training since it forces the training to infect causal, unconditional relations between events and actions, leading to the development of strategies for handling unforeseen events and initiating and promoting self-regulatory motivational processes (Burke et al. 2006).

Taking a few minutes to review what has been learned from an experience, even outside of the training environment, and asking questions about the experience is known as reflection. For safety trainers, reflection and debriefing are very similar.

Retrieval

Many facilitation techniques involve trainers using some sort of retrieval activity, and done properly, this can aid long-term retention. The act of retrieval forms the basis for most of the safety training activities in this book, including flash-card activities, Braindump, Safety Lotería and Safety Sequence, and work with case studies. Retrieval is also demonstrated in activities such as a Hazard Hunt where trainees rely on past experiences and information learned in order to complete a new activity that is in an environment they have not seen before. Another way to add retrieval practice into a safety training class is by helping trainees find ways to relate the information to what they already know. One of the easiest ways to do this is to explain it to somebody else in your own words. Richard Feynman, discussed in Chapter 4, proposed that one of the best ways to learn new information is to teach others. This form of learning is discussed in detail in Chapter 18 on teamwork.

Metaphors and Analogies

Another facilitation technique that can aid in memory retention is the use of metaphors. In order to learn, a trainee must be able to link a current experience with prior learning, and metaphors and analogies are ways to do that through association and categorization.

Metaphors are what thought is all about. We use metaphors, consciously or unconsciously, all the time, so it is a matter of mental hygiene to take responsibility for these metaphors, to look at them carefully, to see how meanings slide from one to the other. By recognizing similarities, metaphors bring different kinds of knowledge together (Bateson 1994). As facilitators, it is necessary to remember that everything ever learned is based on metaphors and analogies because these are the reference points the brain uses (Taylor and Marienau 2016). In secondary school, many children are introduced to the idea of metaphors as a figure of speech to learn about and use in their writing, but "Metaphors are not just linguistic elements that people use to communicate; metaphors are fundamental vessels through which people understand and experience the world around them" (Zhong and Leonardelli 2008).

Technical and difficult topics can be explained to others through the use of analogies (Spiro et al. 1988). For example, trainers delivering safe lifting training may want to convey the idea that the discs between the vertebrae in the spinal column are soft and when too much pressure is placed on them, such as when bending incorrectly, the walls of the disc can become weak, allowing fluid to seep out and cause pain. To use an analogy to explain this, the trainer could explain how the discs are like jelly donuts that when pressured too much may leak their contents. This could even be demonstrated in a training class using real jelly donuts and small blocks in the place of vertebrae. When analogies are used, learning can be transferred between the simpler concept or task and the complex concept or task. Although this analogy may seem quite unusual, it is likely to stay in a trainee's mind longer. Memory experts have long known that a trick to remembering information is to make its presentation so unusual or strange that it is difficult to forget. While this would not be appropriate for much of the learning that occurs in a safety training class, it can help in creating analogies that will stick with trainees.

Emotions

Proper facilitation of training activities not only increases the attentiveness of the trainees, which in turn extends their retention, but can also help trainees experience different emotions. The more emotions connected to an experience, the better it will be remembered (Taylor and Marienau 2016). That is why things like storytelling are such a valuable part of safety training. A good story told well will cause trainees to experience various emotions, making it more likely to be remembered. Storytelling is discussed in detail in Chapter 9, "Making it Real."

For many adults, the fear of being singled out and asked a question in front of their peers may trigger negative emotions that are more closely related to a serious physical threat than learning. Trainees all have stress-related hormones that can either help or hurt training. A moderate amount can help by increasing the attention a trainee gives to the trainer.

A learning environment, such as a safety training class, should be low stress, enjoyable, and stimulating. Stress and anxiety are two emotions that inhibit learning by sending the amygdala into overdrive. The amygdala is where emotional learning takes place, especially learning related to fear and threat response. When learners experience stress they go into a hyperstimulated state known as the affective filter, which inhibits information from passing through the amygdala to the information processing parts of the brain. Emotions can also serve to distract when they trigger a threat response. Trainees that are upset about a personal or work issue may have a difficult time learning (Taylor and Marienau 2016).

In order for learning to occur, safety trainers need to reduce stress, anxiety, and even threat within the classroom and create an environment where learning is enjoyable and exciting. Exciting and enjoyable learning environments will cause a dopamine release that can lead to memory building (Halls 2014). Most memories people can recall easily are tied to emotional moments and situations. This is because the hippocampus is kicked into high gear and accelerates the formation of memories. The optimal state for learning is believed to be a moderate amount of positive emotion. This level of positive emotion is found to promote creativity, insight, and perception (Dixit et al. 2019).

Training Environment

The ANSI standard on the accepted practices in safety, health and environmental training specifies that a training environment should also consider safety, climate, noise, lighting, and ergonomics (ANSI/ASSP Z490.1). The trainee will learn best when comfortable—not only mentally but physically as well. If a trainee is forced to sit on an uncomfortable chair with an attached desk in a hot training room with poor lighting and a lot of background noise, it will make it more difficult to focus and pay attention.

According to Dixit (Dixit et al. 2019), safety trainers can encourage positive emotions in their training classes by:

- Maximizing novelty
- Creating positive anticipation
- Incorporating rewarding social experiences in which learners can connect with other people

A safety trainer can maximize novelty by adding in new training experiences that will surprise the trainees. For example, if trainees show up to a scheduled training class and sit at desks expecting to be shown another safety video followed by a request to sign an attendance sheet, a safety trainer could instead base the entire class on an interactive safety training activity. Having props or other visual aids present at the beginning of a training class can also add novelty. When presenting training related to musculoskeletal disorders, a trainer could have a full-size skeleton in the training room so that when trainees enter the classroom their attention will be drawn to the skeleton, and they will know that things will be different than they are accustomed to.

Novelty and curiosity often go hand-in-hand as novelty often increases curiosity, and as most people know, it is hard not to pay attention when curious. Giving trainees a problem that needs to be solved is a great way to do this. The use of case studies is discussed in Chapter 9. They can be slightly modified so they can be provided to trainees without the ending or the solution. Trainees can be told they need to work with others to come up with what they believe to be the end to the story. After all groups of trainees have shared their answers, the trainer can share what actually happened.

To create positive anticipation, a trainer can use preclass communication (discussed in Chapter 8) to his or her advantage. Attendance confirmation and agenda emails can mention interactive activities that are planned, guest speakers that may be invited, or even snacks that may be served. If trainees will receive a certificate, or better yet, a badge or other token that is part of a planned gamification effort, this can also be communicated early in an effort to increase anticipation.

To incorporate rewarding social experiences, trainers simply need to plan class activities that allow trainees the opportunity to interact with one another. A training class may be the only time a trainee gets to see and interact with others. Interactive class activities based on teamwork not only lead to positive emotions but provide rewarding social experiences as well. A variety of interactive class activities are provided in the chapters at the end of this book.

Motivation

There is a difference in motivation to learn and motivation to transfer the learning content back to the job. *Motivation to transfer* can be explained by the desire of the trainees to use the knowledge and skills that were mastered in the training program on the job when the training is over (Noe and Schmitt 1986). Research has shown that the amount of training transferred back to the job is highly dependent on the trainee's intention to apply the learning (Knox 1988) and that the motivation to learn and a positive pretraining attitude positively correlate with the amount of learning that occurs. One particular study found that the level of pretraining motivation increases when the training is perceived as mandatory (Baldwin and Ford 1988), which if true, would be a positive factor in safety training transfer. The decision to learn and then transfer the learned information back to the job ultimately lies with the trainee, and trainees will make their own choices about what to pay attention to and plan to use and what to ignore.

One model that attempts to predict the decision-making process a trainee goes through when deciding whether or not something is important enough to learn and remember includes three decisions the trainee must make (Yelon et al. 2004):

- Is the information credible?
- Are the skills practical?
- To what extent are the knowledge or skills needed?

If these really are the three decisions a trainee makes internally before deciding if he or she will pay attention and remember a topic, then it may be important to have a subject matter expert assist with the training if one is not already scheduled to deliver it directly. Mental models were discussed in Chapter 3, and a trainee's preexisting mental model may come into play when considering these three decisions. If a trainee sat through safety training where the trainer did not know what he or she was talking about or focused on things that were interesting to the trainer but of little interest to the trainee, his or her expectations of the training class will already be unfairly skewed.

Four Motivation Principles

In addition to the three questions trainees ask themselves when deciding whether or not to pay attention, there are four principles that motivate trainees to learn and apply the content. If a safety professional can identify and incorporate these principles, the training is likely to be more successful.

The four main principles that govern the motivation to learn include inclusion, attitude, meaning, and competence. Trainees need to feel included. They need to feel they are in a safe environment and can express their opinions and thoughts and offer questions without being afraid of any kind of retaliation or negative feedback. Many trainers start off training classes with some kind of icebreaker or warm-up session in an attempt to make all trainees feel included and comfortable. Naturally, these openers should relate to the safety content.

The effects of emotions and motivation are discussed earlier in this chapter. A trainer can facilitate a classroom activity in ways that create a learning environment that promotes positive attitudes that will contribute toward learning. One of the best ways a trainer can do this, although it is not always possible with compliance training, is to offer choices to the trainees about how they'd like to learn or what exactly they would like to learn. Mandatory safety training may not offer much flexibility with this, but there are ways to allow the trainees to be more in control of their own learning. If it is possible to let trainees choose between an in-person class or e-learning, or the day and time of a class, that is a start in giving the trainees some control. If a trainer can offer several different in-class activities for the trainees to participate in, that is another way to let them make choices that affect their learning experience.

Additionally, the trainer can create positive attitudes by making the training content personally relevant. The importance of trainees understanding what's in it for them is discussed throughout this book. When training has meaning, trainees will pay more attention, because an adult never wants to pay attention and learn things that have no use for them personally. One way to create meaning is through engaging experiences, including interactive activities and games and clear information on why the content is important.

Trainees of all types want to be competent. Trainers can help trainees feel confident about their competence by giving them a chance to apply or practice what they have learned and to receive feedback. Timely feedback will let them know how well they are learning the information.

Extrinsic versus Intrinsic Motivation

Many people learn about intrinsic and extrinsic motivation when they take their first psychology class, whether that's in high school or later on in college. *Intrinsic motivation* is when an individual (e.g., a trainee) wants to do something on his own, and *extrinsic motivation* is when an individual does something to make someone else happy. It is likely that participation in safety training is extrinsically motivated. It would make sense then, if trainees are really motivated to learn, they are going to pay more attention to the content, which is the first step in helping them remember it after completing the class. In general, it is beneficial for the safety trainer to include both intrinsic and extrinsic motivation in training programs. Trainees will experience intrinsic rewards when they have a sense of accomplishment after learning something new. Trainees will experience extrinsic rewards when they receive something tangible for their learning. Some trainees like the idea of getting a small token as a reminder after a training class. It helps them associate their learning with pleasant experiences. Certificates, hard-hat stickers, or even workplace posters showing the names of trainees who successfully completed the training class can be great motivators.

Self-Determination Theory

Self-determination theory suggests that people are more motivated to do something when they believe what they do will have an effect on the outcome. In Ina Weinbauer-Heidel's book, *What Makes Training Really Work: 12 Levers of Transfer Effectiveness*, she refers to the importance of self-determination theory in the following way: "At its core, the question 'is the act in itself fun or not?' is replaced by 'do I want it for myself or do others want it?' Self-determination theory assumes that humans have an innate basic need for autonomy and self-determination. Like Maslow's theory which places self-realization at the top of a hierarchy of needs, this theory also holds that humans pursue what we ourselves want to do; that it is conducive—but not essential—to this pursuit if the activity itself gives us pleasure (intrinsic motivation); and that we tend to tackle things with great (and sustainable) motivation if they have positive and desirable consequences for us" (Weinbauer-Heidel and Ibeschitz-Manderbach 2018).

To use this theory and Dr. Weinbauer-Heidel's ideas about safety training, safety trainers must find ways to motivate trainees to follow the new safety rules or procedures they are learning about. If trainees are told they have to follow the rules because that's just the way the company operates, that would be an example of extrinsically controlled motivation. If trainees are told they need to follow the safety rules, and they believe it's because it will keep them safe and injury free for their families, then that is an example of extrinsic autonomous motivation. If a trainee thinks, "I will follow all of these safety rules because I don't want to get hurt or hurt others," that is an example of intrinsic motivation.

Extrinsic motivation can work. Research has shown that the amount of training used on the job is increased when there is external pressure from department supervisors enforcing the training (Gegenfurtner 2013). Since this is the way most trainees are likely motivated, safety trainers have probably realized this is not the best way to operate. Self-determination theory says this is not going to bring about a lasting change. The best way of motivating trainees to change for the long term is to place a greater emphasis on autonomous forms of motivation, as described in the earlier example of trainees who follow the safety rules because they want to be safe.

It can be difficult for a trainer to get trainees to be self-motivated when the safety training content is going to make their day-to-day job a little or a lot more difficult, or slower, or uncomfortable. If a new safety rule requires trainees to take an extra step to get a work permit completed before proceeding with a project, the new safety-related step is going to slow things down, and it's unlikely to be a popular new procedure. If the new safety rule is going to require the use of a full-face respirator, initially many trainees would not be excited about this change since it will take some time to get used to breathing in the additional personal protective equipment, and it may make them uncomfortable, especially during exertions.

Getting trainees to follow new procedures will require that they truly understand the benefits of doing so. The benefits of compliance, or reduced lost time and other injury costs, are not going to motivate trainees. Trainees need to see that by following the information provided in the safety training class they are choosing to do what is best for them personally. This must be continually stressed. One of the first things many trainers learn about how to deliver training is that trainees must understand what's in it for them, and although this is an overused phrase, it is still extremely important. The trainees must understand the reasoning behind the standard or the new procedures or the new policy and not just be told that's the way it is. If training focuses on interactive learning activities that make the trainees active participants in their own learning, they are more likely to have autonomous transfer motivation and be able to see how it applies to their situation. More information on the benefits of interactive learning are discussed in Chapter 5 on accelerated learning.

A good way to encourage autonomous transfer motivation is to use language that implies autonomy rather than control (Weinbauer-Heidel and Ibeschitz-Manderbach 2018). For example, in a safety training class on forklift safety, instead of saying "you must remove the keys from the forklift when you are more than 25 feet away," a trainer could consider posing the solution (removing the keys when 25 feet away) as a question, such as "Why do you think OSHA requires that keys be removed from a forklift when the operator is 25 feet away?" or "How far do you think you can walk away from a forklift before OSHA requires that you remove the keys?" The correct information will still be communicated but in a much less threatening manner.

Organizational Culture

Culture is usually identified as a set of shared values, language, and rituals that guide the interactions and operations of an organization (Marquardt 2002). "A learning culture can be described as an organizational culture that is oriented toward the promotion and facilitation of worker learning, participation, and dissemination, in order to contribute to organizational development and performance" (Rebelo and Gomes 2009).

As mentioned in Chapter 2, "Why Safety Training is Different," a trainee's culture can have an effect on individual and group motivation to participate in safety training. Not only can a company's culture affect the number of accidents and incidents that occur in a workplace, a company's safety culture can also have a profound effect on the amount of learning that is transferred back to the job after a training class. The training transfer climate is established by company leadership, supervisors, coworkers, and trainers, and can be impacted by employee reward systems, recognition systems, and the types of support in place after a trainee has left the training class. If there is a great safety training transfer environment, this can lead not only to better safe behaviors but to better application of the training content back on the job and also to the inspiration of coworkers, which affects their safe behaviors as well (Huang and Yang 2019).

To establish an excellent safety training culture, it may be wise to start at the supervisory level. Often the supervisors' support of safety training is already affected by the overall safety culture of the company. As long ago as 1957, research was conducted to show the link between an unsupportive organizational culture and transfer failure (Mosel 1957). These studies concluded that training only transfers to the extent that supervisors support and practice the same behaviors that staff is taught in the training environment. Safety professionals have long known that without having a supervisor who backs up safety procedures and policies, it's unlikely workers at all levels will support those same policies. If trainees learn one thing in a safety training class and then return to the work site and learn something else by watching coworkers and management do things a different way, the training from the classroom is not going to be transferred in an effective way. If the organizational culture supports not only training but also the use of the safe behaviors learned once trainees are back on the job, there will be a greater amount of transfer (Foxon 1993).

Instead of relying on chance and hoping for the best, trainers must use strategies that improve the odds in favor of transfer and maintenance of training information. If a trainer works on strengthening the supports that will be necessary back on the job, as well as minimizing the factors that may inhibit the trainees from using that information, the likelihood of training transfer is greater. A positive transfer climate provides adequate resources and opportunities to apply new knowledge and helps to remind learners of lessons learned (Ford 1992).

Peer Support

Peer support is also an important piece in understanding how to improve motivation and training. "The workplace can train people far more efficiently than even the best training department can train people" (Brinkerhoff and Gill 1994). Imagine that a trainee leaves a training class fully excited and ready to apply on the job what was just learned. However, if that atmosphere leads to harassment for following the rules or taking the extra steps to be safe, the trainee risks not being accepted by the group and not fitting in. No matter how good the training class or how skilled the trainer, if coworkers are not supportive of the information delivered in the training class, that training will prove useless. Support from peers is a crucial ingredient in transfer success (Blume et al. 2010).

When we talk about trainees' peers there are actually two separate groups that need to be considered. The first group consists of the other trainees in the class. The second group includes the people working around them when they go back to their day-to-day jobs and begin to apply what they learned. If these groups of people are different, the amount of influence those groups have on the trainee might be quite different, although the need to feel connected is equally present in both groups (Weinbauer-Heidel and Ibeschitz-Manderbach 2018).

Experts that study how trainees transfer information back to the workplace suggest that one of the best ways to provide training is to have it occur in natural groups. A *natural group* is a group that works together all the time. For example, instead of having two electricians from every location in a large corporation come together for a full week of electrical safety training on similar work duties, choose to train a natural group of all the electricians that work together every day in a single place. Although there are many benefits to having trainees from a variety of locations attend a training class outside of their normal environment with people they do not normally get to work with or possibly even know, researchers have found that it is better for training transfer when the group works together in the course of their normal workday (Saks and Monica 2006).

Motivation to Pay Attention

The importance of getting the attention of trainees was discussed in Chapter 1, and it is the first step in the learning process described by Gagné in Chapter 3. Most good safety trainers know that, if they don't get the attention of trainees at the beginning of a training class, the trainees will be lost for the rest of it. It's important to open a training class in a way that not only gets attention but also motivates the learners to keep paying attention throughout the whole class. It's remarkably useful to get trainees' attention the minute they walk into the room. If trainers give them a chance to sit down, pull out their phone, pull out a newspaper, or start chatting with coworkers seated around them, it's going to be harder to pull their focus back to the training class content. The following are ways to direct attention to the topic immediately upon starting the class:

- Show preclass slideshows. A preclass slideshow is a set of slides that are interesting enough that the trainees will want to watch them while they wait for class to begin. It's best if they relate in some way to class content, but anything safety related will work. Photos of people doing stupid things related to safety can be used as well as safety-related jokes or memes. Safety trivia questions can also be used with one slide showing the question and a second showing the answer. PowerPoint slide shows can be set to autoplay so the trainer is freed up to do other preparations before the class starts.

- Distribute a training activity for the trainees to start working on as soon as they arrive. The activity can already be placed on desks or chairs, or handed out to trainees as they walk in, or be included on a PowerPoint slide. These activities can be as simple as a crossword puzzle related to the class topic or something that requires teamwork. There are many options available in the chapters at the end of this book.
- Provide instructions for trainees to begin working on an activity and include directions written out on a flip chart, whiteboard, or a slide in the front of the room. The trainer may also need to walk around the room and gently remind trainees of the activity that needs to be completed.
- Hand out preclass evaluations as soon as trainees are seated and tell them to try answering all the questions before class begins.
- Have a paper with a QR code at each desk, or better yet, hang four pieces of paper with different QR codes on different sides of the room and inform trainees that each QR represents a different class assignment. Tell them to pick just one and scan it to discover their assignment. If trainees are not accustomed to using QR readers, the trainer can also provide instructions on how to add QR code readers to their phones. Additionally, many mobile phones are able to simply scan a QR code using the phone's camera so an external application is not needed. (This is great information to include in preclass communications).
- Have a senior leader of the company attend the beginning of the class and provide the kickoff. This may help trainees realize the importance of the information they are about to hear. It is also important for senior leaders, managers, and supervisors to publicly show their support of the topic and the program so trainees are more likely to act on what they've learned during the class once they are back on the job.
- Create curiosity by using a variety of props. Activities at individual workspaces sealed in envelopes and different-from-expected room arrangements are examples.

It is important for a trainer to facilitate the training experience in a way that gets and keeps attention during the entire session. No one likes to sit through a long lecture, especially considering the content covered in safety training. Therefore, it is important to vary the stimulus. A trainer should strive to add some type of interaction every 10 to 12 minutes, even if that interaction is simply asking the class a question. Good facilitation skills and motivation strategies can be effective in increasing retention and transfer.

Review and Retention Activity

The Red Light/Green Light activity is described in this chapter.

On a sheet of paper draw two columns, and at the top of the column on the left, draw a green light. At the top of the second column draw a red light. In the "green-light" column, brainstorm plans to implement the content of this chapter. In the "red-light" column, list activities, procedures, or training techniques that will no longer continue.

References

Baldwin, T. T., and J. K. Ford. 1988. "Transfer of Training: a review and directions for future research." *Personnel Psychology*, 41(1):63–105.

Bateson, M. C. 1994. *Peripheral Visions: Learning Along the Way*. New York: HarperCollins Publishers.

Blume, B. D., J. K. Ford, T. T. Baldwin, and J. L. Huang. 2010. "Transfer of training: a meta-analytic review." *Journal of Management*, 36(4):1065–1105. doi: 10.1177/0149206309352880.

Brinkerhoff, R. O., and S. J. Gill. 1994. *The Learning Alliance: Systems Thinking in Human Resource Development*. Jossey-Bass. San Francisco, CA: Pfeiffer.

Burke, M. J., S. A. Sarpy, K. Smith-Crowe, S. Chan-Serafin, R. O. Salvador, and G. Islam. 2006. "Relative Effectiveness of Worker Safety and Health Training Methods." *American Journal of Public Health*, 96(2):315–324.

Dixit, J., J. Thompson, and M. Slaughter. 2019. "The AGES Model can help learning stick." *Chief Learning Officer*. November 12, 2019. https//www.chieflearningofficer.com.

Ford, J. K., M. A. Quinones, D. J. Sego, and J. S. Sorra. 1992. "Factors affecting the opportunity to perform trained tasks on the job." *Personnel Psychology*, 45:511–527.

Foxon, M. 1993. "A process approach to the transfer of training, Part 1." *Australian Journal of Educational Technology*, 9(2):130–143.

Gegenfurtner, A. 2013. "Dimensions of motivation to transfer: A longitudinal analysis of their influence on retention, transfer, and attitude change." *Vocations and Learning*, 6(2):1–19, 187–205.

Gradous, D. 1991. "The Development and Validation of a Transfer-of-Training System. Project Number Forty-Five." St. Paul, MN: Minnesota University, Dept. of Vocational and Technical Education.

Halls, J. 2014. *Memory and Cognition in Learning*. Alexandria, VA: ATD Press.

Huang Y-H, and Yang T-R. 2019. "Exploring On-Site Safety Knowledge Transfer in the Construction Industry." *Sustainability*, 11(22):6426.

Knox, A. B. 1988. "Helping adults apply what they learn." *Training and Development Journal*, 42(6):55–59.

Marquardt, M. J. 2002. *Building the Learning Organization: Mastering the 5 Elements for Corporate Learning*. Palo Alto, CA: Davies-Black Publishing.

Matthews, A. 2012. *How to Design and Deliver Great Training: Learn How to Turn Any Material into Lively, Engaging and Effective Training*. Scotts Valley, CA: CreateSpace Independent Publishing Platform.

Mosel, J. D. 1957. "Why training programs fail to carry over." *Personnel*, 34(3):56–64.

Noe, R. A., and N. Schmitt. 1986. "The Influence of trainee attitudes on training effectiveness: test of a model." *Personnel Psychology*, 39:497–523.

Rebelo, T., and A. Gomes. 2009. "Different types of organization, different cultural orientations towards learning: What factors explain this?" In K. A. Fanti, ed., *Applying Psychological Research to Understand and Promote the Well-Being of Clinical and Non-clinical Populations*, pp. 175–186. Athens: ATINER.

Ritter, F. E., G. D. Baxter, J. W. Kim, and S. Srinivasmurthy. 2013. "Learning and retention." In J. D. Lee and A. Kirlik, eds., *The Oxford Handbook of Cognitive Engineering*, pp. 125–142. New York: Oxford University Press.

Saks, A., and B. Monica. 2006. "An investigation of training activities and transfer of training in organizations." *Human Resource Management*, 45:629–648. doi: 10.1002/hrm.20135.

Spiro, R. J., R. L. Coulson, P. J. Feltovich, and D. K. Anderson. 1988. *Cognitive Flexibility Theory: Advanced Knowledge Acquisition in Ill-Structured Domains*. Ft. Belvoir, VA: Defense Technical Information Center.

Taylor, K., and C. Marienau. 2016. *Facilitating Learning with the Adult Brain in Mind: A Conceptual and Practical Guide*. Jossey-Bass. San Francisco, CA: John Wiley & Sons, Inc.

Weber, Emma. 2018. "The Missing Link in Learning: Transfer." *Science of Learning*. Volume 35, Issue 1816, July Bonus 2018. Alexandria, VA: ATD Press.

Weinbauer-Heidel, I., and M. Ibeschitz-Manderbach. 2018. *What Makes Training Really Work: 12 Levers of Transfer Effectiveness*. Hamburg, Germany: tredition GmbH.

Yelon, S., L. Sheppard, D. Sleight, and J. K. Ford. 2004. "Intention to transfer: how do autonomous professionals become motivated to use new ideas?" *Performance Improvement Quarterly*, 17:82–103. doi: 10.1111/j.1937-8327.2004.tb00309.x.

Zhong, C. B., and G. J. Leonardelli. 2008. "Cold and Lonely." *Psychological Science*, 19:839–842. doi: 10.1111/j.1467-9280.2008.02165.x.

Part 2

♦

Make It Stick

Chapter 8
Preclass and Postclass Communication

As a demonstration of one of the learning retention strategies described in this chapter, the following Prereading Quiz is provided. Readers should now complete this Prereading Quiz.

Prereading Quiz: What Do You Know?

1. Why is preclass communication important?
2. Name a benefit of preclass communication.
3. Name three examples of preclass activities.
4. What is the Transtheoretical Model?
5. Describe an example of postclass communication?
6. Name two ways to provide reinforcement back on the job.
7. What does the Pygmalion effect have to do with safety training?

Preclass Communication

The communication trainees receive before a formal training class occurs can help increase retention of the training material. Trainees need to understand what to expect from a training class with respect to transferring those skills back to the job, and a good place to insert some information regarding this is in a preclass communication. Motivating trainees before they attend a training class will get the class off to a good start. Also, pretraining motivation has been shown to have an effect on posttraining motivation and the trainee's determination to apply the learned knowledge and skills (Colquitt et al. 2000).

When a safety trainer is working on the design of a program, it's important to decide what must happen before a learning event to ensure participants are prepared, and what must happen after the training event to make sure the trainees are contributing to the overall goals of the organization. Preclass communication could have the following focus:

- Prepare trainees for what's going to happen in the training class and set expectations. "The first stage of the learning transfer process is to generate understanding among learners about the importance of transfer for themselves and their organization. Linking this to the business results the organization is looking to achieve posttraining will help them create their own personal action plan as part of the learning journey" (Weber 2018).
- Advise the trainees' supervisors of what will occur so they can support the transfer of the new knowledge back to the job. Trainers should be sure to clarify what the trainees will be expected to do differently or in a better way and how this aligns with the overall business goals.

In addition to simple communication efforts, there are a number of preinstructional activities that a safety trainer can use to prepare trainees for learning before the class. Preclass activities can be used in both the online training environment and in face-to-face classes. A great benefit of preclass activities is that they can help shorten the amount of time the trainees must actually sit in a training classroom or in front of a computer.

Preclass activities could include assigned short readings, requests for examples or photos related to the class content, short quizzes, or surveys that the trainees are asked to complete before attending class. These small steps can make a training class run more smoothly. Having the trainees participate in this type of preclass activity also means they will be hearing some of the training content before the class actually begins. In this case, when the material is presented during the class, it will be the second time (at least) the trainees are hearing the information. As discussed in Chapter 10, repetition is an important part of increasing learning retention.

Flipped Classrooms

The idea of a flipped class is becoming more widely known in the university setting, but in many workplaces the idea of the flipped classroom, or at least a modified version of it, can be a way to shorten the amount of time a trainee needs to be away from his or her job. With the *flipped classroom model*, the trainee, possibly in conjunction with a supervisor, is learning a lot of the material on his or her own. Self-instructional packages can be developed and delivered to the trainee for completion before the actual class. When this is done, training class time can be spent focusing on reviewing the information the trainee worked on, class activities to help reinforce the content, and evaluations. This means using a hybrid learning model where a trainee first reviews and completes some activities online or through the use of other technology and then attends an in-person event for review, further activities, and the evaluation portion of the learning experience.

The Transtheoretical Model

The transtheoretical model (TTM) proposes that people pass through a series of steps during the behavior change process. Their success in passing through each of the steps can predict whether the behavior change will stick. Since various stages of the TTM can be affected by preclass communication, the model will be discussed here (Prochaska et al. 2008).

The six stages in the transtheoretical model are:

1. Precontemplation (no intention of making a change)
2. Contemplation (intention to make a change)
3. Preparation (intention to make a change and actions to prepare for the change)
4. Action (initial change of behavior)
5. Maintenance (sustained change of behavior)
6. Termination (no temptation to relapse and 100 percent confident of change being maintained)

Stages 1, 2, and perhaps even a part of stage 3, can be implemented to some extent in preclass communication.

In stage 1, precontemplation, the trainees probably don't even realize they will have the opportunity to change. They may receive a training class announcement and may not even begin to think about how they need or want to change.

In stage 2, contemplation, the trainees will begin to decide to make a change. For example, if a training class announcement were advertised as a way to learn how to use a new type of fall protection harness, the trainees hopefully will realize that they will be taking positive steps to protect themselves by learning to use the harness correctly and thus will intend to make a change. The objective of learning to use the new harness and the goal of the training—to work safer—can both be communicated in the preclass communication. An individual's psychological preparedness to change a behavior will influence important training antecedents and outcomes (Steel-Johnson et al. 2010).

In stage 3, preparation, the trainees will consider what they must do to learn the new information. Actions to prepare for change include attending the training class and getting hands-on practice with the new equipment. This includes asking questions and receiving feedback from the trainer, as well as learning from mistakes.

Applying the transtheoretical model to safety training would mean that the safety trainer assesses where a trainee is in the six stages and then incorporates this information into the training design. For example, a trainee who has been doing a certain task for a long period of time in a particular way and has never experienced an injury would likely be in the precontemplation stage, as he or she would have no desire to make a change. A trainee in the middle of the six stages (contemplation, preparation, and action) is more motivated to learn new safety behaviors because he or she has a greater awareness of the benefits. If a trainee is in the maintenance stage, he or she probably has attended safety training before and has seen the importance of the information presented in keeping a trainee safe on the job and is also looking forward to maintaining the current safe behavior. Knowing where each trainee sits in the scale can help direct preclass communication and even the training design itself.

Communication of Objectives

Before any trainees attend a safety training class, it is best to communicate the objectives of the class ahead of time. The objectives should not simply state, "Work safely around XYZ," but should be specific to observable and realistic changes. In the case of an electrical safety class, it would not be sufficient just to say work safely around electricity. Instead, a better objective would be that all trainees should be able to successfully complete a lockout-tagout permit before servicing electric machinery in their work area. A well-written objective like this will give trainees and supervisors better information about what will occur in the training class as well as what the trainees are expected to do after the class. Well-written objectives also are extremely important when accurately evaluating the success of the class.

Another important consideration of safety training is to include all levels of leadership in the training initiative. This may mean offering a mini-class, an informational webinar, or at a minimum, a descriptive email, about the safety training topic to the trainees' management. The leadership and supervisors of the people attending the training class should have an idea of what is being learned in the class, why it is important for trainees to attend, and what they should be able to do after the class is completed. The objectives should be shared with the trainees' supervisors who will then be able to help with opportunities to practice the newly acquired information back on the job and therefore increase the amount of training transfer.

Influencers and Subject Matter Experts

If the group of trainees is large, executing a trial run of the class that includes highly visible and highly influential employees can be beneficial, especially if it's important to build interest and buy-in for the training topic. In a union shop, this may mean the union safety representatives or other well-respected employees. It is also beneficial to run the training content and design of the class past these "influencers" before the training session is finalized. They will not only appreciate being asked but will often suggest valuable changes.

In addition to getting buy-in from influencers, it is important to request and gather input from subject matter experts (SMEs). This is especially important if the trainer is not a subject matter expert in a particular area. Having material reviewed by someone within the company who is highly respected for their knowledge in that area can help ensure that the trainer is presenting realistic and credible information. If trainees do not believe a trainer, their attention will be lost early, and retention of the content will be unlikely.

If possible, the SME can attend the training class and be a very valuable asset, supplying expertise by answering specific questions that may come up during the class. If credibility has been a problem in the past, it may also be beneficial to include in the preclass communication that the SME has helped to create the training content so that additional credibility is given to the class overall.

Role models can be highly influential in the workplace. Consciously or unconsciously, employees often pattern their behavior after that of those around them. This is better known as *vicarious learning*, which means using the observation of others to acquire new experiences and skills (Broad 2007). If safety trainers can identify influential workers to serve as informal role models to the trainees, it can be helpful to have a discussion with those individuals. They may or may not realize they are seen as being in this position. The added responsibility of serving as an example for newer and younger workers may be enough to encourage the role models to behave appropriately themselves. In many work situations, the most powerful role model for the training is the supervisor (Fleishman et al. 1955), but this may not be the case in every facility.

Management Support

The importance of involving safety trainee supervisors and managers has been discussed in several chapters of this book, but one of the most important places to involve this group is in the preclass communication as a manager's impact may be greatest before the class even happens. If a trainee's supervisor or manager has expressed support and interest before the class occurs, hopefully the trainee will approach the class with an improved mindset and attentive attitude. The supervisor and manager should make it known that the trainee will be expected to apply what he or she learned in the training class once back on the job. In order to get the supervisors and managers to support the safety training, it may be necessary to spell out in clear and simple terms why the training is important. In addition to the obvious information, such as helping to reduce accidents and injuries, support can also be gained by tying the overall company goals to the objectives of the training class.

When American Express studied how effective a blended learning approach was for one of their programs, they found that the influence of an immediate supervisor had enormous impact, and they found that this impact began before the training class even commenced. The American Express study found that having a supervisor who clearly shows support for the training class is a key factor in whether or not the training will be transferred back to the job (American Express 2007).

Advanced Organizers

In terms of preclass communication that serves as part of the planned learning methods, advanced organizers can be used as a form of priming. *Advanced organizers* can be described as "appropriately relevant and inclusive introductory materials ... generality, and inclusiveness" (Ausubel et al. 1978). Advanced organizers help trainees make sense of the content they are about to hear. Advanced organizers provide information about what the trainees already know and help them connect the new information to it, providing some focus for the trainees so they understand what is important in the training session they are about to complete (Schunk 2004). A few simple ways for safety trainers to take advantage of the benefits of advanced organizers follow:

- Sharing an overall safety procedure with a blank section included where the new safety and health information to be presented will be added. This will help trainees see how a new policy fits in with the overall safety program.
- Providing an outline with spaces for notes so trainees can add what they learn, and also see how different aspects of the new information fit together in accordance with the outline.
- Showing a visual representation of how different safety policies are connected with a particular policy or procedure. For example, the illustration shown in Figure 8.1 for a hypothetical drum handling safety training class could be given to trainees at the beginning of a class and used to provide a quick review of the existing safety procedures already in place that are related to the topic at hand.

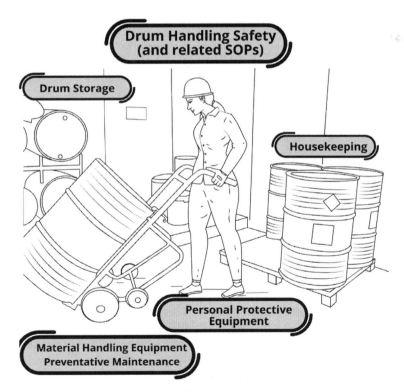

Figure 8.1 ✦ Safe drum handling illustration

Postclass Communication

Like preclass communication, the information a trainee receives after training is completed is equally as important. In the six stages of the transtheoretical model described at the beginning of this chapter, stage 5, maintenance, can be supported by postclass communication.

- Postclass communication could include support for trainees in the form of written materials as well as access to online materials. After the training class these materials can be used to support and reinforce training.
- Clarification of the safety trainer's role and responsibilities after the class is completed should be shared with stakeholders. If the trainers are not safety professionals or SMEs, this type of support is going to be different than if the safety professional or SME were delivering the training.

Evaluations

As with all training, it is important to collect data afterwards regarding the amount of change in behavior. For example, data collected before and after can show the results of trainees attending the class. This will help the trainer adjust the class as necessary going forward and improve it so that retention is greatest.

Evaluations of the training material can be formative or summative evaluations. The formative evaluation will help trainers make adjustments to their training class as it is being developed; the summative evaluation is completed some time after the end of the training class and is based on the results of the changes that were made by people attending the class. A *formative evaluation* seeks to improve a solution. A safety trainer can perform formative solutions by testing out training class content, interactive activities, and delivery methods as the class is being created instead of looking only at evaluations of the program at the end. *Summative evaluations* are completed after training is complete and aim to determine the effect the training had on the organization.

Organizational Goals

Another important way of reinforcing training program content is to be sure the content is tied to the overall programs and goals of the company. Safety training classes should not be seen as standalone programs. The trainer needs to show how one safety training class is part of the bigger picture, including the company's overall goals and mission. To the individual trainee, one 60-minute class may not seem like it contributes much to the company's overall success so it's important to point out how the trainee's attendance and participation is going to help the company meet its goals.

As discussed in Chapter 7 on facilitation and motivation, it's important to have managers and leadership buy into the training ahead of time so they can actively encourage trainees to practice what they learned and help facilitate the transfer of the safety training information after the class has been completed. Managers and company leaders may be more concerned and familiar with top-level goals. Stressing the connection of the company objectives to the training class objectives before and after the training class can effectively increase their support.

Consistency

When designing and presenting safety training, it's important to consider how the class information is talked about in the normal course of a workday and to use the same types of images, phrases, and words in the class that are used on the job. For example, if trainers refer to "energy control procedures" in an electrical safety class, then "energy control procedures" should be the terminology used in the workplace. If instead of "energy control procedures," "LOTO" is used, this may cause confusion. Even though it seems like a simple thing, there may be some people who do not realize these words and abbreviations mean the same thing, even if it seems like it would be obvious. If a trainer is talking about how to fill out a lockout-tagout permit for example, the actual permit that trainees are going to be expected to complete should be used in the training and not a generic form, which may be part of an off-the-shelf training program.

Five-Minute Refreshers

During future safety meetings or at safety meetings held prior to a shift, such as toolbox talks or huddles, it is great to provide a quick 5-minute refresher on topics covered in previous safety training classes. This quick refresher will do a lot to help trainees remember the content they learned days, weeks, or even months before. If a safety trainer is not participating in these shorter training sessions, a supervisor or safety representative can provide the refresher instead.

Postclass communication is a form of reinforcement and can take many forms. Postclass activities should serve to increase retention as well as help the trainees transfer the information learned in a training class to their day-to-day jobs. Postclass communication in the form of activities can help keep trainees engaged with the content long after the class has ended.

Experts and Coaches

When possible, it can be advantageous to assign topic experts, ambassadors, or coaches in each work area so trainees have someone who quickly can provide answers and clarification as well as additional coaching for new safety training topics they have learned. If these individuals are assigned before the class occurs, they can be named during the class as resources for trainees to access when back on the job.

It is also helpful to provide a place for postclass discussion or questions. Trainees need to be encouraged and perhaps told how to ask questions about the training class content after the class has concluded. A new employee might not know how or where to share concerns and questions, so this information should be made very clear during training. In many situations, an online forum may not be accessed easily by many of the trainees, so something as simple as a paper question box or a dedicated number to call or text, especially if it's anonymous, can provide valuable assistance. Answered questions can be promoted, and the answers can be provided to the entire group of trainees. If one person had a question or problem with one part of the content, it was most likely a problem for other people as well.

A simple follow-up game could also be created using a similar box. A question related to the training class could be sent out by email or text, or posted on a bulletin board, and if trainees remember the answer, they can write it on a piece of paper along with their name and put it in a collection box. Names and answers can be drawn randomly and prizes awarded. All entries could be eligible if the idea is simply to encourage trainee participation. Once the contest is over, the question and matching correct answers should be sent out or posted to all participants, which will provide an additional level of review. Prizes do not have to be costly if the budget is small and can simply be a voucher for a free cafeteria coffee or lunch or even a preferred parking place for a week.

If there is pushback to a trainer's attempt at reinforcing the content once it has already been presented, it is important to remind trainees and supervisors that training is an investment. If the training content is forgotten quickly, the time spent preparing and delivering the training, as well as the time spent away from the job by the trainees, will be wasted. It may be necessary to point out to company management that even small pieces of reinforcement of training content will go a long way in supporting what was learned, and this will further increase the value of the training and hopefully prevent it from being necessary to retrain employees in the future on the same topic.

Posttraining Follow-Up

If the trainees' supervisors and managers reinforce the training, there is less chance the training will be considered a waste of time. Trainees need to understand they will be supported when they begin to implement the lessons that were learned. Supervisors need to understand they have a role in increasing trainee retention, too. After a training class has been completed, supervisors should be notified if one of their employees attended the training and be reminded of the purpose of that training program. The supervisors should also be asked directly to support the trainee's efforts to apply the training. Suggest they have a brief conversation with the trainee immediately after returning from the training class. The supervisor should also be encouraged to have an additional conversation with the trainee several weeks later. A few sample questions a supervisor can ask the trainee who has returned from a training class include:

- What was the most valuable part of the training?
- How are you going to use it?
- Is there any additional help that you need?

Additional reinforcement several weeks after the training class has concluded can be especially helpful in increasing retention. Sample questions a supervisor can ask at this time include (Pollock and Jefferson 2012):

- How have you applied the training to your job?
- What have you achieved as a result?
- What helped you the most?
- What did you learn that prevents you from having an accident or injury?
- Do you have any advice for other people attending the same training class?

Reinforcement can happen in a variety of ways. It can include tangible or digital follow-up documents, and activities related to the training content can act as memory joggers for the information that was covered in the class. Reinforcement can also be personal, and if delivered by someone in authority or someone the trainee may look up to, it provides acknowledgement the trainee sees as positive. If supervisors and managers are not comfortable giving positive feedback, that is probably a sign that training in this area (i.e., giving feedback) is necessary. There are many applications based on psychology of how to reinforce good behavior, but in general, effective reinforcement needs to be given only when following the observation of the desired behavior and making clear the connection between the behavior and the reward. Under these conditions, positive reinforcement can be highly effective for cementing a pattern of desirable work behaviors and stimulating their repetition (Broad 2007).

On-the-Job Support

There are many ways to provide reinforcement of the learned material for trainees to reference once back on the job. The general term for things that can help the trainees is *performance support*. There are many different types of performance support that a safety professional may consider. The following list provides a few ideas:

1. Job aids such as
   - checklists
   - forms
   - reference cards
2. Electronic performance support systems (EPSSs) such as
   - embedded tutorials
   - chatbots
   - databases
   - internal document libraries

Supervisors are often instrumental in helping trainees find opportunities to practice the skills they learned in the training class. Trainees may never be expected to use the information learned in some types of training, and in these cases, especially without any type of reinforcement, the training probably will soon be forgotten. If supervisors can assign trainees job tests or special projects that will allow them to use what they learned, it will go a long way in increasing the trainees' retention of the material. The American Express study mentioned earlier found that climate factors can quite literally make or break a company's training investments and understanding and creating a high transfer climate should swiftly move to the forefront of any training initiative (American Express 2007).

Job Aids

Job aids, discussed in Chapter 7, are another way of providing reinforcement on the job. They are frequently found in the workplace and can provide just the right amount of guidance and support at the time they are needed. An example would be the visual instructions available inside the covers of most automated external defibrillators (AEDs). Especially in a time of high stress, having instructions available when and where they are most needed is very helpful for trainees who once may have learned how to use an AED in a training class. The job aid helps them to remember and apply this information.

A safety professional might consider designing the job aid first (if one doesn't already exist) and then work backwards to design the training around the job aid. The entire safety training class could be focused around showing trainees how to use the job aid. Not all jobs are good candidates for job aids, but if they are, this reverse training design idea can be effective in improving retention. Job aids traditionally include things such as checklists, diagrams, pocket cards, posters, or laminated instructions posted where needed. Today, job aids can also include applications on mobile phones and things like Alexa skills or chatbots or QR codes that link to the job aid. Even if the best job aids are created and given to trainees, they still might not serve the intended purpose unless the supervisors make sure they are used. Job aids should be introduced and shared in class so they are more likely to be accessed when needed.

Removing Constraints

Sometimes a better way to reinforce training lessons after a class has concluded is to work more on removing transfer constraints than trying to force trainees to apply what they learned. This relates to a theory known as *Lewin's Force Field Analysis*. Lewin's force field model explains that there are many ways to encourage change, and it's not always best to push harder. Kurt Lewin's Force Field

Analysis identifies two types of forces: driving and restraining. *Driving forces* support a change and *restraining forces* are those that will get in the way.

If there is difficulty getting safety trainees to use what was learned on the job, trainers can identify what driving forces and restraining forces may be in play. For example, a driving force may be that a trainee truly wants to follow the rules and do what is possible to work safely. A restraining force may be pressure from a supervisor to take shortcuts to get work done quicker even if that means working unsafely. To change the situation, a trainer can identify how to make the driving forces stronger and how to make the restraining forces weaker. In this example, the trainee could be given more reasons to work safely, perhaps in the form of additional recognition or responsibilities. To weaken the restraining forces (i.e., the pressure from the supervisor), the trainer can work with managers higher up the chain to instruct and make it clear to the direct supervisor that safety is valued over productivity. Supervisors can make it easier for trainees to use what they learned if they can help relieve job pressures the trainees might experience when trying to follow the new procedures and policies that were included in a safety training class. For example, a manager could reduce some of the forces that could stop a trainee from applying what was learned simply by enforcing whatever safety policies or procedures the trainee hopes to apply. If a trainee returns to work and coworkers are not performing their job as the trainee was just instructed to do, it is up to the supervisor to correct the other workers so it's easier for the trainee to do what is needed.

Another way the supervisor could make it easier for trainees to use what they learned is to follow up with them while they're working and ask if there's anything that would make it easier for them to apply the training. For example, if a trainee had just spent a day learning about the importance of completing work permits for various types of work projects, but the trainee soon finds out that blank permits are never available nor is anyone available to sign off on them, this would be a major problem for a trainee trying to use what was learned. If this information is brought up to the supervisor, the supervisor can take the necessary steps and remove the barrier to applying the training.

Another approach that can positively affect transfer after a class is for the supervisor and managers to meet with the trainer and discuss any issues that may have become apparent during the training class that may affect the likelihood of the training being applied. Often trainees will talk freely in a training class, and things may be said that would not be said directly to supervisors. If for example, a group of trainees snickered when a trainer stated that a set of safety procedures needed to be followed before starting a job, the trainer, if paying attention, can note that this probably is going to be a problem, and the training may not be applied. Hopefully the relationship between the trainer and the trainees is one where an open discussion can be held and the trainer, especially if a safety professional is providing the training, can and should take action to make it as easy as possible for the safety training to be used.

For noncritical but infrequent situations, training can be provided as needed, such as for walking on ice or working outdoors in cold temperatures when this is not the norm. For training skills and knowledge that are very important to remember but seldom used, the problem of forgetting over time is much more significant. An example of this is the AED example described earlier. For these types of skills, trainees need reinforcement of the material. It's not just nice to provide it; the reinforcement is absolutely necessary. This could be through simple reminders or more formal classes.

Publicize Success

Many facilities do a good job of celebrating successful safety programs. With a little effort, the benefits of attending safety training programs can be included in these celebrations. If an employee is recognized for putting out a small fire, the fact that the employee learned the skills to do this at a company fire safety training class should be publicized. If an employee were able to lead a coworker to an eyewash after a chemical splash, and assist the affected coworker in using the eyewash, and performed procedures learned in a training class, this should be rewarded as well.

Because safety training is often just one of many responsibilities of a safety professional, safety professionals may have little time for following up with trainees after a training class has been completed. If a facility is small and a safety professional who is also serving as a trainer knows the trainees and gets to work with them daily, this can be a big plus. A few suggested ways to provide support and reinforcement follow.

The Pygmalion Effect

The *Pygmalion effect* is "the phenomenon whereby one person's expectation for another person's behavior comes to serve as a self-fulfilling prophecy" (Saxena

2016). To use this idea in safety training, trainees can be provided with documentation that states they are qualified to perform a particular activity safely. Alternatively, the names of all trainees successfully passing a class can be posted or shared via company emails or newsletters. If a warehouse trainee is provided with a certificate stating he or she is now a trained "Safe Forklift Driver," this can be a self-fulfilling prophecy according to the Pygmalion effect. The trainee, having been formally named as a safe forklift operator, will then operate a forklift successfully. If members of the Fire Safety Committee are given jackets, badges, or hard-hat stickers that say as much, this can affect their actual behavior when it comes to following and enforcing fire safety procedures (Broad 2007). If a fire safety committee member or trained fire marshal is walking around a building while wearing a fire marshal jacket and sees an emergency exit door propped open, the Pygmalion effect phenomenon would say that the employee would take the time to correct the situation and not walk by and simply ignore it.

Reinforcement

A safety trainer can create and design a variety of reinforcement materials—everything from workplace posters to microlearning modules delivered by text message—but the trainees still must decide to use the materials in the best way possible. A trainee could look at a safety poster that summarizes and highlights the key points of a training class and mentally review the information, or the trainee could ignore the poster completely. Trainees might have much less control over whether they participate in a microlearning program, but they can choose to take it seriously and put effort into refreshing their memory by fully engaging with the information, or they can decide simply to glance at the content and only do what is necessary to complete the course.

Safety training activities can be used to provide reinforcement after training classes are completed and can be a great way to remind trainees of what was learned. Consider the following ways that safety training can be reinforced through postclass communication:

1. Emails
   - send reminder emails
   - ask for success stories
2. Text messages
   - share success stories and tips
3. Assignments
   - assign activities such as Letter to Self or TABB (described in Chapter 7)

4. Group activities
   - schedule follow-up events for trainees to meet with or without a trainer to discuss progress applying what was learned
5. Infographics
6. Coaching
7. Marketing materials (continue marketing it—follow up with goals, benefits, procedures)
8. Refresher or practice classes

Review and Retention Activity

This activity is the second part of the example of pre- and postclass communication activities as described in this chapter. The Prereading Quiz was presented at the beginning. Readers should now complete this Postreading Quiz.

Postreading Quiz: What Do You Know Now?

1. Why is preclass communication important?

   _____

2. Name a benefit of preclass communication.

   _____

3. Name three examples of preclass activities.

   _____

   _____

   _____

4. What is the Transtheoretical Model?

   _____

5. Describe an example of postclass communication?

   _____

6. Name two ways to provide reinforcement back on the job.

   _____

   _____

7. What does the Pygmalion effect have to do with safety training?

   _____

References

American Express. 2007. "The Real ROI of Leadership Development: Comparing Classroom vs. Online vs. Blended Delivery." http://blog.2edu.pl/wp-content/uploads/2011/04/CLOspr07.pdf.

Ausubel, D. P., J. D. Novak, and H. Hanesian. 1978. *Educational Psychology: A Cognitive View*. 2d ed. Montreal: Holt, Rinehart and Winston.

Broad, Mary L. 2007. *Beyond Transfer of Training: Engaging Systems to Improve Performance*. San Francisco, CA: Pfeiffer.

Colquitt, J. A., J. E. LePine, and R. A. Noe. 2000. "Toward an integrative theory of training motivation: A meta-analytic path analysis of 20 years of research." *Journal of Applied Psychology*, 85:678–707.

Fleishman, E. A., E. F. Harris, and H. E. Burtt. 1955. "Leadership and supervision in industry; an evaluation of a supervisory training program." Ohio State University. *Bureau of Educational Research Monograph, 33*, xiii; 110.

Pollock, R., and A. Jefferson. 2012. *Ensuring Learning Transfer*. Alexandria, VA: American Society for Training and Development (ASTD) Press.

Prochaska, J. A., C. A. Redding, and K. E. Evers. 2008. "The transtheoretical model and stages of change." In K. Glanz, B. K. Rimer, and K. Viswanath, eds., *Health Behavior and Health Education. Theory, Research, and Practice*. 4th ed. pp. 97–121. San Francisco, CA: John Wiley & Sons, Inc.

Saxena, S. 2016. "Pygmalion Effect: An Innovative Tool to Increase Motivation." *CPJ Global Review*, 8(1):105–8.

Schunk, D. H. 2004. *Learning Theories: An Educational Perspective*. Upper Saddle River, NJ: Merrill.

Steele-Johnson, D., A. Naryan, K. M. Delgado, and P. Cole. 2010. "Pretraining influences and readiness to change dimensions: a focus on static versus dynamic issues." *The Journal of Applied Behavioral Science*, 46(2):245–274.

Weber, Emma. 2018. "The Missing Link in Learning: Transfer." *Science of Learning*. Volume 35, Issue 1816. July Bonus 2018. Alexandria, VA: ATD Press.

Chapter 9
Making It Real

"Practicing the actual production of the knowledge and procedures that are the target of the training is essential: One chance to actually put on, fasten, and inflate an inflatable life vest, for example, would be of more value—in terms of the likelihood that one could actually perform that procedure correctly in an emergency—than the multitude of times any frequent flyer has sat on an airplane and been shown the process" (Bjork 1994).

The above quote sums up the importance of making safety training as realistic as possible. Most experienced safety trainers realize the benefits of adding practice opportunities to safety training classes. Not only do hands-on experiences get and keep the attention of trainees, but they make it easier to learn and remember. If something as common as riding a bicycle is used as an example, it's easy to see why practice opportunities are preferred. If someone were given instructions to read or shown a video on how to ride a bike, it is unlikely they would successfully master the skill. Just like many procedures taught in training classes, soft skills and hard skills are understood better once trainees get the opportunity to practice.

Adding practice to safety training classes is an important part of making training as realistic as possible. Anytime safety training is tangible and hands on, the trainees are going to pay more attention. There are many ways to make safety training more realistic, which will in turn make it more useful for the trainee and more likely to be remembered. These include experiential learning such as simulations, virtual reality, augmented reality, and tabletop exercises.

Experiential Learning Activities

Experiential learning activities in a safety training class help trainees learn new skills by letting them process the new information in a real or a simulated environment. Generally, it is not safe, or it is too expensive, to practice safety training activities in a real environment. In these cases, experiential learning can be a great way to present this type of learning. Through simulations, the trainee can experience a variety of problems and challenges that tie back to training class content. When trainees have to deal with these types of challenges, they will also be receiving feedback related to their reaction, their answer, or the way they handled a particular situation and whether it was correct or incorrect. When the trainee's answer or response is not correct, this situation can lead to the benefit of learning through failure, which is discussed later in this chapter.

Simulations

There are two kinds of simulations that can be used in safety training: an open model simulation and a closed model simulation. With an *open model simulation*, the outcome can change depending on who is playing it and who else is participating. The trainees will respond based on their past knowledge, experience, and beliefs. In a *closed model simulation*, the outcome is predetermined. All activities are stacked toward achieving a particular outcome. If no one survived a fire safety simulation, that would be an example of a closed simulation. A simulation-type game can create understanding of the different positions people may find themselves in.

One way to improve trainee retention in simulations is to have trainees create avatars or characters. When they create avatars, they will be embedding themselves into the training situation more easily. When possible, simulations should be designed so that the lessons learned are more memorable, because possible outcomes are dramatic when either a right or wrong decision is made. "The outcomes of bad decisions need to be vivid and memorable" (Weinstein 2015).

Simulations are now being used to train everyone from line workers at meat processing plants on safety and compliance to retail employees on using empathy and emotional intelligence when interacting with customers. Simulations create an environment and a model of reality that help trainees feel and experience situations that are comparable to or symbolic of real-world situations. Imagine a safety training simulation game that puts managers or supervisors in the place of an average line worker. By adding random gamified elements, such as instructions that tell the participant to stop working and walk to the supply room or suddenly begin to cover two workstations because a coworker is sick or stop a machine because of a missing label, the ultimate goal of the game, which may be to finish production quickly and safely, is compromised. In this case, the supervisors or managers might begin to feel what it's like to be a line worker trying to work safely and still accomplish all of the goals they need to as part of their normal job. Hopefully, in that situation, they'll begin to think about possibilities and other interventions that can improve the situation.

Serious games are often part of learning through simulations, but there is one big difference—a game introduces the element of winning whereas a simulation does not (Stadsklev 1974). For more on games and gamification, see Chapter 16 on gamification.

Simulations don't have to be high tech. The focus should be on the strategy and reasons for using simulations, not on high-tech bells and whistles. If there is no budget or willingness to purchase or create an advanced simulation, a low-tech simulation can be created. Cardboard, masking tape, room dividers, and props can be used to create room parameters and contents. Safety training topics like first aid and CPR have long used relatively inexpensive props like CPR manikins or real first-aid treatment materials to practice with fake injuries.

An essential part of any simulation is the postexercise debrief, in which learners reflect on actions and identify areas of strength and opportunities for improvement for themselves as well as the system (Kolb 2020). Debriefing is discussed in detail in Chapter 7.

Virtual Reality

As seen with simulations, a big benefit of using virtual reality is that trainees are not actually exposed to the hazardous situations they are experiencing. "While providing safety training in the environment where the actual skills will be needed might not be feasible due to the work environment, the same work environment portrayed in a virtual reality headset may aid retention of the information. Research in cognitive psychology has shown that recall is superior in the same environment in which the training took place" (Godden and Baddeley 1975). Virtual reality may provide such a situation (Krokos et al. 2018).

Virtual reality (VR) is technology that takes place entirely in a virtual world. Simulations, discussed earlier, sometimes use virtual reality and at other times use mock exercises. Virtual reality and other immersive digital tools are gaining in popularity and are being used in many different industries for a variety of purposes. The plumbing and heating industry is using VR to improve its certification training programs; the medical field is using virtual tools to help students learn anatomy, develop better communication skills with patients, and even learn surgical techniques from more experienced surgeons; and UPS is using virtual reality training modules to prepare its drivers for potential hazards on the road (Bhargava 2020).

A recent study from the National Commission for Certified Crane Operators (NCCCO), an organization that promotes construction industry safety, looked at the value of virtual reality with respect to crane operator certification. The results of its study showed that a certification test taken in a virtual reality environment is a highly reliable measure for predicting passing scores on an actual crane operation test (Judd 2020). These certification tests were taken using a VR desktop simulator, which greatly enhances the realism of the experience. In this case, the certification exam presented the same situation that was present in the actual certification test. A sample testing setup is shown in Figure 9.1.

Virtual reality is also being used in areas of safety training like hazard recognition, fall protection, and emergency situations such as mine and rescue escape. Figure 9.2 shows a screenshot of an aerial lift recognition simulator, available free online.

However, virtual reality learning is not for everyone. Some people become disoriented when participating in activities in the virtual world. Virtual

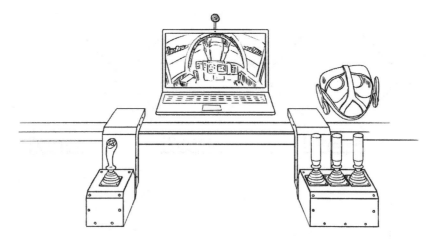

Figure 9.1 ✦ Illustration of desktop simulator (Adapted from Judd 2020)

Figure 9.2 ✦ NIOSH's Aerial Lift Hazard Recognition Simulator (Source: NIOSH 2016)

reality should be used as an add-on for other types of safety training and used in short duration. A 20-minute rule for VR training is recommended (Bailenson 2019).

Augmented Reality

Augmented reality (AR) is a technology that overlays virtual objects onto a physical background. It can help learners interact with learning content directly, and this can increase retention because trainees are having a real-world experience. Most AR technology can be simply accessed through a trainee's phone or on a mobile tablet, but AR can also be used with special headsets or glasses. The trainee can see real-time data (that is stored in the cloud) about an object and can control the data through screens, voice control, or hand/arm gestures. With AR, trainees are creating their own learning, which is best for retention. For this reason, AR is increasing in popularity. "Worldwide spending on AR and virtual reality (VR) was forecasted to reach $17.8 billion in 2018, an increase of nearly 95 percent over the $9.1 billion spending that International Data Corporation's *Worldwide Semiannual Augmented and Virtual Reality Spending Guide* shows. Worldwide spending on AR and VR products and services will continue to grow at a similar rate throughout the remainder of the 2017–2021 forecast period, achieving a five-year compound annual growth rate of 98.8 percent" (Richards 2019).

AR can be especially useful when trainees must learn a particular technique. As discussed in Chapter 24 on image-based safety, illustrations and images go far in helping trainees to understand content. AR can take that one step further by making those images and illustrations interactive. Imagine training someone on lockout-tagout procedures. A trainer could show a step-by-step list of what to do or could show a step-by-step list of what to do alongside images and illustrations of each of those steps being completed. The trainer could take this one step further by creating an augmented reality situation where a trainee would look at a piece of equipment, and the data necessary to lock out or deenergize that piece of equipment would appear through the lens of the augmented reality viewer. While many procedures can be demonstrated in the classroom, classroom experiences are not always repeatable on demand. Augmented reality provides that option.

AR markers are the two-dimensional images that are used for activating AR experiences and can be used to create interesting microlearning programs. The AR markers can be placed in prominent places around a facility. Places where trainees may congregate, such as outside elevator doors, in break areas, near time clocks, or by vending machines, can be great locations to provide microlearning content and/or gamified content to the workforce. The content the AR markers point to can change frequently, which will keep trainees interested and even help set up a serious companywide game. AR markers can garner trainee attention over time, and their use is only limited by a trainer's creativity.

There are a few ways to experiment with augmented reality in a safety training program. There are various vendors already in this marketspace that would be happy to provide a demonstration. A trainer wishing to create augmented reality projects in house, without the aid of an outside vendor, could try out one of the many applications that provide free trials and paid subscriptions.

Stories

Just like the experiential learning activities described earlier, training aids in the form of stories, case studies, and lessons learned can increase retention. "The more attention we pay to something, the more likely we are to file it—

and its associations—in long-term memory" (Liebermann and Hoffmann 2008). Training activities that prompt trainees to remember something clearly will help trainees pay attention, focus, and more easily transfer the information back to the job.

Stories evoke salience—the state of being important or conspicuous—through human interest and can be triggered by the use of "aha" moments (Liebermann and Hoffmann 2008). Aha moments exhibit a certain pattern of events. They begin with a difficult question and a struggle to find a solution, followed by a moment of insight, and end with happiness and satisfaction at having found the answer. Think of something related to the training material that always seems to baffle people but actually has a clear answer. Present the problem and let the trainees struggle with it for a while until they have the moment of insight—or the trainer helps them find the answer.

People remember stories better than boring lectures (Boris 2017). Consider trying to convince a group of safety trainers to add interactive activities to safety training classes. They could be told that by adding safety training activities the trainees will be involved in their own learning. Alternatively, they could be told a story about a group of stubborn, grumpy trainees who showed up for a training class in a defensive and bad mood but surprisingly were very engaged and animated when presented with the chance to participate in fun, yet informative, interactive activities. Which one of these statements would make a bigger impression on safety trainers?

A *story* is "an account of events that take place over time. An effective story describes a single event that has powerfully affected the life of one person (or one group)." (Ricketts 2015). In the context of this book, the idea of stories is used interchangeably with lessons learned and case studies. Lessons learned are basically case studies and examples that include many details, insights, surprises, and even possibly some drama. Lessons learned can be found in accident reports, in newspaper articles, in "Fatal Facts" reports provided by OSHA (see the example in Figure 9.3), in hazard alerts provided by WorkSafe BC, and even by talking with older, more experienced workers.

Stories have been shown to be a great way to educate, inform, change, and develop adaptive thinking within organizations (Gold et al. 2002). Older, experienced employees may be better able to react to an unusual situation because they have years of experience with a variety of scenarios. On the other hand, younger employees with very little experience will encounter a greater challenge when faced with something unknown. By sharing stories that include

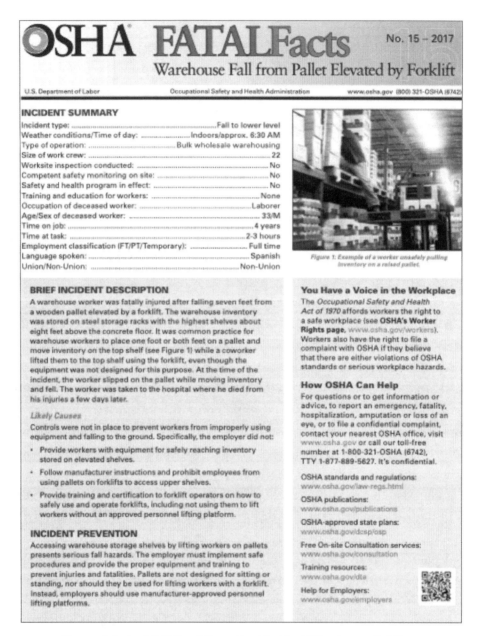

Figure 9.3 ✦ OSHA Fatal Facts No. 15–2017, Warehouse Fall from Pallet Elevated by Forklift (Source: OSHA 2017)

a wide variety of scenarios, all trainees will have more of a background from which to make future decisions (Joung et al. 2006). Even though lessons learned might not be lessons learned personally, a trainee can still learn by living through others' experiences vicariously. With exposure to many types of stories and examples, a trainee can develop adaptive expertise (Hesketh 1997).

Adaptive Expertise

Adaptive expertise, or adaptability, has been identified as an important part of the performance of many jobs. The phrase *adaptive performance* refers to an individual's capacity to deal with changing work environments, and in particular, new or unusual situations (Hesketh 1997). Many safety training scenarios presented to trainees require them to exercise adaptive performance. Training classes such as Hazwoper provide needed skills to trainees, but trainees are still expected to be able to take that knowledge and apply it to an unpredictable situation. The key to adaptive performance is that trainees are able to look at a situation, look at how it's being handled, identify any potential problems, and then come up with a new set of alternative actions that will enable them to foresee what could possibly happen with any unusual events that could occur.

OSHA recognizes the value of learning from past experiences and using those in training environments. OSHA's HAZWOPER standard (29 CFR 1910.120) includes instructions to include a critique of incidents that have occurred in the past year that can serve as training examples of related work and other relevant topics. A critique of past incidents can lead to stories that can be used in training in the form of lessons learned. Since stories trigger brain activity that mirrors the experience of living through an actual event, using lessons learned is effective in tapping into trainees' emotions, which has been shown to increase memory. These stories are also a great way to bring reality into safety training. Often safety trainers use lessons learned to communicate what others have learned through their past mistakes, although sometimes successes are shared in lessons learned as well.

Error-Exposure Training

By sharing case studies, in particular ones that apply directly to a facility or group of trainees, trainees can more realistically visualize how they would use the new knowledge that they're gaining in their day-to-day jobs. Case studies and lessons learned that minimize errors have been found to be less effective than case studies that are based on error-exposure training. In *error-exposure training*, trainees make their own mistakes or watch someone else make a mistake and then receive feedback. When case studies are used that do not include errors, trainees do not have the opportunity to learn from mistakes. Further, case studies and lessons learned that do not include mistake making may lead to the effortless acquisition of skills, which is fine for routine performance but not helpful when a trainee is expected to deal with new and complex situations (Joung et al. 2006). Error-exposure training will lead to more active processing and problem solving, and its benefits appear to be retained longer when performance is assessed after long delays. Error-exposure training also produces better transfer to new situations (Charney et al. 1990).

Research has found that *story-based interventions* can lead to important and lasting changes in people's behavior. Workers tend to change their safety-related behavior after hearing compelling stories about others who have suffered injuries and illnesses. Stories capture attention, stimulate deep reflection, trigger powerful mental images, alter perceptions of new situations, and influence behavior (Ricketts 2015).

The following are a few research-based tips for developing effective story-based communication (Ricketts 2015).

1. When working with stories, try to balance the story with general information in order to capitalize on the strengths of each. Although the story will provide interesting information in a way trainees can easily relate to, it's still necessary to provide facts and procedures that the trainees can learn from. Stories are a great way to start off a training class, not only as a way of getting trainee attention, as discussed in Chapter 7, but also to help trainees see themselves in a particular situation. Once trainees see themselves in a particular situation, it is easier to discuss the basics behind the safety training content. Since trainees already have an idea of how this information will apply to them in their day-to-day jobs, the "boring part of the content" will make more sense and hold their attention longer.
2. Use stories that explain and highlight focal message points without creating any distractions (Rey 2012). Superfluous details may be amusing to the trainees, but having unnecessary information in the story or case study will be distracting. In addition to unnecessary details, another type of distraction is when the story may touch on a sensitive topic or issue. For example, if a certain group of trainees is always being blamed for doing something by management or another department, a story that discusses an accident that happened to a trainee related to the same issue may cause trainees to be distracted by the situation they are experiencing (Ricketts 2015).

3. The best stories demonstrate convincing cause-and-effect relationships. Stories are most effective when they include clear connections between causes and effects (Voss and Sandak 1999). If a strong cause and effect is not evident in the story, it is probably better to use a different story. If trainees cannot clearly understand what caused a particular accident after hearing the story, they may not be getting the intended message. Similarly, if trainees hear the cause of an accident and never really get to hear the effect, they may think the situation was fine or acceptable. The best way to make sure the cause-and-effect relationship is evident is to tell the story in chronological order and use only stories in which the cause and effect are indisputable (Voss and Sandak 1999).
4. Stories used in safety training are more effective if the trainees can connect to at least one of the main characters in the story (Dal Cin et al. 2004). If a story is about a construction worker that has 30 years of experience and always works outdoors on the side of the highway, and the trainees work in a similar situation and have a similar experience, they will be more likely to connect to the main character in the story. If the same story is shared with a group of healthcare professionals, it is unlikely they will be able to identify with the main character, and the story will not be as effective. If a story is about a trainee that had an accident because he did not have a strong command of English, when all workplace warning signs were in English, an audience consisting of all native English speakers will probably not be able to relate well to it.
5. The best stories describe situations that are familiar enough that trainees will understand them but have outcomes that are surprising enough to keep their interest and make them think about what they actually learned in the story (Schank and Abelson 2008). Imagine telling a story about a company electrician who needs to repair a piece of energized equipment. When a trainer begins a story like this, the trainees are probably expecting a certain outcome—the electrician failed to follow some type of lockout-tagout or deenergization procedure. However, if that electrician had an accident that was based on something completely different, such as falling off of a ladder or making contact with stored energy that the electrician did not account for even though the material or machinery was locked

out, this would be an unexpected outcome that would spark interest and hopefully get the trainees thinking about how that same situation could happen to them one day.

6. Stories used in safety training should also emphasize preventive measures that the trainees can realistically use on their jobs. Trainers should not share stories that trainees see as unpreventable or with situations that are out of their control. If a story is shared about a drunk driver that hits a worker on his way to work, through no fault of the worker, there's nothing in that situation that the individual was able to control. Trainees will learn nothing from that type of story (Glanz et al. 2008).

7. All good stories, whether used in the workplace or elsewhere, have some element of suspense. There are numerous books on storytelling that can be helpful in crafting safety training stories. If a story has trainees wondering what will happen next, they will not only pay more attention, but their emotions will be involved as well, and that is important for remembering the training. Research has shown that stories should deal with serious rather than trivial outcomes. Suspense can be generated by inserting a brief time delay at the end of the first part of the story. During that pause, ask the trainees to predict what happens next before finishing the story and sharing the outcome (Ricketts 2015).

As a safety training activity, photos can be used to help teams of trainees create their own stories. To use this storytelling activity, trainers can give each team a photo of a workplace and tell them the photo was taken right before an accident occurred. Each training team's mission is to come up with a story about what they believe happened next. After teams have had a chance to create their stories, the trainer should stop the activity. The trainees will be expecting to hear what happened next, but instead, the trainer simply says that they will come back to the story. This is an example of using suspense with a story as a safety training aid. The benefit of this activity, aside from creating suspense, is that in the process of creating a story about what happens next, the trainees are now forced to think about what they have learned or are learning in safety training classes and how that applies to the situation shown in the photo. This will help the lessons be transferred back to the day-to-day job. By withholding the real results of the story, trainers can create suspense, which will keep trainees focused. Additional details about using a What Happens Next? training activity are provided in Chapter 18 on error-based examples and activities.

8. The best stories are those that would have very different outcomes if the main characters had acted differently. Story-based messages are especially persuasive when audience members imagine that characters could have avoided tragedy by making better decisions (Connelly and Rebb 2005). For example, a story about a machine operator who violated a fixed machine guard, which resulted in a serious injury, would be one where trainees could easily identify an action that would have led to a different result.

9. As discussed in Chapter 24 on image-based safety training, complex ideas work best when communicated through the use of appropriate and relevant images. Information is more easily understood when it is presented using a combination of words and images rather than words or images alone. While images are helpful for all audiences, they are especially important for those with limited language skills (Houts et al. 2006).

Stories are everywhere, and once a trainer knows what types of stories are best to use in safety training, it will be easier to find them and use them as learning tools. Many organizations publish injury reports that are easy to find through a simple search online. Some examples are the fatality assessment and control evaluation (FACE) reports and fatality and catastrophe investigation summaries provided by OSHA. Insurance companies and workers compensation carriers may also provide a variety of reports to their clients. The news is unfortunately also a source of case studies that can often be modified and used in the safety training setting. It is very easy to set up news alerts in search engine providers such as Google so that news stories related to a particular topic are delivered straight to an inbox. While many of these may not be useful for a particular situation, these sources can provide news stories that can be used as case studies and provide content that otherwise might never be seen. Finally, many social media groups that exist on LinkedIn, Facebook, and Twitter often share worst-case scenarios or stories of accidents that occur elsewhere. When using any of these stories, it is important to remember that news stories involve real people, real accidents, and real tragedies, and care needs to be taken not to trivialize them.

Tabletop Exercises

Tabletop exercises are drills that professionals working in emergency response may have had the benefit of experiencing. Tabletop simulations used in safety and environmental training can offer the same benefits. While high-tech, full-scale simulations of hazardous emergency situations, such as hazardous waste spills, are a great way for safety, health, and environmental professionals to practice and put classroom training to the test, not every facility can afford them. In such instances, a tabletop exercise can be designed and used instead. Central to a successful tabletop exercise is that it involves more than one sector with responsibilities under the plan being practiced. In *tabletop exercises*, prepared situations and problems are combined with role-playing to generate discussion of the plan, the procedures, the available resources that can be called upon, and the policy to be adhered to in making decisions (Wisner and Adams 2002). A successful tabletop exercise can point out any gaps in procedures, knowledge, necessary coverage, equipment, or anything else that needs to be added before a real-life emergency would occur. Full-scale simulation exercises are much more involved but serve the same purpose as tabletop exercises. They provide a realistic experience for those learning the information so there will be greater retention.

Tabletop exercises can improve group problem solving under pressure and elevate trainee preparedness for emergency situations. An effective tabletop exercise needs to be properly designed, carefully conducted, evaluated when complete, and include careful analysis of the results of the evaluation. There is no value in a tabletop exercise if the results—good or bad—are not acted upon. At the Business Preparedness for Pandemic Influenza Second National Summit hosted by the Center for Infectious Disease Research and Policy in February 2007, experts Kristine Moore and Jill DeBoer presented the following 10-step process for implementing tabletop exercises (Rothstein 2007):

1. Review the plan.
2. Define a goal for the exercise.
3. Form an exercise design team.
4. Develop exercise objectives.
5. Develop the exercise scenario.
6. Identify the players.

7. Decide on a format.
8. Develop scripts and data injects.
9. Address facilitation issues.
10. Plan an after-action report.

When designing any safety training program, it is recommended that similar steps be followed. Safety training activities involve viewing plans ahead of time and determining what the desired program design outcome includes. It is suggested in the ten steps that the individuals designing the exercise are not the same individuals who participate in the activity. Steps 4 and 5, developing the exercise objectives and the exercise scenario, are also related to the development of any safety training activity. Number 6 states that the players should be identified. In general, the safety trainer is not going to select who needs to participate in a training class; that is most likely determined by job title or the department that an individual works in, but when designing a safety training activity, it is still important to keep the audience in mind. Step 7 requires that the individual planning the tabletop exercise decide on a format, which is very similar to safety training where the trainer must decide on the best method of delivery for a particular audience. Unlike most safety training activities, number 8, which calls for developing scripts and data injects, is something that is not commonly done in a safety training class. Data injects can be thought of as curveballs that a safety trainee may have to deal with unexpectedly. During the course of a tabletop activity, several different *curveballs* could be added to almost any safety training exercise. Steps 9 and 10 are also closely related to most safety training activities. Chapter 7 describes the importance of facilitation in detail, and after-action reports are very similar to evaluations conducted after a safety training activity. The value of posttraining communication such as this is discussed in Chapter 8.

Tabletop exercises have the benefit of offering trainees a very realistic experience that can be directly related to potential actions they may need to take on the job. A mini-tabletop exercise involves a great deal of emotion, and trainees are expected to act appropriately under pressure, similar to what they would need to do in the real situation. Tabletop activities are a great way to increase retention by not only adding emotion to the experience but often also letting trainees participate in an exercise that will be very similar to what is expected of them—including the need to handle curveballs.

Review and Retention Activity

Stories used as experiential learning activities are described in this chapter.

Review this case study, an example of such an activity.

Case Study

A safety trainer was assigned to deliver a 3-day training class on supervisor safety skills. The attendees at this class were field supervisors and not willing participants. The list of subjects to be presented over these 3 days included many soft skills, such as how to give feedback and how to be a better listener. On the first day of class, the trainer noticed that all the trainees entered and took their seats with arms crossed in front of them or quickly opened newspapers and held them in front of their faces. This trainer had recently learned about accelerated learning principles and had made the risky decision to implement numerous interactive learning activities throughout the supervisor safety skills class.

    The learning activities were presented approximately every 10–15 minutes, over 3 days, where there were natural breaks in class content. Much to the trainer's surprise, trainees paid attention and were highly engaged. Activities ranged from small group discussions to competitive team games, all focused on the training content. About halfway through the 3-day class, several attendees approached the trainer and thanked her for giving them the opportunity to do something during class and not just be forced to sit and listen to a lecture or watch videos endlessly. Although it may seem that many trainees would not be willing to participate in interactive class activities, done well, most trainees—even the unexpected participants—appreciate the opportunity to be involved in their own learning, while at the same time paying more attention and learning more content. Trainers that doubt the ability to use interactive activities with their workforce are encouraged to give accelerated learning principles a try because, as demonstrated in this story, classes consisting of even the most difficult trainees will often be surprisingly receptive to taking a more active role in their own learning.

References

Bailenson, J. 2019. *Experience on Demand: What Virtual Reality Is, How It Works, and What It Can Do.* New York, NY: W. W. Norton and Company, Inc.

Bhargava, R. 2020. *Non-Obvious Megatrends: How to See What Others Miss and Predict the Future.* Oakton, VA: Ideapress Publishing.

Bjork, R. A. 1994. "Memory and metamemory considerations in the training of human beings." In J. Metcalfe and A. Shimamura, eds., *Metacognition: Knowing about Knowing,* pp. 185–205. Cambridge, MA: MIT Press.

Boris, V. 2017. *What Makes Storytelling So Effective For Learning?* Harvard Business Learning, Corporate Learning Blog. Dec. 20, 2017. https://

www.harvardbusiness.org/what-makes-storytelling-so-effective-for-learning/.

Charney, D., L. Recher, and G. W. Kusbit. 1990. "Goal setting and procedure selection in acquiring computer skills: a comparison of tutorials, problem solving, and learning exploration." *Cognition and Instruction*, 7:323–342.

Connelly, T., and J. Reb. 2005. "Regret in Cancer Related Decisions." *Health Psychology*, 24(4S):S29–S34.

Dal Cin, S., M. P. Zanna, and G. T. Fong. 2004. "Narrative persuasion and overcoming resistance." In E. S. Knowles and J. A. Linn, eds., *Resistance and Persuasion*, pp. 175–191. Mahwah, NJ: Lawrence Erlbaum Associates.

Glanz, K., B. K. Rimer, and K. Viswanath, eds. 2008. *Health Behavior and Health Education: Theory, Research and Practice*. Jossey-Bass. San Francisco, CA: Pfeiffer.

Godden, D. R., and A. D. Baddeley. 1975. "Context-dependent memory in two natural environments: On land and underwater." *British Journal of Psychology*, 66(3):325–331. doi: 10.1111/j.2044-8295.1975.tb01468.x.

Gold, J., D. Holman, and R. Thorpe. 2002. "The role of argument analysis and story telling in facilitating critical thinking." *Management Learning*, 33(3):371–388.

Hesketh, B. 1997. "Dilemmas in training for transfer and retention." *Applied Psychology: An International Review*, 46:317–339.

Houts, P. S., C. C. Doak, L. G. Doak, and M. Loscalzo. 2006. "The role of pictures in improving health communication: a review of research on attention, comprehension, recall and adherence." *Patient Education and Counseling*, 61(2):173–190.

Joung, W., B. Hesketh, and A. Neal. 2006. 'Using "War Stories" to Train for Adaptive Performance: Is it Better to Learn from Error or Success?' *Applied Psychology*, 55:282–302. doi: 10.1111/j.1464-0597.2006.00244.x.

Judd, W. 2020. "Virtual Reality: Does it have a role in certification testing?" National Commission for the Certification of Crane Operators (NCCCO). March 2020. http://www.ncccofoundation.org/wp-content/uploads/2020/03/Virtual-Reality-in-Certification-Testing.pdf.

Kolb, Gretchen. 2020. "Simulation as a Lever for Change." *TD Magazine*, June 2020:56–61.

Krokos, E., C. Plaisant, and A. Varshney. 2018. "Virtual Memory Palaces: Immersion Aids Recall." *Virtual Reality*, 23(1):1–15. doi: 10.1007/s10055-018-0346-3.

Liebermann, S., and S. Hoffmann. 2008. "The impact of practical relevance on training transfer: Evidence from a service quality training program for German bank clerks." *International Journal of Training and Development*, 12:74–86.

National Institute of Occupational Safety and Health (NIOSH). 2016. Aerial lift hazard recognition simulator. Accessed June 11, 2020. https://www.cdc.gov/niosh/docs/2017-103/pdfs/2017-103.pdf?id=10.26616/NIOSHPUB2017103.

Occupational Safety and Health Administration (OSHA). 2017. *OSHA Fatal Facts: Warehouse Fall from Pallet Elevated by Forklift*. Washington DC: U.S. Department of Labor. https://www.osha.gov/Publications/OSHA3916.pdf.

Rey, G. D. 2012. "A review of research and a meta-analysis of the seductive detail effect." *Educational Research Review*, 7:216–237.

Richards, D. 2019. *Seeing the Possibilities with Augmented Reality*. Alexandria, VA: ATD Press.

Ricketts, M. 2015. "Using Stories to Teach Safety: Practical Research Based Tips." *Professional Safety*, May 2015:51–57.

Rothstein, N. 2007. "Designing, Conducting, and Evaluating Tabletop Exercises: A Primer on Optimizing This Important Planning Tool." Center for Infectious Disease and Research Policy. University of Minnesota. May 3, 2007. https://www.cidrap.umn.edu/news-perspective/2007/05/designing-conducting-and-evaluating-tabletop-exercises-primer-optimizing.

Schank, R. C., and R. P. Abelson. 2008. *Scripts, Plans, Goals and Understanding: An Inquiry into Human Knowledge Structures*. Taylor & Francis Group. New York: London Psychology Press.

Stadsklev, Ron. 1974. *Handbook of Simulation Gaming in Social Education*. Institute of Higher Education Research and Services. The University of Alabama.

Voss, J. F., and R. Sandak. 1999. "On the use of narrative as argument." In S. R. Goldman, A. C. Graesser, and P. van den Broek, eds., *Narrative Comprehension, Causality and Coherence: Essays in Honor of Tom Trabasso*, pp. 235–252. Mahwah, NJ: Lawrence Erlbaum Associates.

Weinstein, M. 2015. "It's not all fun and games." *Training*, September/October 2015:36.

Wisner, B., and J. Adams, eds. 2002. *Environmental Health in Emergencies and Disasters: A Practical Guide*. Geneva, Switzerland: World Health Organization.

Chapter 10
Repetition, Spacing, Retrieval Practice, and Interleaving

If training were thought of as learning occurring over time and not as a one-time event, it would be more effective. That goes for just about every area of our lives. Many people work their way through higher education by cramming information into their heads in order to pass an exam. This method of studying for an exam has actually been shown to be effective, but only if the material needs to be retained for a short period of time. Learning information this way can help someone to pass a test, which may be acceptable to the trainee, and sometimes to a trainer as well, but over the long term, this way of learning is not going to result in trainees being able to use and apply the new knowledge back on the job.

In order for anyone to remember something long term, repeated exposure to the material over a period of time can be highly effective. In most safety training classes, trainees just need to pass an exam at the end of class for the training to be considered a success. Training is more valuable and serves its true purpose when trainees are able to remember the information weeks, months, or even years later. Some ways to get training content into the stored memory of trainees so it is remembered longer is to use the concepts of repetition, spacing, retrieval practice, and interleaving. These techniques are not very common in safety training at this time, but with a little preplanning, safety trainers can use these techniques to greatly improve the retention of the material that is delivered in safety training classes. It's not just safety trainers who often do not take advantage of these strategies. A recent study conducted by the Association for Talent Development found that interleaving, spacing, and retrieval practice are among the least considered of eight different strategies training professionals often use to present content (Association for Talent Development 2019).

Definitions

Repetition occurs when a trainee sees the same content repeatedly. When repeating information over and over in an attempt to remember it, the trainee is using repetition as a learning strategy. For example, if the same five-step safety procedure is sent out to trainees every Monday with the intent that it would eventually sink in, a trainer is using repetition to ensure the material will be remembered. *Spacing* occurs when the content is repeatedly delivered at intervals. Retrieval practice is sometimes called the testing effect (retrieval methods are discussed in detail in Chapter 11, and the testing effect is further discussed in Chapter 13). *Retrieval practice* is different from repetition since the material is not simply being reviewed multiple times; instead, the content is being pulled from memory. When content is spaced out over time and also includes retrieval practice (i.e., testing), the greatest benefits can be seen in the amount of material that is retained. *Interleaving* is probably the least well known because it takes more planning than the other training strategies and is counterintuitive. With interleaving, a trainee begins learning something, but before finishing it, switches to learning a new topic. Before finishing the new topic, the trainee goes back to the first or another new topic. Interleaving is similar to spacing and retrieval practice but with added difficulty. All four of these methods are further discussed in this chapter.

When deciding whether or not to include these methods in a safety training program, consider the following research findings (Thalheimer 2006):

- Repetitions, if well designed, are very effective in supporting learning.
- Spaced repetitions are generally more effective than nonspaced repetitions.
- Spaced repetitions benefit both the new presentation of learning material and retrieval practice of previously learned information spaced out over time.
- Spacing is particularly beneficial if long-term retention is the goal.
- Spacing helps minimize forgetting.
- Wider spacings are generally more effective than narrower spacings, although there may be a point where spacings that are too wide are counterproductive.
- Spacing the repetitions over time can hurt retrieval during the actual learning events, while it generates better remembering in the future.

This means safety trainers would be wise to include some type of repetition, retrieval practice, and spaced learning in their safety training programs.

Repetition

As a trainer, it's important to build in opportunities for trainees to review and try out what they are learning. By asking trainees to practice what they have just learned, they are adding the new knowledge they just gained to the mental models they already have established. As described in Chapter 7, it's important to facilitate debriefing sessions after training activities as a way of adding in repetition of content and as a way of helping trainees move new information into their long-term memory. One study conducted with nursing students found that repetition through the use of text messages after a learning event increased overall retention (Bowling 2017). This is not only an example of repetition but also microlearning, which is discussed in Chapter 14. Repetition is fine, but multiple studies have shown that spacing out repeated encounters with the material over time produces superior long-term learning (Kang 2016), and this type of repetition leads to the spacing effect.

Spacing

Spaced repetition produces more learning and better long-term retention than repetitions that are not spaced (Thalheimer 2006). If a group of safety trainees are in a classroom for 5 days straight, and every day they are presented with the same information, after 5 days and five separate repetitions of the same information, they will remember the content for awhile, but their time would be better spent attending a similar class 1 day a week over 5 weeks. Longer spacings tend to produce more long-term retention than shorter spacings (Thalheimer 2006).

Why does the spacing effect work? It is believed that the longer the time period between when a trainee first hears information and when it is repeated, the more trainees must use extra effort to remember what was previously learned. This extra effort compels them to remember the information better. Additionally, having wider spaces between content delivery means there will be a greater amount of forgetting when the trainee is relearning. This may seem counterintuitive, but it will result in trainees using different strategies to help them remember in the future.

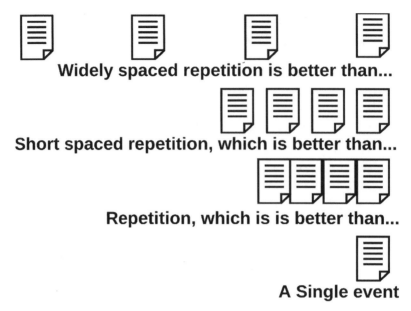

Figure 10.1 ✦ Types of repetition and their effectiveness
(Adapted from Dellarosa and Bourne 1985)

Spaced repetitions will allow trainees to store information in their memories in a manner that makes the information more resistant to forgetting than if they had learned it through nonspaced repetitions. Research has shown that widely spaced repetition is more effective than more frequent repetition, and in turn, spaced repetition is more effective than nonspaced repetition. Nonspaced repetition is more effective than trainees hearing information only once in a single presentation (Dellarosa and Bourne 1985). Figure 10.1 shows the relationship of the various types of repetition to effectiveness.

Repetition spaced out over time is better than all alternatives with one exception—when the information must be recalled immediately. If an exam is being taken immediately after learning the content, learning through repetition without delays is more effective. Many people know this exercise as cramming. The problem with cramming is that the information will not be remembered in the long term. Longer spacing of repetition is better when the information must be remembered in the future.

Another way trainers can benefit from the spacing effect is to add the opportunity for trainees to be exposed to the content before the class as well as after the class. That way, in addition to the time spent in the formal learning portion of the safety training class, trainees would be exposed to two additional repetitions of the material spaced over time. Before the class meets, a trainer could send out a simple one-page infographic that displays the content and ask trainees to read through it and be prepared for a quiz when they arrive in class. Although the quiz will not be counted, it is another important part of the testing effect, which is discussed in Chapter 13. This would also prompt the trainees to read through the information and understand it instead of simply ignoring it. When trainees come to class, an activity can be presented that acts as a pretest of their knowledge. The class content can then be presented as planned.

After the trainees are finished with the training content, a trainer can follow up with them in a way that presents the content a third time. For example, the trainer could request trainees to fill out a second quiz or complete a task. Something as easy as asking trainees to take a photo of themselves using the new skill in the workplace and to send it back to the trainer would require them to recall what they learned and would serve as repetition. The trainer could also create and share a video or podcast that recaps the content. A detailed work poster could also be put in their work area. These suggestions for additional steps don't entail much more effort than is already being put forth, but would easily insert repetition and spacing into an existing safety training program.

The spacing effect can involve only a handful of repetitions or many repetitions over a much longer period of time. To use the spacing effect appropriately, the exact wording and the same delivery method does not need to be shared with the same group of trainees over and over again. If the repeated delivery of information were exactly the same, this would be boring, and the trainees probably would ignore it after the second or third time they were exposed to it. Instead of sharing the same word-for-word text, PowerPoint presentation, video, or e-learning modules with trainees, the information can be slightly rewritten or recreated. It can be presented in a different format, or it can be presented in a different style. For example, instead of using a lecture-based format, the same content can be covered in a case study or with a visual aid, such as an infographic, or with a training activity.

In addition to different formats, different delivery methods can be used to share information over and over but still provide a little bit of variety. If a group of trainees were presented the content while they were sitting in the classroom, the same information can be repeated in an online training situation for the second exposure. A trainer could also record the information and share it as a podcast or other type of audio file. Another option would be to set up and send a series of texts that break down the content into smaller pieces. The number of ways a trainer can repeat content is only limited by the imagination. With the increased use of technology, and since the majority of people have mobile phones, it's easier than ever to get information out quickly, easily, and inexpensively.

An added benefit of the spacing effect is that spaced repetitions may be beneficial in making ideas more persuasive (Casebourne 2015). Safety trainers often need to rely on persuasion when presenting information in a safety training class as well as outside of the classroom. Trainers often try to persuade trainees to follow safety rules, act in a safe way, or do a certain set of steps in a particular order so the trainees will be able to work in a safe way.

For example, trainers that work for companies where chemical hazards are the primary safety concern may want to spend the majority of the trainees' allotted time for learning on various chemical hazards and how to prevent those hazards from leading to accidents. Instead of presenting a multiday class that covers all of these hazards, this information could be spaced out over time. Much of the information would be exactly the same with only a small change in content based on the particular type of chemical being discussed. The same information delivered to trainees every few months (but with a slight twist) would be an example of spaced repetition—the content is the same, it's just presented in a slightly different way. There are definite benefits to delivering training in this way. For instance, in between each of the sessions a trainee is likely to have some exposure to the content in a real-world application setting and thus will be able to relate to the content more fully and bring the experience back to the next training class. Even better, if trainees can share that information with others in the training class, it would create an environment of collaboration and social learning. The benefits of collaborative learning are discussed further in Chapter 5 on accelerated learning principles.

Repetition and spacing work hand in hand. If content is repeated too quickly, the benefits will not be as great as when the content was spaced out over time, but it will still produce better results than if no spacing were done at all (Thalheimer 2006). The longer the time period between learning events of the same information, the longer the retention will be. There is a point, however, where the time between repetitions is too long, and the effect will not be the same.

Another possibility is to gradually increase the spacing. For example, the training content can first be repeated after 1 week, and then 10 days can pass before it is repeated again, followed by 14 days for a third repetition. This type of spacing can be even more effective than having long delays (Morris et al. 2005).

When considering how to incorporate the spacing effect into a safety training program, it is important to realize that in general, more complex and more substantial content will require more repetitions (Thalheimer 2006). Spaced learning is extremely effective. "Nothing in learning science comes close in terms of immediate, significant, and reliable improvements to learning" (Carey 2015).

The Ebbinghaus forgetting curve was discussed in Chapter 3 and shows how forgetting occurs over time. Spaced learning can change the way this curve looks. With spaced learning, trainees will not learn the information as quickly, but it will be remembered longer and can be used once they are back on the job. Learning can seem more difficult when spaced repetitions are used, but in the long run, the information is more likely to be remembered when it is needed. If a trainee receives important safety information in a 1-day class but won't need that information for several weeks, the information probably will be forgotten by the time it is needed. If on the other hand, the information is repeated in spaced intervals, the repetitions will come closer to the time it is actually needed, which can make a big difference in the amount of learning transferred to the workplace. Using spaced repetitions will minimize the amount of forgetting that trainees do but may also create minor and temporary difficulties in learning the information the first time. If the training content is truly important to the safe work of the trainees, spaced repetition of the material will be worthwhile. If trainers must present certain training classes only to meet regulatory requirements, but there is no expectation that the trainee will use the information later on, spaced repetition may not be worth the effort.

Retrieval Practice

The importance of retrieval practice and possible methods to encourage retrieval are presented in detail in Chapter 11 but are also mentioned here because the benefits of retrieval practice are greatly increased through spacing. Learning content that is spaced can include presentation material, or it could include a retrieval practice such as a self-test or a more formal quiz. Presentation material is typically what a safety class is based upon. Examples are a PowerPoint presentation with case studies, illustrations, or maybe even a hands-on demonstration. In these classes, trainees see and hear the content first hand. Retrieval practice, on the other hand, includes things such as pre- and postevaluations/tests and an opportunity to practice skills after learning the content. Activities where trainees must call upon their memories to recall what was learned in previous safety training classes also serve as retrieval practice. Spacing out retrieval practice is more effective than spacing out the presentation of content, so when deciding what information to space out to trainees, the focus should be on things that require trainees to retrieve what they learned and not necessarily on the review of content that was already presented or the presentation of new material. Sending out informal quizzes, requests for analyses of case studies or lessons learned, and opportunities to practice what trainees learned is central to effective retrieval practice.

A simple way to demonstrate reinforcement of content as a form of retrieval practice is placing posters in the workplace that provide visual summaries of key points but leave out important information. Unlike standard safety posters, safety posters used for retrieval practice do not include all of the information a trainee needs. The modified posters created for retrieval and reinforcement purposes remind trainees of what they learned without telling them everything.

Figure 10.2 shows a poster created to reinforce content from a class on fire extinguishers and to function as a retrieval tool. In this poster, P.A.S.S.—a common acronym used in classes on fire extinguisher use—is shown. The letters stand for "pull" (the pin), "aim" (at the base of the fire), "squeeze" (the handle), and "sweep" (the spray from side to side). The poster only shows the acronym and not what each letter stands for, so the trainees will have to pull that information from their long-term memory. This will help the trainees remember the fire extinguisher training content longer.

Spaced retrieval practice can also be built into existing safety training classes so the classes are not just based on presentation. As discussed earlier, one way to do this is by using interactive safety training games and activities. Many of the safety training games and activities provided later in this book are a type of retrieval practice. Although they are not presented as quizzes and evaluations, they are in effect testing the trainee on knowledge previously learned in the training class, requiring the trainee to recall the information from memory. These activities can also be sent as follow-up materials, which will provide additional retrieval practice and reinforcement through spacing.

Figure 10.2 ✦ Fire extinguisher P.A.S.S. poster (Source: Tapp 2017)

Embedding new learning in long-term memory requires a process of consolidation in which the new information is strengthened, given meaning, and connected to prior knowledge. This process unfolds over hours and may take several days. Durable learning requires time for mental rehearsal and is what makes spaced repetition work better. "The increased effort to retrieve the learning after a little forgetting has the effect of retriggering consolidation, further strengthening memory" (Brown et al. 2014). This tells safety trainers it is important to give trainees the time to have new safety training information sink in before revisiting the content. This may seem like a luxury that many safety trainers cannot afford, but there are easy ways to add this type of repetition into existing safety training programs. Various techniques are discussed throughout this book and include things such as microlearning as a form of reinforcement, discussed in Chapter 12, and the use of short quizzes as a way to reinforce training content and important points, discussed in Chapter 11.

Forgetting

This chapter focuses on trainees' abilities to remember information, but the other side of this coin is to use forgetting to actually increase learning. The effect of spaced learning and repetition involves forgetting as a way of increasing retention.

Forgetting can be beneficial. When we ask a safety trainee to remember something and he or she can't, this serves as a warning to the trainee, but this also provides important feedback for the trainer. If the trainer had not asked the question and given the trainee the opportunity not to know it, the safety trainer would not be able to modify and adjust the content and delivery as necessary. If safety trainees fail in their attempt to remember something, future opportunities to learn the same information related to the previous failure generate more vigorous and constructive learning behaviors. Most retrieval failures happen when trainees can't remember the information and not when they remember the wrong information, although both types of this failure to remember seem to motivate learners to use more energetic and better encoding strategies when they get the opportunity to learn the same information again (Thalheimer 2006).

Interleaving

Interleaving is the process of learning new information by mixing up two or more related topics. This is done by spacing out the training sessions and mixing up the skills that are presented to trainees each session. Training often focuses on one topic, start to finish, until trainees have learned the content. With interleaving, one topic is presented, but not all of it. By moving on to a new topic before a trainee feels ready, trainers are encouraging some level of forgetting. During the next training session, a second topic is presented, but again not everything that should be included with that topic is shared. At the third class, the content from the first class is quizzed and revisited. This sounds confusing, but interleaving is based on the concept of distributed retrieval practice combined with the mixing up of different topics. Interleaving refers to the practice of spending some time learning one thing, and then pausing to concentrate on learning a second thing before having quite mastered the first thing, and then returning to the first thing, and then moving onto a third thing, and then returning to the second thing, and so forth. In short, it involves the processes of repetition, spacing, retrieval practice, and mixing learning activities—the spacing happening by virtue of the mixing. An example of how this could be used in safety training follows.

> Training day 1: Scaffolding safety, part 1
> Training day 2: Excavation safety, part 1
> Training day 3: Scaffolding safety, part 2
> Training day 4: Fall protection, part 1
> Training day 5: Excavation, part 2
> Training day 6: Scaffolding safety, part 3
> Training day 7: Fall protection, part 2

Interleaving can be thought of as a spiraling series of exercises that cycle back to skill sets in a seemingly random sequence that adds layers of context and meaning at each turn (Brown et al. 2014). Trainees learning this way may feel like it's going slower and experience frustration. This is often the reason this method of providing new information to trainees is skipped or overlooked, but "research shows unequivocally that mastery and long-term retention are much better if you interleave practice than if you mass it" (Brown et al. 2014).

When delivering class content, the safety trainer can plan to switch to a new topic before trainees have had a chance to master the first topic or could switch topics before the trainees have had a chance to practice the original content. For example, if a trainer is presenting 10 steps for a safe lockout-tagout procedure and normally would ask employees to practice identifying those 10 steps in the correct order, the trainer could add in the benefits of interleaving by moving on to a new topic before the trainees are able to identify those 10 steps in the correct order. A separate but somewhat related topic would be presented next; perhaps training on proper machine guarding could be discussed. Again, the trainees could practice identifying the correct sequence for the machine-guarding topic, but before the trainees accomplish this, the safety trainer would return to the first topic.

Since initially this may seem frustrating to the trainees, it's important to explain the science behind it. This varied practice helps trainees assess changing conditions and environments and prompts them to respond appropriately. Learning in this way may be frustrating because trainees are unable to successfully complete the tasks as they are presented, but it will have lasting beneficial effects.

Interleaving is the opposite of *blocking*, which occurs when one topic is learned at a time before moving on to the next. "Blocked study or practice deepens our association between a learned skill or concept and the specific context in which we learned it; interleaved learning, by contrast, forces us into frequent transfers of information and skills across contexts, which helps us develop the ability to recognize when a learned skill might apply in a new context" (Lang 2016). The way most safety training classes are conducted—one topic is presented and then mastered/tested and then the next topic is presented/tested—does not require the trainee to decide which knowledge to apply and when. For example, if different types of chemical hazards were being presented to a group of trainees, and the first 30 minutes were spent reviewing flammables, followed by a quiz, and then the second 30 minutes were spent reviewing combustibles, followed by a second short quiz, the trainee would not necessarily discern the difference between a flammable and a combustible since they were taught at different times, as described here.

Interleaving is believed to work because it improves the brain's ability to discriminate between concepts. By mixing up the topics, the brain needs to do more searching for the correct answer when it's time to practice or recall the information. Another reason interleaving might work is because, when the information is learned that way, it cannot stay in short-term memory. Simply put, when a new topic is learned, the old information is pushed out. When new material is learned through blocking, it stays in short-term memory, and that is sufficient. Interleaving requires the previously learned information to be pulled back to short-term memory multiple times, and this reinforces neural connections and enhances learning. In any event, interleaving involves more of a struggle to remember information, and this is a good thing. The idea of not doing well or having trainees experience frustration may prevent safety trainers from trying this technique, but as discussed in Chapter 14, allowing trainees to fail in a safe place does more for long-term memory retention than if the content and the process of learning were easy. The added effort of learning through interleaving can lead to better, longer-lasting results. "Research has shown that interleaving helps learners learn better how to assess context and discriminate between problems, selecting and applying the correct solution from a range of possibilities" (Brown et al. 2014).

Interleaving multiple subjects or training topics can also provide a type of spacing. This is important because, when topics are presented separately in an interleaving fashion, the trainees are able to discriminate better among different types of challenges they face on the job. Many safety hazards that arise are often due to something unusual occurring, and the specific incident the trainee is faced with may not have been specifically mentioned during a training class. If the trainee is able to pull from a toolbox of learned skills, hopefully he or she will be able to successfully meet any challenge. Interleaving topics can help trainees build that skill.

Some research has shown that interleaving is more effective for a variety of topics. Other research has shown that interleaving works best when the students have at least a little familiarity with the subject beforehand, or when the materials can be quickly or easily understood. Nevertheless, the interleaving process has proven to provide long-lasting benefits with less forgetting of the material over time.

There's only so much that blocked practice can do in helping trainees learn how to transfer information from the original context in which they learned it into unusual and new situations. It is very difficult to achieve transfer. This is especially disturbing considering how important almost all safety training information is in preventing workplace accidents and injuries. If a safety trainee attended confined space training that involved practice entering a tank, that trainee may or may not be required to enter other confined spaces similar to the tank used during the training class. If a second situation not included in the formal safety training program arises, the specific safety skill a trainee learned may not automatically apply.

To add benefits of interleaving into a safety training class, a trainer could start integrating these principles with evaluations given at the end of class. If a safety trainee is required to attend a series of classes, this works especially well. This may be the case if a new hire must attend consecutive training classes on a variety of topics before being allowed on the job. In this situation, after the second topic or class has been completed, the final quiz/evaluation can also include questions related to what was learned in the first class. In the third training class, the new hire could further deepen learning and retention if the safety trainer includes questions related to the first and second class on the exam for the third class, and so on. In classes where pretests are given, a similar change can be made to these quizzes, where questions related to previously learned material are included.

Another small action that can be taken to include the benefits of interleaving is to ask the trainees at the end of an interleaved training class to create a test question based on the new material they just learned. Make sure they know this test question will be presented back to them in the future. These test questions can be used in future classes or sent out as reinforcement in the form of weekly texts or emails.

As stated earlier, repetition, spacing, retrieval practice, and interleaving are not frequently used strategies in training programs. Safety trainers can stand out by creating and delivering programs that show a positive return on investment by applying learning science research, including the strategies discussed in this chapter.

Review and Retention Activity

These learning and retention activities are based on the principles of repetition, spacing, and retrieval practice discussed in this chapter.

Complete activity 1D. One week later, complete activity 1W. In 1 month, complete activity 1M (Figure 10.3). Check the answers using the answer key provided (Figure 10.4). It is suggested that appointments for these be added to a personal calendar as a reminder to complete activities 1W and 1M. If possible, take a photo of each activity and attach it to the calendar event, or alternatively, send the future activities as part of an email that is created now but scheduled to be delivered at the appropriate time in the future.

Activity 1D (to complete now)

1. Training would be more effective if thought of as occurring over time and not as:
    something mandatory   being boring   being optional   a one-time event

2. Repeated exposure to training material is called:
    repetition   duplication   multiplication   association

3. Repetitions are more effective if they are:
    done quickly   occuring only yearly   spaced   not done

4. Spaced repetitions are not best for content that must be remembered:
    in 6 months   in 2 years   never   immediately

5. Repetition of material should be in the exact form and have the exact wording as the original material.   True or False

6. More complex training topics will require _____ repetitions.
   less   more   zero   100

7. This curve reflects the amount of forgetting that occurs over time.
   Arnie   Ebbinghaus   Seuss   Heinrich

8. The act of forgetting can be used to increase:
   frustration   attention   learning   repetition

9. The process of mixing up two or more related topics is known as:
   confusion   mass-learning   repetition   interleaving

10. Interleaving is believed to work because it improves the brain's ability to:
    function   discriminate between concepts   learn quickly   rest

Activity 1W (to be completed in 1 week)

1. Training would be more effective if thought of as occurring over time and not as a _____.

2. Repeated exposure to training material is called _____.

3. Repetitions are more effective if they are _____.

4. Spaced repetitions are not best for content that must be remembered _____.

5. Repetition of material should _____ in the exact form and have the exact wording as the original material.

6. More complex training topics will require _____ repetitions.

7. The _____ curve reflects the amount of forgetting that occurs over time.

8. The act of forgetting can be used to increase _____.

9. The process of mixing up two or more related topics is known as _____.

10. Interleaving is believed to work because it improves the brain's ability to _____ between concepts.

Activity 1M (to be completed in 1 month)

Repetition, Spacing, Retrieval Practice, and Interleaving

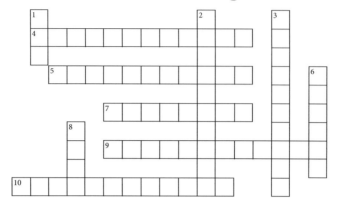

ACROSS
4 Training would be more effective if it were thought of as occurring over time and not as a _____ (3 words).
5 Spaced repetitions are not best for content that must be remembered in this time frame.
7 The act of forgetting can be used to increase this.
9 Interleaving is believed to work because it improves the brain's ability to do this between concepts.
10 The process of mixing up two or more related topics.

DOWN
1 Repetition of material should ____ be in the exact form and have the exact wording as the original material.
2 Repeated exposure to training material.
3 This curve reflects the amount of forgetting that occurs over time.
6 Repetitions are more effective if they are _____.
8 More complex training topics will require _____ repetitions.

Figure 10.3 ✦ Repetition, spacing, retrieval practice, and interleaving crossword puzzle

Answers to Activity 1D and 1W

1. Training would be more effective if thought of as occurring over time and not as **a one-time event**.

2. Repeated exposure to training material is called **repetition**.

3. Repetitions are more effective if they are **spaced**.

4. Spaced repetitions are not best for content that must be remembered **immediately**.

5. Repetition of material **should not be** in the exact form and have the exact wording as the original material.

6. More complex training topics will require **more** repetitions.

7. The **Ebbinghaus** curve reflects the amount of forgetting that occurs over time.

8. The act of forgetting can be used to increase **learning**.

9. The process of mixing up two or more related topics is known as **interleaving**.

10. Interleaving is believed to work because it improves the brain's ability to **discriminate** between concepts.

Answers to Activity 1M

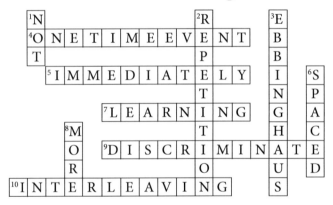

Figure 10.4 ✦ Answer key for repetition, spacing, retrieval practice, and interleaving crossword puzzle

References

Association for Talent Development (ATD). 2019. "State of the Industry" report. Alexandria, VA: ATD Press.

Bowling, Judy, 2017. "The Effect of Repetitive Text Messages on the Retention of Knowledge Among Clinical Staff." https://www.scholarlycommons.baptisthealth.net.

Brown, P. C., H. L. Roediger, and M. A. McDaniel. 2014. *Make It Stick: The Science of Successful Learning.* Cambridge, MA: Belknap Press, an imprint of Harvard University Press.

Carey, B. 2015. *How We Learn: The Surprising Truth about When, Where, and Why It Happens.* New York, NY: Random House.

Casebourne, I. 2015. "Spaced Learning: An Approach to Minimize the Forgetting Curve." *TD Magazine.* January 27, 2015. https//www.td.org/insights/spaced-learning-an-approach-to-minimize-the-forgetting-curve.

Dellarosa, D., and L. E. Bourne. 1985. "Surface form and the spacing effect." *Memory & Cognition*, 13:529–537. doi: 10.3758/BF03198324.

Kang, S. H. 2016. "Spaced repetition promotes efficient and effective learning: policy implications for instruction." American Educational Research Association. *Policy Insights from the Behavioral and Brains Sciences*, 3(1):12–19.

Kolb, D. A. 1984. *Experiential Learning: Experience as the Source of Learning and Development.* Englewood Cliffs, NJ: Prentice-Hall.

Lang, J. M. 2016. *Small Teaching: Everyday Lessons from the Science of Learning.* Jossey-Bass. San Francisco, CA: John Wiley & Sons, Inc.

Morris, P. E., C. O. Fritz, L. Jackson, E. Nichol, and E. Roberts. 2005. "Strategies for Learning Proper Names: Expanding Retrieval Practice, Meaning and Imagery." *Applied Cognitive Psychology*, 19(6):779–798. doi: 10.1002/acp.1115.

Tapp, L. 2017. *Five for Fire: Safety Training Activities for Fire Safety.* Madison, NJ: Enninsmore Publishing.

Thalheimer, W. 2006. *Spacing Learning Events Over Time: What the Research Says.* Somerville, MA: Work-Learning Research, Inc. https://www.worklearning.com/wp-content/uploads/2017/10/Spacing_Learning_Over_Time__March2009v1_.pdf.

Chapter 11
Retrieval Methods

The act of retrieval practice has long been known to aid in memory retention. For more than 100 years, the benefits have been tested and shown with groups of students as diverse as those ranging from sixth graders to college students to medical residents (Dobson 2013).

Put simply, to retrieve knowledge from memory you have to practice retrieving knowledge from memory, and the more time a learner practices remembering something, the better he will be able to do it in the future. The ability to remember important information from a safety training class once the class is finished is critical. One of the most common ways to encourage retrieval practice is by administering tests and quizzes, but retrieval practice is not limited to these two methods.

The very act of retrieving information from the brain is by itself a learning event, because every time the information is recalled, it becomes easier to recall it in the future. "The act of retrieval is a memory modifier" (Bjork 1975). Additionally, retrieval practice combined with feedback offers an unbeatable way to help trainees learn new information and remember it when necessary (Thalheimer 2006).

Retrieval practice is a powerful means of increasing learning and memory, and the more difficult the retrieval practice the better it is for long-term retention (Agarwal and Bain 2019). For example, remembering an answer to a safety training question will be better for remembering the material long term than if the trainee were asked to look up the information. Similarly, the flashcard activities described in Chapter 21 are more effective as learning activities if the trainee flips over a flash card and has to write down the correct answer instead of merely flipping over the flash card quickly to see the answer. Making training activities a little more challenging and making the information a little more difficult to recall when tested, will help trainees remember the information longer. When trainers make training activities easy, the learning will be more short term. For example, if trainees are given a quiz with multiple-choice answers, the trainees only need to identify information previously seen in order to answer correctly. In this case, the trainee will not have much of a mental struggle to come up with the right answer. Alternatively, if the trainee is presented with a quiz that requires the trainee to write in a short answer, the trainee will have to work harder to come up with the right answer. Although this may cause some frustration, the trainee will remember the information better in the long term.

Free Recall

Research has pinpointed differences between students who learned new information by either trying to write down everything they could remember about a topic and students who reviewed a past test or highlighted notes. Self-testing, such as forcing oneself to write down whatever can be remembered about a particular topic, works because of the feedback that is received (Young 2019). If trainees arrive at a refresher class believing there is nothing left to learn, and then attempt to write down everything they know about the topic, they soon realize that they don't know as much as they thought they did. This realization acts as a type of feedback. When class notes are simply reviewed there is no feedback, so learners don't really apprehend what they know and don't know. In *free recall* (such as the writing exercise just described) the students don't have any feedback about what they missed or what they got wrong. "The act of trying to summon up knowledge from memory is a powerful learning tool on its own beyond its connection to direct practice or feedback" (Young 2019).

The concept of *desirable difficulty* states that more difficult retrieval leads to better learning, provided that the active retrieval in itself is successful (Bjork 1975). One safety training activity called Braindump takes advantage of the idea of free recall mentioned earlier. In Braindump, trainees are asked to write down as much as they can remember about a particular topic in a limited amount of time. This can be a great way to start a refresher class, as many trainees will come to these classes believing they already know all there is to know. If instead the trainees were presented with a worksheet that gave them hints about what they needed to remember, their retention would not be as good after the class was over. For example, in a first-aid class the trainees could be given a worksheet that simply asks them to write down what they can remember about the various types of first aid they might be expected to personally deliver (including cues). Some examples follow:

- A coworker's hand is bleeding badly. What first-aid techniques would you use?
- A coworker fell off a ladder and is unconscious but breathing. What would you do next?
- A visitor has burning, tearing eyes and can't stop coughing. What would you do?

While questions such as these will do a good job of jogging trainees' memories of what they have learned in past classes, it would be better to ask them to simply write down all they can remember about first-aid techniques that they are able to deliver. Consider the following replacement question:

"You have just been promoted! Congratulations! Your promotion requires you to work in a new facility. Since you are already certified in first aid, you will be expected to provide first aid as needed in this new work location. When your new supervisor asks you what type of first aid you are trained to deliver, along with a request for you to name three important things you know about each type of first aid you describe, what would you say?"

In this situation, the trainee will most likely have to struggle to provide comprehensive, detailed answers. For this reason, "cued recall tests, in turn, are better than recognition tests, such as multiple-choice answers, where the correct answer needs to be recognized but not generated" (Young 2019). A safety trainer can take advantage of this idea by providing safety training exams that require more fill-in-the-blank questions and free-recall requests than multiple-choice or matching questions. Making the retrieval of information more difficult should not be seen as an obstacle but as a way to make training more effective.

Suppose that the scenario around first-aid training involved the following sample preclass quiz questions:

1. Is a tourniquet appropriate for a major laceration to an artery? T/F
2. What does the C stand for in CPR?
3. Will a coworker suffering from heat stress have cold, clammy skin or hot, sweaty skin?

These three examples will serve the purpose of jogging the trainees' memory of what was previously learned but will not be anywhere near as effective as the other two sample question sets described earlier. Making quiz questions as easy as these examples, especially when given only two or more choices as shown in questions one and three, will not work to increase learning.

Desirable Difficulty

Although desirable difficulty can be beneficial, it is important to mention that it will be undesirable if it becomes so hard that retrieval is impossible. If trainees are asked to recall information from too long ago, the information may be forgotten entirely. The trainer needs to find the right midpoint so that the testing occurs long enough after the material is presented to make the trainees experience some difficulty in remembering the answer but not so long after the training class that they will have remembered nothing. If safety professionals passed a certification exam 20 years ago, they would probably have forgotten some of the information they learned for the exam but never had to apply. If they were asked these questions now, they might experience too great a struggle to remember content without first experiencing some kind of refresher learning event. On the other hand, if a newly certified safety professional were asked sample certification test questions 6 months or a year after passing the exam, there would be a much more desirable level of difficulty.

Spacing, described in Chapter 10, can be used for presentation of new material and for retrieval of previously learned information. Retrieval practice is actually one type of spacing. We often think of spacing as including just the presentation of new information, but spacing includes two types of repetition: one being presentation of information and the second being retrieval practice, which includes things like tests and quizzes. When a quiz or test is used as a method of retrieval practice, the trainee gets the question and then has to retrieve the information from memory and then respond to the original question. Research has shown that by gradually increasing the time between opportunities for retrieval practice, there will be greater benefits from that retrieval practice than if the presentation of information were the only thing being spaced. Gradually increasing the time between each retrieval practice provides benefits, while expanding the time between spacing that involves only explanations and descriptions (i.e., presentation of material, for example) does not (Thalheimer 2006).

The idea of testing oneself is not used frequently in real life or in safety training, and as stated previously, this process makes it difficult to know how well something has been learned. When looking over notes from a training class, trainees may have a general feeling about how well something is understood. Alternatively, if trainees feel like they don't know something, they will probably feel that it hasn't been learned. Many people feel like they're learning more when they read a book than when the book is closed and they're trying to remember what they just read—but this isn't true. When this has been tested, students realized days later that the retrieval practice produced better results than the passive review (Karpicke and Roediger 2008). The passive review (e.g., looking at class notes) may provide better results immediately after the review is undertaken, but it is not as effective as retrieval practice for increasing retention of the material long term.

The Value of Evaluation

Chapter 13 on predicting and evaluations covers evaluations in greater detail, but in relation to retrieval practice, there are a variety of testing activities, and each one will help solidify knowledge. Testing in this case refers to forcing learners to recall learned information, concepts, or skills from their memory (Lang 2016). Tests given in a training class enable trainers to

- find out what a trainee already knows when deciding on which classes a trainee needs to attend based on their preexisting knowledge
- find out what the trainees already know, so that the trainer knows what to spend more or less time on during a training class
- inform a trainee about the information that will be covered in a training class
- measure the amount of learning that took place during a training event
- identify how much learning was retained after a period of time
- review what was just covered in a small segment of the training class (like end-of-chapter tests or tests embedded within the flow of online classes)

Additional tests will not be especially welcomed by trainees. Make sure they know why they're being tested—so the trainer will know what material to cover and what material should be reviewed in the future. Sharing the science behind the benefits of additional testing may help trainees understand the need and benefits of these evaluations.

Much research has been done on how much humans can actually remember, but there is a "wide consensus among memory researchers that long-term memory is essentially unlimited" (Miller 2017). The problem is not how much trainees can remember, but how they can retrieve it from their long-term memory once it has been learned. Whenever something is remembered, we are strengthening the neural pathways that lead from our long-term memory into our working memory where we can use that information and transfer it to the actual tasks involved with the job. If information is pulled from long-term memory frequently, as is the case with retrieval practice, that pathway becomes more and more defined.

Retrieval Practice Options and Activities

As mentioned earlier, training quizzes and tests are not the only options a safety trainer has to implement retrieval practice. Retrieval practice can be added into a safety training class in very small steps and still be effective. Retrieval practice can appear in the beginning of a training class or at the end of a class, and it can also work in online and blended classes.

Questions

One of the easiest ways to integrate retrieval practice into training classes is to start a class with a simple question: "What do you remember about the last training class on this topic?" This would obviously work much better for a refresher class, but it could also be used for a class that has never been offered before because many trainees most likely had some exposure to the topic somewhere in their career. Trainees could also be given sticky notes when they arrive to a training class and asked to write down a topic that they believe will be covered in that class. Trainees should be encouraged to write out as many sticky notes as they can. Once they have their notes written, they should stick them on the wall. This simple act of asking the trainees to think back to a previous learning experience is a form a retrieval practice.

This type of activity can also be done in an online environment. There are a variety of collaborative websites that allow trainees to create virtual sticky notes and share them on screen. Virtual whiteboards trainees can use serve the same purpose, but a low-tech version that involves trainees writing down their topics on a sheet of paper and holding it up to the webcam also will achieve the same purpose.

In addition to opening a training class with questions, closing questions are another way to use retrieval practice to increase retention. When using closing questions, it's important to focus on the key concepts from the training class. The other techniques described above can also be integrated and used with closing questions.

Another way to add retrieval practice is through the use of interactive training activities. Many of the activities in this book ask a trainee to remember information previously learned. Examples of these types of activities can be found in the chapters at the end of this book.

When using retrieval practice activities, one option is to have all trainees write down answers instead of simply answering orally. Questions asked orally can still provide retrieval practice, but there will be many trainees that will not have to respond to the question, and probably won't. Asking all trainees to write has the added benefit of getting all trainees (and not just the especially vocal or confident ones) to participate. A word of caution though—not all trainees will be literate. Trainees should be allowed to write their answers in their own language, but even when that is clearly stated, not all trainees will have good writing skills, so the trainer should keep that in mind when asking for this at the beginning of class. The trainer should also make it clear that their answers won't be collected or shared.

Training Tutor

The Training Tutor activity is described in Chapter 15. This activity is another form of retrieval practice, as trainees will need to work together in teams to retrieve previously learned information. In this activity, the safety trainer puts trainees in teams and asks each team to prepare a 3-minute presentation on the safety training topic. At the end of the 3 minutes, the trainer goes around the room and asks the different teams to give their brief report. This is not a quiz, but it can have a similar effect when used as retrieval practice.

Safety Lotería

In Chapter 24, the safety training activity Safety Lotería is presented along with examples. Safety Lotería is usually used at the end of a training class as a way to reinforce what was presented, but Safety Lotería can also be used as a way to encourage retrieval practice in the beginning of a class if it is slightly modified from the way it is presented in Chapter 24. To use Safety Lotería in the beginning of a class, the Safety Lotería sheets can be given to trainees when they arrive for training, and the trainees can be asked to identify what each of the images on the Safety Lotería card represents. If the trainees are familiar with the Safety Lotería game, a trainer can take it one step further and ask trainees to write the clue that represents each square. After they have done this opening retrieval activity, Safety Lotería sheets can be collected and at the end of the class used again with unmarked sheets as the closing activity. Alternatively, if trainees have been asked to create clues for the images on their lotería sheets, these clues can be used in the actual game and at the end of the class.

Covert Retrieval Practice

Another idea is to use something called covert retrieval practice. *Covert retrieval practice* asks trainees to simply think about something and not speak out loud or write any of the answers. The trainer needs to make sure that enough time is given for the trainees to think about their answer. Awkward silences are difficult for many people, and a trainer may be tempted to rush through and start the training class, but taking a few minutes to let trainees pause and think will greatly increase their retention. In research studies, retrieval practice, even covert retrieval, was still shown to increase retention (Smith et al. 2013).

Agendas

In longer safety classes where there are a variety of topics to be covered, preparing a written agenda for an 8-hour or longer class can also be beneficial as a retrieval aid. After the first day of class, the trainer should ask trainees to pull out their agendas and make a note next to the topics that were covered on day one and write down a few things they remember about each. This can continue throughout the class since having trainees simply look back for a few moments will help increase retention.

Trainees may complain when they first experience a safety trainer's increased desire to use retrieval practice in training classes, especially when it's in the form of quizzes, so briefly explaining the science behind it can be helpful. If the trainees realize that trainers are adding it to training programs as a way to help trainees remember important safety information that can make a big difference in whether or not they have an accident in the future, hopefully they will see the benefit of those few extra tests.

Review and Retention Activity

These learning and retention activities are based on the idea of covert retrieval practice discussed in this chapter.

Recall the key points described in this chapter. Do not write them down. Simply think about the material presented and what you would tell someone about retrieval methods.

References

Agarwal, P. K., and P. M. Bain. 2019. *Powerful Teaching: Unleash the Science of Learning.* Jossey-Bass. San Francisco, CA: John Wiley & Sons, Inc.

Bjork, R. A. 1975. "Retrieval as a memory modifier." In R. Solso, ed., *Information Processing and Cognition: The Loyola Symposium*, pp. 123–144. Hillsdale, NJ: Laurence Erlbaum.

Dobson, J. L. 2013. "Retrieval Practice Is an Efficient Method of Enhancing the Retention of Anatomy and Physiology Information." *Advances in Physiology Education*, 37:184–191. doi: 10.1152/advan.00174.2012.

Karpicke, J. D., and H. L. Roediger. 2008. "The Critical Importance of Retrieval for Learning." *Science*, 319(5865):966–68. doi: 10.1126/science.1152408.

Lang, J. M. 2021. *Small Teaching: Everyday Lessons from the Science of Learning.* 2d ed. Jossey-Bass. San Francisco, CA: John Wiley & Sons, Inc.

Miller, M. D. 2017. *Minds Online: Teaching Effectively with Technology.* Cambridge: Harvard University Press.

Smith, M. A., H. L. Roediger, and J. D. Karpicke. 2013. "Covert Retrieval Practice Benefits Retention as Much as Overt Retrieval Practice." *Journal of Experimental Psychology: Learning, Memory, and Cognition*, 39(6):1712–25. doi: 10.1037/a0033569.

Thalheimer, W. 2006. *Spacing Learning Events Over Time: What the Research Says.* Somerville, MA: Work-Learning Research, Inc. https://www.worklearning.com/wp-content/uploads/2017/10/Spacing_Learning_Over_Time_March2009v1_.pdf.

Young, S. H. 2019. *Ultralearning: Master Hard Skills, Outsmart the Competition, and Accelerate Your Career.* New York City: Harper Business.

Chapter 12
Microlearning and Chunking

The idea of microlearning has been gaining in popularity in recent years, mostly because of the greater use of technology and mobile devices (Shail 2019). Research conducted by Microsoft in 2015 found that the average person's attention span may be decreasing (Microsoft 2015). Another study found that trainees have trouble focusing on a topic for more than 20 minutes at a time (Islam 2013). This last finding is one reason why interactive activities should be dispersed throughout a training class, but in the context of microlearning, this information provides strong support for breaking down training into smaller pieces that can be consumed in a shorter amount of time.

Challenges and Benefits of Microlearning

As there are more and more demands on the workforce, and now more and more workers working remotely, microlearning can be effective in getting educational material in front of trainees and allowing them to focus on a small piece of content at a particular time instead of having to sit in a classroom for multiple hours. Today, just about everyone owns a mobile phone, affording endless opportunities for distractions. If training is not designed in a way that increases or encourages learning retention and transfer, trainees may not remember the content shortly after returning to work. If so, time and money have been wasted. Microlearning can provide solutions to many of these challenges.

In-person training is no longer the most desired delivery method in the workplace. Benchmarking results indicate that managers prefer on-demand learning and access to up-to-date information in a timely manner. By delivering discrete chunks of information in short bursts of time, often via social media, microlearning can be a strategy that complements more comprehensive classroom and web-based training, reinforcing concepts in between tasks performed in the office or working as job aids on the production floor (Overton 2011).

Presenting learning in small chunks has another advantage; it interferes less with the productivity of workers. No matter how supportive a company seems to be of safety training initiatives, almost all companies would prefer to have trainees spending more time on their day-to-day responsibilities than sitting in a classroom or in front of a computer. Microlearning can supply clear information on important learning topics, fitting it in between tasks or at the beginning and/or end of a shift without interrupting the trainees' daily schedules. Trainees can learn and perform better when they can access small pieces of meaningful content at their own speed as opposed to trying to absorb large amounts of material in a single sitting (Mayer et al. 1999). Microlearning has been reported to make the transfer of learning 17 percent more efficient (Gutierrez 2018).

Microlearning also speeds up the learning process overall since it creates less mental fatigue, and mental fatigue can lead to serious cognitive decline (Shail 2019). Sitting in a training class, in person or virtually, and trying to learn a lot of new information can cause fatigue and less focused attention, and that provides less than ideal conditions for learning. By breaking down and spacing out the content, trainers can help avoid this mental fatigue. It is important to note that this type of spacing out is different than the spacing discussed in Chapter 10, because spacing out in this context means breaking down content into smaller pieces to be delivered over time instead of in one setting. The spacing discussed in Chapter 10 refers to the spacing of the same information, possibly in different formats, over a period of time.

Microlearning can also work well with the concept of interleaving, which is discussed in great detail in Chapter 10. Interleaving has been shown to increase retention and combined with microlearning it can be especially effective. To use interleaving with microlearning, the individual microlearning modules would be somewhat related but cover different safety topics. Interleaved microlearning schedules would include plans to revisit earlier topics. A microlearning schedule could present one topic, then move on to a new topic, and perhaps on to another new topic, before going back to build on the first topic presented. This is in contrast to a program without interleaving where only one topic would be presented over the same period of time.

Microlearning Defined

What exactly is microlearning? There are many definitions, but the term microlearning generally refers to small, condensed pieces of content that take less than 10 minutes to complete. Content is usually delivered to trainees on a mobile device, but it doesn't necessarily have to be conveyed that way. Some people think of microlearning as a form of training that should be able to address the desires of trainees to learn at any time and any place. None of this necessarily tells us what microlearning is; it tells us what it needs to be. Basically, *microlearning* is an approach to training that delivers content that is short and presented in focused bites. We are not making learning easier by breaking it down, instead we are making it more focused. The most important thing to remember about microlearning is that information is broken down into chunks, and those chunks should focus only on what is most important. No extraneous information should be included.

Will Thalheimer describes microlearning in the following way: "Relatively short engagements in learning related activities—typically ranging from a few seconds up to 20 minutes (or up to an hour in some cases)—that may provide any combination of content, presentation, review, practice, reflection, behavioral prompting, performance support, goal reminding, persuasive messaging, task assignments, social interaction, diagnosis, coaching, management interaction, or other related methodologies" (Thalheimer 2013). These attributes are discussed in various chapters throughout this book.

Although the amount of time that a microlearning class should take seems to be thought of differently by different practitioners, the shorter amount of time it takes to digest information makes it a very good match for social media. The short timeframe of microlearning also makes it very easy for first-time users to grasp. As individuals experience more and more microlearning experiences, they can expand their knowledge incrementally for effective knowledge retention.

The Adaptability of Microlearning

Microlearning can be used to teach just about everything, from an informal topic such as communication tips to more complex material that is broken down into smaller, more manageable pieces, although highly technical topics may not be a good fit. One advantage is that it can be customized more easily for company- and job-specific aspects of training content. A full-size, off-the-shelf, generic product may be difficult to make location specific, but when training is presented in smaller chunks, it's easy to customize one, two, or even three of the smaller chunks of information. "Rich, precise, and geared towards a specific audience, engaged and empowered learners retain more information because they decided, with guidance from their supervisors, what they need to learn to perform their jobs better" (Emerson and Berge 2018).

Three Elements of Microlearning

Microlearning consists of three main elements: the instructional unit; a shortened time commitment; and engagement, which presents itself in three different ways. The first element is the *instructional unit*, which refers to the entire course of microlearning from start to finish. It can be in the form of a text message, short video, or learning activity. It can be as simple as a flash card. When these variations are considered, it's evident that microlearning can last anywhere from a few seconds to 20 minutes or longer.

The instructional unit can be described as having a title, a body, and an evaluation question. The title is what causes trainees to pay attention to it, deciding whether or not to go through with the microlearning experience. The body of a microlearning module should direct the trainees toward what to think about and possibly do. This section often has images and related video; this type of microlearning has been found to deliver the greatest impact (Paul 2016). The third section of the instructional unit is evaluation. This section helps trainees make deeper connections to the content, which in turn helps store the content in long-term memory. Asking questions further helps trainees see where the information is most applicable to them and their responsibilities.

The second element of microlearning is that it has *a shortened time commitment*. It's not meant to be long. Without any fluff or extraneous information, trainees can concentrate only on what's important. The time commitment associated with a particular microlearning event depends on the type of engagement that's involved.

The third element of microlearning is the actual engagement. Without some type of *engagement*, or method to hold the participant's attention, there would be no value in microlearning. If the intent of microlearning is to get people to pay attention for a short period of time, but the trainees don't do that, then the program is not working. Information may be sent out, but it may not be effective.

Three Types of Engagement

There are three actual types of engagement: forced, sensory, and self-prompted. *Forced engagement* is a type of gamification. If a short assignment is sent as a text that must be completed in order to maintain a streak, this is an example of forced engagement. *Sensory engagement* involves some kind of buzzing or beeping sound that comes from an educational application. Many people use smart watches that run a variety of applications and provide sensory engagement by buzzing, beeping, or vibrating to motivate the wearer to do something. This type of sensory engagement could also work with training engagement efforts. *Self-prompted engagement* is a need-to-know type of engagement that usually occurs in the form of workflow learning when a trainee needs to know information on the spot.

Just like regular training, people learn best when learning is not passive. Trainees can't be expected simply to sit and absorb information like a sponge. Microlearning is most effective when it causes people to interact with the information and complete an activity. This could be as subtle as a mental activity that asks trainees to think about a time when they needed to follow a particular procedure, or it could be more structured like a training game they need to participate in. Games used in microlearning can take place over a period of days, weeks, or even months.

Six Types of Microlearning

Six types of microlearning have been identified. When deciding to use microlearning, safety trainers can review the six types and consider what type might work best for a particular topic and organization. The six types include pensive microlearning, performance-based microlearning, persuasive microlearning, postinstruction microlearning, practice-based microlearning, and primary microlearning (Kapp 2019).

In *pensive microlearning*, trainees are asked to think about an idea, situation, or learning task. By asking the trainee to take a few minutes to think about something, the information will move into long-term memory. An example of this in a safety training microlearning program would be a question such as "Where are three areas you can use this information?" Chapter 11 on retrieval methods discusses how even covert retrieval practice (i.e., asking trainees to simply recall information by thinking of the answer) has a positive effect on retention.

The second type is *performance-based microlearning*; this is used to help a trainee perform an immediate task. This kind of microlearning can be selected or called upon by the trainee at the time he or she needs to do something specific. For example, there could be a library of short, 1-minute videos that tell trainees how to safely do specific procedures. Many people are already familiar with using YouTube to find out how to do something quickly, so the idea of accessing information on the spot and when needed, will be welcome. For example, if a trainee has a question about where to store a particular product, they could quickly get the answer if an easy-to-access video library containing product storage information is available.

The third type is *persuasive microlearning*. This is used to modify learners' behavior. It reminds trainees of the goals and prompts behaviorally focused actions. This could be as simple as reminding people to stay safe, or reminding trainees of a particular hazard on a job. During the cold months, a microlearning module could remind people of the proper way to walk on ice. It could show a short video of how to do that safely. It's important to include something trainees need to do as a result of engaging with the microlearning module.

The next one is called *postinstruction microlearning*, and this is a targeted follow-up to the regular training event. It includes reminders and quizzes—what is described in the repetition and spacing chapter as a way of sending information out after formal training has concluded to supply reinforcement. After a training class, a trainer could inform trainees that the end-of-class quiz will be sent out in parts over the course of several days.

The next is *practice-based microlearning*, and this is a reminder to practice. This type of microlearning can coach people to do things the right way. An example of this would be a short reminder on safe lifting procedures sent several days after safe lifting training has been delivered.

The last type is *primary microlearning*. This type of microlearning is set up as a series of planned learning initiatives to prepare trainees for a larger event or all-day class session. It could be used as a refresher or could consist of new, general content. For example, if there is a longer event scheduled to cover the Global Hazard Classification System (GHS), a trainer could make each of the sixteen areas of the GHS into a short microlearning segment, so each module only touches on one specific topic. The modules could then be sent out to trainees, one at a time, over a period of days or weeks before the longer event. This is a form of repetition as well because trainees are seeing this information in the microlearning format before the class, and it's being presented again during the formal class. Trainees will also have the opportunity to see it again when follow-up is part of postclass communication efforts.

One use of microlearning is to provide a drip feed of short, regular (even daily) bursts of information (e.g., instructions, tips, quizzes, etc.) to individuals in order to stimulate activity and social interaction on a continuous basis. As a form of primary microlearning, these tiny bursts of information could be structured into some logical sequence and could form a tiny course or stand-alone training event. They might also be a series of unstructured items that build up over a set time period into a useful body of knowledge (Hart 2014). The GHS example described above could be used in this way.

Opportunities for engagement in a tiny course for safety training include:

- Daily tips, such as unusual safety concerns to watch out for
- Daily instructions
- Daily terminology or vocabulary
- Daily articles, blog posts, or longer text messages
- Daily learning puzzle or game
- Daily chance to enter a contest based on successful completion of an activity
- Daily quiz question
- Daily photo or image

Designing Microlearning Programs

It's also important to remember that microlearning must intentionally be designed as microlearning. It may seem possible to create a microlearning class by taking an 8-hour course and dividing it into sixteen 30-minute sections, which are then sent out over a period of time, but this is not how good microlearning programs should be created. Just as with all training design, before a safety professional or trainer starts to create training and plan the associated activities, it's best to consider what the final outcome should be. What should the trainees be able to do or understand after the microlearning program is finished? Once this is known, it is better to work backwards, designing the individual segments of the microlearning program with the end in mind.

Microlearning is not meant for every type of safety training. It is best for declarative and conceptual knowledge but not as good for problem solving or life-and-death situations that may require a high level of depth and expertise (Kapp 2019). For example, if employees need training on how to safely enter a confined space, microlearning is not the best way to do it. Alternatively, if there is a new type of gas monitor in place and trainees are already familiar with how to operate a different brand of gas monitor, a short microlearning program might be acceptable. Some studies have found that microlearning may not be the best tool when the student is learning something for the first time or learning a complex skill (Fox 2016).

Additional suggestions for creating microlearning programs can be found in the section on chunking.

Technology Reinforces Microlearning

Microlearning can take place on multiple platforms. Typically, it is delivered in a format highly reliant on different types of media. Microlearning can provide just-in-time knowledge and is usually available on multiple platforms at the same time, including tablets, smartphones, desktops, and laptops. Some studies suggest that using mobile technology is a great way to get the attention of trainees since it is so prevalent in their lives to begin with and since they are generally distracted by it anyway. Using this force for a good purpose can get important information to trainees on their time schedules and in ways that are very familiar to them. Providing microlearning on mobile devices offers the added benefit of giving learners the ability to pause learning and consume information at a pace that is best for them. Also, by consuming small bits of information at a time, which happens with well-designed microlearning programs, trainees can also check their understanding of small chunks of the material and make corrections as they go along.

When redesigning a longer compliance class, a trainer should consider if it's possible to take each of the separate lessons in that longer class and provide summaries for each topic in the form of a checklist or short video. Subject matter experts can be recruited to record the videos or other short messages. With mobile phone technology, short videos are not difficult or expensive to create. The videos could easily be distributed to trainees so they can watch the different topics on their own time, and if desired, can replay the content if they feel they need additional clarification or reinforcement.

Microlearning Implementation

The Association for Talent Development (ATD) issued a report that provided the following recommendations to follow when implementing a microlearning program (ATD Research 2017):

- *Make learning only as long as needed.*
  If possible, it's always a good idea to present the minimum amount of information that learners must know so they are not overwhelmed. If trainees are given too much to absorb at once, they will be overcome with excessive cognitive load. Microlearning can prevent that. Unfortunately, safety training content may be mandated by regulations requiring that it be delivered in a particular way or over a certain length of time. Whenever possible, training should only be long enough to cover the key parts of the training class information.
- *Get buy-in from leaders.*
  Similar to all types of safety training, buy-in from leaders, in particular trainees' managers, is very important to the success of a training initiative. Keeping trainees motivated to use a microlearning system requires that they see the program being supported by management. One of the barriers discussed with microlearning is often a lack of accountability; having buy-in from a trainee's supervisor is one way to alleviate that problem.
- *Identify learning objectives first.*
  Again, as with most training programs, and as described in the instructional design chapter (Chapter 6), learning objectives are very important. A microlearning program should not be undertaken without a clear goal in mind. A safety trainer needs to understand what the trainees need to be able to do as a result of completing the individual segments.
- *Realize knowledge quizzes may not always be the right choice.*
  Be careful about using quizzes, because they are going to take up the limited time available when sending out microlearning content. Think twice before deciding if quizzes really need to be included.
- *Consider integrating hands-on activities and simulation.*
  According to ATD, research reveals that organizations that incorporate hands-on activities or simulations into microlearning activities are more likely to see their microlearning efforts be highly, or very highly effective.

These elements may be a more engaging choice than other options and can also provide greater variety. The opportunity for trainees to practice and apply skills where there's no pressure is very valuable.

A few ways a safety trainer can give trainees the opportunity to participate in hands-on activities as part of a microlearning program include:

- Requesting employees to send photos related to the training topic back to the trainer
- Assigning one-question quizzes
- Providing the opportunity to play a quick training game
- Sending links to mini-audio files or podcasts
- Emailing mini fill-in-the-blank tests
- Texting a fact of the day along with a request for a response
- Asking for postclass survey completion to gauge retention from a recently completed training (this in and of itself can help increase retention)
- Providing directions to AR markers or QR codes strategically placed around the facility (both should provide material related to training content)

A few more best practices to consider when implementing a microlearning program follow:

- Send microlearning emails that don't require scrolling.
- Include distilled bullet points at the top of the message.
- Add microlearning-related agenda items to all staff meetings.
- Personalize microlearning messages if possible.
- Use leaderboards to track and share participation in microlearning efforts.
- Implement progress bars so trainees can track their progress.
- Check the compatibility/appearance on mobile phones.

Microlearning and Gamification

In Chapter 16, the use of gamification in safety training is discussed in detail. Gamification can also be a successful part of a microlearning program. Microlearning often uses what is known as structural gamification, which is the application of game elements to propel a learner through content without altering the content (Kapp 2019). An example would be an experience where a learner receives points for answering questions correctly, and the points are then applied toward some type of reward.

Short Sims

Although simulations are discussed in Chapter 9, it is important here to discuss how microlearning can work with simulation programs, in particular, short sims. The *short sim* concept was pioneered by Clark Aldrich (Aldrich 2020). He defines it as an interactive experience that takes a user between 5 and 15 minutes to finish. In a short sim, trainees interact with a character in the simulation and have to make realistic choices, receiving feedback on their input. Short sims, by their very nature, are based in reality. (The importance of creating training that is based on realistic experiences is also discussed in Chapter 9.) Short sims should also be based on an actual situation that a trainee might encounter. The advantage of a short sim is that, while a full-blown simulation can take a long time to develop and deliver, a short sim can focus on one element and can be created in much less time (Aldrich 2020). In a short sim, there is only one short goal. Once the short sim is completed, there is not any other work to do as part of the module. This helps keep trainees focused and provides a quick way for trainees to practice and learn something. Short sims aren't about receiving new information, they're about actually doing something, so it's important that trainees have an action to take when they're participating in this kind of activity.

If there's no behavior or action trainees need to learn or figure out how to resolve, then a short sim should not be used as part of a training program. With any learning program, the trainer needs to know how success will be measured.

Chunking

Chunking is a strategy of breaking down content so that the brain can process it more easily. Different people are able to remember and process different amounts of information at a time, but generally, it is easier for individuals to process information divided into chunks. *The Art and Science of Training* (Biech 2017) includes the following tips for chunking training content:

- Start at the highest level by taking a large amount of content and dividing it up into reasonable smaller parts. If the larger amount of

content was to be put in outline form, each section would be a good place to separate the larger piece.
- Next, each of those sections should be broken down into smaller chunks that become the individual lessons.
- The lessons are broken down one more time into topics. Each topic can be covered by the presentation of some form of content, such as a short reading assignment, video, mini-lecture, or training activity.
- Always look to eliminate unnecessary content. Extraneous information increases the cognitive load.
- Review the design and decide if trainees will need to retain more than a few things in memory at the same time. If there is still too much content, the content should be broken down further.

Although the term "microlearning" is heard more frequently than "chunking," they are closely related. Microlearning is one type of training delivery method that takes advantage of chunking, but there are other ways safety trainers can use the benefits of chunking to increase retention. "According to cognitive principles, the brain seeks to arrange incoming information and put it in some type of order to help learners process materials more efficiently. Well organized materials make it easier for a person to learn and recall information" (Simmons 2013).

Cognitive Load

John Sweller introduced *cognitive load theory* in 1988 (Sweller 1988). He developed the theory to help explain why people have much more difficulty learning complex content. Simply put, the theory states that when training is designed, the content needs to be broken down into more manageable chunks, which allows the brain to convert information from short-term memory into long-term memory and application.

Cognitive load theory proposes that there are three types of loads that a learner must manage. The first type of load is called *intrinsic load*, which is how difficult the learning is on its own. For example, learning complex calculus calculations is likely to have a bigger intrinsic load than learning something that involves simple math such as the 4:1 rule for ladders. The second type of load is called the *extraneous load*, and this is information that is not really necessary but extra. Since the trainee's cognitive load is a combination of these three types of loads, extra information (i.e., extraneous load) is contributing to the overall cognitive load, and that is not a good thing. An example of content that would be considered an extraneous load is the history of a particular OSHA standard that is presented along with the technical training content that is actually required by the standard. Illustrations added to presentation slides or handouts that are purely decorative or meant to be amusing are also examples of things that can increase the extraneous load. The third type of load is called the *germane load*. The germane load is information that helps the learner process the new information. Examples of things that contribute to the germane load include graphs, charts, and images that directly support the content. It is also recommended that germane information be presented in various formats. This will help to form various neural pathways to the same information, thereby helping the trainee remember the content, retrieve it more easily, and apply it where necessary (Meacham 2017). By breaking content down into smaller chunks, the brain has a chance to reset and reenergize so it can retain more.

The intrinsic, extraneous, and germane load all combine to equal the total cognitive load. One way to lessen the total load is through the use of chunking. In addition to breaking up content into smaller pieces or delivering the smaller pieces of content over time, the idea of chunking to reduce cognitive load can also be used in longer classes. If trainees are scheduled for an 8-hour class covering eight different topics, chunking can still be applied. To do this and reduce the cognitive load of such a long class, each topic can be presented followed by an activity that will let trainees practice, become more comfortable with the topic before moving onto the next one, and have a chance to reset. Also, if the content can be spread out over 2 days, a week, or longer, the mind will have even more time to reset.

Safety trainers can help reduce cognitive load by keeping the following in mind:

- When creating safety training, all extraneous information should be put into a separate reference document—if it's necessary to include it at all. Miscellaneous content that does not add value to the training should be eliminated.

- When using illustrations, the explanatory text should be shown clearly alongside the illustration it goes with. If there is confusion, it will increase the cognitive load and make it more difficult to remember.
- Information presented in a table, chart, or map is easier to manage than information presented in a paragraph (Mayer 2010).

A few suggestions to organize (chunk) training content include:

- Use different objects to represent different parts of the training content when chunking information in a longer class.
- Try using different types of graphic organizers, such as flow charts and infographics, to break the training down into smaller parts.
- Create outlines (see the description and benefits of advance organizers in Chapter 8 on preclass communication).
- Break content into separate modules.

The Association for Talent Development found that 81 percent of training professionals use microlearning to reinforce and supplement training, and 79 percent of that microlearning is delivered by video, 79 percent is self-paced e-learning, and 62 percent uses visuals (ATD 2017). Microlearning, an example of chunking, is likely to increase in popularity as more and more trainees have access to, and become comfortable with, technology. Further, microlearning is an effective way to increase retention by providing opportunities for repetition, reinforcement, distributed practice, and interleaving, which have all been shown to be effective in helping trainees remember information longer so it can be transferred back to the job. Even when training programs are delivered in a traditional classroom environment, the science behind microlearning, such as the benefits of chunking content, is important to consider in training design so that training has the intended effect of being remembered and used on the job.

Review and Retention Activity

The microlearning infographic as a review technique is discussed in this chapter.

Review the infographic on microlearning and chunking shown in Figure 12.1.

Figure 12.1 ✦ Microlearning infographic

References

Aldrich, C. l. 2020. *Short Sims: A Game Changer*. Boca Raton, FL: CRC Press.

Association for Talent Development (ATD). 2017. *The Science of Learning: Key Strategies for Designing and Delivering Training*. Alexandria, VA: ATD Press.

Biech, E. 2017. *The Art and Science of Training*. Alexandria, VA: ATD Press.

Emerson, L. C., and Z. L. Berge. 2018. "Microlearning: Knowledge management applications and competency-based training in the workplace." *Knowledge Management & E-Learning*, Vol.10, No. 2., June 2018, pp. 125–132. doi: 10.34105/j.kmel.2018.10.

Fox, A. 2016. "Microlearning for Effective Performance Management," *TD Magazine*, 70(4):116–117.

Gutierrez, K. 2018. "Numbers Don't Lie: Why Microlearning Is Better for Your Learners (and You Too)." SHIFT eLearning Blog. September 27, 2018. https//shiftelearning.com/blog/numbers-dont-lie-why-bite-sized-learning-is-better-for-your-learners-and-you-too

Hart, J. 2014. *Social Learning Handbook 2014*. Raleigh, NC: Lulu.

Islam, K. 2013. "Attention Span and Performance Improvement" Training Industry Blog. March 1, 2013. https://trainingindustry.com/blog/performance-management/attention-span-and-performance-improvement/.

Kapp, K. M., and R. A. Defelice. 2019. *Microlearning: Short and Sweet*. Alexandria, VA: American Society for Training and Development (ASTD) Press.

Mayer, R. E. 2010. *Multimedia Learning*. New York: Cambridge University Press.

Mayer, R. E., R. Moreno, M. Boire, and S. J. Vagge. 1999. "Maximizing constructivist learning from multimedia communications by minimizing cognitive load." *Journal of Educational Psychology*, 91:638–643.

Meacham, M. 2017. "TMI! Cognitive Overload and Learning." *ATD Insights*, July 13, 2017. https//www.td.org/insights/tmi-cognitive-overload-and-learning.

Microsoft. 2015. "Attention Spans: Consumer Insights." Microsoft Canada. https://advertising.microsoft.com/en/WWDocs/user/display/CL/research report/31966/en/Microsoft-attention-spans-research-report.pdf.

Overton, L. 2011. "Benchmarking can help improve learning and development initiatives." *HR Magazine*, June 27, 2011. https//hrmagazine.co.uk/

articles/benchmarking-can-help-improve-learning-and-development-initiatives.

Paul, A. M. 2016. "Microlearning 101." *HR Magazine*, 61(4):36–42.

Shail, M. S. 2019. "Using Microlearning on mobile applications to increase knowledge retention and work performance: a review of literature." *Cureus*, 11(8):e5307.

Simmons, P. 2013. "Safety and Health Training Theories and Applications." In Joel M. Haight, ed., *Hazard Prevention through Effective Safety and Health Training*. Des Planies, IL: American Society of Safety Engineers.

Sweller, J. 1988. "Cognitive load during problem solving: Effects on learning." *Cognitive Science*, vol. 12, no. 2, pp. 257–285.

Thalheimer, Will. 2013. "Definitions of Microlearning." Work Learning Research Blog. https://www.worklearning.com/2017/01/13/definition-of-microlearning/.

Chapter 13
Predicting Results and Testing

Prereading Quiz

1. What is the value of asking trainees to make predictions about the training content before it is presented?
2. How are emotions connected to the act of predicting outcomes?
3. Describe the Pause–Predict–Ponder activity.
4. What is the importance of curiosity on learning and retention?
5. Explain the testing effect.
6. How does the forward testing effect help prepare the mind for learning?

Predicting Results

Increasing learning retention by predicting results is probably something many safety trainers have not considered before. The idea of predicting results is intended to get trainees thinking about what something means or about the outcome of some event. It provides a way for trainees to revisit their predictions at the end of the class and cement new knowledge, so it can be retrieved when needed. "Making predictions about material that you wish to learn increases your ability to understand that material and retrieve it later" (Lang 2021).

One way to do this is to start off a safety training class by introducing a case study that ends with some type of accident or incident. If the main part of the case study is shared, but not the final outcome, trainees could be asked to predict what happens in the end. By asking the trainees to predict the ending, they will be paying closer attention to the material as it is covered. Making a prediction is similar to making a guess about who will win a race or other sporting event and adds an emotional component. Chapter 5 on accelerated learning principles explains why tying emotions to safety training is an important way to help move content into long-term memory.

Although both of the examples in the above paragraph are very relatable, there is actually real research behind the value of making predictions at the beginning of a class. "Taking a few seconds to predict the answer before learning it, even when the prediction is incorrect, seems to increase subsequent retention of learning material. This was true even when that prediction time substitutes for—rather than supplements—conventional forms of studying" (Kornell et al. 2009). So, even when a safety trainee predicts something incorrectly, there is still great value in making the prediction. Imagine a safety training class where a variety of unsafe and safe scenarios are presented early in the training class. Trainees could be asked to predict which ones resulted in an OSHA fine. The answers should not be given to the trainees until the end of the class. If these various situations come up again, the trainees will think back to the original scenario, and they will also pay more attention than they would otherwise since they want to know the true answer that will come out in the end.

Pause–Predict–Ponder

Safety videos are a common way to provide safety training, and very often safety videos involve a reenactment of some type of accident. A safety training video could be used to reinforce trainee prediction in the following way. The video can be shown and stopped right before the reenactment of an accident occurs, and trainees could be asked to predict what happens next. After the video plays, the trainees will see if they were right or wrong, and a discussion can be had about the situation. This type of activity can be described as "pause–predict–ponder" (Ogan et al. 2009).

The What Happens Next? activity is described in Chapter 9 and Chapter 18. In this activity, a photo of a workplace is shown, and trainees are told to predict what happens next. In reality, these photos do not have to represent a situation that actually resulted in an accident, but the idea is to get trainees to think about the situation, what could go wrong, and what the outcome might be. If the pause–predict–ponder formula were used, the trainees would pause and look at the photo and then predict the outcome. After all trainees have had a chance to pause and predict the outcome, results could be shared with the training class and *pondering* could occur. Pondering is more beneficial if facilitated by the safety trainer who can help trainees ponder additional possibilities they may have overlooked, as well as help them see the importance of the activity.

Using Prediction in Safety Training

Why does predicting help with retention? "Predictive activities reshape our mental networks by embedding unfamiliar concepts . . . questions we at least partly comprehend . . . even if the question is not entirely clear and it's solution unknown, a guess will in itself begin to link the questions for possible answers. And those networks light up like Christmas lights when we hear the concepts again" (Carey 2015). This tells safety trainers that the major reason *prediction* helps trainees retain new information is because predicting things prepares the mind to learn and make new connections that will help them make an accurate prediction.

This can be modified into a safety training activity where trainees are encouraged to make connections to what they have learned in the past. For example, when starting a safety training class, a trainer could ask about the topic being presented, "Why is this like . . .?" and encourage the trainees to think of ways the current safety training topic and safety training information they have learned in the past are similar. To make this into a team activity, each team could be presented with the same question and asked to come up with a list of possible topics that are similar to the current topic. The trainees should be told that whichever team is able to come up with the most similarities and/or connections will be declared the winner. By asking trainees to make these connections, they are embedding the new information more deeply into their memories and will remember it in what are seemingly unrelated situations. Since the previous information is already in their memory bank, when the new information is attached to it, the trainees will have an easier time recalling it when they need it. For example, when presenting a class on silica awareness, a trainer could start off by asking trainees how the topic is similar to asbestos. If the trainee has had previous experience with asbestos, the silica awareness training information will be easier to learn and the brain can attach the new information to the previously learned knowledge.

Similarly, a safety trainer could ask the teams "What is this like?"—a variation of the "Why is this like . . .?" question. This variation will have a similar effect as trainees will have to think about what else they know, and how it could be related to the current topic. Assume that a group of trainees is sitting through a training class on precautions to protect oneself from an infectious disease, such as Covid-19. Instead of presenting the topic as brand new information, the trainer can start off by asking what the topic being presented is similar to, and ask trainees to predict the expected similarities. A trainer could then address those predictions throughout the class.

Technology can be used in the process of making predictions as well. Clickers are becoming more and more common in training classes. Even if clickers are not available, there are many apps that could be used on mobile phones that do something similar. Clickers can be used as a simple way to ask questions in the beginning of a class when trainees must take a guess at answering. In this case, the trainees are predicting the correct answer. More ways to use clickers are discussed in Chapter 21 on retrieval activities.

Another type of simple technology that works with prediction is the use of word clouds. Word clouds are graphic illustrations of words or phrases based on the popularity of that word or phrase. For example, if trainees were asked a question, and 20 trainees gave answer A, 10 trainees gave answer B, and 10 trainees gave answer C, answer A would appear largest in the word cloud. There are many free applications that can create word clouds on the spot that can be shared with the training class. In a class on soft skills, such as best practices for giving feedback, a trainer could ask trainees what they think is the most important thing to do when providing negative feedback. The trainer would then add the responses to the word cloud application. After all guesses are in, the completed word cloud could be shown. Whether right or wrong, the exercise of predicting, followed by review, will help trainees focus their attention and remember key facts.

To use a similar type of feedback activity without technology, trainees could be asked a prediction-type question and instructed to put their answer on a sticky note on the wall. When all answers are posted, the trainer can rearrange the sticky notes by answer to form a low-tech type of word cloud. If a photo is taken of the sticky note word cloud, it can be sent out after class as an additional form of reinforcement.

Curiosity as a Training Tool

Research has shown the importance of curiosity on learning and retention. "Curiosity is an emotion that has been recently demonstrated to boost memory when it is heightened prior to exposure to new material. Curious minds showed increased activity in the hippocampus, which is involved in the creation of memories. Curiosity and anticipation of an answer, taken together, lead the brains of the subjects to snap to attention and form deeper and longer memories" (Yuhas 2014). By asking trainees to predict something, trainers are also creating curiosity, which can increase retention.

Curiosity is a great tool to include in the kickoff of a safety training class. As safety trainees enter a classroom, an activity or prop that makes trainees curious will go far in getting them to pay attention right away. A simple way to do this is to have an empty box with a question mark drawn on it on a desk in the front of the room. The trainees will take special notice if this is something new that they haven't seen done before. When the training class begins, the trainer can make a reference to something in the box, and the trainees can start to use their imaginations to guess what it is. The item in the box should not be something random, but should be related to the class content. A trainer could simply ask the trainees to make a prediction about what is in the box, but they should first be told that the item in the box serves a very important purpose in relation to the topic of the safety training class. Throughout the class, the trainer can give additional clues about the item in the box. At the end of the training class, trainees could be asked to write down their names and their guesses on a piece of paper and put their guesses in the box. Their answers could then be drawn from the box, and the first correct answer to be pulled could receive a small prize.

Tests as Learning Events

Much research exists around the testing effect. The *testing effect* refers to the increase in likelihood that information will be remembered in the long term when an attempt is made to retrieve that information from testing (Okano et al. 2018). Memory gained through testing outlasts gains made through repeated study (Karpicke and Blunt 2011). Testing as a retrieval method is described in Chapter 11 and has been shown to increase retention of the learning material. The idea of testing knowledge before a trainee either feels ready or is actually ready to be tested is not commonly used in safety training, but it can be very effective.

"It appears that a successful retrieval can be considerably more potent than an additional study opportunity, particularly in terms of facilitating long-term recall" (Bjork 1994). Learners who are forced to recall new information immediately in the days after they've been trained are much more likely to retain that information over the long term (Brown et al. 2014).

Retention can be measured by assessing how much of the training content is being transferred to the day-to-day work of the trainee. A skills evaluation such as this can be a good indicator of retention. Can it be observed that the training content was transferred to the job? Is the job, or are certain tasks, being performed more safely or more in accordance with procedures? This is a very important part of training evaluation, but it is not done as often as it should be. If this type of postevaluation is planned for and carried out, it can be a great help in demonstrating ROI.

To measure this type of job transfer, a list of important things to be learned in the training class (tied to the objectives, of course) needs to be developed along with some type of scoring system. The example below could be created and given to a supervisor for completion.

	Before Training Score (1–5)	After Training Score (1–5)
Energy control procedures followed before regular cleaning		
Permit completed correctly		

The next example could be created and given to the trainees after they have been working on implementing a new skill or using new knowledge.

	Did Well Before Training Score (1–5)	Did as Well Now Score (1–5)	Did Better Now Score (1–5)
Energy control procedures followed before regular cleaning			
Permit completed correctly			

Forward Testing Effect

The *forward testing effect* shows that retrieval not only helps enhance what was previously learned, but can help prepare the mind for future learning. Some researchers believe this works because, even if the trainee does not have the knowledge yet, this process helps to reinforce search strategies that can be used once the information is learned at a later time. Other researchers believe that forward testing may work because the mind will focus attention on resources that are related to the missing information. For example, if safety trainees are asked to find a way to guard a machine, and they have no experience in machine guarding, their minds will automatically start to search for possible solutions they may be able to use when they face the experience again. The forward testing effect implies that testing trainees before they themselves or the trainer think they're ready, either because they haven't spent enough time with the material, or perhaps it hasn't even been presented yet, can help increase learning (Yang 2018). "Taking a practice test and getting answers wrong seems to improve subsequent study, because the test is directing the learner in some way to the kind of material that is needed to know" (Carey 2015). Not doing well on a pretest also helps trainees understand what gaps they actually have in their knowledge. Imagine a group of trainees coming to a refresher class that they have attended many times before. Naturally, they are feeling very confident. A pretest can help them evaluate their true knowledge more accurately. The benefit of practicing retrieval this way will greatly enhance learning and retention of the information.

It is important to remember that, in order for predicting and pretesting to be valuable in increasing retention, trainees need to receive feedback on their answers and predictions as soon as possible. If they do not, the wrong answers leave a deeper impression than the correct ones. Additionally, trainees will pay more attention to feedback when it's delivered immediately, but interests start to wane with a delay of results (Metcalfe 2017).

Frequent testing can also be used in training classes that present videos. If there is no planned activity associated with a safety training video, it is easy for trainees to tune out and not pay attention. One study showed that by requiring trainees to answer questions throughout a training video, retention was increased when checked at 25–30 hours after watching the video (Okano et al. 2018). Evaluations do not always mean some form of quiz at the end of a training class, but when trainers begin to use evaluations as tools to help increase learning, the effectiveness of training classes can improve.

Review and Retention Activity

The quiz questions presented at the beginning of this chapter, and the answers to those questions provided at the end, are included to demonstrate the forward testing effect discussed in this chapter.

Answers to Prereading Quiz

1. What is the value of asking trainees to make predictions about the training content before it is presented?
   Answer: Making predictions increases the ability to understand material and retrieve it later.
2. How are emotions connected to the act of predicting outcomes?
   Answer: Making a prediction, especially about how a story or case study ends, involves emotions, and as discussed in Chapter 5 on accelerated learning principles, emotions are important in remembering training content.
3. Describe the Pause–Predict–Ponder activity.
   Answer: An activity that can be used along with the viewing of a training video that involves stopping the video right before a major event occurs, asking trainees to predict what happens next, and then discussing (pondering) whether or not the predictions were correct.
4. What is the importance of curiosity on learning and retention?
   Answer: Curiosity has been shown to boost memory when it is heightened prior to exposure to new material.
5. Explain the testing effect.
   Answer: The testing effect is the likelihood that information will be remembered in the long term when an attempt is made to retrieve that information through testing.
6. How does the forward testing effect help prepare the mind for learning?
   Answer: Testing before content is learned will help the mind focus on resources that are related to the missing information.

References

Bjork., R. A., (1994). "Memory and metamemory considerations in the training of human beings." In J. Metcalfe and A. Shimamura, eds., *Metacognition: Knowing about Knowing*, pp. 185–205. Cambridge, MA: MIT Press.

Brown, P. C., H. L. Roediger, and M. A. McDaniel. 2014. *Make It Stick: The Science of Successful Learning*. Cambridge, MA: Belknap Press, an imprint of Harvard University Press.

Carey, B. 2015. *How We Learn: The Surprising Truth about When, Where, and Why It Happens*. New York, NY: Random House.

Karpicke, J. D., and J. R. Blunt. 2011. "Retrieval Practice Produces More Learning than Elaborative Studying with Concept Mapping." *Science*, 331:772–775.

Kornell, N., M. Hays, and R. Bjork. 2009. "Unsuccessful Retrieval Attempts Enhance Subsequent Learning." *Journal of Experimental Psychology: Learning, Memory and Cognition*, Vol. 35, no. 4, pp. 989–998.

Lang, J. M. 2016. *Small Teaching: Everyday Lessons from the Science of Learning.* 2d ed. Jossey-Bass. San Francisco, CA: John Wiley & Sons, Inc.

Metcalfe, J. 2017. "Learning from Errors." *Annual Review of Psychology*, 68(1):465–89. doi: 10.1146/annurev-psych-010416-044022.

Ogan, A., V. Aleven, and C. Jones. 2009. "Advancing development of intercultural competence through supporting predictions in narrative video." *International Journal of Artificial Intelligence and Education*, 19(3):267–288.

Okano K, J. R. Kaczmarzyk, and J. D. E. Gabrieli. 2018. "Enhancing workplace digital learning by use of the science of learning." *Plos one*, 13(10):e0206250. doi: 10.1371/journal.pone.0206250.

Yang, C. 2018. "Enhancing learning and retrieval: the forward testing effect." Ph.D. dissertation, University College London.

Young, S. H. 2019. *Ultralearning: Master Hard Skills, Outsmart the Competition, and Accelerate Your Career.* New York City: Harper Business.

Yuhas, D. 2014. "Curiosity Prepares the Brain for Better Learning." *Scientific American.* October 2, 2014. https://www.scientificamerican.com/article/curiosity-prepares-the-brain-for-better-learning/.

Chapter 14
Productive Failure

It may seem counterintuitive to make training more difficult for trainees. After all, it's a safety professional's job when delivering training to get trainees to learn and remember the greatest amount of information possible. However, research has shown that techniques used to speed the rate of acquisition by trainees can fail to support long-term posttraining performance, and the introduction of difficulties for trainees enhances posttraining performance (Bjork and Bjork 2011). One of the benefits of a well-designed training program is increasing an employee's comfort level with vulnerability and failure. This is accomplished by introducing challenging opportunities specifically designed to let participants struggle—and sometimes outright fail (Bahm 2020). Interactive safety training games and activities are a great way to do this.

Build Mental Models

Using failures and errors in safety training helps build accurate mental models, which are valuable in learning transfer (Jones and Endsley 2000). When the trainee is allowed to make a mistake, he or she is being allowed to test out ideas about what will and what will not work in a safe environment. Failing at something ordinarily provides instant feedback, and it will draw sharp attention to the problems with the way a trainee may think something should be done. Second, when somebody makes a mistake, it's usually memorable. Allowing trainees to make mistakes in the training class will likely cause them to keep that attempted effort, and the resulting failure, in their memory, which will hopefully prevent repetition of these mistakes in similar situations (Jones and Endsley 2000). Third, errors are associated with surprise, and surprise is important in learning. When someone is surprised, they are going to pay attention. Getting the trainees to pay attention to the content is the first step in helping them to remember the information longer.

Vary Conditions of Practice

One way for safety trainers to introduce opportunities for productive failure into their safety training classes is to vary the conditions of practice. "Introducing variation and/or unpredictability in the training environment causes difficulty for the learner but enhances long-term performance—particularly the ability to transfer training to novel but related task environments" (Bjork and Bjork 2011). A safety trainer could move training outside where trainees must demonstrate a newly learned skill or could present trainees with a quiz when they first enter a training classroom. Both of these activities would most likely be unexpected.

The Benefit of Being Wrong

Trainers can start classes with a question they surmise will result in trainees giving the wrong answer. This will not only get the attention of trainees, but they will be alert and ready to hear the correct answer. (The benefit of adding curiosity to training classes is discussed in Chapter 13.) An example of a question that trainees might get wrong is: "What do you think is the biggest cause of death among hunters while hunting?" Most people will probably think it's accidental shooting, which is actually a leading cause. The correct answer, however, is falls, which equal or exceed the number of deaths by guns (Chávez 2017). According to the National Bow Hunter Educational Foundation, an average of 100 hunters die every year from falls while climbing up to tree stands. After a trainer asks and answers this question, a follow-up question could be asked: "How can this be prevented?" Hopefully the follow-up question causes trainees to have an "aha" moment. The trainees should relate the scenario to what they know about protection from falls at work where safety harnesses are commonplace. Similarly, harnesses are critical in preventing tree-stand fall deaths. The initial question—one the trainees are likely to get wrong—will stay in their minds and help them remember the information longer.

The above example can be used in a class on fall protection and possibly one on confined space entry where trainees will need to use tripods and harnesses. But it may not have the desired effect in training classes on other topics. To find a question that has a counterintuitive answer to use in other classes, trainers can look through the training content for an idea that is important but doesn't seem to make a lot of sense initially. For example, in a fire safety class, a trainer could ask trainees the following: If a coworker wearing a polyester work uniform while attempting to put out a small trash-can fire in his work area got too close and his pants caught on fire, what should he do next? What should coworkers coming to his aid do next? Trainees might say remove the pants, which would seem like the correct answer but is not. Because the individual in the story was wearing a polyester uniform, the pants will have fused with his skin and removing them could do more harm than good. Burn center staff would be much better equipped to deal with this type of serious accident. Being told not to remove the cause of the accident or pain is counterintuitive, so when trainees are told the correct answer, it will stick in their minds longer.

Challenging Tests

Retrieval practice in the form of testing was discussed in Chapter 11. Testing is generally thought of as a way to measure how much was learned, but as discussed throughout this book, it is also a way to increase retention of training material. The importance of making retrieval practice, including testing, more difficult has been studied and found to be an effective way to increase retention. To use the benefits of productive failure with trainee testing, there are several easy ways a safety trainer can add this to existing training programs.

- When administering exams, do not allow trainees to look at their notes or copies of the slides for the answers.
- Create questions that can conceivably result in wrong answers.
- Provide test questions with fill-in-the-blank answers instead of providing questions with multiple-choice answers. Fill-in-the-blank tests are more difficult because the trainee will need to pull the answer out of his or her head instead of simply picking it out of several choices.

"People remember things better and longer if they are given tests so challenging that they are bound to fail" (Brown et al. 2014). Research has shown that students who make an unsuccessful attempt to answer a test question before receiving the correct answer remember the material better than if they simply study the information (Kornell 2009). Psychologists have uncovered a curious inverse relationship between retrieval practice and the power of that practice to entrench learning: the easier knowledge or skills are to retrieve, the less retrieval practice will benefit retention of them. Conversely, the more effort spent to retrieve knowledge or skills, the more retrieval practice will entrench them (Brown et al. 2014). For safety trainers, this means that making tests more difficult will result in better long-term retention among their trainees.

Stories of Failure

Lessons learned, sometimes called war stories, are discussed in Chapter 9, "Making it Real." These stories are another way productive failure can be used in safety training. Error-exposure training that included case studies has been used by firefighters because many firefighters may find themselves in situations that are quite different from the situations and environments where the actual training occurred. In one study done on presenting error-exposure training to firefighters, two different variations of this type of training were used. The first group of trainees was shown case studies that included incidents containing errors with severe consequences in the outcomes. The second group was exposed to the same set of case studies, but these case studies showed the incidents without errors or their consequences. The results of this research showed that it is better to learn from other people's errors than from their successes (Joung et al. 2006). Stories used in safety training should have an outcome—good or bad. Stories where nothing happens or nothing was learned should not be used.

Research has found that error-exposure training can help trainees learn to reason from past errors and failures, which can help them form a strategy to prepare for an existing or future situation (Frese and Zapf 1994). Another advantage of error training is that it helps maintain interaction and attention throughout the training class. As discussed throughout this book, one of a safety trainer's biggest challenges is to get and keep trainee attention. Knowing that they might make a mistake is enough to keep many trainees alert and focused on the content. Unfortunately, too many safety training classes expect passive transfer of information from the trainer to the trainee. Nevertheless, active training is necessary for the information to be absorbed and retained. Research has suggested that error-exposure training will get the trainee to more actively process training content, which will in turn increase the mental effort that's used during training that is known to enhance transfer (Bjork and Bjork 2011).

The ability to react quickly to an unusual situation is important in many professions. This adaptability is extremely important for executing many jobs. A safety trainer can use the knowledge gained from this research by sharing the various types of workplace stories (lessons learned, case studies, war stories, etc.) and selecting those that include errors in judgement and the associated outcomes. Just like many situations that are presented both inside and outside of work, learning from others' mistakes is an effective way to remember what to do and what not to do when challenges present themselves.

Failure in Gamification

Although productive failure is about the importance of adding some type of struggle to the trainee's experience, productive failure is also an important concept in gamification (discussed further in Chapter 16). Gamification is one of the hottest trends in the learning and development industry right now with a 9-billion-dollar market in 2020 projected to grow to over 30 billion dollars in the next 5 years (Gamification Market 2020). A quality learning environment is built on a healthy relationship with failure in play, and although we may have an aversion to both of these terms, we need to pay more attention to this relationship (Provence 2020). Games, both traditional and online, usually involve some type or level of failure because this keeps the participant interested and motivated, and failure can have the same effects when used in training.

Confidence Ratings

Another interesting twist on the use of failure in learning has to do with someone's perception of whether or not they are right. If you ask trainees to place a confidence rating next to their answers on a quiz, this adds another way trainees can learn from their mistakes. Studies have shown that the more confident someone is in a wrong answer, the more likely they will be to remember the right answer once it's learned (Eva 2017). When a learner is highly confident in his or her answer, and the answer turns out to be wrong, not only is the brain quick to overwrite and correct the information, the individual is also more likely to remember the information and learn from that mistake. One instructional design idea presented in Scott Provence's book *Fail to Learn* is to add a confidence rating column on quizzes. Doing this would not add any additional time to the safety training evaluations, but research reports that it will bring added benefits (Provence 2020).

Many of the world's most successful people have found that failing and trying again led to their ultimate success, although many people are brought up to think of failure as a bad thing. If trainers help trainees understand that failing is okay in the training environment and work to provide situations for them to fail in a safe environment with little risk to safety, trainers can help them learn new information and remember it longer.

To help make failing more of a learning option for trainees, a trainer can provide evaluation results as soon as possible. If trainees leave a training room or online training environment without knowing what they got right or what they got wrong, the requirements of a compliance mandate for training and testing may have been met, but a trainer is not meeting his or her responsibility of helping trainees learn. Even if trainees got a particular safety question wrong, learning the right answer by being tested on it and getting feedback quickly is going to do a lot for trainee retention of the material. If safety trainers can provide many opportunities for trainees to fail, that is going to help them not only accept failing as an acceptable alternative but also is going to increase their understanding of the material. Instead of providing one big test at the end of a training class, pretests and several smaller tests or quizzes throughout the course will provide more failure early on but will provide greater benefits in the end. (The effect of evaluations is discussed in Chapter 15 on predicting and evaluations.) Too many training courses combine a low failure rate with high failure costs. More and more studies show this should be turned on its head. Failure rates should increase, and failure costs should decrease. The more trainees are encouraged to try and fail, the better, faster, and stronger their learning will be (Provence 2020).

By making the learning difficult, a safety trainer is making the training more closely apply to the real world. The phrase "practice like you play, and you'll play like you practice," is often applied to athletes and musicians, but it also applies to the world of training transfer. Presenting challenges and difficulties in the training environment will prompt trainees to use the skills they learned later on. The training classroom or online virtual setting is much different from a normal workday environment. By making safety training more challenging, a challenger is also making it more closely reflect reality.

Review and Retention Activity

The value of requesting learners to add confidence ratings along with their answers is discussed in this chapter.

After answering each question, add a confidence rating next to each question.

Confidence   Question
Rating

_____   1. A benefit of a well-designed training program is increasing learners' comfort levels with _____.

_____   2. Mistakes tend to be _____.

_____   3. One way for trainers to introduce the opportunity for productive failure is to vary the _____ of _____.

_____   4. Tests designed with _____ questions are more difficult because trainees will need to pull answers out of their head instead of identifying them from a list of provided options.

_____   5. When using case studies, those that show failure are likely more effective than those that show _____.

Answers: 1. failure, 2. memorable, 3. conditions, practice, 4. fill-in-the-blank, 5. success

References

Bahm, H. 2020. "Design Learner-Centric Development Programs." *TD Magazine.* January 2020:18–20.

Bjork, E. L., and R. A. Bjork. 2011. "Making things hard on yourself, but in a good way: Creating desirable difficulties to enhance learning." In M. A. Gernsbacher, R. W. Pew, L. M. Hough, and J. R. Pomerantz, eds., *Psychology and the Real World: Essays Illustrating Fundamental Contributions to Society*, pp. 56–64. New York: Worth Publishers.

Brown, P. C., H. L. Roediger, and M. A. McDaniel. 2018. *Make It Stick: The Science of Successful Learning.* Cambridge, MA: Belknap Press, an imprint of Harvard University Press.

Chávez, K. 2017. "What Is the No. 1 Cause of Hunting-Related Deaths?" *The Asheville Citizen Times*, October 4, 2017. https://www.citizen-times.com/story/news/local/2017/10/04/what-no-1-cause-hunting-related-deaths/732856001/.

Eva, Amy L. 2017. "Why We Should Embrace Mistakes in School." *Greater Good Magazine*. Posted November 28, 2017. https://www.greatergood.id.

Frese M., and D. Zapf. 1994. "Action as the core of work psychology: a German approach." In H. C. Triandis, M. D. Dunnette, and L. M. Hough, eds., *Handbook of Industrial and Organizational Psychology*, pp. 271–340. Palo Alto, CA: Consulting Psychologists Press.

Gamefication Market. 2020. "Gamification Market Future Growth, Trends and Analysis–2020." March 2020. www.marketsandmarkets.com/Market-Reports/gamification-market-991.html.

Jones, D., and M. Endsley. 2000. "Overcoming representational errors in complex environments." *Human Factors*, 42:367–378.

Joung, W., B. Hesketh, and N. Andrew. 2006. 'Using "War Stories" to Train for Adaptive Performance: Is it Better to Learn from Error or Success?' *Applied Psychology*, 55:282–302.

Kornell, N., M. Hays, and R. Bjork. 2009. "Unsuccessful Retrieval Attempts Enhance Subsequent Learning." *Journal of Experimental Psychology: Learning, Memory and Cognition*, 35(4):989–998.

Provence, Scott. 2020. *Fail to Learn: A Manifesto for Training Gamification*. Independently published.

Chapter 15
Teamwork and Collaboration

One of the principles of accelerated learning states that trainees learn better when they learn from their peers. "Teams are the heart of effective training programs" (National Research Council 1994).

Benefits of Teams

Teams are useful in training programs for a number of reasons. First, in order to be able to do a job, trainees must understand what they're supposed to do, and the best way to do that is to have trainees explain that to each other. "When team members explain to one another what they're learning, the material is learned better, retained longer, and transferred to actual job situations more frequently" (Johnson and Johnson 2013). Second, team members can provide the type of feedback to other members of their team that the members would not be able to get if they had been learning something on their own. Third, team members can encourage and motivate one another to work hard and learn the training content. Fourth, in order for trainees to be successful back on the job, they need to have a number of relevant attitudes and values related to doing the job well, and working with others can help make this happen. Fifth, when trainees learn how to do their job well, it will affect their view of themselves as well as their self-confidence.

The benefits described above are why the safety training games and activities described in this book are based on teamwork and not necessarily on individual efforts. A trainee would rather sit and talk and learn and share with coworkers or other trainees than work solo or simply sit and listen to one expert. Trainees are most likely to learn more when they hear the information from their peers.

"A team is a set of interpersonal interactions structured to achieve established goals. More specifically, a team consists of two or more individuals who are (a) aware of their positive interdependence as they strive to achieve mutual goals, (b) interact while they do so, (c) are aware of who is and who is not a member of the team, (d) have specific roles or functions to perform, and (e) have limited life span of membership. Teams not only meet to share information and perspectives and make decisions, they produce discrete work products through members' joint efforts and contributions" (Johnson and Johnson 2013). A team is more than the sum of each individual's effort (Katzenbach and Smith 2015). Interactive safety training activities based on teams can be short term or long term, but the effect of learning from peers will be an important part of increasing trainee attention and retention of training material.

While a formal definition of "team" is prescribed above, teamwork is defined slightly differently. *Teamwork* is a form of cooperative learning and can be described as a group of people of equal status working together to enhance their individual acquisition of knowledge and skills (National Research Council 1994). Teamwork in a safety training class is closely related to team learning, where a group works closely together to understand and learn new information. Although the definition of teamwork says members must be of equal status, this does not necessarily mean equal status within the company, but it does mean that all members of the team are equal to one another for the purposes of the teamwork.

Research has shown that working in teams results in higher individual productivity than working competitively or individually. Working in teams also promotes more positive relationships and social support among members, as well as greater psychological health, self-esteem, and social competencies. There are a number of influences on team productivity, including prior experience doing the specified task, practice, complexity of the task, and amount of interaction among team members, among other things (Johnson and Johnson 2013). Teams in the context of this book refer to small groups formed for the purpose of completing an interactive training activity.

Forming Teams

When using teams in safety training, three issues should be considered when forming them: the size, the selection of team members, and a plan for appropriate team resources.

Teams should be kept relatively small. In general, four to six people work well for most activities in this book. The larger the group, the smaller the percentage of individuals who will contribute to the team activity. The more anonymous members feel, the less involved they will be, and the less responsible they will be for the team's success. A trainer observing a large team working on a group activity will notice how several people hang back, check their phones, look around the room, and overall, are not involved. When groups have too many people, it is easy for uninterested trainees to just blend in and not contribute to the overall goals of the team. If the activity is very short, a smaller group, say two to four people, will work nicely. For longer, more complex activities, a group of five or six may be necessary. It is also important to consider the size of the class. If there are twelve trainees, the activities would probably work better with three or four groups of four or three, respectively, than two groups of six since there would be a definite loser and a definite winner in games requiring competition.

Knowing the approximate number of trainees is helpful when planning the number of teams that will be needed for a particular activity, and it is helpful to figure that out ahead of time. Teamwork can help break up what is sometimes called information dump. Information dump occurs when a trainer is talking for longer than 20 minutes straight. Team-based activities can provide a much-needed break for trainers and trainees alike and can be used to wake up trainees and get them to refocus on the topic.

The second issue, team member selection, is important to consider for teams that will work on longer and more complex projects, but for many simple and quick safety training activities, random team assignments can be made, but these will also benefit from being prearranged. For longer and more complex activities, such as tabletop exercises, it is important to consider creating teams that have the expertise and skills necessary for the task or the potential for trainees to develop the needed expertise and skills. If possible, the team members should all bring different skills to the table as this will fuel productivity.

Also, when preassigning team makeup before a training class, individuals with the skills necessary to complete the task effectively should be deliberately put on various teams based on their knowledge and expertise. A trainer will know what will be needed by each team ahead of time and can make team assignments that will work best. It is better for the trainer to assign teams rather than to allow employees that are sitting near each other form the teams. This is because friends often sit near each other, and they act differently when put into a small group. Having trainees get up and move to other parts of the room where they are formed into a team with people they do not know as well has several benefits. It may help keep the side conversations under control, but it also builds social connections with people or trainees who may never normally work together. Finally, having trainees move to a different part of the room for a training activity gets them up and gets their blood moving, which is another key part of accelerated learning.

It is very difficult for a team to work effectively if they do not have the adequate space and resources. If a training class is taking place in an auditorium-type setup and team members are told to simply turn around and work with those behind them, this will result in teams working very close to each other, which will not only be distracting but may influence the work of the individual teams. Trainees will also be uncomfortable and may not give the activity their full attention. In addition to adequate space, enough materials should be available for each team to work appropriately. Teams should be given a specified amount of time to work on their activity as well, so they can plan appropriately. Finally, if there are a large number of teams, it is best to have additional facilitators or trainers who can move around the room and assist the teams as necessary. A confused training team will waste valuable time, so it's important to make sure training teams clearly understand what they need to do before breaking into their small groups.

Traditionally, teams are formed right before an activity is introduced and disbanded after the activity has been debriefed. With more and more training being delivered online, it is important to include safety training teams in interactive activities that are delivered virtually as well. Although virtual teamwork would seem to be more challenging, the participation of teams that communicate electronically tends to be more equalized and less affected by prestige and status (Johnson and Johnson 2008). When teams communicate online, they often feel freer to say what they really think, offer new ideas and information, and disagree with other team members who may have more experience or higher status within a company. Virtual teams can also be created with individual members from a variety of geographic locations, which is not possible when all potential team members are located in the same room.

When teams compete virtually, it is important to pay special attention to the facilitation of the activity, and in particular, to the respect paid to each team member by other team members. Since individuals feel more unconstrained when speaking to each other virtually, things could get out of hand when virtual teams are very competitive. There is often a greater sense of anonymity, less empathy, and less influence by established norms of behavior (Johnson and Johnson 2008).

Problem Behaviors

Not all teams are created equal. Some team behavior can be problematic. It is important for the trainer to pay close attention to any behaviors that may adversely affect the learning during a training class. A few things to look out for include maturity, a team member's history, the motives of individual team members, and disruptive behavior by certain team members. Some disruptive behaviors may include talking too much, dominating the conversation, starting arguments, trying to intimidate others to think their way, changing the topic, demanding that their point of view is right, and trying very hard to take control of the outcome of the training activity. A trainer must also be on the lookout for trainees that are showing passive uninvolvement, active uninvolvement, independence, and attempts to take charge (Johnson and Johnson 2013).

In the Hazard Hunt activity described in Chapter 18, a trainer may witness a team member hanging back and not contributing. This could simply be a lack of confidence around more experienced team members. *Active uninvolvement* occurs when a trainee does not see the importance or need to participate in the team activity and may stubbornly sit there and not contribute. Another team member may decide to work on the team activity alone and not share any of his or her thought processes or results with the other members. Finally, a team member may be domineering and insist on things being seen his or her way. This last warning signal will be harmful, as other team members will not be able to learn from one another, and the views of the dominating team member will be imposed on the overall activity.

If it is common that team members are *passively uninvolved*, activities can be redesigned so that each team member has something that other people in the team will need. If passive team members do not see that they need to offer up material they have in order for the group to be successful, the other team members will likely be more direct in requesting the information. An example of a safety training activity where each team member is given part of the activity is Safety Sequence, which is discussed in Chapter 19 on sequencing activities. In Safety Sequence, each team member is given a step in one part of a safety procedure that requires a certain number of steps to be performed in a certain order. Team members work to arrange themselves in the correct order based on the step they have been assigned. If a passive team member has a step in the process, it will be very difficult for that member to sit back and do nothing because the overall team will not be successful in putting the steps together without every person in the team contributing.

If a team member is showing active uninvolvement by deliberately not working on the team activity, or actively tries to distract others from participating, the behavior can be curtailed by assigning the actively uninvolved team member a specific role, such as organizing the others in the group or presenting the results of the activity to the class when completed.

If a team member is working on the training activity *independently*, and not working as part of the team, there are several options. First, the materials necessary for the activity can be reduced in a way that requires the team members to share the resources needed for completing the activity. Instead of giving each team member a copy of the training activity to refer to while working as a team, fewer resources can be distributed. Also, similar to the corrective measures suggested for passive uninvolvement, when a lone wolf is part of a training activity team, resources can be distributed in a way that will make it impossible for the independent team member to work alone and still complete the activity.

If the opposite is occurring, and one team member is dominating and trying to *do all work alone* without asking for input from other team members, one suggestion is to assign specific roles to each team member, ensuring that the dominating member cannot do everything alone. As suggested for the other disrupting types of team members, resources for team activities should be distributed in such a way that the domineering team member cannot do the activity without getting input from other team members.

Cooperative learning research looks at the creation of positive interdependence among group members as the critical step in promoting successful cooperative learning (Johnson and Johnson 1989). To create positive interdependence, teams can be assigned team goals, incentives, tasks, instructions, and assignments that make it clear to the trainees that their individual success is positively linked to the success of the other group members. It is believed that this positive interdependence will lead to productive activities (Drukman and Bjork 1994).

In some cooperative scenarios, trainees are expected to promote each other's success by giving and receiving assistance, exchanging information, giving and receiving feedback about performance, challenging each other's ideas, building trust, mutually influencing each other, and reducing each other's anxiety about failure. These behaviors are part of many serious games. Many of these actions can be seen in the Hazard Hunt activity described in Chapter 18.

Collaboration

Collaboration is closely tied to teamwork and can be defined as working alongside other people to constructively explore ideas, discover new solutions, and explore unique thought processes. Ultimately, the end goal of collaboration is to accomplish something as a team (Carter 2018). When trainees experience teamwork and collaboration as part of their learning, the information will be retained longer, and they will be able to transfer those skills back to the job. "A research study found that participants with high transfer rates had talked with colleagues before taking training, learning from them how the class would help them with their jobs, things to watch out for and other tips for learning and using the information and skills. Another study found that trainees who were paired up with peers who had previously taken the training received valuable advice and assistance from them, that enabled the trainees to put the knowledge to use more easily" (Carnes 2013).

Connectedness

A basic human need is connectedness. Another need described by many is the need for growth and learning. When connectedness and growth and learning are combined, it leads to opportunities for teamwork and collaboration that can be beneficial. *Connectedness* refers to our desire to be accepted by those around us, and to get praise, attention, and encouragement. These needs for recognition and growth can complement each other perfectly with respect to learning transfer (Weinbauer-Heidel and Ibeschitz-Manderbach 2018). Again, interactive activities and games can fulfill these needs.

When trainees are learning together, they may be inclined to ask—and will probably be asking—questions of one another. The trainees may not be experts in the field, but they will see themselves as peers, which is not the relationship that the trainee is going to have with the instructor. The person or the other team members the trainees are working with will probably speak like them and use the same type of terminology that they do, but this may not be the case with a formal class instructor. "Workers on a team are 2.3x more likely to be fully engaged than those who are not on a team" (Hayes et al. 2019).

One of the best ways to learn something is to teach it to someone else. "In the process of explaining and discussing, the subject is repeated, and the fresh knowledge deepened, and the greater processing depth enhances internalization and sustainable memorization" (Weinbauer-Heidel and Ibeschitz-Manderbach 2018). When trainees are put into smaller teams, and they work together through a training activity or assignment, they are discussing what they have learned and are benefitting from hearing the experiences and interpretations of the other trainees in their group. If the training activity is designed correctly, the trainees will also be discussing how the new information can be applied to their own job.

The *helper therapy principle* states that when one person helps someone else, the helper also benefits. "Helpers operating in a teaching context, again both as professionals and nonprofessionals, may profit more from the cognitive mechanisms associated with learning through teaching. They need to learn the material better in order to teach it" (Riessman 1965). Individual group members are aided by helping other members in the group, but the group as a whole may be greatly strengthened as well (Riessman 1965). In Chapter 1, various training delivery methods were shown in the learning pyramid. The bottom of the pyramid shows that teaching others is a great way to learn. The helper effect is also known as the protégé effect, which refers to the process that occurs when people learn more by teaching others. Research has found that the teacher in this case will work harder to understand, recall, and apply more material accurately and effectively (Hollins 2017). This also ties in with the Feynman principles discussed in Chapter 4 that show how learning can be increased when explaining ideas to someone else.

These principles are based on the belief that people who are supporting others have a sense of competence and self-confidence, as well as feeling that they are needed. If a group of trainees who normally work together served as helpers for each other during a training class, they could work to apply what they learned in the class together after the class is over, and this would be highly beneficial. If the performance of a particular training team were tracked and monitored with appropriate feedback, the team could take steps to support each other in the application of the safety information they just learned.

Toolbox Training

Toolbox training classes are fairly common in industries that provide a lot of training on safety and health and are often delivered away from a training classroom, such as at a work area or job site. Some companies that use toolbox training materials alternate who is responsible for delivering the training. A system like this could be as simple as having a binder that contains 52 different training topics (one for each week), and workers are asked to take turns being the trainer. In these situations, the worker who may have zero training experience only needs to remove the prepared packet from the toolbox training binder and read through the materials as described. The best toolbox training talks also provide discussion questions and a form of evaluation or quiz. While these toolbox topics may meet requirements for training found in various standards and help form a sense of community and teamwork, a toolbox training program such as this is unlikely to contain many of the elements necessary to increase retention. On the positive side, trainees will be learning from one another and probably paying more attention to their coworkers when the information is presented in that way. If a trainer can supplement the information in a toolbox training binder with specific company and job-title interactive activities that directly relate to the training topic, the effectiveness of off-the-shelf toolbox training materials can be greatly improved.

Teamwork Activities

Most of the activities described in Chapters 18–22 involve teamwork. One activity, Training Tutor, relies on a group of trainees working together to develop their own miniature training class. The main benefit of this activity is allowing trainees to explain to others what they know, which in turn is helping them to have greater retention themselves. It requires trainees to form a team and helps them learn to work better together. The Training Tutor activity works best for refresher training or other training topics where trainees are quite knowledgeable in the topic already. Many times, trainees walk into a refresher class and roll their eyes, or otherwise show very little excitement for being there, because they have heard the topic over and over for many years.

These topics are often required by various regulations, and delivery of this information cannot be avoided.

Safety Consultant for a Minute

Another teamwork type of activity that can be beneficial and relates to peer-to-peer learning is called Safety Consultant for a Minute. A typical Safety Consultant for a Minute game involves posing a collection of workplace challenges to a group of trainees that are already put into teams. For example, if there are six different challenges that can be effectively addressed through a safety training class, each of these challenges can be written on a separate piece of paper and will form the basis of this activity. Trainees are put into groups of six and are preferably set up at different tables around the training room. Each trainee at each table receives a piece of paper with a different challenge written across the top. (If there are four tables of six trainees, each will need its own set of the questions). The trainees should be told to act as if they are highly paid safety consultants who have been brought into their workplace to solve the challenges on their paper; luckily, they can have the help of team members sitting around them. The trainer starts a timer and tells trainees that they have 1 minute to quickly jot down their solution to the training challenge. At the end of 1 minute, time will be called, and trainees will need to pass their challenge paper to the trainee sitting to their right. This activity continues until every trainee has had a chance to answer every challenge on the six different pieces of paper. If six challenge questions are used, the activity will take approximately 6 minutes. After the activity is complete, each trainee at each table should be given time to review what other trainees have written and decide on the best solution to their challenge. If possible, additional time should be given for trainees at each table to discuss their challenge and final solution with the others in their group. After several minutes have passed, the trainer should request that a few trainees share their challenge and final solution with the rest of the class. If multiple teams were involved, trainees from other teams may be able to add additional solutions that have not been considered before, and this can lead not only to a great discussion but also to greater learning.

Teamwork is a learning strategy that is easy to implement in most safety training programs. In addition to complementing accelerated learning principles discussed in Chapter 5, teamwork also helps maintain trainee attention, creates a positive learning environment, and takes advantage of other theories, such as the helper principle. All of these things stimulate trainee learning, which will hopefully help them remember the training content when it is needed most.

Review and Retention Activity
The Quiz Creator activity is discussed in Chapter 22, "Summarizing Activities."

Create a short quiz for another reader of this chapter on teamwork. If possible, exchange quizzes and attempt to complete each other's quiz. When finished, review the correct answers with the quiz creator.

References
Carnes, B. 2013. *Making E-learning Stick*. Alexandria, VA: American Society for Training and Development (ASTD) Press.

Carter, R. 2018. "What Is Collaboration? Connecting Teams and Getting Stuff Done." *UC Today*. December 23, 2018. https://www.uctoday.com/collaboration/what-is-collaboration/.

Druckman, D., and R. A. Bjork, eds. 1994. *Learning, Remembering, Believing: Enhancing Human Performance*. Washington, D.C: National Academy Press.

Hayes, M., F. Chumney, C. Wright, and M. Buckingham. 2019. "The Global Study of Engagement: Technical Report." Roseland, NJ: ADP Research Institute.

Hollins, P. 2017. *The Science of Accelerated Learning: Advanced Strategies for Quicker Comprehension, Greater Retention, and Systematic Expertise*. Scotts Valley, CA: Createspace Independent Publishing Platform.

Johnson, D. W, and F. P. Johnson. 2013. *Joining Together: Group Theory and Group Skills*. Boston, MA: Pearson.

Johnson, D. W., and R. T. Johnson. 2008. "Cooperation and the Use of Technology." In J. M. Spector, M. D. Merrill, J. J. G. van Merrienboer, and M. P. Driscoll, eds., *Handbook of Research on Educational Communications and Technology*. 3rd ed. pp. 401–423. New York: Lawrence Erlbaum (Taylor & Francis).

Johnson, D. W., and R. T. Johnson. 1989. *Cooperation and Competition: Theory and Research*. Edina, MN: Interaction Book Company.

Katzenbach, J. R., and D. K. Smith. 2015. *The Wisdom of Teams: Creating the High-Performance Organization*. Boston: Harvard Business Review Press.

National Research Council. 1994. *Learning, Remembering, Believing: Enhancing Human Performance*. Washington, DC: The National Academies Press. doi: 10.17226/2303.

Riessman, F. 1965. 'The "Helper" Therapy Principle.' *Social Work*, Vol. 10, Issue 2, April 1965, pp. 27–32. doi: 10.1093/sw/10.2.27.

Weinbauer-Heidel, Ina, and M. Ibeschitz-Manderbach. 2018. *What Makes Training Really Work: 12 Levers of Transfer Effectiveness*. Hamburg, Germany: tredition GmbH.

Chapter 16
Games, Gamification, and Technology

Games and gamification are often incorrectly used to mean the same thing. A *game* is a structured form of play that is usually fun and involves rules, goals, challenges, and interaction, while *gamification* can be defined as "a careful and considered application of game thinking to solving problems and encouraging learning using all the elements of games that are appropriate" (Kapp 2012). Both have their place in safety training, especially in plans to increase retention of training material. Safety training games, many of which are presented in Chapters 18–22, can be gamified if desired. Not every game needs to be gamified though. The end goal of a game or of gamified content is especially important, and decisions need to be made accordingly. With any training activity, games and gamified content used in a training program must directly relate to the class content and objectives. They should not be included just for the sake of adding fun to a class.

Why Games Work

Games can be a great way to get trainees to pay attention, learn while having fun, and learn from one another. Games can also help trainees imagine themselves as using the training content in their day-to-day job, which is critical to retention. Often, a well-designed training game will also build upon a trainee's past knowledge and experience and this is also extremely important for increasing retention. Games that challenge can be great. Some games are difficult, and the trainee may not be successful when playing them, but this is not always a bad thing, as explained in Chapter 14 on productive failure.

People are attracted to games for a variety of reasons, and people of all ages love games. The NPD Group, a data analytics company, reports that 73 percent of Americans ages two and older play video games (The NPD Group 2019), and the Entertainment Software Rating Board study showed that 67 percent of American households play computer or video games, and surprisingly, 26 percent of those people are over the age of fifty (Entertainment Software Association 2018).

Some of the major ways to increase learning retention discussed in this book can be enhanced with gamified content. A well-designed safety training game can work with preexisting knowledge and be designed so that trainees will be accessing their prior memories when playing the game. The trainees are reviewing that prior knowledge and building on it without even realizing they are learning. Some of the games described later in this book rely on organizing, sorting, and matching information. As trainees go through this process, they are relying on their past knowledge as well as helping others, and they are actively participating in their own learning.

Gamification also improves engagement. Einstein once said that the key to learning is to make it so much fun that you don't realize that you're learning at the same time, and gamified training content can do just that. If something is fun, it creates less resistance to learning, and it's also less stressful. This helps people to pay attention and absorb more information. Gamification also works with traditional training techniques. Many games involve things such as repetition, association, elaboration, and the use of stories. These things are related to the science of learning and have been shown to particularly increase retention.

Many of the safety training games provided in this book are somewhat competitive. To make any training game competitive, adding a time limit or rewards is sometimes all that is needed. It is important, however, to know the characteristics of trainees, and if a number of ultracompetitive individuals are in attendance, the competitive part of the game may need to be removed. Competition should not distract from the learning nor intimidate other trainees. An uncomfortable trainee is not going to be learning well, as discussed in Chapter 7 on facilitation and motivation.

Facilitation of Games

Any time a game is used, good facilitation skills are needed to keep the game from taking over a training class. Time management, which includes time to help trainees who are stuck, as well as keeping trainees on task and focused on the activity at hand, are critical to a successful game experience.

The importance of debriefing is also discussed in Chapter 7. Because debriefing is very important when using games and activities in safety training classes, it will be explained further here. Trainees make sense of any type of training activity through proper debriefing. A safety trainer's role in debriefing consists of asking questions that can lead to reflection and guiding discussion, which helps trainees better understand what they learned through the activity and how it applies to them. Since many safety training games are fun, they might not be treated as a learning event, but debriefing, when done well, can tie all the pieces together. Without debriefing, the activity will probably be a waste of time. If trainees participate in an activity without any postactivity discussion to help them reflect on what was learned by participating, the value of the activity will be negligible.

Gamification works particularly well with training programs when the subject matter is not engaging, or when learner resistance is high (Kapp 2012). Gamification can be used to get people engaged in their own learning when and where it's convenient. Information distributed over a longer period of time and not consumed in one setting can be a great help in increasing the amount of retention, as discussed in Chapter 12 on microlearning.

Technology and Gamification

Technology can provide ways to add gamification to safety training programs and especially help with distributing the content over a few days, weeks, months, or even longer. The advantages of spacing out information, whether gamified or not, are discussed in Chapter 10. Technology often plays a part in gamification programs. Several types of this technology are discussed below and also in Chapter 9, "Make it Real."

As chatting by text becomes a more and more common way of communicating, chatbots are increasingly being used in the training arena. *Chatbots* are virtual assistants that can provide information on any topic. Workflow learning, or learning on the job, is important in the learning and development world, and chatbots can be a powerful part of a workflow learning program. Equally as important is the use of these chatbots to provide refreshers of information previously learned so there is greater retention of the completed training.

Siri by Apple and Alexa by Amazon are common products that act as chatbots. Anyone can create a simple chatbot that can be accessed by voice using Amazon's Alexa system by simply following the instructions for building a custom skill on the Amazon website. The simplest of chatbots consist of basic questions and answers. As far as safety training is concerned, there are numerous areas where a chatbot could be beneficial. After a standard safety training class is delivered, either in person or online, a list of questions related to the topic, along with the corresponding answers, can be created and used to provide refresher training on an as-needed basis. Similarly, chatbots could be used to provide short follow-up tests that cover the class information. Some certification exam organizations already are experimenting with the use of chatbots, such as Alexa, to provide exam review questions and answers.

Game Versatility

Gamification in safety training it also great for a wide variety of workforces. With gamification, the trainer is able to adjust the content based on the audience members, their backgrounds, their cultures, their languages, and even their generations, and the game will still have the same effectiveness. Effective safety training games should be flexible and easily adaptable. If trainers find that the activity is too challenging for a particular group of trainees, trainers should be able to quickly modify the game based on the abilities of the class. Good safety training should also be flexible enough so that it can occur in a variety of locations. When using a safety training game, a trainer should ask, "Is the game easily understood?" If there is any confusion at all as to what the team should be doing after the trainer gives instructions, trainees will lose interest and the game will not have the desired results.

Computer games often follow a particular storyline. When safety training games are also based on a story, learners' brains are naturally attracted to listening and finding meaning in what they are hearing. Storytelling can be a great asset to gamified content. Many games can be replayed over and over, and the outcomes will be different. This is a great way to refresh the information in the trainees' minds as well as not bore them with repeat information in the same format. Many employees hear the same information year after year in refresher training for a variety of topics, but if this type of training were gamified, the employees could have the information repeated to them over and over, but it would be in an entirely different context that would be more fun and more memorable.

Game Effectiveness

What makes a game effective? Safety training games should incorporate a combination of chance and skill whenever possible. If too much chance is involved, the game becomes nothing more than time wasted with a mindless activity. Imagine throwing a pair of dice for 20 minutes straight just trying to get the highest number. That would be boring because the game would rely solely on chance. Alternatively, a list of jeopardy-style questions that do not involve any type of chance, and all of which must be answered, involves too much skill. In this case, the game quickly becomes a quiz. Although quizzes have their place in safety training, you do not want to turn the training game into a test—especially if it's called a game.

The game should be fun. If it's enjoyable, trainees will want to take part and be more involved in the activity, which will result in greater learning. Fun games also keep trainees' attention longer and will relax them.

Practical Information for All Games

Before using any game in a safety training class, a safety trainer should practice the game to make sure of the following:

1. The game works.
2. The game is not threatening or too difficult.
3. Adequate time is allotted to play the game.
4. The necessary materials are available. Props used in safety training games may get lost, break, or inevitably travel home with some employees. Basic materials include flip-chart paper, pens, markers, and so on. It's important to make sure all supplies are available before they are needed.

5. The answers to quizzes, or any other game answers, are available so feedback can be given immediately.
6. Safety game instructions are clear and complete. If a trainer has to stop and correct himself, or repeat directions, trainees will stop paying attention, and the trainer could lose credibility. For longer activities, clear, written instructions might be necessary.
7. Have more materials on hand than thought necessary.
8. Have adequate space available for trainees to comfortably perform the activity.

Most of the training activities included in this book involve putting trainees into small teams. Creating teams is not only an easy way to incorporate aspects of accelerated learning into training classes, but it can also make a significant difference in the quality of the learning that goes on. In 1983, professors Donald Finkel and Stephen Monk wrote about something called the *Atlas complex* (Finkel and Monk 1983). This refers to the idea that instructors feel they're responsible for an entire learning process. By dividing training classes into smaller groups, the Atlas complex can disappear and trainees can now be responsible for each other as well as themselves. Within any training team there is bound to be a pool of existing knowledge and experience. Interactive training activities and good facilitation draws on that knowledge and helps everyone learn.

Dividing the training class into teams works well for most training games. The benefits and suggestions for effective teams are provided in Chapter 15. Studies have shown that the social interaction involved with training teams leads to greater learning. Teams also encourage more participation and ideas. The number of members on each team will affect the length of each activity. Teams of four or more often need a leader and usually take longer to work on an activity than a team of two or three.

Fun and Games

Fun is an important part of many safety training games. It's not uncommon for safety professionals to believe that nothing about safety should be fun. In fact, safety is a serious business, and there are serious consequences if safety procedures aren't followed. Does fun have a place in occupational safety? Fun added to any workplace has a series of benefits (Tews et al. 2017, Georganta and Montgomery 2016), but unfortunately many adults reject the idea of having fun, or simply playing, because they don't understand the need for it as they grow older (CRMGamified 2018). Many people believe that a serious person doing serious work should be serious. Research has shown that removing joy and comfort from learning actually distances students from effective information processing and long-term memory storage (Pelling 2011). Fun can be an important part of a safety training program, as described in Chapter 5 on accelerated learning.

Serious Games

There is often confusion about the differences between serious games and traditional games. A *serious game* is a game developed for the main purpose of teaching and not for entertainment. Many people think serious games are only computer based, but they can be like a traditional board game that one would play with the family. Online, serious games can have an advantage though, since millennials appreciate playing video games more than past generations (Gale 2011). Students may also improve knowledge retention through experiential learning in the game environment (Din and Gibson 2019). There have been many studies that look at the characteristics of younger generations and how they may interact with serious games. Studies have shown that these students can thrive in this type of learning environment. Additionally, serious games can increase social interaction, and trainees can benefit from experiential learning, constructivism, and cognitive learning achievement (Din and Gibson 2019).

Studies have been done in the aviation sector, where the effectiveness of mobile virtual reality and serious games were tested to determine their effectiveness in the delivery of aircraft safety briefings. The results were compared with the training delivered using the traditional briefing card. The study found the interactive approach yields a higher level of efficacy of the training (Chittaro et al. 2018). Anyone who has flown on an airplane and watched the reactions of passengers as a safety video played while simultaneously being acted out by flight attendants can probably imagine how a serious game would be a great improvement in relaying important air-travel information. Even OSHA has realized the potential of serious games in safety training. The Occupational Safety and Health Administration provides an interactive, online, game-based training tool to help teach the main concepts of hazard control.

Games as Evaluations

A great way to use games in safety training is to make the safety training class itself the game and to make the game a form of assessment. Often when trainees hear that they're going to have to take an evaluation or a test at the end of class, they will be concentrating only on what they need to know in order to pass that test. The trainees may also tense up and start to worry about the outcome before the class has even begun. Imagine that a trainer kicks off a training class playing a serious game that is actually the content and the evaluation all tied into one. If a trainee or group of trainees failed the game, they can learn from their failure. This does not necessarily mean that they failed the class, but it's a learning opportunity that can be taken advantage of. If a safety training game is offered to a training class, and the class soon learns that the game makes up all of the content of the class, they will hopefully loosen up and begin to relax and have fun. A well-designed training game will help them learn all of the important information they need to learn. In the chapter on accelerated learning, the importance of trainees being responsible for their own learning and the importance of trainees working together can both be accommodated in a well-designed game. Most popular games provide multiple opportunities for failure. There will not be one right or wrong answer for the entire game, instead there will be little challenges throughout the course of the game, allowing people to make mistakes and correct them as they go through it. In safety training games that are well designed, trainees are going to be receiving feedback on all of their decisions in real time, as opposed to waiting for a graded evaluation to be reported back to them sometime after the class is over.

Failure in Games

It's also important to realize that, in order for games to be fun, they have to include an element of failure, and that enjoyment comes from overcoming unnecessary obstacles. If the game is too easy for trainees, they will get bored quickly. If a training activity is too difficult, they may give up before they've ever learned anything. It's important to have the right balance.

In Scott Provence's book, *Fail to Learn* (Provence 2020), Provence suggests a few ways to add failure to gamification efforts. A few are discussed below along with suggestions for implementing them in a safety training class.

1. *Include a replay option.*
   In video games, a replay button gives players the chance to go back and try again. In training, an option can be inserted allowing trainees to go back and review the content one or more times. Safety trainers can use this option to permit the replay of a video or to choose to retest.
2. *Use humor to deescalate fears of failure.*
   As described throughout this book, fun has many benefits.
3. *Incentivize losing.*
   This is an interesting idea that can be applied to training evaluations that don't really mean that much, such as preclass evaluations. To incentivize losing, the trainer would announce that there would be a prize for the most questions answered incorrectly. In order to correctly select the incorrect answer to every single answer on a quiz, the trainee will actually have to know which answers are right. This can also help communicate the message that it's okay to make mistakes in the training environment.
4. *Include confidence ratings.*
   The idea of using confidence ratings to help increase retention is described in Chapter 14. This can be added to safety training games by asking trainees to add a confidence rating to any answers they submit as part of a game.
5. *Make feedback immediate.*
   The importance of immediate feedback is discussed in Chapters 6 and 25. It is also important in safety training games. Trainees should not need to wait until the end of class (or even later) to know if their answers were right or wrong. In order for a safety training game to be an effective activity for learning and retention, trainees need to know as soon as possible if their actions and answers are correct or not.
6. *Make bendy rules.*
   In safety training, the games and game rules are not set in stone. The goal is learning and engagement, and it's important to keep that in mind. The A–Z Race game, discussed in Chapter 22 on summarizing activities, is a good example of a safety training game that includes *bendy* rules. In this game, trainees work together in teams to come

up with a word or phrase related to the safety training class topic for every letter of the alphabet. When a team gets stuck on a letter like Q or X, trainees are told to be creative. For example, for the letter "X" trainees could answer with "X"it (instead of exit). If trainees are told they must strictly follow the rules, they would quickly become disillusioned and realize there is no way to win. Since the objective is learning, bendy rules are okay.

Types of Players

When selecting or creating a safety training game or attempting to gamify a training activity, it is helpful to consider what motivates a particular group of trainees.

One way to do this is to attempt to find out what motivates trainees. There are many models to help trainers identify what type of game player a trainee is. Of course, the simplest way is to ask trainees which of four types of game players they are. In addition, ask them what types of games they like to play. Before any training session is created, good safety trainers know that it is important to know their audience—background, level of experience, and more—so that the training can be designed in a way that is most effective. Similarly, when using gamification as part of a safety training program, it is best to know what type of games will work best with a particular group. If a trainer finds that most of the trainees are one type of game player, the decision is easy, but even if there is an equal mix of player types, games can be made that include at least a small part that will attract each type of player. In 1996 Richard Bartle identified four main types of game players.

The four types of game players are (Bartle 1996):

1. *Socializers*
   The socializers are more interested in the social aspects of a game and don't really care about the game itself.
2. *Explorers*
   The explorers like to play games where they can do what they want, whenever they want. They like to investigate and discover new things.

3. *Achievers*
   The achievers like to collect accomplishments. They like to see what they have accomplished and show off their achievements to others.
4. *Killers*
   The killers are similar to the achievers, but the killers enjoy when others lose in order for them to win.

Another way to get an idea of what might motivate a group of trainees to be interested in a safety training game is to ask them what games they like to play, and what they like best about them. If trainees say they like the game of Risk, they are probably motivated by strategy. If trainees prefer combat games like Dark Souls, they are most likely motivated by vengeance. If trainees like Jenga, they are probably motivated by hands-on activities and skills.

One thing that is very common in game design, but not well known among occupational safety professionals, is the development of learner personas. Personas are closely related to finding out what motivates trainees when it comes to playing games. Using personas to create and select safety training games is discussed more in Chapter 17, "Choosing the Right Activity."

Review and Retention Activity

Flash cards as a learning and retention technique are discussed in Chapter 21 on repetition and retrieval activities.

Make a copy of Figure 16.1 and Figure 16.2; cut on the solid lines and fold on the dashed lines. Alternatively, simply use the terms on the left side, matched with the definitions on the right side, to create flash cards. Look at each term one at a time and only flip over the card to see the correct answer after an attempt has been made to define the term correctly. If the term is defined correctly, the card can be placed to the side. If the definition is not easily recalled, it should be placed at the bottom of the pile. All cards should be reviewed until all are in the completed pile.

Figure 16.1 ✦ Gamification flash cards, page 1

Figure 16.2 ✦ Gamification flash cards, page 2

References

Bartle, R. 1996. "Hearts, Clubs, Diamonds, Spades: Players Who Suit MUDs." *Journal of MUD Research*, 1(1):19.

Chittaro, L., C. I. Corbett, G. A. McLean, and N. Zangrando. 2018. "Safety Knowledge Transfer through Mobile Virtual Reality: A Study of Aviation Life Preserver Donning." *Safety Science*, 102:159–168. doi: 10.1016/j.ssci.2017.10.012.

CRM Gamified. 2018. "Top 6 CRM Gamification Mistakes (And How to Avoid Them!)." CRM Gamified. April 23, 2018. https://crmgamified.com/the-top-6-crm-gamification-mistakes/.

Din, Z. U., and G. E. Gibson. 2019. "Serious games for learning prevention through design concepts: An experimental study." *Safety Science*, 115:176–187.

Entertainment Software Association. 2018. "Essential Facts About the Computer and Video Game Industry." https://www.theesa.com/wp-content/uploads/2019/03/ESA_EssentialFacts_2018.pdf.

Finkel, D. L., and G. S. Monk. 1983. "Teachers and Learning Groups: Dissolution of the Atlas Complex." *New Directions for Teaching and Learning*, 1983(14):83–97. doi: 10.1002/tl.37219831411.

Gale, M. T. 2011. "Gameplay in higher education: the use of serious games vs traditional instructional methods in learning." Auburn University, OroQuest Dissertation.

Georganta, K., and A. Montgomery. 2016. "Exploring Fun as a Job Resource: The Enhancing and Protecting Role of a Key Modern Workplace Factor." *International Journal of Applied Positive Psychology*, 1(1–3):107–31. doi: 10.1007/s41042-016-0002-7.

Kapp, K. M. 2012. *The Gamification of Learning and Instruction*. San Francisco, CA: John Wiley & Sons, Inc.

Peling, N. 2011. "The (Short) Pre-History of Gamification." Funding Startups (& Other Impossibilities) Blog. August 9, 2011. http://www.nanadome.wordpress.com/2011/08/09/-the-short-prehistory-of-gamification/.

Provence, S. 2020. *Fail to Learn: A Manifesto for Training Gamification*. Independently published.

Tews, M. J., J. W. Michel, and R. A. Noe. 2017. "Does Fun Promote Learning? The Relationship between Fun in the Workplace and Informal

Learning." *Journal of Vocational Behavior*, 98(February):46–55. doi: 10.1016/j.jvb.2016.09.006.

The NPD Group. 2019. "According to The NPD Group, 73 Percent of U.S. Consumers Play Video Games." October 8, 2019. https://www.npd.com/wps/portal/npd/us/news/press-releases/2019/according-to-the-npd-group-73-percent-of-u-s-consumers-play-video-games/.

Part 3

Applications and Activities

Chapter 17
Choosing the Right Activity

Other chapters in this book have already discussed the importance of using interactive activities in safety training classes. Trainees should be involved in their own learning and discussions rather than spending all of their time listening to someone lecture. Safety training games can create memorable events in the trainee's mind through the use of visual aids, role-playing, videos, and other forms of active learning (Slavin 2000). Activities are important because the brain needs to interact with new material, process it, and do something with it in order for it to be understood and retained (Matthews 2012), but it is important to consider what the desired outcome is before randomly selecting a game.

Is it Appropriate?

Before a procedure for choosing the right activity is discussed, it's important to consider if it's appropriate to use any type of activity. Questions to ask include:

- Does the activity cover and raise the learning points that are part of the course curriculum?
- Is there time after an activity for discussion that is structured and helps bring meaning to the work the trainees just did?
- Will the activity work within the allotted amount of time?
- Will the activity keep people interested and help them to focus on the content?
- Are the instructions for the activity clear and easy for people to understand?

There are many types of training activities that a safety trainer can pick from when planning a safety training class, with many taking the form of games.

In *Rapid Instructional Design*, Piskurich lists the following items to consider when choosing games (Piskurich 2000):

- What purpose do you hope to achieve?
- Does the game's focus relate to one (or more) of your objectives?
- Is the group the right size for the game?
- Do all trainees have the right experience and background to play the game effectively?
- Is the purpose of the game to introduce new material, demonstrate a concept, or reinforce learning?
- Is the game simple to play?
- Are the directions complete?
- Will the game be fun?
- Is there time to both play and debrief?
- Are there better ways to do what you think the game will do?

When choosing an activity, it is best to know the audience. Are trainees high-energy or low-energy participants? Are they happy to be there or not? Are they willing to participate in discussions? Even if a group of trainees seems like they will not want to do anything that seems fun or interactive, safety trainers may be surprised at how willing they are to participate. When given a choice between watching a video or listening to an instructor for half of a day or even a few hours and getting up, moving around, and having fun, most trainees will choose the active learning option.

When selecting a particular training activity, the physical requirements should also be considered. Does the activity require people to stand for a while or walk around or be able to throw or catch? Are there training activities that require people to crouch down or even sit on a floor? Activities like this may be very difficult for a number of trainees. For example, some training activities are best played when various game parts are spread around on the floor so team members can spread out and participate, but if trainees have poor eyesight or trouble bending over, the floor would not be the ideal place to set up the activity.

Another important consideration when selecting a particular training activity is the environment. Will the training activity be performed somewhere that's noisy? If the activity requires trainees to have conversations with one another and for teams to have conversations that other teams won't be able to hear, consider if that will be possible in the location where the training will be delivered. Will the training be presented in a room that is too small for trainee teams to move adequately away from one another? If so, plans to have some of the teams work outside the training room for the duration of the activity may be necessary.

Cultural Differences

Other considerations in choosing the right safety training activity include the experience, culture, and native language of the trainees. A training activity that works well and is enjoyed in a training class that consists mainly of Americans may not work well at all, or even cause discomfort, for an international audience. One important cultural variable to consider is power distance. *Power distance* refers to the emphasis and importance that society places on status and authority. Trainees from a high power distance culture may need to be told very directly and clearly to participate in training activities and to ask questions. Cultural differences may cause trainees to say things that don't match what they actually do. For example, a trainee may say he or she understands class material in an attempt to please the trainer but then go back to the work area and act as if the information presented in the training class was never heard. Different cultures and backgrounds may also cause individuals to be reluctant to speak up or make eye contact. There are also cultural differences in how far or close trainees may feel comfortable standing next to each other and the trainer (Rhinesmith 1996). All of these things need to be considered when deciding on the appropriate training activity. If a trainee is uncomfortable or not used to questioning and speaking up, some of the activities in this book may not work as intended and could cause unnecessary stress in a training environment.

Locus of Control

Locus of control is a phrase that refers to an individual's internal belief system regarding the cause of his or her experiences and the factors to which that person attributes failure or success. This is somewhat similar to the growth mindset described in Carol Dweck's popular book titled *Mindset*. Dweck explains that often we have not examined our mindsets in any depth, but a strong and wrong mindset can interfere with learning (Dweck 2017). People with an internal locus of control believe that they control what happens to them and people with an external locus of control believe that if they succeed in something, it is due to luck or fate. The internal locus-of-control individuals will expect to succeed due to their own efforts and will be more motivated to learn. If training activities help shift trainees' beliefs to an internal locus of control, that training is more likely to increase the transfer of learned safety knowledge and skills. If individuals have an external locus-of-control viewpoint, they could potentially be more influenced by environmental cues, such as the safety training transfer environment. The transfer environment, discussed in Chapter 4, refers to the culture and training transfer support at a given company. If a trainee has an external locus of control and returns to the workplace with full support to transfer what was learned to day-to-day activities, a positive learning retention and transfer experience can occur. Knowing how trainees view their success, achieved through their own hard work or through luck, can help a safety trainer make the right design decisions when creating safety training programs that include games (Krauss et al. 2014).

Training Design and Outcomes

Training design characteristics can predict training outcomes (Gegenfurtner 2013). In "Training Transfer: An Integrative Literature Review," the authors report that "46% of ASTD members indicate they use specific training design strategies to improve learning transfer" (Burke and Hutchins 2007). A training design strategy includes the decision about whether or not to include training games and activities. Instructional design is extremely important in predicting training transfer, primarily by building in processes that increase learner engagement in the training program (Krauss et al. 2014).

Certain training methods foster trainee engagement more than others. A meta-analysis of 95 safety training studies found that trainee engagement, which was influenced by training delivery method, significantly predicted training transfer (Burke et al. 2006). When trainees are engaged and participate, they are experiencing deeper learning, so it is important to include interactive safety training activities where possible. "Engaging safety training is three times more effective in fostering training transfer than non-engaging training" and "organizations should invest resources into incorporating interactive and experiential learning opportunities into safety training." This investment may be particularly worthwhile when high-risk hazards are the focus of safety training (Burke et al. 2006).

Humor and Fun

When selecting safety training activities, it is best to include those that are not only best for a particular group of trainees, as discussed in other chapters, but also some that include an element of fun. Often safety trainers believe that safety should be serious and there's really nothing to laugh about. Although there are plenty of instances where laughter and fun are not appropriate, studies have shown that humor can have positive effects both physiologically as well as psychologically. Psychologically, humor can reduce stress and anxiety levels, enhance self-esteem, and increase self-motivation. It's very difficult to train or teach stressed out or anxious students, as discussed in Chapter 7 on motivation. Humor can help create a positive emotional and social environment that will help trainees lower their defenses and enable them to focus more clearly on the material being presented. Trainees in a good mood are going to pay more attention, be more involved, and retain more information. If their mind is elsewhere, they're not going to be paying attention. Humor can help pull them back. It's very hard to ignore information that's funny if everyone else is laughing and having a good time.

In 1986, William Glasser, MD, proposed that the five primary needs of humans are survival, belonging, power, freedom, and fun. He also pointed out that all of our behavior is a constant attempt to satisfy one or more of these needs. In his book, *Choice Theory: A New Psychology of Choice Freedom*, Glasser states, "fun is difficult to define but is associated with laughter, play and entertainment." The activities shared in this book are intended to take advantage of at least two of these needs—belonging and fun (Glasser 1999).

Research has also shown that humor can increase students' interest in learning and that students taught with the use of humor will have better retention of the information (Kuhrik et al. 1997). If the classroom is more relaxed and spontaneous, trainees may be more willing to participate in risk-taking as well since mistakes are more acceptable in this type of atmosphere. Physiologically, humor and laughter affects trainees by improving respiration and lowering their pulse and blood pressure. Laughter is also commonly associated with release of endorphins into the bloodstream. Studies in the medical world have looked at how laughter can help patients heal by lessening stress and anxiety and increasing mental sharpness. Again, these are all great things to have in the training environment and are important, as discussed in Chapter 7 on motivation and facilitation.

Most of the games and activities found in Chapters 18–22 could be modified for use with a variety of topics. Once the basic structure of a game is established, it is usually only a matter of substituting the props and/or instructions to make it applicable to a different topic or audience. The title of the game might also need to be changed, but often the trainer is the only one that sees the title. By using imagination, often a trainer can simply adapt, shorten, or lengthen most games and activities based on the needs of the class, the delivery method, and time constraints.

Game Mechanics

An important part of gamification is game mechanics. Game mechanics are the things that make any game work and include things such as competition, surprises, leaderboards, memory, trading, randomness, leveling up, and many more. One of the most important parts of selecting an appropriate game or creating a new game is to match what motivates trainees to specific game mechanics. For example, a training game based on competition and vengeance might appeal to a certain type of trainee but may not appeal to trainees who prefer cooperation and teamwork. By identifying personas (described below), the best mechanics, and in turn the best game, can be selected.

Personas

The use of learning personas is popular in the world of gamification and game design but might be new to safety trainers. *Personas* are fictional characters created based upon specific research that considers different types of players. Personas should not be confused with demographics. For example, it might be known that a training group consists of all men with more than 20 years of experience at a company, who all have the title of senior XYZ technician. Information such as years with the company and job titles are examples of demographic information and not examples of learner personas. The main difference between demographic information and personas is that the demographic information is not going to tell you what type of things motivate or demotivate the trainees. The persona information, on the other hand, will help you identify what will resonate and drive interactivity in the training class. A key to creating personas for use in safety training is to think about the trainees at the emotional level.

For most safety training classes, several personas will be needed. It is highly unlikely that all trainees in a training class are going to be represented by the same exact learner persona. The type of information that goes into creating a *learner persona* includes things such as pain points; goals; preferences for finding needed information; free time choices, such as hobbies; and things that are important or a priority for the trainee.

If a trainer works with coworkers every day, it will be much easier to create learner personas for them than if the trainer is an outsider or consultant. In the second instance, trainers can talk with the safety professionals or other employees at that company to try to gather as much of this information as possible. Knowing this information ahead of time will help the safety trainer create a training program that will appeal to most of the group. Even if a trainer has worked with this group of employees for many years, it is still a good idea to informally interview a cross section of trainees. This information could be gathered from simply talking to people when walking through work areas or when seeing them in break areas. Once a safety trainer knows the reasons people do things, those will be central to figuring out their motivations, which can lead to changing their behaviors. Knowing this information will help in designing a training class that will address trainee likes and dislikes and pinpoint which game mechanics will personally motivate them.

For example, if a safety trainer finds that trainees often go to YouTube to learn how to do something, even when they are home, it can be a good idea to include video clips in the training class. If trainees often learn new information by talking with peers, planned opportunities to learn from others through teamwork can be attractive. If trainees frequently visit a source on the company intranet or rely on postings in the work area, these locations can be leveraged and built into a training game.

The persona a trainer creates will not be a real person but a character that symbolizes trainees. As mentioned above, most companies will have more than one learning persona. Two sample learning personas are described below.

Mike the Mechanic

Mike is 22 and has been at the company for 2 years. He started as a mechanic right after trade school. He loves working with his hands and spends the weekend tinkering with an old Chevrolet Camaro he hopes to get running one day. When he needs a part or needs to figure something out, he first looks on YouTube for instructions. Mike played soccer in high school. He is part of a competitive paintball league outside of work and is the shortstop on the company softball team. He considers himself very competitive. He is not married and lives with two friends.

Pauline the Packer

Pauline is 35 and has worked in packaging for almost 10 years. She is married and has three children in grade school. She enjoys reading mysteries and lately has been spending a lot of her free time (which isn't much) watching TikTok videos. She loves to do crafts with her children and considers herself very creative. She often plans craft activities for her children's school holiday events. She finds a lot of great ideas for these activities on Pinterest.

If Pauline the Packer and Mike the Mechanic were in the same training class, would it be possible to find a training activity or two that would appeal to both of them? Consider the following information, which can be extrapolated from their personas.

- Mike grew up on social media.
- Mike likes hands-on activities.
- Mike likes trial and error (productive failure).
- Mike is a problem solver.
- Mike prefers to learn by watching.
- Mike is athletic.
- Mike is very competitive.

- Pauline is very comfortable with social media.
- Pauline likes surprises.
- Pauline is a problem solver.
- Pauline enjoys videos.
- Pauline likes to create with her hands.
- Pauline likes to help others.
- Pauline is creative.

By looking at these two personas that represent two trainees, it is easier to figure out which training activities would appeal to the group and which activities are better avoided. Both types of trainees would be very comfortable with an activity that involves accessing content online, and visual aids, especially video, would appeal to both types of trainees. They are both problem solvers, so training activities that provide a task that needs solving would be effective. Both personas also enjoy hands-on activities, so training methods that include the opportunity to touch, build, create, and/or manipulate would also be good choices.

When looking over available options for interactive training activities to include in a training class, trainers should keep the personas for their trainees in mind. Although they are made up, if they were created using information gleaned from a cross section of interviews with the actual group to be trained, the training material is much more likely to work well and be a success than if this type of information were not considered. It is important to be as detailed as possible when creating personas, as demonstrated in the descriptions shown above.

Pivotal to instructional design, as discussed in Chapter 6, is that the training program should be designed for the learner. Defining a learner involves more than simply determining someone's age and/or gender. Learner personas can prompt the individual creating the safety training to occasionally stop and ask, "Would this be an activity that Mike would like?" or "Would Pauline be excited about this activity or bored by it?" By constantly thinking of the personas when designing all aspects of the training, the trainer will have a much easier time keeping the learners' needs in the forefront. If a trainee is more interested, pays more attention, and is more actively involved in a training class, the overall retention of the material will be greater.

It's important to keep in mind that personas are not stereotypes but instead are considered generalizations about a group of trainees. Stereotypes can be defined as a list of traits assigned to all members of a group, whereas generalizations are descriptions of a group based on its members. When trainers start to create personas for safety training programs, it may become obvious that additional personas are needed. For example, a trainer may know that two or three other individuals who will be in the training class are not comfortable with social media and would much prefer listening to information and asking questions about it. It may become obvious that not all of the personas previously created are going to cover the needs of one particular training class and new personas will need to be created. When creating personas, it's a good idea to think about how many trainees each one of the personas represents. If a persona represents less than 10 percent of the learners, it is not necessary to create a different persona just to cover the needs of one or two individuals.

Often, safety training programs are developed strictly with the organization's goals in mind. While this is an important thing to consider, no program can achieve a return on investment if it's not designed with the learners' personal goals in mind as well. Without learner buy-in and engagement, no development program can truly succeed (Bahm 2020). Considering the likes and dislikes of trainees promotes training design that will truly resonate with them and provide greater benefits long term. Keeping learner personas, as well as trainee experience, culture, and personal factors in mind will help ensure that the best training game is selected.

Review and Retention Activity

Checklists as training aids are discussed in Chapter 8 on preclass and postclass communication. Review the checklist in Figure 17.1 before adding a training game to a training class to help ensure the most effective activity is chosen.

Choosing the Best Training Game

Adapted from *Rapid Instructional Design* (Piskurich 2000)

- [ ] The purpose of using the selected game has been identified.
- [ ] The game's focus relates to one or more objectives.
- [ ] The class is the right size for the game (and vice versa).
- [ ] Trainees have the right experience and background to play the game effectively.
- [ ] The purpose of the game is to introduce new material, demonstrate a concept, or reinforce learning.
- [ ] The game is simple to play.
- [ ] The game directions are complete.
- [ ] The game includes elements of humor and fun.
- [ ] There is adequate time to play the game as well as debrief.
- [ ] There is not a better alternative to do what the game is intended to do.
- [ ] The game aligns with the culture of the trainees.
- [ ] The game is appropriate for the persona(s) of the learners.
- [ ] Game mechanics included in the selected activity are appropriate for the specific group of trainees.

Figure 17.1 ✦ Checklist for choosing the best training game

References

Bahm, H. 2020. "Design Learner-Centric Development Programs." *TD Magazine*. January 2020, pp. 18–20.

Burke, L. A., and H. M. Hutchins. 2007. "Training Transfer: An Integrative Literature Review." *Human Resource Development Review*, 6(3):263–296.

Burke, M. J., S. A. Sarpy, K. Smith-Crowe, S. Chan-Serafin, R.O. Salvador, and G. Islam. 2006. "Relative effectiveness of worker safety and health training methods." *American Journal of Public Health*, 96(2):315–324.

Dweck, C. 2017. *Mindset*. London: Robinson.

Gegenfurtner, A. 2013. "Dimensions of motivation to transfer: A longitudinal analysis of their influence on retention, transfer, and attitude change." *Vocations and Learning*, 6(2):1–19, 187–205.

Glasser, William. 1999. *Choice Theory: A New Psychology of Personal Freedom*. New York: HarperCollins.

Krauss, A., T. Casey, and P. Y. Chen. 2014. "Making Safety Training Stick." In S. Leka and R. R. Sinclair, eds., *Contemporary Occupational Health Psychology: Global Perspectives on Research and Practice*, Volume 3. Chichester: Wiley-Blackwell. doi: 10.1002/9781118713860.ch12.

Kuhrik, Marilee, Paula A. Berry, and Nancy Kuhrik. 1997. "Facilitating Learning with Humor." *Journal of Nursing Education*. 36(7):332–34. doi: 10.3928/0148-4834-19970901-10.

Matthews, Alan. 2012. *How to Design and Deliver Great Training: Learn How to Turn Any Material into Lively, Engaging and Effective Training*. Scotts Valley, CA: CreateSpace Independent Publishing Platform.

Piskurich, George M. 2000. *Rapid Instructional Design: Learning ID Fast and Right*. Jossey-Bass. San Francisco, CA: Pfeiffer.

Rhinesmith, S. H. 1996. "Training for Global Operations." In Robert L. Craig, ed., *The ASTD Training & Development Handbook*. 4th ed. New York: McGraw-Hill.

Slavin, R. E. 2000. *Educational Psychology*. Boston: Allyn and Bacon.

Chapter 18
Error-Based Examples and Activities

Error-based examples involve showing trainees how not to perform a skill and is one of the least known instructional strategies that has been found to support better transfer (Carnes 2013). When using error-based activities, examples of errors that are shown to trainees must be different enough from what is actually correct so it is easy for trainees to tell the difference. For example, if an illustration used to show the importance of proper storage of chemicals in a lab showed an uncapped chemical bottle and another illustration showed the cap properly sealed, these illustrations would be different enough for the trainees to know what is safe and what is not. If the same two illustrations showed one chemical bottle that was properly sealed and a second chemical bottle that had the lid slightly ajar, it would be more difficult for the trainees to learn from the second illustration. When trainees are able to experience and see how something is being done incorrectly and then see how it can be done correctly, they are more likely to learn from the example and use what they learn.

Ask the Experts

When using error-based training activities, it can be helpful to talk to experts on the topic to ask for suggestions about possible incorrect uses and techniques. For example, if a trainee is attending a class on material handling procedures, and a common incorrect use of a tool has led to injuries in the past, having this example of an incorrect use as part of a training activity would be an example of an error-based learning event. If a trainer is preparing a training class for machine shop operators, it can be helpful to talk with longtime, experienced employees in that area and ask them about the craziest thing they ever saw someone do in a machine shop. It is probable that experienced employees have many stories to share.

Another thing to consider is asking trainees in an interactive activity what kind of mistakes or misjudgments people might make with regard to a specific safety procedure. A trainer can also ask for examples of things that should not be done when performing a particular activity. Similarly, the trainees can be asked what the consequences would be if something were not done the correct way.

One way to use these ideas is to incorporate activities such as What Happens Next? This activity is described in Chapter 5; an example is shown in Figure 18.1.

In this type of activity, the photo is shown to teams of trainees, and each team is asked to come up with a story about what happens next. Depending on the topic, the trainees can be told that this photo was taken right before an accident occurred and that they need to discuss with their teammates what could have caused the accident and what accident actually occurred. This activity can be amplified by asking trainees to discuss and be ready to share how the accident could have been prevented.

There are many opportunities available to find error-based examples online. "Fatal Facts," available on OSHA's website, and other similar case studies,

Figure 18.1 ✦ Sample photo for the What Happens Next activity

Figure 18.2 ✦ OSHA FatalFact No. 14–2016 (Source: OSHA 2016)

can be presented to teams of trainees, and similar discussions can ensue. If a small budget is available or a company has an internal graphic design department, these fatal facts and other case studies can be given to an illustrator and then presented as an image instead. While it is not in good taste to show a photo of an actual devastating accident, an illustration that provides much of the same detail can be very effective. Take a look at Figure 18.2 that was created based on OSHA's FatalFact No. 14–2016 titled "Crushed by Carriage During Skyline Skidding Operation." Instead of showing a photo, the incident was recreated in the form of a black and white illustration.

Sometimes the use of error-based activities can also be amusing. It is important, however, not to make fun of tragic accidents. One way to add humor with the use of error-based activities is for the trainer to be self-deprecating or to show examples that are so obviously incorrect that they are amusing. Some of the best times to use this type of amusing activity is when providing training on soft skills. Soft skills are usually not the first thing that comes to mind when thinking of safety training, but soft skills are important if trainees are going to learn to communicate effectively with coworkers and management about safety. Common soft skills that are closely tied to safety include things such as listening skills, how to provide feedback, observation skills, and leadership skills. If trainees are attending a training class on delivering appropriate feedback, a mock presentation that shows a coworker delivering feedback to someone acting unsafely will be interesting, but if the mock scenario shows the feedback being delivered so terribly that it's humorous, this would not only get the attention of trainees but would also surely result in laughs.

Sometimes video clips from popular television shows, such as *The Office*, can be used in this way. As discussed in Chapter 7 on motivation, trainees are much more likely to learn when they are comfortable and do not feel threatened. It is hard not to pay attention when other trainees are laughing and when something is enjoyable. Even if trainees are irritable and annoyed about being forced to attend a training session, they will have a difficult time not participating if there is laughter in the room, and these exaggerated examples can do just that.

In addition to live demonstrations (safely staged) of error-based examples, images and illustrations are also highly effective and are probably more available then live demonstrations of an unsafe act—and for good reason. With safety training, which is different than many other kinds of training, an unsafe act can have serious consequences, and the act of doing something unsafely on purpose as a training class demonstration is almost always not warranted. Some e-learning courses show accidents, but these accidents usually are performed by stunt people in a controlled setting. Unless the same controls (and insurance) are in place, it is not recommended that these types of videos be staged.

The use of standalone photos can be effective in error-based activities as long as the photo of the incorrect activity or condition is equally compared to the correct conditions. Figure 18.3 shows an overloaded electrical outlet shown next to an electrical outlet that is used correctly.

Safety Sort Activities

The use of safety sort activities as a way of increasing trainee retrieval of previously learned information is discussed in the Chapter 20 on sorting activities. Potential workplace errors can be incorporated into a safety sort activity to provide error-based learning. For example, a list of ten possible incorrect steps trainees may be able to make in the course of their normal day can each be written on a separate index card. A set of these ten incorrect activities can be made for each participating group of trainees. When each group of trainees has a set of the cards, they should be asked to put them in order of consequence, with the activity having the most potential for negative outcome placed first in the pile and the last activity in the pile being the activity with the least likelihood of causing an adverse effect. This type of activity will lead to much discussion about the effects of negative consequences and errors that may

Incorrect

Correct

Figure 18.3 ✦ Electrical safety comparison photos

be experienced in the workplace and will lead the trainees to think, perhaps subconsciously, where that error was made or where they might commit that same error when back on the job.

Another variation of this type of error-based sorting activity would be to set up the activity the same way but ask trainees to sort the error cards into three piles. The first pile should reflect the errors that would have fatal consequences. The second pile should reflect errors that would cause serious injuries or property damage. The third pile should reflect errors that would result in very little negative effect or are bound to go unnoticed by those around them. There are no right or wrong answers in these two activities. The important benefit is that they lead to discussion and reflection on the training content and help trainees realize the importance of the training to them personally. Such activities also help trainees remember the information and be more inclined to apply key concepts when performing their own job.

A Hazard Hunt

Hazard hunt photos can provide another example of error-based safety training. Photos for this activity may already be available in your workplace, but if not, they can be temporarily staged in order for a photo to be taken. It is important to note that an unsafe situation should never be created. If a hazard cannot be demonstrated safely, a different type of training activity should be selected. If there is a particularly unorganized work area, this is usually a good place to start, because there will be more items to consider when the activity is used in the classroom. To help stage an area for a hazard hunt photo, a cord could be temporarily laid across the floor, a fire extinguisher could be temporarily unmounted from a wall and positioned on the floor, a wrapper from someone's lunch could be placed in an area where eating is not allowed, or an empty chemical container could be put on a desk without a lid. Once the photo is taken, the temporarily hazardous situations that were staged for the photo should be corrected immediately. Once the photo is created, it should be printed in color and copies made.

To use a hazard hunt activity in a training class, trainees should be put into small teams of approximately four to six people. Each team should be given a copy of the hazard hunt scene. The trainees should be instructed to work together to identify all of the unsafe conditions found in the photo. At the end of the activity, trainees should count up the number of items found and report them to the instructor. It is highly unlikely that different teams of trainees will come up with the same number, which will lead to vigorous discussion. Often there is no right or wrong exact answer, but the benefit of this activity, like several others described in this book, is the discussion that ensues.

A focal point of this activity is the debriefing session. To debrief the hazard hunt activity, the first step is to ask trainees to identify the hazards they found. Each of these hazards should be discussed, and trainees should be asked what the correct situation would look like. To further discuss the activity, trainees should be asked why they believe that different teams of trainees had different answers. This will generally lead to a variety of answers, but usually includes things like different backgrounds, different levels of experience, different types of safety knowledge, and the tendency to focus on things we know best. For example, an electrician may focus on the electrical hazards in the room, while someone who works in an office may not notice the electrical hazards but may notice a cord running across the floor. Once this discussion is underway, trainees should be asked how this could make a difference in their own workplace safety. Possible discussion might include what happens when trainees complete safety inspections of their own work area and why teamwork is important. It is also important to discuss how trainees can be well rounded in identifying various types of hazards.

Serious Error-Based Games

Serious games, as discussed in Chapter 16 on gamification, are those that are developed for the main purpose of teaching rather than entertainment and can be used to introduce error-based activities in a safe way. Serious games have been used for a long time in the defense industry, education, healthcare, and emergency management. Serious games may still be fun, but that is not their primary purpose. A serious game can introduce a safe place for trainees to make mistakes and learn from their mistakes. In Chapter 14, the idea of productive failure as a learning method was discussed. It's okay for trainees to make errors, and sometimes the most valuable learning experiences come from those activities.

A game that has serious consequences, such as someone experiencing a fatality due to a mistake made, is not going to be a game that is intended to create fun for the trainees. In fact, it may cause a high level of stress and emotional involvement. As seen in Chapter 7, emotional involvement and personal connections are very important in increasing retention of training material. While it is important to reduce stress in order to have trainees feel comfortable for some types of training, it is sometimes important to have the dire consequences of an unsafe act more fully realized, and this could be accomplished through serious games. "Serious games constitute an alternative for safety training, and they are becoming popular mainly because of their potential to allow learners to get involved in scenarios that would not be feasible in a real-world context because of cost, time or safety reasons, either on their own or as a supplement to other existing more formal ways of safety training" (Martínez-Dura et al. 2011).

The construction industry, which is known to have one of the worst fatal injury rates of any industry (Bureau of Labor Statistics 2020), has a variety of situations that could benefit from the use of serious games. A study conducted in

2011 studied the effect of serious games designed to increase safety of those working in trenches. In this and most serious games, a realistic environment is provided along with a wealth of interactive content that provides trainees with opportunities to practice the applicable knowledge. In the trench safety game evaluated in this study, students were able to move around freely in a 3-D environment as if they were working and use a mouse to control their viewpoint. Additionally, objects could be viewed simply by clicking on them. In this serious game, which involved a variety of scenarios, one outcome was serious injuries to an avatar that represented a coworker (Dickinson et al. 2011). In a game such as this, there are serious consequences, such as injury to a coworker that would be the result of an error made by the participant. Emotion is surely involved in this type of training scenario, and this emotion as well as the application of real-world scenarios, makes this type of serious game appropriate for increasing training retention.

Other serious games that are designed to help trainees learn from their errors are frequently used in public safety. Serious games used in this arena focus on situations that require strategy, tactics, coordination, and communication (McGowan and Pecheux 2008). There are many situations in environmental health and safety where similar topics are extremely important for the workforce to understand. Often, if workers are not skilled in these topics, disastrous consequences could result.

In the use of serious error-based games, annotations on potentially dangerous actions should be included. In order for trainees to learn from their mistakes, they need to know what was wrong and not simply be able to skip to the next section. The feedback will contribute to trainees avoiding the mistake in future games as well as in real life (Martínez-Durá et al. 2011).

Review and Retention Activity

The Safety Sort training activity is described in this chapter.

Sort the cards (from Figure 18.4) into two piles: one with the safety training activities that are more likely to increase retention and transfer and the other with activities that are less likely to do so. To accomplish this, copy the image with the 12 cards and cut out each one, or simply mark each card with either a "+" to represent something that should be done or a "–" to represent something that should not be done.

Great Safety Training Sort

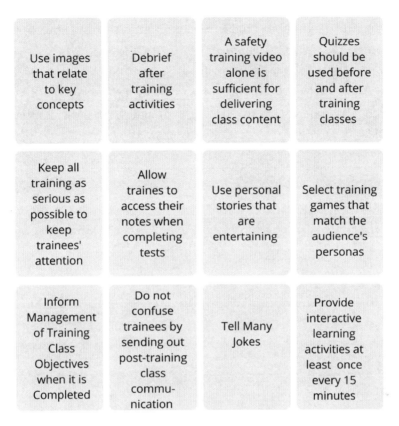

Figure 18.4 ✦ A great safety training sort activity

References

Bureau of Labor Statistics. 2020. "National Census of Fatal Occupational Injuries in 2019." Washington, D.C.: U.S. Department of Labor. Accessed December 20, 2020. https://www.bls.gov/news.release/pdf/cfoi.pdf.

Carnes, B. 2013. *Making E-learning Stick*. Alexandria, VA: American Society for Training and Development (ASTD) Press.

Dickinson, J. K., P. Woodward, R. Canas, S. Ahamed, and D. Lockston. 2011. "Game-based trench safety education: Development and lessons learned." *ITcon*, Vol. 16. *Special Issue Use of Gaming Technology in Architecture, Engineering and Construction*, pp. 119–134.

Martínez-Durá R. J., M. Arevalillo-Herráez, I. García-Fernández, M. A. Gamón-Giménez, and A. Rodríguez-Cerro. 2011. "Serious Games for

Health and Safety Training." In M. Ma, A. Oikonomou, and L. Jain, eds., *Serious Games and Edutainment Applications*. London: Springer. doi: 10.1007/978-1-4471-2161-9_7.

McGowan, C., and B. Pecheux. 2008. "Serious games that improve performance." *Sigma: information technology*, June:22–26.

Occupational Safety and Health Administration (OSHA). 2016. "Crushed by Carriage During Skyline Skidding Operation." *Fatal Facts*. Washington, D.C.: OSHA, No. 14-2016. https://www.osha.gov/Publications/OSHA3884.pdf.

Chapter 19
Sequencing Activities

Sequencing activities are interactive safety training exercises that can be used with any type of safety procedure or policy that involves the use of a specified set of steps that must be followed in a particular order. For example, the policies of many companies regarding energy control include specific steps for lockout-tagout procedures that must be followed by all employees. Other examples of such policies or procedures include fire extinguisher use, steps to follow when donning a safety harness, and safe steps to follow when cleaning up a hazardous waste spill. These policies may vary slightly from facility to facility, but in general, the order of the steps is the same. One workplace may have a ten-step procedure for deenergizing equipment safely, and another facility may have eight steps in its procedure. The exact number of steps is not important, what is important is that the trainees understand what is required in their specific facility. Sequencing activities are effective because they rely on a trainee's ability to remember information that was learned and to look critically at each step to decide where it best fits into an overall procedure.

The activities presented in this chapter include the use of teams, which further increases the value of sequencing activities. Very often, when these activities are used, there is a debate among team members about the correct order of the specific steps. This is important in helping trainees learn from one another. In sequencing activities, it can also be beneficial to add in a time component so that teams are racing against each other. When a team finishes the activity, the instructor performs a review, and if mistakes are found, the team must go back and try again. This is also beneficial because it includes the aspects of productive failure, as discussed in Chapter 14.

Sequencing Activities and Accelerated Learning
Safety sequencing activities also contain many of the major components of accelerated learning, including learning from one another, hands-on activity,

fun, and visual images. Trainees are working in teams while participating in safety sequence activities, and as discussed in Chapter 15, there are many learning benefits of teamwork. These activities, when used with a little bit of competition among the teams, also produce a level of fun, which increases trainee attention. Since most safety sequencing activities consist of an illustration of each step of a safety procedure printed on a separate paper or card, these activities provide the benefits of being hands-on learning and include the benefits of image-based safety training.

Creating Sequencing Activities

Safety sequencing activities are easy to create and have little or no expense associated with them. These activities can also be easily modified for groups of trainees that do not have a strong command of the English language or that may be illiterate. The benefits of image-based safety training are discussed in Chapter 24.

To create a new safety sequence activity, a safety procedure needs to be broken down into specific steps. Each step should be clearly explained and either written on an index card (one step per card), or preferably, illustrated with one image per card. If illustrations are not available or cannot be created in house, an alternative is to have an employee assist in the preparation of the activity by posing for a photograph while completing each step. The series of photographs can then be used in place of cards with text or cards with illustrations. Nevertheless, when using photographs or illustrations, it is also beneficial and recommended to use a small amount of text to accompany each photo or illustration for the purpose of providing further clarification. Once the steps are broken down and displayed on cards, copy the set of cards so that each group of trainees has a complete set. If there are four teams of trainees in the training class, each team should receive its own set of cards. It is important to mix up the cards before giving sets to teams. The best-case scenario occurs when the number of team members equals the number of steps in the procedure. For example, if there are ten steps in a lockout-tagout procedure, there should be ten team members in each group and at least two groups. If it is possible to match each team member to a step in the card stack, then each team member can be responsible for one particular step of the procedure. If this cannot happen, the steps should still be divided equally, if possible, between the members available. To illustrate how this activity works, the following describes a procedure for donning a fall protection harness.

Eight cards illustrate eight different steps involved with successfully donning a fall protection harness. The steps may be slightly different in different workplaces, but the steps shown in Figure 19.1 can easily be adjusted accordingly. In this example, imagine there are four teams of eight members each. Each team would receive one set of eight cards with each card having a different step of the donning procedure. It is important that the cards are not in the correct sequence when they are given to each team. The teams are told to have each team member be responsible for one step and then to arrange themselves in line in the correct order of the procedure. For example, the first step in putting on a harness is to "inspect the harness," so the team member holding that card

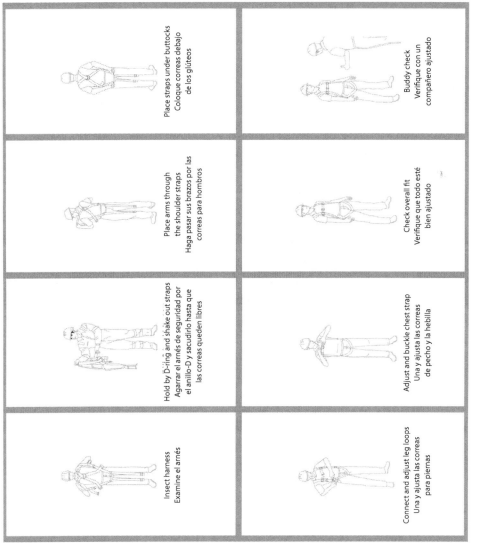

Figure 19.1 ✦ Fall protection harness safety sequence (Source: Tapp 2015)

would stand first in line. The last of the eight steps in this sample activity is "buddy check," so the team member holding that card would stand last in line.

When there is more than one team working on this interactive activity at the same time, an extra challenge can be posed to the teams by adding in competition. The teams can be told that there is a race to see which team can get its members into the correct sequence as quickly as possible and that the first team to do so correctly will be declared the champion. When this activity is used at the end of a safety training class, trainees should be told that they are not allowed to look back at their class notes. Whether or not the time variable is added, individual teams should still work together to determine the correct sequence of steps in the procedure. When one team believes it has finished, the members should raise their hands, and all teams should stop working while the instructor reviews what the team believes to be the correct sequence. As the facilitator reads out each step in a team's order, other teams may or may not be in agreement with the sequence that the supposedly winning team has come up with. If the team that thinks it has finished first does not have the steps in the correct order, the facilitator or instructor should tell the other teams to continue working and tell the first team to try again. Again, when one team thinks it has the correct order, members should raise their hands. The activity stops, and the facilitator again reviews the steps. Very often teams agree on all steps except for one or two, which they may have switched with another. This often leads to robust discussion as to why different teams believe different steps to be correct. When the instructor finally reviews the steps in the correct order, an additional level of review is being presented to the trainees. This repetition and reinforcement is important in increasing retention. This activity also serves as a type of evaluation since trainees are being required to show how well they have learned the material. Additionally, if they fail, this is going to increase learning as discussed in Chapter 14 on productive failure.

Debriefing Sequencing Activities

When the activity is complete, it is important to debrief the trainees on what they just learned from the activity and any other important observations that can be shared. In this instance, many teams will have rushed through the activity in order to come up with the solution faster than the other teams, and often this leads to mistakes. If the winning team's first attempt was not correct, then a discussion can be initiated about the negative effects of rushing to get something done and the consequences, particularly with respect to safety procedures. Questions can also be asked of the trainees regarding what process they went through to determine the correct order and how the teammates worked together to come to a consensus of what was right and what was wrong. This too can be turned into a discussion about how others can be influenced in the workplace when following safety procedures. If a more experienced, older employee insists that something is correct, does the group tend to follow that employee's advice even if some members have questions about its legitimacy? If this happened in a sequencing game, what would be the consequences if the same thing happened in the real world? The key to debriefing is to encourage discussion and reflection about the activity and what can be learned from it.

Applying Variations to the Activity

A variation of the sequencing activity can be achieved by removing one or more of the cards from the packs provided to each group of trainees before each team receives its cards and starts the exercise. For example, in the sequencing activity that covers the steps for donning a fall protection harness, two or more steps of this sequence could be removed before the activity begins. If these steps were removed or skipped in real life, there could be dire consequences, and the fall protection would not work as planned. In this variation, the cards should be given to the teams, and each team should be able to identify what important steps are missing after attempting to put the cards in the correct sequence. The activity could be made even more difficult by not informing teams of how many cards are missing. When a team identifies a step that should be included but is not, the members can approach the instructor and ask for the missing card. If they can describe what is illustrated on that card, the instructor can give them the missing card. Every time a team of trainees believes it has identified another missing step, it can approach the instructor and describe what is missing, and if that is indeed a missing step, the instructor gives the team that card. This activity should continue until each team believes it has the full set. As a bonus activity, the trainees could be told that they can propose additional safety steps if they think they are needed.

Blank cards could be available for safety training teams to write out or illustrate the new steps.

The additional modifications suggested in the previous paragraph add increasing levels of difficulty to the sequencing activities. As discussed in Chapter 11, adding difficulty or challenges to safety training activities is a great way to increase learning and retention. Activities shouldn't be so difficult that trainees give up and become frustrated, but a low level of difficulty can be highly beneficial.

Sample debriefing questions that could be used in this type of sequencing activity include questions such as:

- How did you identify what steps were missing?
- What can you do to remember the necessary steps once you are back at work?
- Are there any steps that could be combined?
- Are there any steps that could be eliminated?
- What additional steps would you like to add?
- How did the team work together to determine what steps were missing?
- What would happen if the missing steps were overlooked during the actual job?
- What would the consequences be?

As with other activities, the debriefing step is meant to increase discussion and may also bring to light any lack of understanding that may exist. By asking what the consequences would be if the step were skipped when the job was performed in the real world, the instructor is helping the trainees make the connection back to the job, which will in turn increase retention and transfer.

Review and Retention Activity

Sequencing activities are described in this chapter.

The following nine squares represent Gagné's Nine Events of Learning (discussed in Chapter 3), but as shown, they are not in the correct order. Make a copy of

Figure 19.2 ✦ A sequencing activity for Gagné's Nine Events of Learning

Figure 19.2, cut out each square and try to put the nine steps in the correct sequence. Alternatively, simply write a number (1–9) in each box to reflect the proper sequence of the nine events.

References
Tapp, L. 2015. *Safety Sequence: Putting Your Safety Training in Order.* Madison, NJ: Ennismore Publishing.

Chapter 20
Sorting Activities

Sorting activities in safety training classes are a great way to encourage teamwork and learning from peers. These activities are relatively easy to set up and can be specific and made to reflect a particular company or work area. Sorting activities are a type of retrieval practice that also leads to much discussion among trainees. Like some of the other activities described in this book, the end of the activity does not always result in correct answers, but instead the value is in the discussion that results. It is not uncommon to hear trainees argue a point in front of the class or with other teams when they believe their choice is correct. While this may initially seem like it would not be beneficial, the idea of having a trainee be so passionate about a safety topic or situation is very valuable. On many levels, the way the sorting activities are structured also makes it easy to have trainees imagine these situations and how they could affect day-to-day responsibilities, and this is important for information to be retained.

How to Use Sorting Activities

Safety Sort is an activity where trainees are asked to look at a list of hazards or conditions, usually written or printed on index cards, and then sort them into a variety of piles. Just like safety sequence activities, sorting activities are very inexpensive to use and create.

One way to use the safety sort activity is to ask trainees to sort the cards based on three conditions:

> Pile 1: hazards or conditions that would require immediate shut down of a work area

Pile 2: hazards that would require a priority work order and are expected to be completed by the end of the day

Pile 3: regular work-order requests or an email to department management with the expectation that the hazard would be taken care of in the very near future

Another way to use Safety Sort is to ask trainees to sort various work conditions into piles as described above, or in an order from most to least dangerous. This will involve teamwork and much discussion among team members. After the teams of trainees have sorted piles as directed, the trainer should facilitate a discussion that addresses why the teams sorted the piles the way they did. This activity will highlight where there may be differences in beliefs and where additional or follow-up training may be needed. Figure 20.1 shows a sample safety-sort card set created for a scaffolding safety class.

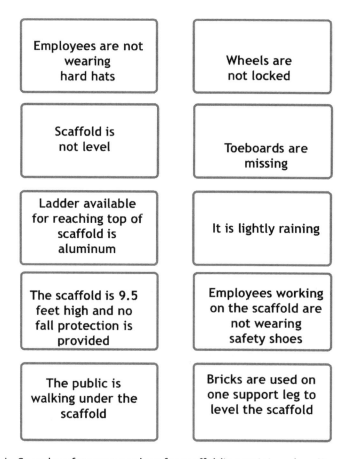

Figure 20.1 ✦ Sample safety-sort card set for scaffolding training class (Source: Tapp 2018)

Sample Sorting Activities

Lone Ranger

The Lone Ranger is an activity similar to Safety Sort. For the Lone Ranger sorting activity, a group of ten or more work orders with work requests are given to each group of trainees, and they are told to imagine that they are the sole maintenance engineer in their facility. Their job is to look at the ten work requests and prioritize them based on urgency. The Lone Ranger is good for training classes focused on a particular topic or related to a general work area. After each group of trainees has their items in priority order from one to ten, each group is asked to share what work order it would work on first and what work order it would address last. In almost all instances, groups of trainees are not going to have their ten work orders in the same order as other teams. While there is not necessarily a correct answer for this activity, the debriefing questions are key to its effectiveness. The trainer should ask things such as "Why do you think different teams had work orders placed in a different order?" and "What could be the result if different departments see things as a higher or lower priority than other departments?" This is an example of an activity where the discussion is significant. Another common discovery after this activity is completed is that a lack of information, diverse backgrounds, and a variety of experiences among trainees can result in different perceptions, and these can affect safety actions.

While You Were Out

When doing this activity with a group of supervisors or management, a simple variation can be added to the activity. This safety sorting activity is called While You Were Out. It is similar to Lone Ranger, but in this instance, phone messages are written with requests related to safety from various departments. The trainees are told that they just returned from vacation and are given the stack of messages. Each message presents a different situation or concern within a department or across the entire facility. Their job is to again prioritize the concerns and decide what they will work on personally, what they are able to delegate, and what can be ignored. Having trainees sort information in this way requires them to rely on all of their past experiences and many of the past training sessions they have attended in order to make wise decisions. Whenever they reflect on what they learned in the past to solve current problems, they are making valuable connections that will help them retain information longer.

This activity can easily be customized to a particular workplace, making it even more relatable to groups of trainees. As an example, take a list of the most frequent safety inspection findings over the past year or across several years. Each of these findings can be generalized and listed as a separate item on one of the cards to be sorted. If that information is not available or if a wider variety of items are needed for sorting, similar information can usually be found for different industries online. The main idea is to include different conditions or findings that the trainees might actually face or find in their workplace. This version of safety sort presents them with the challenge of deciding what is more hazardous in their actual work environment and why.

Match Game

Another type of sorting activity that is more hands on is Match Game. This can be used for safety procedures where decisions must be made from a variety of choices, such as container labeling or personal protective equipment selection. To use Match Game as a safety training activity for a class on personal protective equipment (PPE), a number of different types of PPE should be written on index cards and a stack should be given to each group of trainees. Each team's stack of cards will be the same, but each team should write a team name on each of their cards. It is usually necessary to include multiple copies of each type of PPE in each card set since the same PPE will probably be necessary for the various jobs/tasks in the activity. Before the class, the trainer needs to identify at least ten different jobs/tasks in the facility and write those jobs/tasks on cards or pieces of paper. Once in the training room, the cards should be distributed around the room in different locations. Trainees should be told to meet with their team and look through the PPE options included in their stack of cards and begin to think about which jobs/tasks require which pieces of PPE. When the trainer instructs trainees to start, the teams should walk around the training room and place the appropriate PPE cards in front of the job or task cards that would require that type of PPE. The PPE selected to go with each job/task should be the PPE that is necessary for that job or task to be completed safely. When all cards have been placed, trainees should return to their seats, and the trainer should go to each job/task card and read out the PPE cards that have been placed in front of each. The trainer can verify if the teams accurately placed the PPE with the right jobs/tasks and lead a discussion about the choices that were made. This provides a review and reinforcement that will help retention of the content. The activity also helps trainees to learn how to make decisions about PPE selection, and this skill can be transferred back to the work environment.

A similar Match Game and setup can work well with safety training classes addressing chemical storage. To set this up, a photo of storage options available in a facility can be placed around a classroom. Storage options may include locations such as fume hoods, lab refrigerators, flammable storage cabinets, or designated hazardous material storage areas. Teams can be given cards with different chemicals or products written on them and instructed to place the cards with chemical or product names in the proper storage location. Better yet, and only if it can be done safely, empty chemical or product containers could be given to teams and they can place the containers in the appropriate storage locations in the training room.

For a chemical labeling exercise as part of a class covering the Global Hazard Classification System (GHS), teams of trainees could be given GHS symbol stickers, and various chemicals and products can be placed around the room. Teams would then need to walk around the room and place the appropriate stickers on the images or the empty containers of the chemicals and products. Match Game can work well for any topic that requires trainees to know information before making the best choice from a variety of options. Although Match Game isn't as obvious a sorting activity as the other sorting activities mentioned earlier, trainees are still required to sort through the information in their minds and sort through a variety of options.

Sorting by Probable Cause

Accident causes can also be sorted in a training activity and would be a good way to get trainee attention at the beginning of a class. A one sentence description of a number of accidents can be written on index cards. After each team has a set of cards, preferably 20 or more cards per set, the trainer should instruct the teams to sort the accident cards by probable cause. The trainer can let the teams come up with their own categories or can provide four or five general, high-level categories. The teams should be given time to discuss the accidents and decide together on a probable cause. The accidents on the cards can be accidents that actually occurred within an organization (with all

BORED TRAINEES	SUPERVISORS NOT SUPPORTIVE	TRAINEES TALKING	TRAINEES NOT RETURNING FROM BREAK
TRAINEES FAILING QUIZ	TRAINEES NOT VOLUN-TEERING	TRAINEES MISSING SCHEDULED MAKE-UP CLASSES	NOT ENOUGH TRAINING SUPPLIES
PROJECTOR BREAKING MID-CLASS	TRAINEES CONFUSED BY TRAINING GAME	TRAINEES NOT WILLING TO PARTICIPATE IN GAME	TRAINEES NOT REMEM-BERING CONTENT IN 1 MONTH
TRAINEES NOT USING WHAT THEY LEARNED IN CLASS	TRAINEES NOT KNOWING WHERE TO ACCESS INFO AFTER TRAINING	TRAINEES SLEEPING	NO FUNDING FOR TRAINING PROGRAMS
SUPERVISORS ASSIGNING TRAINING AS CORRECTIVE MEASURE	TRAINEES SKIPPING REFRESHER SAFETY TRAINING	TRAINEES TEXTING TO FRIENDS DURING CLASS	TRAINEES GIVING POOR EVALUATIONS TO TRAINER
SUPERVISORS SKIPPING TRAINING CLASSES	TRAINING BUDGET SLASHED	FIRE DRILL DURING TRAINING CLASS	HYPERLINKS IN ONLINE TRAINING CLASS FAIL

Figure 20.2 ✦ Probable cause sorting activity

personal information removed) or made up of the typical types of accidents that might occur in that industry. After the teams have finished their sorting, the trainer should lead the discussion and review, asking what causes teams identified and what specific accident cards were assigned to each cause. This activity is valuable because it follows the principles of accelerated learning, plus it forces the trainees to reflect on how specific accidents could have occurred. If they later find themselves in a situation that equates to an identified probable cause, the exercise will hopefully help them recall the accident that followed it and will remind them to follow the safety procedures they have been trained to use.

Review and Retention Activity

Probable cause sorting activities are described in this chapter.

Each card in Figure 20.2 lists a brief description of a training challenge or situation. Sort the cards into piles by probable cause of the challenging situation. One pile should reflect challenges or situations that are attributed to the trainer; a second pile should contain challenges and situations that are probably due to the actions of management; and a third pile should reflect those reasonably attributed to the attendees themselves. This figure can be copied, and the cards cut out and sorted, or alternatively, an initial representing each group (T for trainer, M for management, and A for attendee) can be written in each box.

References

Tapp, L. 2018. *Activities for OSHA Outreach Trainers*. Madison, NJ: Ennismore Publishing.

Chapter 21
Repetition and Retrieval Activities

The importance of using repetition and retrieval to increase retention and the likelihood that training content will be remembered when needed has been described throughout this book. Repetition activities can be as simple as getting trainees to rephrase what they learned or more formally planned through the use of reinforcement activities. The value of repetition can be even greater if the frequency of repetitions are increased and spaced out over time.

Getting Started

For longer classes, such as those that last 8 hours or more over the course of several days, the repetition can begin during the class and can continue throughout the entire class. A safety trainer can add in repetition activities throughout a training class by simply providing a quick review or summary of the class material. If the trainer repeats this review, preferably in different formats, throughout the class, this is an easy way for a safety trainer to add in repetition. For example, if a safety trainer is discussing five safe steps involved with performing a certain procedure, those five steps could be shown at the beginning of the class and then again after one or two other topics have been covered. Coming back to those five steps, and simply asking trainees to remember and state what those five steps were, is also repetition. After this second review, the trainer should continue on with the lesson. After another short period of time, the trainer again says, "Okay, one more time, what were those five steps?" Every time a trainer asks for the five steps to be repeated, and allows trainees the time to guess what those five steps were, and follows up with feedback on the correct answers, a trainer is helping them retain important information longer. The first time a trainer asks for the five steps, the trainees could be provided with a piece of paper that simply shows the numbers 1 to 5, and they should be asked to write each of the five points in the appropriate area. The second time the trainer provides an opportunity for repetition, an image could be provided that illustrates all five points with no text at all. For this review, the trainer would ask trainees to write what is represented by each image. The third time the trainer provides an activity for repetition, a simple training game could be used.

Snowball Fight and Ask in the Airplane

Snowball Fight is an example of a retrieval activity that works great as an opener. Snowball Fight can be played by giving each trainee a piece of paper to write down one of the five points. After each trainee has written down one of the five steps on the piece of paper, the trainer asks the trainees to crumple their papers into a ball. The trainer should then tell them that, on the count of three, they are going to throw their snowball across the room so that it lands near another trainee. This activity usually surprises many trainees since they were probably not expecting to do something like this in a training class, and as discussed in Chapter 7, novelty and surprise are great ways to get and keep trainee attention. Once the paper balls are thrown, trainees should pick up one of the snowballs and read the step on that piece of paper. After each trainee has a new piece of paper, the trainees should be told to stand in line in the order of the five steps. For example, the trainees who picked up step number 1 would stand at the front of the line and the trainees that picked up step number 5 would stand at the end of the line. Once the lines are formed, the trainer can review the five steps once again. This can also help the trainer identify if any one of the five steps seems more difficult for the trainees to remember than others. If no one wrote down step 3 on their paper before throwing it, it might mean that step 3 is the least remembered of the five, and the trainer can make adjustments going forward to make sure that all steps are seen as important and perhaps spend some additional time on that step. By doing the same repetition activity three different ways, the trainees are repeatedly forming connections to the content in their minds, and it will be remembered for a longer time.

Another version of Snowball Fight is called Ask in the Airplane. Instead of having trainees write on a piece of paper and crumple it to form a snowball, they are instead asked to make their paper into a paper airplane. Instead of throwing a snowball across the room, the trainee throws the paper airplane. Depending on the audience, the trainer can select which version is best. The paper airplane method usually takes more time, as some people are very particular about how they like to fold their paper into airplanes. Plus, it is important to tell trainees to be careful not to throw a pointy paper airplane into the face of another trainee.

Repetition through Pre- and Postclass Communication

To increase the number of times a trainee interacts with the content, the first time the information is presented to trainees can occur even before class begins. When inviting trainees to a training class that is going to cover five specific safety steps, those five steps should be included in the precourse communication. If the trainees receive an email or paper notice or even a poster advertising the training class, the five points should be included in all of these types of announcements. This should ensure that the trainees have at least seen the content once before showing up to class. At the beginning of class, when the five steps are covered, it will already be the second time the information is presented to the trainees.

Additionally, the five steps should again be repeated after the class is over. This could be as simple as sending out a text a few days after class that lists the five points, or sending out an email that does the same thing. To break it down even further, step 1 could be sent out on day one after the training class. Step 2 could be sent out the second day after the training class, and so on. If the budget allows, the trainer could set up a simple contest asking trainees to submit their answers to the question "What were the five steps?" in exchange for the chance to win a small prize. Small prizes could be something as simple as a voucher for a free lunch in the company cafeteria or a gift card for a local coffee shop.

For longer classes that take place over the course of a day or more, repetition could be added into the class through the use of beginning- and end-of-day training games. Many of these activities can also be used at various points throughout a training class. Several safety training games that support repetition of safety training content are described later in this chapter.

The benefits of retrieval practice have been described in detail in Chapter 13. Retrieval practice works, but it is difficult and so may be avoided by some people. Integrating the technique of retrieval practice with interactive training activities can provide great learning and retention opportunities. One way to do this is with flash-card activities. Flash-card activities work really well for a specific type of retrieval—when there is a pairing between a specific question and a particular response. An example of this in safety training would be the identification of safety symbols, key safety words or specific knowledge (e.g., crane hand signals), Global Hazard Classification System (GHS) symbols, or safety-related definitions. Many people grew up using flash cards to study and memorize information—and for good reason. Flash cards are effective because they promote learning and retention through repetition, retrieval practice, and spacing.

Flash Cards

The German scientist Sebastian Leitner developed his own system for spaced practice of flash cards, known as the Leitner box system. The *Leitner box system* was a series of four different boxes with the first box containing the study materials that needed to be reviewed frequently because mistakes were often made with those materials. The second box contained flash cards with material the user was pretty good at remembering, and therefore were viewed less often. The third box included flash cards that were reviewed even less often than those in the second box. Finally, the fourth box held cards that were reviewed the least. When using a system such as the Leitner box, flash cards selected and not answered correctly are moved to the next box up, so they will have to be reviewed more often. For example, if a card were drawn from box two, and the answer was not known, it would be moved to box one. The idea behind the Leitner box system is that the better something is known, the less often it has to be practiced, and although a piece of information is known extremely well, it will never completely disappear from the review (Brown et al. 2014).

A safety trainer can create learning activities based on the Leitner box system as a way to increase repetition and add retrieval practice to safety training classes. A series of flash cards could be created based on a particular safety topic. Imagine safety trainees need to learn 100 technical terms in order to do their job safely. Safety trainees could review these cards in teams, and whenever a card is guessed correctly, it would be put into the next box down. (A card from box one would be moved to box two, and a card from box two would be moved to box three, and so on). All of the safety terms would be reviewed in this manner. Teams could work on this activity for a set amount of time based on the length of the class. When time is up, teams should share what cards remain in the first box, that is, the cards that need the most review. By doing this, the trainer not only provides additional focus on the cards that are giving trainees difficulty, but also provides additional review of these cards. The use of a box here is only symbolic, and although the activity could be done with boxes numbered one to four given to each team, asking teams to use four separate piles to represent boxes works equally well.

One type of flash-card activity that relies on repetition is based on the familiar game of Jeopardy. Many safety professionals are familiar with some of the off-the-shelf Jeopardy games available, and these are a good way to gamify content. The version described here, Jeopardy Flashcard, is slightly different and includes opportunities to benefit from repetition.

To create and use a Jeopardy Flashcard activity, a stack of index cards would be needed for each topic in the game. If five different topics need to be covered, a trainer would then come up with ten different open-ended questions for each of those topics and write one on the front of each card. On the back of each card, the answer to each question is written. As teams play the game, cards are recycled and put back in the stack if a training team does not know the answer. Since that card will now get reviewed again, repetition is created. By asking an open-ended question on the front of each card, the benefits of retrieval practice are also included. If trainees are presented with the same game at a future training class, the benefits of spacing are added as well.

Safety Flash

Safety Flash is another flash-card training game that uses the benefits of repetition and retrieval practice. Many people grow up using flash cards to study everything from foreign languages to vocabulary words to math formulas. Many safety professionals use them when studying for certification exams. There are even a variety of applications that take the basic flash-card idea and use a technology-based approach. One of the more popular examples of this is Quizlet. Many people prefer flash cards because they can be carried around easily and can be very effective. One of the main reasons they are effective is because of the repetition of the material. If there is a stack of flash cards for reviewing material, they are not being looked at just once, but multiple times over and over again. Flash cards can be more effective if they are put down and then picked up again several days later so that the review is spaced out. If this process is repeated a week or so later, it is even more beneficial to long-term retention.

In Safety Flash, there are two sets of identical flash cards and two teams of trainees. It can be an especially interesting and inclusive activity if these flash cards are designed to be very large. This can be accomplished by putting the flash cards on poster boards, although this takes a little more planning. To play Safety Flash, the teams or pairs of trainees stand on opposite sides in lines facing each other. Each line has its own stack of cards/poster boards, and the cards in each stack should be in a different order. The first trainee in each line shows a flash card to the person on the other side. The person on the other side must give the correct answer to that card. If a trainee answers correctly, they get to collect that card and add it to their pile. If the trainee does not answer correctly, they do not get to collect that card and it gets put on the bottom of the stack. This continues until either a particular amount of time has passed or until one group of trainees has collected all of the cards from the other team's stack. It can sometimes be better if each stack of training cards is different, but this may not be possible depending on the topic. If it's a safety training topic that covers a large amount of information, it may not be very hard to come up with 40 different flash cards so that 20 can be given to each team. If there are only ten different items covered in the training class, it may be necessary to give the exact same set of cards to each team.

To make flash cards for safety training more useful, they could be created with only one phrase, question, or image on the front and nothing on the back. When the trainees are shown the cards, they should be asked to write or say the answer. Without any information on the back, trainees will not be able to flip the card over quickly to see if they are correct or get a hint about the correct answer. Not being able to access the correct answer immediately is better for increasing long-term memory. Very often the tendency is to flip the card over quickly to see the answer before enough mental struggle has been done to retrieve the answer from memory. It is better for long-term retention to have this struggle.

Depending on the characteristics of the trainees, a trainer may prefer to do Safety Flash as a team activity. Instead of one trainee at a time acting as a team representative, each team can play as one. Each time the other side shows a card, the team can huddle and come up with an answer. The rest of the game would proceed as described above. Similarly, the game can be played with two trainees against two trainees.

Free Recall

As discussed in Chapter 11 on retrieval methods, free recall is an extremely effective way of learning new information and retaining it for the long term. After watching a safety video or attending a safety training presentation, if trainees are asked to write down everything they can remember on a blank piece of paper, they will probably find this very difficult. This difficulty is actually helpful. By forcing the trainees to recall the main points, they'll be able to remember the safety training information better later. Using one-sided flash cards is an easy way to encourage free recall.

A safety training activity based on this idea of free recall is called Braindump. To facilitate the Braindump activity in a safety training class, each trainee is given a blank sheet of paper and something to write with. If this activity is being done virtually, a trainee can simply do the same thing at home or type into an empty word processing document on their screen. After presentation of the training content, the trainee should be asked to write down everything he or she can remember from the training class. After a specified amount of time, the trainees can share what they remembered. It is probable that different trainees will have remembered different aspects of the training, so after everyone has taken turns sharing their braindump, this will have provided a more complete review of the content. Trainees should be told not to look at their notes when attempting free recall activities.

Movie Reviewer

A similar idea can be used with an activity called Movie Reviewer. If a training program relies heavily on safety training videos, the same idea behind Braindump can be used in this context. Instead of simply asking trainees to write down everything they remember, the trainer can ask them to meet with their team after viewing the video and work to identify the main safety points covered and also to note when they were covered in the video. The trainees can also be asked to act as a movie reviewer and discuss whether or not certain points were delivered effectively and what could have been done better. The purpose of this activity is not to tell the trainee what those points were, but to let them first come up with those points before they critique them.

Another type of retrieval activity is to ask trainees to design quizzes for the other members of their class as they are participating in the class in real time. Instead of encouraging trainees to take notes during a topic presentation, the trainees should be told to write questions related to the topic as the topics are presented and that these questions will be used to quiz their classmates after the session. By encouraging trainees to take notes in the form of questions instead of statements, they are creating material that can help them practice retrieval later on. For example, in a machine guarding class, one note a trainee may jot down is that "Nip points are associated with rotating action." If the trainee were taking notes as questions instead, he or she could write,

"What type of motion are nip points associated with?" At the end of the class, trainees will each have a list of questions that could be used as a quiz and also used as a mini-lesson in microlearning. Questions created by trainees can be collected and sent out as texts as a way not only to provide repetition and retrieval but also reinforcement.

To incorporate the benefits of retrieval practice with safety training activities, activities that require all trainees to retrieve the content, and not just one individual, are the best way to make the most of this learning tool. If an individual trainee were called on to answer a question, the benefits of retrieval practice would not be fully realized. For example, an activity like Safety Bingo, described next, requires all trainees to think actively about what the correct answer could be. All trainees would be going through this process at the same time.

Safety Bingo

Safety Bingo is basically played like any other bingo game but with one big exception—most regular bingo games are purely based on luck, safety bingo is based on knowledge. Regular bingo involves the random selection of a letter and number, and if that letter/number combination is found on a participant's game card, it is crossed off. Random letters and numbers are drawn until a participant is able to cross off all boxes down, across, or on a diagonal, and that

Padded Grip	Pinch Point	Correct Tool	Wear & Damage	Moving Parts
Light Curtain	Vibration	Excessive Force	Repetitive Motion	Caustic
Burns	Dermatitis	FREE	Puncture	Lock-Out/Tag-Out
Leather Gloves	Latex Gloves	Jewelry	Missing Guards	Heat
Two-Hand Controls	Away From the Body	Good Housekeeping	RSI	Neoprene

Figure 21.1 ✦ Safety Bingo sample for hand safety

person is then declared the lucky winner. In Safety Bingo, each box on the bingo card is filled with a key word or phrase related to the class content (Figure 21.1). Instead of random letters and numbers being called, the trainer reads a description that is related to the class topic that matches one of the words or phrases found on the bingo card (Figure 21.2). When the trainees hear

---

Hand Safety BINGO Call Sheet

Directions: Explain to the trainees that you will be reading a clue for each of the words on their BINGO cards. If they think the clue you read matches one of the words in a square, they should cross it off. When they cross off 5 in a row (up or down) or on the diagonal, they should yell "BINGO!"

To begin, randomly select one of the clues below and read it aloud slowly and clearly. Be sure to read only the clue and not the answer. Continue until someone yells BINGO. When you have a winner, ask them to read the words in the boxes they crossed off to make sure they selected the right ones for the clues you read. If there is a mistake, continue reading clues until another trainee has yelled BINGO.

Clue 1: A general term for injuries related to poor ergonomics **Answer:** RSI
Clue 2: A workplace hazard that can result in burns. **Answer:** Heat
Clue 3: An alternative to traditional guards. Also considered a presence detection device. **Answer:** Light Curtain
Clue 4: These type of injuries can result from excessive heat or some chemicals **Answer:** Burns
Clue 5: A great glove when working with mercury or pcbs. **Answer:** Neoprene
Clue 6: Good gloves for handling rough objects. **Answer:** Leather Gloves
Clue 7: Doing the same thing over and over may cause this type of injury **Answer:** Repetitive Motion
Clue 8: When this unsafe situation occurs, injuries are more likely to occur because body parts may be exposed to moving parts. **Answer:** Missing Guards
Clue 9: This type of procedure/policy can stop a machine or equipment from being accidentally started while it is being worked on. **Answer:** Lock-Out/Tag-Out
Clue 10: _____ & _____ from normal use of tools, can cause them to not work properly and this can lead to injuries. **Answer:** Wear & Damage
Clue 11: This can help reduce the negative effects of working with vibrating tools. **Answer:** Padded Grip
Clue 12: Keeps an operator's hands away from the point of operation during an entire machine stroke. **Answer:** Two Hand Controls
Clue 13: Rings are one type of this which should not be worn when working with machinery. **Answer:** Jewelry
Clue 14: Keeping tools clean and grease free are this type of activity **Answer:** Good Housekeeping
Clue 15: When using any type of knife, you should cut in this direction **Answer:** Away from the body
Clue 16: Exposure to some chemicals can cause this type of skin condition **Answer:** Dermatitis
Clue 17: A hazard area between moving and stationary parts of a machine where a body part can become caught. **Answer:** Pinch Point
Clue 18: By using this for a specific job, injuries are less likely to occur **Answer:** Correct Tool
Clue 19: Where these exist on a machine, there is an increased likelihood of injury unless some type of guard is in place **Answer:** Moving Parts
Clue 20: Repeated exposure to high levels of this (a physical movement) may lead to injuries such as HAVS. **Answer:** Vibration
Clue 21: This is a major factor contributing to RSIs. **Answer:** Excessive Force
Clue 22: This type of chemical (example sodium hydroxide) can cause burns to skin. **Answer:** Caustic
Clue 23: This type of injury is caused by a pointy object, has a small entry hole and little blood. **Answer:** Puncture
Clue 24: This type of glove is not very resistant to chemicals but good for bloodborne pathogens. **Answer:** Latex Gloves

Figure 21.2 ✦ Sample Safety Bingo call sheet for hand safety

this description, they need to think about what they learned in the class (i.e., retrieve the information) and come up with the correct answer and then look for that answer on their bingo card. If they have the correct answer on their safety bingo card, they can cross it off, and the game proceeds much like regular bingo. The trainer keeps reading clues, and if the trainees have the answer to that clue on their safety bingo card, they cross it off. The first trainee to get all boxes on a particular line across or down or on a diagonal crossed off is declared the winner.

To make Safety Bingo most effective, the trainer needs to review the correct answers after the game is completed. The best way to do that is to ask the winner or winners to read off the words that he or she has crossed off. As the trainee reads off those words, the trainer can ask the rest of the class what clue goes with that word. This step provides an additional level of review for the entire class. The entire activity utilizes retrieval practice, and this secondary review is an additional level of repetition.

Safety Bingo can be a great way to repeat class content in a game form. One issue that may arise is that a group of trainees does not have good reading skills. In this instance, Safety Bingo can be modified to an image-based version called Safety Lotería. Safety Lotería and other image-based safety training activities are described in Chapter 25.

Retrieval activities should be considered ways to help trainees learn and not as ways to test trainees. By keeping the retrieval practice as an activity and not a test, the retrieval activity will not cause anxiety and should make it easier for trainees to understand that mistakes are okay—both major factors in learning, as discussed in Chapter 14.

Feedback is central to using retrieval activities as ways to increase retention. In the activities discussed in this chapter, feedback is especially important in helping trainees learn and retain information. The more detailed the feedback, the better the learning. If trainers only list or present correct answers, the activities will not be as effective as if detailed explanations in the form of feedback were provided.

Clickers and Feedback

Another option for repetition and retrieval activities involves the use of clickers or index cards. *Clickers*, small handheld units or weblinks that send answers to a trainer, are a technology-based alternative to using feedback cards to do the same thing. Clickers or feedback cards can be used to provide mini-quizzes, which can be a great way to keep trainees focused if offered every 10 minutes or so. To use feedback cards—the nontechnological version of clickers—a trainer needs to give four index cards to each trainee along with a marker, and each trainee can then be asked to write the numbers 1, 2, 3, and 4 on the back of each of the index cards. When ready, the trainer can either verbally ask a question that has four different answers or present the question on a slide. The trainees can then be told to hold up the number of the correct answer. When using handheld clickers, the trainees would simply select either number 1, 2, 3, or 4 on the clicker.

One of the benefits of using clickers and this design of feedback cards is that trainees will not easily be able to see others' answers. If the room setup does not allow trainees to answer without fear of being wrong in front of their coworkers, they can be asked to pass their index card to the front of the room instead of holding it up for the instructor to see. When a trainer sees all of the answers at once, either through clicker responses or from feedback cards, the trainer can see what most trainees believe to be the correct answer. Clickers and feedback cards will curtail embarrassment if trainees are unable to see the answers of others.

When trainees answer individually this way, they are also unaffected by what others may think. Since no one other than the instructor will see a particular answer, trainees can select the answer that they truly believe is correct. A trainer can receive valuable feedback as to what may or may not be confusing during the course of the class. By asking short questions throughout a training class, trainers can get real-time feedback on the understanding of trainees instead of waiting to see the results of an end-of-class exam. If a question is asked 10 minutes into a training class and more than half of the trainees answer incorrectly, the trainer can spend more time where needed, which can be especially important in classes where later content builds on foundational information presented in the beginning.

After all trainees have answered, and the correct answer is shared, the trainer should specify why the other answers were not correct and why the correct answer is the one that should have been selected. Although this is somewhat like a quiz, it is not graded and should not be seen as something threatening to the trainees. In this instance, these very short one-question quizzes are a repetition activity and will increase retention. Short quizzes using clickers or feedback cards are also a retrieval activity since the trainees are responsible for recalling the correct answer based on information they previously learned. Every time the information is retrieved, more connections are built for retaining it longer.

To use a similar activity when training is delivered through a platform such as Zoom, trainees could be asked to send their answer to the trainer in the chat box by private message. It may be necessary to show trainees how to send a chat message to one person and not to everyone on whatever platform is being used, but this can be an easy way for trainees to share their answers privately. Applications such as Kahoot can also be used to offer questions with opportunities to provide answers privately during a training class. Applications such as this often provide the option for trainees to submit their answers through their mobile phones, which can work with both in-person and virtual classes.

As with the other activities described in this book, a pivotal step for using it correctly in a safety training class is what happens after the activity is done. Giving feedback, which would involve which answer was correct and why, as well as having trainees think about where this information is going to be useful once they return to their job, is vital to retention. It is also one of the most important reasons for debriefing activities being an integral part of all safety training activities.

Review and Retention Activity

Safety Bingo is one of the repetition and retrieval activities described in this chapter.

Safety Bingo is not intended to be played alone, but for the purpose of showing how this activity can be used to increase retention through repetition, a sample safety bingo sheet focusing on repetition and retrieval activities is provided, as well as a clue sheet. To use this activity as a review, look at the clues and then find the answer to each clue on the bingo card (Figure 21.3). When found, cross it off. In a classroom bingo game, clues would continue to be read until one of the participants has crossed off all squares across, down, or on the diagonal. As a solo review activity, attempt to answer all of the clues. If successful, every box on the bingo card is crossed off.

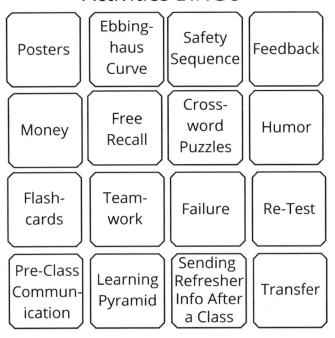

Figure 21.3 ✦ Repetition and retrieval activity—Safety Bingo

Review and Retention Bingo Clues

1. An example of a technique that involves sending out key points to be covered in a training class before trainees attend a class
2. A retrieval activity that takes advantage of the benefits of asking trainees to struggle to remember content
3. A method of repetition involving frequent attempts to recall key facts
4. A simple form of reinforcement in the workplace that can be improved as a reinforcement activity by removing some of the information
5. A form of quiz/evaluation that is disguised as a game
6. An evaluation that serves as retrieval practice
7. Trainees working together to learn from each other
8. This shows the amount of material forgotten (decay) over time
9. Something lost if training is done poorly and does not provide the intended outcome

10. A training activity that works well with safety procedures that involve a particular set of steps that must be done in a particular order
11. The experience of getting something wrong as a way of increasing retention
12. An example of postclass communication
13. An image that is often used to show the effectiveness of different types of learning
14. All learning activities are more effective if this is provided immediately after the activity is completed
15. Adding this, as appropriate, to a training class engenders positive memories, which can increase retention
16. The word for the act of taking what was learned in a training event and applying it on the job when needed

References

Brown, P. C., H. L. Roediger, and M. A. McDaniel. 2014. *Make It Stick: The Science of Successful Learning.* Cambridge, MA: Belknap Press, an imprint of Harvard University Press.

Chapter 22
Summarizing Activities

Some activities are best done after the formal part of the training session has been completed. These types of activities usually involve some type of reflection or the need to ask trainees to summarize important information. By doing these two things, trainers are helping trainees realize how they are going to use this information once they are back at work, and this is central to increasing the chance that the information will transfer. These activities can be as simple as asking trainees questions about the content, but a better approach would be to get the trainees to make up questions and ask them of each other.

Summary Quizzes
Have teams of trainees create quizzes for the other teams of trainees. This will force them to think about all the content that was covered, and they will undoubtedly realize what information they may not have learned as well as they should have. In addition to writing out the quiz questions, the teams will also need to develop answer sheets; however, they will not share the answer sheet until after the other team has had a chance to answer the test questions.

Creative Activities
If trainees are agreeable, trainers can have them participate in a more creative activity. They can be asked to summarize what they learned in class by creating a story using all of the main topics covered in the class. Alternatively, trainees could be asked to draw a picture either individually or with a partner that demonstrates the key concepts. These illustrations could then be shown to the rest of the class to see if they can guess what was drawn. When people try to guess, they are searching through their memories to identify what they learned in the past, and this in itself is a way to increase long-term retention.

Infographics are a great way to summarize focal points from a training class. Although creating infographics might be too detailed and lengthy of an activity for your trainees to do during a training session, infographics created by others can be modified and used as training activities (Tapp 2020). A few ways to do this are delineated below.

Sample Summarizing Activities

Infographics

A one-page infographic is a good example of a summarizing activity because it reflects all of the content from the training class, but it also allows trainees to benefit from the use of retrieval practice. To use an infographic as a

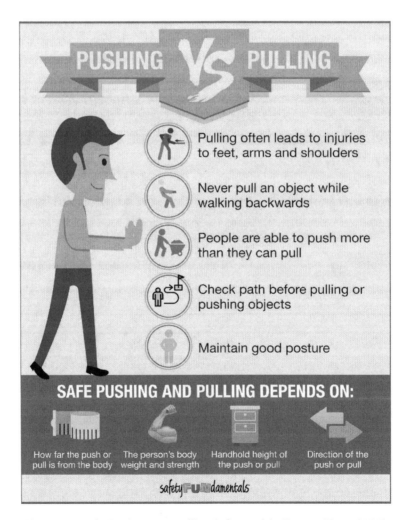

Figure 22.1 ✦ Pushing vs. pulling infographic (Source: Tapp 2020)

fill-in-the-blank activity, the trainer takes an existing infographic and removes some of the basic information. Each team of trainees should be given a copy of the modified infographic and asked to discuss what information should be added to make the infographic complete. This activity is best done after the class information has already been presented to trainees, so they will have heard the information at least once before they attempt to complete the missing information. After trainees have finished completing the infographic, the trainer needs to review the information with the class as a whole, solicit the correct answers from trainees, and then share the appropriate feedback. Figure 22.1 shows an infographic and Figure 22.2 shows the same infographic modified to be used as a fill-in-the-blank training activity.

Figure 22.2 ✦ Pushing vs. pulling infographic as a fill-in-the-blank activity (Source: Tapp 2020)

Figure 22.3 ✦ Most Frequent Violations as a sample infographic (Source: Tapp 2020)

Infographics can also be used to help trainees create a story. When trainees are asked to create a safety training story, they often think back and rely on information they learned during a training class. The sample infographic shown in Figure 22.3 is one that could be used internally as a summary of all the common safety hazards found within a particular facility. Getting the message across about typical safety hazards that trainees work with can be much more interesting when presented as a visual illustration such as this. To use it as an activity for creating a story (Figure 22.4), the infographic can be presented to groups of trainees after the training class has been completed and trainees have been told to make up a story about an accident that was the result of the items shown on the infographic. Trainers need to tell the trainees it is important to be very specific when creating their story. For example, if a common hazard found in the facility is cords across the floor, trainees should specifically say where those cords were located when they create their story. The made-up stories should be specific to the trainees' workplace. After each group has had the appropriate time to create a story, each team needs

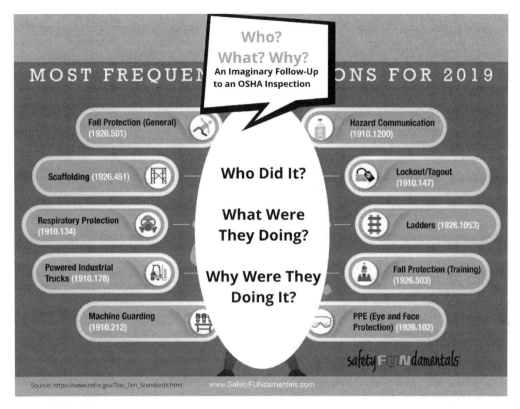

Figure 22.4 ✦ Most Frequent Violations as a safety training activity (Source: Tapp 2020)

to share its story with the rest of the class. This activity is bound to result in a lot of laughs, which are usually welcome in a safety training class. In addition to being humorous and helping trainees to relax, funny stories and laughter will help trainees remember the information longer. Also, when trainees are working to create their story and are thinking of actual locations and situations where the hazards could exist, they are cementing the information in their memories, which helps them realize where it may apply in their day-to-day work.

A–Z Race

Another very simple and inexpensive summarizing training activity is called the A–Z race (see Figure 22.5).

When using the A–Z Race at the end of a training class, the trainees are first put into small teams and given a piece of paper. It's best if these teams are composed of between four and six people. One person in the team needs to take the sheet of paper and draw a line down the center. Next, one member

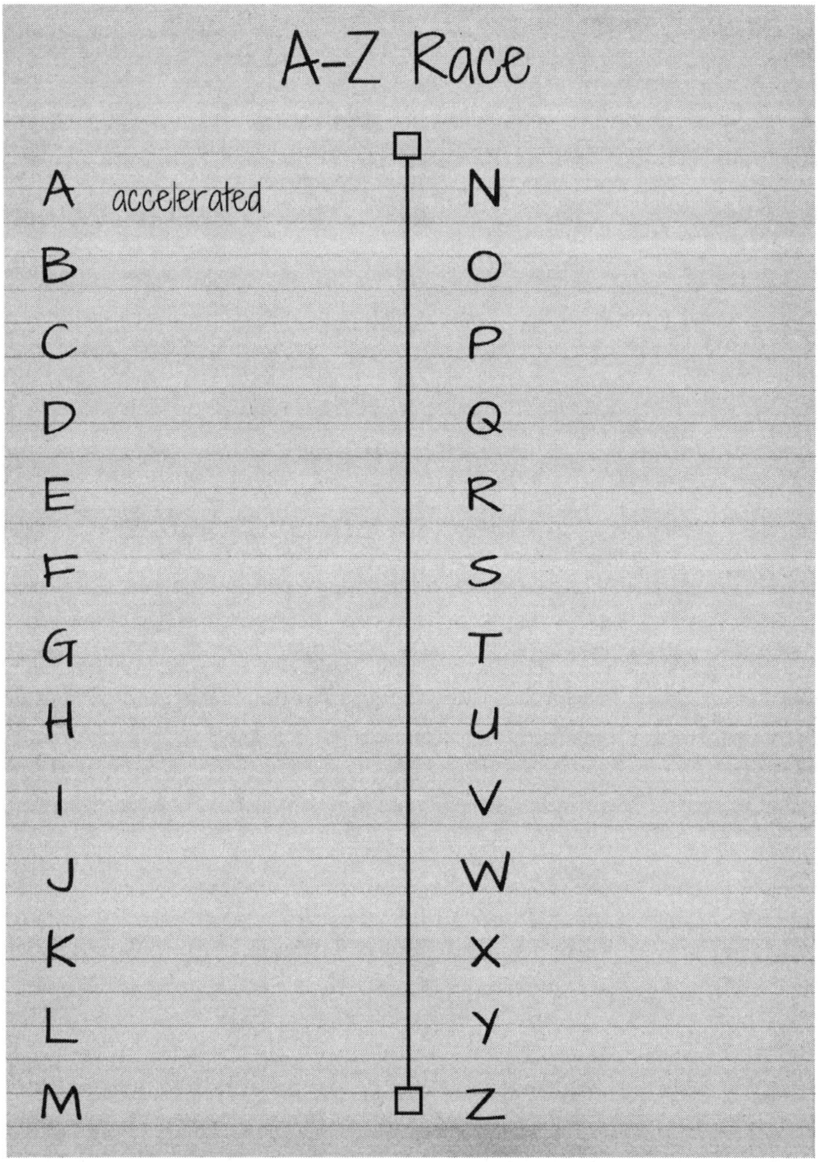

Figure 22.5 ✦ A–Z Race (Source: Tapp 2006)

of the team should be asked to write the letters A through M vertically down the left side of the page and N through Z vertically down the right side of the page. It can be helpful to draw this out on a large piece of paper, such as one from a flip chart, but any size paper will do. Before the activity begins, the trainer announces that this is a race to see which team remembers the most information from the training class. Their assignment is to think of a word or phrase related to the content that begins with each letter of the alphabet. The trainees also should be told that the first team to write down an answer for every letter would be declared the winner. It's also wise to tell teams that there can be some flexibility with difficult letters, such as "Q" and "X", and that teams should be creative. In the end, there is not necessarily a right or wrong answer for any of these letters, but the overall goal is to get trainees working together to discuss, summarize, and remember all of the content from the training class. After the activity is finished, and one team has declared itself the winner, it is important to review all of the answers for each letter. When one team has stated it has completed the A–Z sheet before other teams have finished, that victory-touting team should be asked to read off every letter on its paper followed by the word or phrase team members wrote next to it. This will often result in some heckling from the other teams, especially when there are creative words or phrases provided by the winning team, but the end goal of summarizing all content is still accomplished.

When the trainer reviews all of the information on the A–Z sheet, an additional summary review is being conducted, although the trainees are unlikely to realize that they are benefitting from this form of repetition. This same summarizing activity also enables trainees to leave the class with the completed A–Z sheet to use as a memory jogger in the future. The trainer can take a photo of each team's completed A–Z sheet and can send them out to team members a week or more after the training class as reinforcement of the training material.

To add an additional challenge, a blank A–Z page could be sent out to the trainees after the training class is over, requesting they individually attempt to complete the A–Z sheet once again and return it to the trainer. For each completed A–Z sheet that is submitted during this follow-up exercise, the training team will receive one point. The team with the most points will be eligible to win a prize, or at least be named the winner. This type of activity provides benefits on many levels and is an excellent way to provide reinforcement of the training class content. As described in other chapters, prizes can be as inexpensive as a free lunch voucher or preferred parking space.

Shopping for Safety

The Shopping for Safety activity will work for safety training classes that involve trainees learning how to protect themselves from certain types of workplace hazards. After the content has been delivered, trainees are divided into teams, and each team is given a supply of fake money. Trainees are then asked to work together and spend their money on anything that will help prevent accidents or incidents in their workplace from occurring. The only accidents or incidents they can focus on at this time are those involving the hazards that were presented in that particular safety training class. The trainees should be told to assume that, at the current moment, there is no protection in place (even if some protections already exist in the workplace, such as personal protective equipment), and they need to designate an amount of money to spend on protecting one person. Teams should get as close as possible to the actual price of each protective measure. If necessary, they can use their phones to look up prices for different materials. Trainees can select everything from barrier guards to personal protective equipment.

An alternative would be to present a photo of a workplace, preferably one very similar to where the trainees actually work, that shows a variety of hazards that are related to the safety training topic. The trainees should be told they are responsible for making that work area as safe as possible and given a certain amount of fake money to spend (usually between 1000 and 10,000 dollars). Trainees need to come up with a shopping list that, once purchased, would make this area safer. When a team of trainees does this kind of activity, they are not only reflecting on what they know about the various types of hazards in the workplace, but they're thinking of how they would apply their new knowledge, and this is a great way to increase retention.

Ten-Cent Summary

If groups of trainees are comfortable with their reading and writing skills, a more challenging activity called the Ten-Cent Summary can be used. At the end of a training class, trainees are put into teams and told that each team needs to write a summary of the information that was learned in the class. The challenge is that each word in the summary document is worth ten cents. At the end of an allotted amount of time, each team should be told to count up the words in its summary and come up with a total dollar amount. The trainees should be told that filler words like "a," "the," "an," and "and" do not count, and that the same training ideas cannot simply be repeated over and over. The group of trainees with the highest dollar value should be declared the winner. This is another activity where trainees work together to review everything they have learned during class. It can also be beneficial to collect these summaries and send them out after the training has been completed as an additional reminder of the class content. This additional level of repetition increases retention and transfer.

This activity can be a great follow-up event to use in a future training class. At the beginning of the class, the trainees are given the same exact assignment. They should be asked to work together recreating the summary they wrote in the original instance. This will be very difficult for them, but as described in Chapter 14 on productive failure, the added difficulty aids long-term retention of the safety training content.

Summary Group Grids

Another type of summarizing training activity is based on a grid that focuses on the major aspects of a particular training topic. As with the other types of activities in this book, this activity is best completed with trainees in teams. An example of a group grid that can be used for safety training is one on personal protective equipment (PPE). To create a group grid activity for a PPE class, the general types of PPE should be listed in the boxes across the top of the grid and the various work areas should be listed down the side of the grid (Figure 22.6). Trainees can then work together to identify what should be written in every box. This is a way of getting trainees to think back on what they learned during the class and summarize that information on a one-page grid.

PPE by Task Grid				
Warehouse	Picker	Packer		
Lab	Technician, Analyst		Technician, Analyst	Technician, Analyst
Mfg.	Packer, Supervisor	Packer, Supervisor		

Figure 22.6 ✦ Sample summary group grid

In addition to a PPE grid, another example would be to base a grid off of the hierarchy of controls. The hierarchy of controls could be written across the top of the grid and a variety of common workplace hazards could be written down the left side. Teams of trainees would then be requested to fill in the boxes. For example, if the first box on the top left shows "Engineering Controls" and the top box on the left shows "dust," the teams would need to come up with an engineering control for addressing a dust hazard and write it in the appropriate box. Teams would work on the activity until as many boxes as possible have been filled in.

Word Cloud

Word clouds were described in Chapter 13 as ways to use the benefits of predicting to increase attention and retention, but they can also be used to summarize the content of a training class. Word-cloud summarizing activities require the use of a free website or application for creating the word clouds. The trainees should again be put into teams and then told to write out a minimum of ten key words related to the training content. If the trainees have access to a laptop or mobile phone, they can go to websites such as WordArt, Word It Out, or Mentimeter and create their own team word cloud. If they do not have such access, they can show their ten words to the trainer or other assistant in the class who can quickly and easily add the ten words to a word cloud website or application and create a word cloud for them. The finished word cloud can serve as a reminder of class content and is more interesting than reviewing just a simple list of words or phrases. If a printer is not available, the word cloud can be downloaded and then emailed or texted to the attendees after the class is over. After each team has created their own word cloud, the teams can also be asked to vote for their favorite word cloud, but trainees must be told they cannot vote for their own word cloud.

Quiz Creator

At the end of a class, a trainer can announce to the group that instead of having a formal evaluation to judge how much they paid attention and learned, they will be creating a quiz for other trainees instead. If there are multiple sessions of the same class, this can be very effective, as the trainees can be told that they are creating a quiz for their co-workers who will be attending the class later. If this is the case, the activity can be done with the class as a whole, and various trainees can offer suggested quiz questions. The trainer would write these questions on a flip chart, and when approximately ten questions have been submitted, the trainer will then review the ten questions with the class, asking for the correct answers as well, with a promise to share those ten questions with other training classes. If the class is only presented one time to one group of trainees, the teams can work together in small groups to create shorter quizzes for other teams in the class. For example, if team A creates a six-question quiz, that quiz can be given to team B when they are finished. Team B can create a six-question quiz and give their completed quiz to team C. Team C can create a six-question quiz and give the quiz they created to team A. In this way, all of the training teams have a different quiz created by their peers. When creating the questions, the trainees must work together to think about the important points that were covered in the class. It is also probable that trainees writing the quiz will come up with much more difficult questions than if the trainer created the quiz questions.

Timeline

An interesting summarizing activity that can be used in certain training classes involves asking trainees to create a timeline of important safety procedures or precautions that must be followed in order for workers to complete a task and remain safe. The trainees will need to think of every possible scenario and create a list of activities that must be completed for the activity to be performed safely. Once this list is complete, each team should work together to put those steps in sequential order. When a team has its list of steps in the correct order, the team members should draw the steps out on a timeline and share it with the rest of the class. The class as a whole can then discuss and review what each team has presented.

Mind Maps

Mind Maps are a great way to summarize information and also to provide memory joggers for the future. Trainees may not be familiar with this type of note taking and summarization, so it may be necessary to provide a brief overview of what a mind map is and the technique. One way to use a mind map as an effective summarizing activity is to provide a partially completed mind map to the trainees and have them work together in teams to fill in the blanks and add additional branches as they see fit. Again, doing this type of

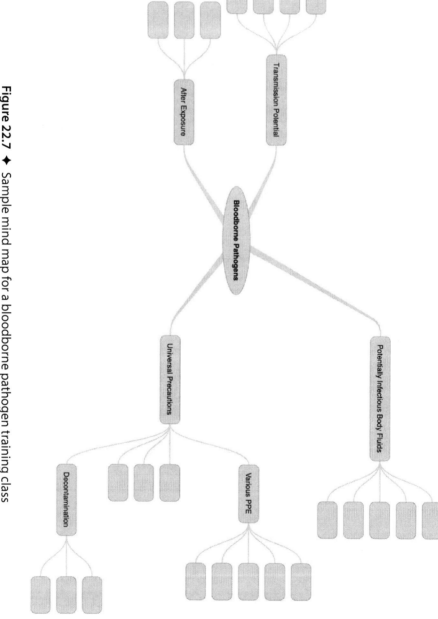

Figure 22.7 ✦ Sample mind map for a bloodborne pathogen training class

activity will cause trainees to revisit all of the content they just learned and will also get them to see connections they may not have seen before. An example of a blank mind map activity that could be used in a bloodborne pathogen training class is shown in Figure 22.7.

Sherlock (Safety) Holmes

Sherlock (Safety) Holmes is a type of summarizing activity, but it requires safety trainees to imagine that they are responsible for investigating a serious accident or incident. Trainers will need to have a prepared accident or incident story that will be read to the trainees at the end of a training class. Alternatively, a trainer can have several different preprinted accident or incident stories and give a different one to each group of trainees. To be most effective, the story must relate directly to the training class content. The trainees should be told to come up with a reasonable explanation, based on the information they learned in the training class, for how the accident may have occurred and how it could have been prevented. They should be told to make sure they include answers to who, what, why, where, and how in their investigative findings. This activity also provides a way for trainees to look at the training content that was presented as a whole, and the storytelling aspect will ensure the information is remembered longer.

Summarizing activities done at the end of training class or after trainees are back on the job are an important part of training reinforcement. By asking trainees to think back and use a lot of the information they learned during a training experience, they are making connections that will store the information in long-term memory where it will more likely be recalled and transferred to the job when needed.

Review and Retention Activity

The A–Z Race is an activity described in this chapter.

On the A–Z activity sheet (Figure 22.8), write a word or short phrase related to the content of this book that begins with each letter of the alphabet.

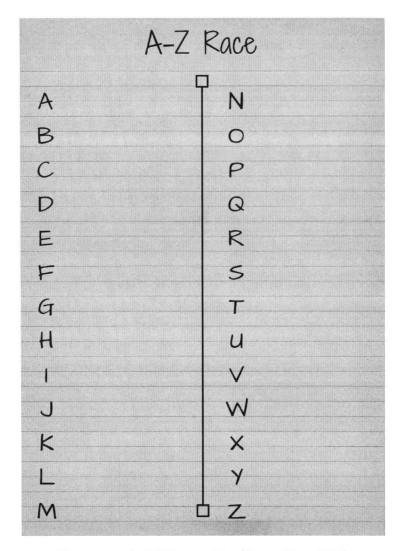

Figure 22.8 ✦ A–Z Race activity (Source: Tapp 2006)

References

Tapp, L. 2006. *SafetyFUNdamentals: 77 Games and Activities to Make Training Great!* Cherry Hill, NJ: Ennismore Publishing.

Tapp, L. 2020. *Safety Training Infographics: Communicating with Visual Images.* Madison, NJ: Ennismore Publishing.

Part 4

◆

Special Considerations

Chapter 23
Retention Techniques for Online Learning

In this chapter, online learning refers to several different types of training delivery methods, but all have one thing in common. Online training has a different time and/or place of delivery than traditional face-to-face training where instructors and trainees are all in the same place at the same time. Online learning is sometimes called e-learning or virtual training or even a webinar. *Online learning* refers to training conducted using an electronic platform that allows learners and trainers to be in different places and learn either at the same time or at different times. The retention techniques discussed in this chapter refer to all forms of online training.

While most of the learning retention and transfer strategies discussed in this book are focused on classroom interactions, the principles also apply to online learning but may pose unique challenges when adapting them to this delivery mode. With more and more learning being conducted online and/or virtually, it's important to consider how to use methods of learning retention and transfer appropriately.

According to *Training Magazine*, in 2020, 29 percent of training hours were delivered online or through computer-based technologies, 10 percent were delivered through mobile technologies, and 33 percent of training hours were delivered through blended learning. In contrast, mandatory or compliance training, which includes safety training, was provided mostly online, with 92 percent of organizations surveyed delivering at least some of it online and 42 percent delivering it entirely online (up from 29 percent in 2019). As expected, all of these numbers are up from previous years, most likely due to restrictions in place due to the Covid-19 pandemic (Freifeld 2020).

During a live training class, the trainer is able to interact on a much different level with the trainees in the class. On a subconscious level, the trainer is better able to note when a trainee is not comprehending the material that is being delivered. In a virtual training environment, using a platform such as Zoom, a trainer often only sees the faces of trainees and cannot easily evaluate body language. If a trainee experiences instruction purely online, such as through a learning management platform, and no trainer or instructor is present at the time of training, the challenges become even greater.

Distractions

Online learning, especially learning that takes place remotely, is prone to many distractions. When trainees learn from home, they face even more potential interruptions. Especially with asynchronous training (i.e., training that happens when the trainee and trainer are not online at the same time), learners may multitask while participating in a training program, and this lack of focus leads to poor retention. Even with a live online training class where a trainee has close contact with an instructor, it still may be challenging to keep the attention of a trainee. One study has found that, once interrupted, a learner will take 30 percent more time to complete the training—if they complete the training at all (Mansi 2011).

Testing

As research has shown, when implemented appropriately, testing can be used to significantly enhance learning. When tests are interspersed throughout an online training session, trainees focus their attention on the content in a way that minimizes mind-wandering and participation in activities not related to the training class (e.g., checking email, responding to text messages, etc.). Interspersing tests throughout an online class decreases mental distraction by half, increases note-taking by three times, and increases overall retention of the material. While learning improves, it has also been shown that frequent testing reduces test anxiety when it comes to a final exam (Szpunar et al. 2013).

Part of the success of intermittent testing is that learners recognize they will need to show they understand the content. If learners are also asked to think of specific and distinct instances where the training can be applied back on the job, the effect on retention, and more importantly on transfer, will be greater. Quiz questions interspersed throughout an online training class that focus on application serve more than one purpose. In addition to helping trainees maintain focus and attention, the forward testing effect described in Chapter 13 is also utilized. By showing trainees how and where the training class content can be applied, a well-designed online program can help them move the training information into their long-term memory.

Social Learning

The advantages of social learning have been discussed in Chapter 15 on teamwork and collaboration. Social learning can also be advantageous in an online learning environment but may be slightly more difficult to arrange and facilitate.

The most commonly used methods of adding interactivity and social learning to online learning environments are chats, breakout rooms, and polling. These are some of the most basic and easiest ways to interact within an online training environment, and these features are built into many online platforms. As more and more companies move to online learning because of desire or necessity, these and additional add-ons will become more prevalent and more advanced, and better methods of interacting online will become available as a result.

Digital Assistants

Researchers found that when trainees work harder, they apply themselves more to the learning, have higher test scores, and improve their transfer rates by as much as 30 percent when there is a digital assistant present (Carnes 2013). Many e-learning programs have some type of option to incorporate a digital assistant, usually in the form of an avatar. It has been suggested that a cartoon avatar is less likely to distract a learner than an actual photo of a real person, since the photo of a real person may remind the trainee of someone or something and provide a distraction.

As with face-to-face training, the ultimate goal of an online learning class is learning transfer. It is important to remember that training should not be a one-time event but should be part of an ongoing effort to increase learning and to practice what is learned. This is true for both face-to-face training and online learning. Just like face-to-face training, what happens before and after an online training class will strongly influence whether the training content is remembered and transferred back to the job. Training should be designed to include activities and techniques that can be used before and after the training occurs, whether or not that training is online or not.

Some Disadvantages of Online Learning

Asynchronous online learning can have many benefits, such as allowing trainees to learn the information at their own speed and/or review information as needed. However, there are disadvantages as well, including the added distractions mentioned earlier. Also, online learning is often set up in a way that provides limited opportunities for trainees to ask questions and get feedback. In an e-learning program where a single trainee sits in front of a computer, and possibly has access to a trainer, there will be no opportunity for interaction and learning from classmates. Interactive activities will be limited to those that can be done solo. Further, depending on a trainee's level of comfort with technology, the technology itself may impose an additional hurdle. If a trainee is struggling to figure out how to raise a virtual hand or type in an answer to a question, a low level of stress is introduced, which is going to distract from the main purpose—learning the important safety information that is being presented.

There are many opportunities in online learning to try out the latest and greatest additions to online learning platforms. Safety trainers need to be careful they are not adding the latest products to their training just to bring bells and whistles into a training class. Sometimes the addition of multiple animations, for example, can be distracting rather than productive. Adding too much complexity to an online course can have more of a negative effect than if that complexity were added in a face-to-face environment since there is no one to provide immediate explanations and assistance if needed.

Learning Theory and Online Training

There are many studies and theories on learning transfer, but most don't take into account whether those same research studies apply when the learning is not face to face. There has been some effort to adjust models of training transfer to include the effects of technology. Some of the key points in these new models include reliable technology, trainee interaction, synchronized media, and computer confidence (Carnes 2013).

Reliable technology is critical in creating an effective online safety training environment. If an online platform is freezing or shutting down unexpectedly, requiring a trainee to log back in and either start over or try to pick up where he or she left off, it will cause frustration and make it difficult for the trainee to learn the information. Some geographic locations may present more challenging environments for online training, so the reliability of the internet connection and online platform need to be considered. When training is developed for online learning, it is also imperative that all links and any other interactive elements are tested and validated. Sometimes links change or no longer work with very little notice given, so if links are embedded into an online training program, they should be checked frequently.

Synchronized media is an important aspect of online training if trainees are going to be able to focus and pay attention to the class material. For example, if an online training video requires trainees to stop, go to a different website to complete a quiz, and then return to the original site to finish participating in the training class, potential problems are being added to the process. If a virtual training class requires trainees to spend time in a breakout room, this experience can only be beneficial when it is seamless. Suppose trainees participating in an online training event being held on one of the popular virtual meeting platforms are asked to use their mobile phones to join group texts, as opposed to using the built-in chat feature that is part of the learning platform. This means they will need to leave one online area to do something different, which can create a distraction. Multiple platforms should be avoided, if possible, since they add in unnecessary complexity and chances for disruptions.

Computer confidence may vary wildly among different trainees. Some trainees will be very comfortable logging in to complete a class online, while others may find this very difficult. It's important to consider the demographics of the trainees before implementing many online safety training programs. If trainees are not very confident with the use of technology, and online training is the only option, it would be best to keep the training simple and direct. If trainees are more accustomed to using technology, adding interactivity options would be more appropriate.

When using any type of technology for training, it is always wise to include a lesson on the technology itself. This could be provided by an introductory video and practice time at the beginning of a session, or preferably, the mini-technology lesson could be sent out beforehand for trainees to try on their own time. The preinstruction "how to" video can also be optional, so that those who have more experience with online learning and technology can opt out if they choose.

The trainee's involvement in the course—called interaction, engagement, or building community—is critical if an online class is to be more than a lecture-oriented course in which interaction is primarily between the learner and the content or the learner and the instructor (Conrad and Donaldson 2011). In the past, content may have been the primary focus, but today it is interactivity that drives learning (Norris et al. 2003). Many believe that the most important role of the instructor in online classes is to ensure a high degree of interactivity and participation. This means designing and conducting learning activities that result in engagement with the subject matter and fellow students (Kearsley 2000). Numerous experts in the field of online learning agree that interaction is the key to effectiveness (Conrad and Donaldson 2011).

Integrating interactive activities into online learning is possible, although additional planning steps are needed. Sometimes a classroom-based activity can be used as is, or it might be adapted for use online, or an entirely new activity might be designed that meets the needs of the learner. Extra thought will have to go into how the instructions, objectives, and goals of the learning activity will be communicated to the trainees. When creating an online activity, it is important to consider what tools will be needed by the trainee and whether those tools, in addition to the technology, need to be nearby. In an in-person training class, the trainer can easily hand out extra pens or paper if necessary, but this is not the case in an online environment. Many training activities rely on social interaction between trainees, so a clear plan for how this aspect of a live training class will be incorporated needs to be laid out. Finally, a trainer must decide how to handle questions or any problems that come up.

Trainee interaction is an important part of learning retention and transfer back to the job. Any interaction will be different when learning is online. Some online learning programs have robust chat rooms that can be very beneficial but can also distract from the content while it's being presented. If a trainer or instructor is leading a live virtual class and trainees are asking questions in a chat box, it is very difficult for the trainer or instructor to monitor the chat box and facilitate the class at the same time. This can result in frustration and disappointment among the participants because their questions are not being seen and not being answered. One solution is to have a second person act as a moderator who will monitor the chat box and either answer questions directly or be responsible for stopping the instructor to ask the question so it can be answered.

Using Interactive Activities

When interactive classroom activities are used with a live audience, it is usually necessary, and definitely recommended, that the trainer walk around and make sure that trainees are clear on the instructions for completing the activity. When an online training activity uses breakout rooms, providing this type of oversight is more difficult if there is only one trainer or instructor involved. It is important that everyone is clear on what is expected before getting split up into breakout rooms. It is also recommended that the trainer or instructor move between breakout rooms during the activity to address any concerns or questions that may arise.

One possible way to add an interactive activity to an online training class is to introduce the activity at the beginning of the class and focus all of the training material presentation on that activity. The different topics in a training course can be tied back to the activity, so the activity is an ongoing process and not a one-off that is completed in a breakout room or at the end of the session. This will give added opportunities for questions and concerns to be brought up while the entire class is together.

For example, if a new employee training class will be covering a variety of workplace hazards, the class could start off with the Hazard Hunt activity (see Chapter 18). Since multiple kinds of hazards are presented in this type of activity, a trainer could break the training class into modules based on the different hazards. As each type of hazard is discussed, the trainer could ask trainees to work on the activity for a few minutes at a time and try to identify where that particular hazard is found. It is important to point out that, although a hazard is found, it may or may not pose a risk. If the proper controls are in place, the existence of the hazard can still lead to discussion that will increase learning. At the end of the class, the activity will be complete, as well as the delivery of all training class modules.

When an online training activity is going to require the use of small teams, it is a good idea to decide if the membership on those teams is an important part of the learning process. If the learning activity can successfully be completed with a random mix of trainees, many virtual platforms can randomly assign individuals to a breakout group. It is also usually possible to preassign individuals to teams, and this can be beneficial for different types of activities, especially where different points of view and experiences are an important part of the activity. There is no right or wrong way to assign members to teams, but this is a point that should be considered and planned for ahead of time. Just like in a live classroom, if there is a group of trainees who are best friends and more likely to have side conversations and not participate when together, it is good to know this for the online training environment as well so teams can be assigned appropriately.

Online learning activities that produce an end result, such as a final completed project or group activity, will be slightly more challenging to share with the entire class in an online environment. Still, sharing is possible, and is usually a good idea. If trainees are comfortable with technology, many online platforms allow participants to share their screen. If one person in a breakout group is told to be the scribe, the notes for the group can be shared if they were taken in an online document creation tool.

If the interactive training class activity involves something like the team working jointly on a handout, the trainer has at least two options. First, before the online class begins, trainees can be emailed or texted the activity in the form of prework, although they will not need to do anything with the activity before class other than print it out. If all trainees have printed out the page ahead of time, they can all work on it together with one person in the team being responsible for capturing everyone's contributions on their page. When it is time for the teams to reconvene and share their results, the work of the team can simply be held up to the webcam for all to see.

The second option takes advantage of the many available online collaboration platforms. Many of the options, similar to online whiteboards, are easy to integrate with existing platforms. In online collaboration environments, all trainees can see what others are doing in real time and add their own notes, for example. Since this type of collaboration takes place online, it is very easy to share with everyone.

Since trainees are sitting in front of a computer or mobile phone anyway during the online training experience, it is easy to integrate the use of email and texting into the training. One way to encourage trainees to do this is to ask them to create an action plan. Ask trainees to think about how they will use the training content once they return to their job. They should also be asked to make a commitment to do so and document their agreement by writing an email to the trainer or supervisor right then and there, stating how they expect to use what they learned once they are back on the job. The email should be sent to themselves, as well as to someone else that they will be accountable to. This could be a co-worker or even a family member. If trainers receive copies of these emails, most email systems will allow the user to set a later time for the email to be redelivered to the inbox. If an email program does not support this, the email can be saved, and a note can be added to the calendar as a reminder to resurface the email at a designated date and time. Another option is to set up questions about future plans in a free online survey tool. Trainees can easily provide short answers to the survey questions, and trainers can treat these like the emails described above. A week or two after the online training class has been completed, a trainer can forward the email or survey questions back to the trainees as a reminder of what they had committed to along with questions to follow up on how well they believe they have implemented the online learning. There are various websites and applications that enable emails to be written and delivered at a later date.

Similar to the action plan idea just discussed, another way to increase retention in online training classes is to encourage trainees to think about where the information will be applied or how it will be useful to them. In a face-to-face class, asking such questions may result in only one or two hands being raised, or as many trainers know, often these types of questions will go completely unanswered. Getting trainees to consider these questions in an online environment may be easier because there is some anonymity associated with sitting behind the camera. Trainees can be further encouraged to share this type of reflective information if it is in the form of a team activity. Additionally, trainees may be more likely to share this information with a small group rather than with the entire class.

Infographics

An *infographic* is as simple as the word sounds—it's information presented graphically. The use of infographics as training activities is briefly discussed in Chapter 22 on summarizing activities. Chapter 24 reviews the importance of using images in safety training, and infographics are a great way to do this even when the training is presented online. In fact, many infographics are better viewed online because the format of an infographic is often designed to be read on a mobile device while scrolling. A custom infographic specific to the workplace is a great way to capture trainee attention and also engenders reflective activity.

Trainees, once divided into smaller groups, can each be given or shown a copy of the infographic and asked to identify at least two places where the items shown in the infographic may actually be found in their workplace. Once teams have gotten the chance to work on this individually, they can report back to the larger group with their examples. In an e-learning environment, the same infographic can be shown and space for the trainees to type in their responses to the same question can be provided directly on the page they are viewing. This type of reflective activity can work well for many safety training topics but may not be as appropriate for topics that focus strictly on a particular procedure that is needed at a particular place or time. For example, workers taking training on slips, trips, and falls focused on scaffolding may only be able to think of one or two instances where they could use that information on the job. In this case, reflection would not be as meaningful.

Grab Their Attention

Just like in a regular classroom training presentation, it's beneficial to get the trainees' attention as soon as they walk into the room. Whether they are entering an online or in-person classroom, there is a temptation to begin checking phone messages and emails or begin chatting with other trainees. If trainees have something to do as soon as the learning program begins, it will be easier to keep them on track.

There are many ways to engage trainees immediately in a live setting. Most of these can also be applied to the online classroom. In a virtual setting, a training activity related to the content can be displayed on the welcome screen along with instructions that the trainee can easily follow. If the training content is focused on hazard recognition, an illustration or photo showing an area that contains many hazards can be displayed, and trainees can be asked to look at the image, identify hazards, and be ready to discuss them when the training class begins. This kind of activity not only gets their attention immediately but also gets their minds set for learning. Additionally, in order to complete this activity, the trainees must think back on what they already know. This is a form of retrieval, as discussed in the Chapter 11. Instead of providing busywork for trainees to complete when they enter class, an activity that's directly related to the content can be a great training opener.

Video

If available technology is adequate for showing an uninterrupted video, a small video thumbnail can also be present on the screen in an online classroom. Trainees can watch the video to get an introduction, or better yet, they can watch a video that would require them to do something. For example, if the training class is on safe lifting procedures, the video could show the basic steps in safe lifting or could show someone lifting an object incorrectly. The trainees could be asked to practice the safe lifting procedures shown in the video while they wait for class to begin, or they could be asked to identify what the actor in the video is doing wrong. Many trainees come to training classes having already attended other classes on the same or a closely related topic. If so, trainers can take advantage of this preexisting knowledge.

It is generally believed that giving trainees a good deal of control during a training session is beneficial. In most instances, this is true. However, studies have shown that if the training to be delivered is complex, more direct learning guidance is necessary. When material is complex, the learner should not have control over the sequence, the time spent on the material, or other variables that are often offered in self-paced e-learning classes (Granger and Levine 2010). Some online training programs, such as how to use a fire extinguisher, are relatively simple. In such a case, the trainee could control the speed at which he or she goes through the information. Other complex training topics, such as process safety or assessing fall protection anchor points, are better delivered online when supervised and more tightly controlled.

To address these issues, trainers can consider the following suggestions:

- Determine the level of complexity by looking at how many different key points of information the trainee is expected to learn.
- Simplify the content by spreading these points out over several classes. It is suggested that three to five concepts be presented per module (Carnes 2013).
- Trim the content. As described in the chapter on microlearning and chunking, identify areas in the training materials that are simply nice to know but are unnecessary for the trainee to perform the procedure safely. Information that is nice to know can be provided in a separate reference document or online on a company wiki page if one is available.

- Add restrictions for using features available on the learning platform. Such features may include requiring a trainee to spend a certain amount of time on each screen or activity. Additionally, many learning systems can be set up to require trainees to learn concepts in a particular order or successfully answer online questions before proceeding.
- Require trainees taking complex training online to achieve a high score when tested in order to pass the class.
- Trainees should successfully complete each of the modules in the order they are presented before being allowed to begin the next one (Carnes 2013).

QR Codes

QR codes—short for quick response codes—are popular since they allow people to scan an image and get immediate access to a wide variety of information. QR codes are used in some workplaces to provide everything from lockout-tagout procedures for a particular piece of equipment to information on personal protective equipment required in a specific area. QR codes can also be effective in training programs and can provide instant access to valuable safety information when and where it's needed.

In the online environment, the use of QR codes can also be helpful. Before an online or e-learning class that incorporates QR codes is delivered, it is important to instruct trainees in how to scan these codes. There are a variety of free applications available that can be installed on a trainee's mobile device before the training class begins. While many QR codes are placed in physical locations, QR codes can also be integrated into slides and other online delivery materials. Trainees can simply scan the code they see on the screen in front of them and get instant access to learning material, including pdfs, training games, and videos. If a particular set of steps is part of a safety training class, it is important the trainees remember those steps when they are back on the job. A QR code can be placed at the actual spot where a trainee works to serve this purpose. When the trainee is on the job and needs the information immediately, he or she can scan the code and instantly receive the needed information. The ability to access this information after completing a training class will aid retention and stimulate transferring what was learned and applying it when it's actually needed. In addition to many available QR readers, there are also a number of QR code creators. Some are free, while others may charge a small fee.

Chapter 9, "Make it Real," discusses the importance of making training seem realistic to the trainees, and this is one area where online training has an advantage. In a classroom environment, it may be necessary to show a realistic activity being performed by video, but in an online setting there are more options. It is possible for the trainer to travel to a work area and live stream a task or work area related to the safety training class. It is probably necessary to talk to a company's human resources and/or legal department before live streaming co-workers to a training class.

Drag and Drop

Drag and drop activities are another way to engage online trainees. There are a variety of online collaboration tools that can be used for this purpose. Several of the activities described in chapters 19 and 20 on sequencing and sorting activities rely on the ability of trainees to arrange information in the best way possible. "When a person does a drag and drop activity, the physical exercise in cyberspace increases memory, retention, and learning compared with a less physical exercise such as taking a multiple-choice test. Thus, the drag and drop activity has an underlying valid learning principle" (Conrad and Donaldson 2011).

Seek and Find

Seek and find activities take advantage of the trainees' day-to-day use of technology. Many trainees will be comfortable and familiar with searching for information online. Even if they do not do this as part of their day-to-day job, they most likely use a computer or a mobile phone at some time in their off-work hours to search for a variety of information that might be interesting or needed. When trainees are spread out over a geographic distance, or even when they are in the same building but experiencing online training, activities can be based around the trainees' personal use of the technology they have with them. In a seek and find activity, trainees are asked to locate specific information related to the class content. This teaches trainees how to locate information they may need in the future when a trainer or instructor is not there to help. In addition, when individuals search for certain key words on their mobile technology, those words stay in their search history and reappear at a later time. This can serve as a surreptitious way of providing reinforcement of the training point.

For a seek and find activity using teamwork, trainees can be sent into virtual breakout rooms, and each team can be told to use their personal phone or mobile technology to find three specific items related to the class content. For example, in a fall protection class, each team of trainees could be asked to search for an image where fall protection is needed, or they can search for images of three different types of fall protection. At the end of the breakout period, all trainees return to the main area and share the images they found. They can simply hold up their phones showing the image to the camera on their webcam for others to see. If the online chat allows images to be attached, the team's work can be shown in this way.

Interaction

Most people desire to have interactions with other people; this is true of trainees as well. Whether in a classroom or in a virtual setting, research has shown that interaction can increase learning. In a virtual environment, the same research has shown that interaction can lessen the psychological distance involved in online learning (Mayes et al. 2011). In a regular safety training classroom environment, trainees are certain to interact with each other without much preplanning from the instructor. Additional interactions can be provided easily by adding interactive games and activities. The online environment is different. Very little interaction might occur without considerable preplanning of its implementation at the design stage.

Three strategies—related to three types of interaction—that can increase interaction in online learning environments have been defined (Moore 1989). They include:

- Learner–instructor interaction
- Learner–content interaction
- Learner–learner interaction

Interaction between the instructor and the trainees has been found to be the most important type of interaction in an online class and leads to a greater sense of community as well as higher levels of engagement (Brinthaupt et al. 2011). To break this down further, seven factors of successful learner–instructor interaction have been identified (Shackelford and Maxwell 2012).

1. State expectations.

   Just as in a regular safety training class, instructors need to communicate expectations for participation. The safety training class will move more smoothly and be more effective if all trainees have their camera on and are required to participate in things such as polls and surveys. If these are the expectations, they need to be explicitly stated at the beginning of the safety training class. If the class is asynchronous—where the trainees are learning on their own without the benefit of interacting with an instructor—the expectations still need to be provided at the beginning of the class.

2. Require participation in discussions.

   Research has shown that when an instructor is absent during an online discussion, engagement is low (Journell 2008). Trainers need to be involved in an online class in order to provide feedback and guide trainees in staying focused on the content. It is also necessary for the trainer to find ways to connect the content back to the overall learning objectives of the class and to guide the trainees in doing so.

3. Provide support and encouragement.

   In any type of training environment, a trainer can and should provide support and encouragement to trainees. This can be done in a chat box or verbally, and in asynchronous situations, through short videos and audio clips.

4. Provide timely feedback.

   Similar to providing support and encouragement, it is important for an instructor to provide timely feedback whether the training environment is synchronous or asynchronous. The importance of feedback is discussed throughout this book and does not change because the training is presented virtually. In a face-to-face safety training class, the instructor is providing feedback without even realizing it. Smiles, head nods, and other forms of body language provide types of feedback that probably seem unremarkable. In an online environment, it is very difficult to read someone's body language. Feedback can be provided to the group as a whole or individually through the use of text messages and chat boxes. Classes can be followed up with a series of emails or discussion board opportunities that can provide additional feedback to the attendees.

5. Use multiple modes of communication.

   Although it might seem counterintuitive to say that a safety trainer can use multiple modes of communication in an online environment, there are ways to communicate other than what is possible through a computer monitor. If necessary, trainees can meet with the instructor in one-on-one virtual meetings or communicate through email messages and through instructional videos such as screencasts.

6. Model desired behavior.

   When research was conducted on the seven different types of learner–instructor interaction, instructor modeling (i.e., where an instructor models the desired behavior), was found to have the greatest impact on the trainees' sense of community and belonging. It may take additional planning, but trainers should find ways to model behavior in the virtual environment as well as in live face-to-face training.

7. Require participation in learning activities.

   When all trainees participate in learning activities, they will have no choice but to interact with the instructor. Research has shown that, to the extent possible, computer-based training or distance learning should include active participation on the part of the learners, who should also use these seven suggestions in order to increase knowledge acquisition (Burke et al. 2006). A lot of online learning is passive and requires very little of the learner, which adds nothing to the learning experience.

Spaced practice, discussed in Chapter 10, and microlearning, discussed in Chapter 12, work extremely well with online learning, and using technology in this way can "turn online education on its head" (Kerfoot et al. 2007). One way to add spaced practice to an online course is to present the course entirely in a test/question format. New information appears when the correct answer is explained and elaborated upon. When a microlearning course is set up this way, incorrectly answered questions might repeat 1 week later and ones that were answered correctly might reappear 3 weeks later. This is similar to the Leitner box system described in Chapter 21. Material that is well known will be studied less frequently and material that trainees struggle with will be studied more often. Combined with repetition, this type of spaced practice in the form of microlearning can be very effective.

Other Considerations

Just like with classroom training, a needs assessment should be conducted before online learning is even considered as an option for providing safety education to trainees. Training is not the answer for all safety-related issues. Training should only be considered a solution when there is a gap in knowledge or skills. No matter how experienced the trainer, a bad attitude or lack of motivation in a trainee cannot be fixed through safety training. Even if training is a possible solution to address a performance deficit, the needs of the learners must also be considered. ANSI/ASSP Z490.2, Section 4.1, includes the following considerations when completing a needs assessment:

- the availability of quality producers, instructional designers, facilitators, and administrators of e-learning
- electronic technologies, internet connectivity, and/or other methods of training delivery and distribution
- internet service available to learners
- minimum learner literacy and computer skills necessary
- preferences of learners, including their attitudes and cultural/global acceptability of e-learning
- ability to deliver e-learning materials in languages appropriate to learners
- special accommodations required by learners to complete e-learning

The Z490.2 standard also stresses the importance of considering various aspects of electronic devices, such as the available screen space, the need to scroll, the size of buttons, and the ease or difficulty of clicking in the design of the training. For example, if most trainees will be taking the online learning class by accessing it on a mobile phone, it may be difficult to see many items that would be easily seen on a larger screen, such as a full-size computer monitor.

The use of appropriate images is discussed in detail in Chapter 25 on image-based safety training, and the same principles apply in the online learning environment. Visual aids included in online learning should reinforce the content and not distract from it. Additionally, when audio is used, the audio and the visuals should support one another and not make it more difficult for the trainee to focus and pay attention. Audio elements should complement what the trainee sees on the screen and not simply repeat the words that appear there.

As described throughout this book, interactivity is a vital part of increasing learners' attention, retention, and transfer back to the job. This interactivity is also extremely important to include in online learning.

Review and Retention Activity
Free Recall is an activity described in Chapter 21 on repetition and recall activities.

On a blank piece of paper, write down the main concepts you can remember from this chapter covering retention techniques for online learning. Do not refer to notes or the material included in this chapter.

References
ANSI/ASSP Z490.2. 2019. *Accepted Practices for E-Learning in Safety, Health and Environmental Training*. Park Ridge, IL: American Society of Safety Professionals.

Brinthaupt, T. M., L. S. Fisher, J. G. Gardner, D. M. Raffo, and J. B. Woodard. 2011. "What the best online teachers should do." *Journal of Online Learning and Teaching*, 7(4):515–524.

Burke, M. J., S. A. Sarpy, K. Smith-Crowe, S. Chan-Serafin, R. O. Salvador, and G. Islam. 2006. "Relative effectiveness of worker safety and health training methods." *American Journal of Public Health*, 96(2):315–324.

Carnes, B. 2013. *Making E-learning Stick*. Alexandria, VA: American Society for Training and Development (ASTD) Press.

Conrad, R., and J. Donaldson. 2011. *Engaging the Online Learner, Updated: Activities and Resources for Creative Instruction*. 2d ed. Jossey-Bass. San Francisco, CA: John Wiley & Sons, Inc.

Freifeld, L. 2020. "2020 Training Industry Report." *Training Magazine*. https://trainingmag.com/trgmag-article/2020-training-industry-report/.

Granger, B., and E. Levine. 2010. "The perplexing role of learner control in e-learning: will learning and transfer benefit or suffer." *International Journal of Training and Development*, 14(3):180–197.

Journell, W. 2008. "Facilitating Historical Discussions Using Asynchronous Communication: The Role of the Teacher." *Theory & Research in Social Education*, 36(4):317–55. doi: 10.1080/00933104.2008.10473379.

Kearsley, G. 2000. *Online Education: Learning and Teaching in Cyberspace*. Belmont, CA: Wadsworth Thomson Learning.

Kerfoot, B. P., H. E. Baker, M. O. Koch, D. Connelly, D. B. Joseph, and M. L. Ritchey. 2007. "Randomized, controlled trial of spaced education to urology residents in the United States and Canada." *The Journal of Urology*, 177:1481–1487. doi: 10.1016/j.juro.2006.11.074.

Mansi, G. 2011. "Assessment of Instant Messaging Interruptions on Knowledge Workers Task Performance in E-learning Based Training." Ph.D. dissertation, Nova Southeastern University.

Mayes, R., J. Luebeck, H. Y. Ku, C. Akarasriworn, and O. Korkmaz. 2011. "Themes and strategies for transformative online instruction: A review of literature and practice." *The Quarterly Review of Distance Education*, 12(3):151–166.

Moore, M. G. 1989. "Editorial: Three Types of Interaction." *American Journal of Distance Education*, 3(2):1–7. doi: 10.1080/08923648909526659.

Norris, D. M., J. Mason, and P. Lefrere. 2003. *Transforming E-Knowledge: A Revolution in the Sharing of Knowledge*. Ann Arbor, MI: Society for College and University Planning.

Shackelford, J. L., and M. Maxwell. 2012. "Sense of Community in Graduate Online Education: Contribution of Learner to Learner Interaction." *The International Review of Research in Open and Distributed Learning*, 13(4):228. doi: 10.19173/irrodl.v13i4.1339.

Szpunar, K. K., Y. K. Novall, and D. L. Schacter. 2013. "Interpolated memory tests reduce mind wandering and improve learning of online lectures." Proceedings of the National Academy of Sciences, 2013. doi: 10.1073/pnas.1221764110.

Chapter 24
Image-Based Safety Training for Increased Retention

Even the newest safety trainers know visual aids are an important part of safety training. When trainees are illiterate or have English as a second language, graphics and photos are even more important. Image-based communication has been growing in popularity, although images have always been an important part of communication. Images are more popular than ever and are widely used to communicate and often as a primary method of communication. Some of the fastest growing social media applications are image based. Pinterest and Instagram are just two examples. To understand why this is so, consider the following. In 2010, Google CEO Eric Schmidt made headlines when he said, "we now create more information in two days than we created from the dawn of man up until 2003" (Siegler and Schmidt 2010). In 2020, the Information Overload Resource Group reported that "90 percent of the online data has been created in the past two years" (Einstein 2019). With so much information readily available, it is evident why it's so hard to get people's attention—and to get them to remember what they have heard or seen. As the adage goes, "a picture is worth a thousand words," and using visuals can attract attention as well as provide additional clarity for better understanding. If someone has the choice to look at an image in an effort to learn something, or read a paragraph or more of text, the visual option will be much more inviting.

Visual Aids
Visual aids are an effective means to express and analyze complexity in ways that words alone cannot (Chambers 2009). Visuals rearrange the mental load since it's believed that verbal and visual information are processed differently

by the brain. By effectively using both visuals and lecture, trainers can help trainees avoid being overwhelmed by providing them with various ways to digest the information (Dirksen 2016). Visuals are also important because it is often difficult to produce detailed and accurate verbal descriptions. Language differences can make this more difficult. Additionally, describing something accurately might require specialized vocabulary (e.g., technical jargon) that can further confuse trainees. When trainers share information only through words, there is a risk of losing meaning when erroneous or unclear information is shared, and this can have serious consequences in training.

When illustrations or photos are used, they should only be used if there is a very clear connection to the training material (Szudy 1994). For example, if a trainer wants to add a visual aid to a PowerPoint presentation on chemical safety and considers adding a graphic of a tombstone to reinforce the message that chemicals can be dangerous, this type of indirect relationship might be confusing for the trainees. Graphics or illustrations that are more directly related to the slide would be more effective.

The first rule of using visual aids, as described in *The Visual Marketing Revolution* by Stephanie Diamond, is to recognize the power of visual persuasion. Visuals persuade. Educational researchers at the Department of Labor report that over 83 percent of human learning happens visually (Diamond 2013). Since the information being delivered to trainees is so important and can even mean the difference between life and death, it is imperative that visual learning is incorporated into training materials.

Presenting information with visual aids helps establish and maintain attention, and as described in several chapters of this book, getting and keeping the attention of trainees is an important factor in trainee retention. Visuals can also provide information in a form that the trainee can quickly and easily interpret. If a trainee doesn't understand spoken words, retention of that information is an unreachable goal. Many safety trainers attempt to clarify what they say by adding an illustration or two, and these can be very effective, but more can be done.

Humans first and foremost process the world visually. Nonhumans may use smell, hearing, or even radar as their primary way of getting information. Humans are made to be sophisticated seeing machines, and although they use all of their senses to understand information presented in various forms, the eyes are a person's most important tools. Humans acquire more information through their visual system than through all their other senses combined.

This is because visualizations contain certain characteristics called *preattentive attributes*, which the eyes perceive very quickly and the brain processes without any real action by the human being—like force-feeding the mind (Ware 2020). Philippe Kahn of LightSurf Technologies said, "If a picture is worth a thousand words, then a picture with text is worth 10,000 words."

Images Reinforce Learning

Are all images equally instructive? Unfortunately, they are not. Good visual aids are easily recognizable, and easily and universally understood (Hodgdon 2015). A good visual should appeal to the audience while effectively providing knowledge that enables clear understanding. A good visual aid should also foster retention. It should impart memorable knowledge. For the purposes of safety training, the first priority of a visual is comprehension, followed by the ability to promote retention. Finally, appeal is important.

Many trainers may be using visuals strictly for decoration. Although this won't ruin the training class, any unnecessary information, including decorative items, will increase the cognitive load. Their use also constitutes a lost opportunity to increase comprehension (Clark and Lyons 2010). "Decorative graphics are the shallowest type of instructional visual, and should be used with some caution" (Dirksen 2016) as they may also distract from the real message (Thalheimer 2004). In addition to images that are purely decorative, it is wise to avoid visual clichés, such as an image of hands shaking to represent working together or cooperation.

Lefever, the author of *The Art of Explanation: Making Your Ideas, Products, and Services Easier to Understand*, says that good visuals should not be noisy and should be simple (Lefever 2013). For example, at his company, the figures used in communication messages do not have faces because that would be considered "noise." The brain notices the emotions or the look on the face of the image and starts processing it, diluting the core message. At his company, the goal is to have people see themselves in the figure.

Safety trainers can improve their training materials and keep the focus on key information by reviewing images for extraneous information and eliminating what's not necessary. If visual aids are complex and contain too much information, trainees will look away—the opposite of what safety training requires. The best types of visuals have limited information and can be understood with a quick glance.

Many times, when creating safety training programs, it is difficult to find appropriate illustrations and images for the topic being presented. Safety includes many highly technical and job-specific ideas that may not be found on stock image websites that are commonly accessed. If this is the case, one option is to have an image or illustration specifically created to fill the need. Another option is for safety trainers to create their own image. Some safety trainers may have reservations, or even anxiety, around creating their own visual aids. After all, most safety trainers probably have no training in drawing or graphic design. Visual aids do not have to be perfect. The most important thing is that the visual aid is easily understood. It doesn't have to be beautiful. It just needs to do the job it was meant to do—make information clear.

Six Types of Drawings

Dan Roam, author of two books on communicating through visuals, says that anyone can visualize almost any idea by using six basic types of drawings, because there are six basic pathways along which our brains process imagery. He reasons that we can draw just six pictures to illustrate any idea we can think of. Roam's six types of problems and associated visuals include:

1. "Who and what" problems
   "Who and what problems" are challenges that relate to things, people, and roles. For example, in a safety training class on electrical work, there are different types of training (e.g., awareness level), and different authorities or classes of personnel within a facility (e.g., authorized person). By using images of each group and the type of electrical work each may be doing (e.g., changing a light bulb or working with high voltage), trainers are able to represent different kinds of people and make the training story oriented.
2. "How much" problems
   "How much" problems occur in situations where numbers need to be presented. Safety trainers could use a chart to show how many near miss reports were filed or how the number of lost-time accidents changed in a given year, but a visual representation of the same data would be more memorable. For example, if a trainer wanted to show how long an average worker is away from work due to a lost-time injury, the trainer could show a generic calendar month with weeks

highlighted, or if the average time is very long, a pie chart where each quarter represents a season could be used. If the average time away from work is 6 months, showing a pie chart where half of a year is lost will be better than simply saying the average is 6 months.

3. "When" problems

   "When" problems relate to scheduling and timing or topics that need to be expressed with a timeline. A topic like CPR often involves particular timing. A large diagram of a clock with marks to show the progression of time associated with the steps of CPR would be an example.

4. "Where" problems

   "Where" problems are challenges that relate to direction and how things fit together. Safety training often talks about where things are—emergency exits, eyewash locations, hazardous waste storage areas, and hearing-protection-required areas to name a few. Instead of providing a list of the areas, maps showing them are more visual and more memorable. "Where" also refers to "where have I seen this before?" You want an image that is recognizable. Showing actual photos of the locations on the map would be especially beneficial.

5. "How" problems

   "How" problems are challenges that relate to how things influence one another. Flowcharts with visuals are a good way to show these relationships. If information is being presented after a serious accident, a flowchart showing the factors that led to the incident will be understood better than handing out a paragraph listing them. Similarly, diagrams showing how to do something are commonly needed when explaining safety procedures. Step-by-step illustrations accompanied by explanatory text are very effective.

6. "Why" problems

   "Why" challenges are related to guiding others to see the big picture. The images can help others see and understand why something should be important to them or why they should care about a particular procedure or policy. Multiple-variable plots can provide effective ways to explain the why. In Roam's book *The Back of the Napkin* (Roam 2010), he goes into great detail about how to create these plots. Safety training topics that include multiple data points are good candidates for multivariate plots.

Examples of the six types of problems or information follow. Each type has a verbal description and a visual representation of the same information, as shown in Figures 24.1 through 24.6.

Who/What

The Covid-19 vaccine is to be administered to high-risk groups first, with distribution to occur in three phases (Figure 24.1). Further prioritization of the high-risk groups places those in long-term care facilities and medical personnel in the first group. Teachers and emergency responders, food and agriculture workers, utility workers, transportation workers, and correction officers are in the second group. Adults over 65 years of age and those with preexisting conditions are in the third group.

How Much

Both minor and major automobile accidents involving sales representatives occur throughout the day but occur most at dusk. The least amount of accidents occur midday (Figure 24.2).

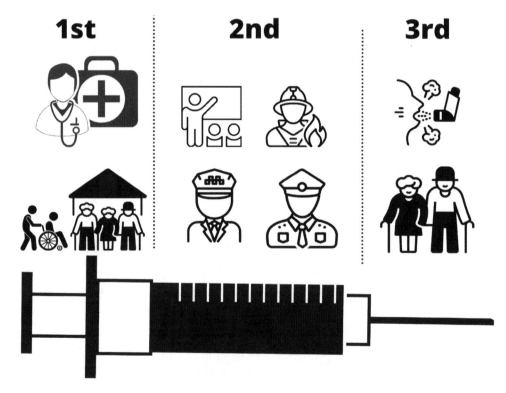

Figure 24.1 ✦ Allocation of initial Covid-19 vaccine (Adapted from: Dooling 2020)

When

If a heavy or large object must be lifted, the lift should be planned in advance. First, the item should be checked for rough or unusual edges, and any available straps or openings that will assist with the lift should be identified. Next, the path the object will be carried should be inspected, and any items that are in the way, such as cords across a walkway, should be removed so the path is clear. When ready to pick up the object, the knees should be bent while keeping the back straight. The object should be firmly grasped and held close to the body while slowly standing up (Figure 24.3).

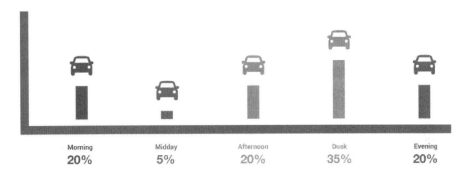

Figure 24.2 ✦ Sales representative accident occurrence by time of day

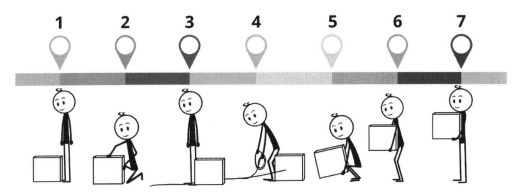

Figure 24.3 ✦ Steps for safe lifting (Source: Tapp 2015)

340 ✦ Make Your Safety Training Stick

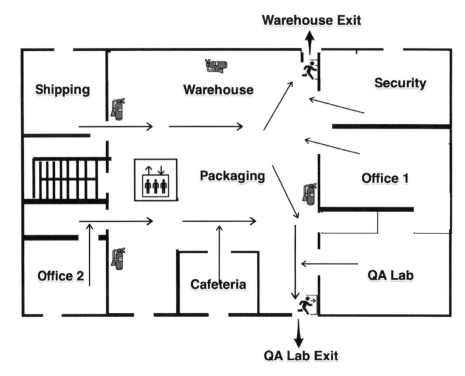

Figure 24.4 ✦ Sample emergency evacuation plan

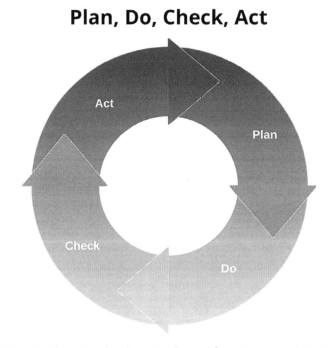

Figure 24.5 ✦ Plan, Do, Check, Act (Adapted from Evans and Lindsay 2008)

Where

If an emergency occurs, all employees must leave the building by exiting through the closest emergency exit. Employees working in the shipping department, the warehouse, office 1, and security personnel should exit by the warehouse exit door. Employees working in office 2, the cafeteria, the QA lab, and the packaging department should leave by the exit next to the QA lab (Figure 24.4).

How

A Plan/Do/Check/Act procedure plan has many uses. When starting a new safety training program, it is necessary to first create a plan, then implement the plan, then check to see the results, and then take action to revise and adjust the plan so that it is better able to meet the desired outcome. After taking action to correct/revise the original plan, the cycle starts again (Figure 24.5).

Why

Lab technicians may not always work with solvents inside a fume hood as required by lab safety procedures (Figure 24.6). Failure to do this, or the decision to work in fume hoods with inadequate fume hood rates, results in both increased numbers of sick days and more reports to in-house medical facilities for first-aid treatment for ailments such as dizziness and headaches.

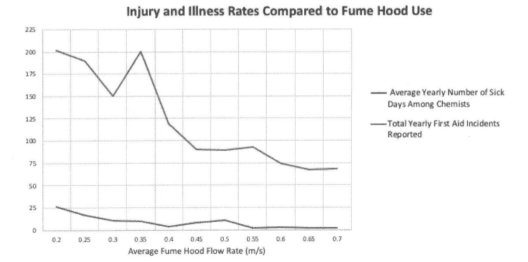

Figure 24.6 ✦ Injury and illness rates compared to fume hood use

Infographics

Infographics, discussed as a tool for summarizing activities in Chapter 22, are usually posterlike visuals that bring information together in a unique and interesting way. Instead of reading an article, it is often possible to gain the same relevant information by reading over and studying a well-designed infographic. Although infographics do contain text, they are primarily visual aids meant to get attention and communicate information quickly. The visual components of an infographic, and how the different components work together, can greatly aid in the understanding and retention of the material. One of the first infographics ever created was by Florence Nightingale (Figure 24.7). When her pleas to Parliament for action regarding the poor health and hygiene of British troops got nowhere, she developed a pie chart to get them thinking a new way about disease. Once they were able to visualize the problem, they took action (Lankow et al. 2012).

"Graphics are able to extend the reach of our memory systems" (Lankow et al. 2012), and they are also important in retention of the information presented. "Visualizations do this by instantly and constantly drawing upon non-visual information that's stored in our long-term memory" (Ware 2020).

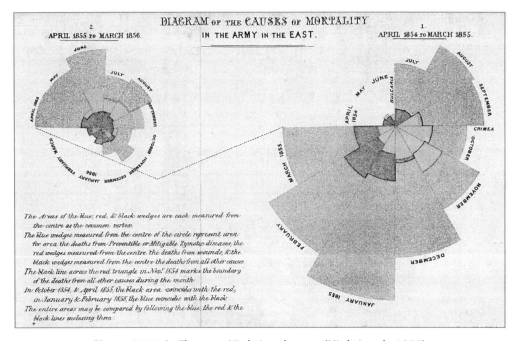

Figure 24.7 ✦ Florence Nightingale map (Nightingale 1858)

Our brains are able to recall things that are familiar to us so we can quickly see and comprehend many visuals. If we use visual aids in safety training that are somewhat familiar to the trainees, they will be more effective.

Illiteracy and Non-Native Speakers

The importance of incorporating opportunities for interactive class involvement has been discussed throughout this book. While interactive activities are a great addition to training classes, most of these activities are based on the premise that the trainees can read and write English. This is why a visual aid can be absolutely necessary during training. According to the National Center for Educational Statistics (NCES), 21 percent of adults in the United States fall into the illiterate/functionally illiterate category (National Center for Education Statistics 2019). Illiterate adults have never been taught to read and write, and functionally illiterate adults have such poor reading and writing skills that they are not able to use them in day-to-day tasks.

A group that is largely overlooked is illiterate workers who are also native English speakers. Illiteracy is a big problem in many areas of the United States. A five-year, $14-million study conducted by the United States government interviewed over 26,000 adults. The study proved that more than 92 million people (more than 47% of U.S. adults) cannot read and write well enough to hold an above-poverty-level-wage job. This study also proved that more than 40 percent of employees in U.S. businesses are functionally illiterate. Many training materials rely on the ability of trainees to read and write. Additionally, most training materials are written at a college reading level. Studies have recommended that training materials should be designed that rely less on reading (Szudy 1994).

When safety training is conducted in the native language of trainees, whether that is English, Spanish, or any other language, the training will still be flawed if it does not account for the literacy level of the audience. Even if training materials are translated and delivered in another language, trainees may not be able to read or write very well in any language, so the use of images is imperative. Sherry Baron, M.D., of NIOSH has reported that the form of the training and not just the language is important. She also emphasized that foreign-born workers may not be literate, so visual aids are more effective than the written word (Nash 2005).

The challenge of providing safe workplaces for non-English speakers has been recognized by industry professionals and government organizations alike. According to the Occupational Safety and Health Administration, language barriers contribute to about 25 percent of all workplace fatalities. Groups such as OSHA have dedicated a great deal of time and money to providing education and materials for Spanish speakers since this is the fastest growing demographic in America. From 2018 to 2028, the U.S. Bureau of Labor Statistics projects the number of Hispanics in the labor force to increase by about 7.4 million—more than any other age, sex, or race or ethnic group. BLS projects the Hispanic share of the labor force will be 20.9 percent by 2028 (Bureau of Labor Statistics 2019).

A great safety training game for most classes is Safety Bingo (discussed in Chapter 21), where key words and phrases related to the class topic make up the squares on the bingo card. Unfortunately, employees who cannot read or write English will have difficulty playing, and thus learning, from this game. Whenever any safety training activity is used, it is very important to make sure that the activity is a good match for the specific group of trainees. This includes making sure that it is easily understandable for everyone in the class. If there are any doubts about the ability of trainees to read or write well enough to participate, interactive activities should be selected that rely on visual aids instead.

Sample Image-Based Safety Training Activities

A few suggestions for image-based safety training games and activities that can be used with trainees who do not read or write English well, either because they are non-native English speakers or because they are illiterate, are described below. These are also great activities for all workers and are based on the principles and techniques explained throughout this book. The prominent use of images makes them appealing and effective for all.

Safety Lotería

Safety Lotería is like Safety Bingo and is a safety version of a popular Mexican game called Lotería. In Safety Bingo, game boards have words or short phrases related to the class topic. Instead of words on the game boards, in Safety Lotería small pictures represent those words. The game could be played by simply following the instructions of a traditional lotería game with the trainer randomly selecting a picture and then showing the card with the picture to the trainees. Trainees having that picture on their card, mark it off. Just like in regular Bingo, the first person to mark off all of the pictures in a line (across or down) wins. Played this way, it's an amusing game, but it does not do a good job of teaching new skills related to safety.

To make the activity more educational, the picture selected should not be shown to trainees. Instead, the trainer can provide a hint or even a small riddle that describes the picture. For example, if the class topic is personal protective equipment (PPE), and the image on a Safety Lotería card is a pair of steel-toe boots, the trainer would ask, "What type of PPE is necessary to protect the feet from forklift traffic?" If a trainee had an image of the steel-toe boots on a lotería card and knew the answer to the question, they would cross it off. The game continues this way with the trainer reading random clues and trainees marking off appropriate images on their cards until a trainee has marked off all images across, down, or on a diagonal on a card. At that point, the trainee should yell "Lotería!" Next, the trainer should ask the trainee to describe the images they crossed off, and together the class should try to remember and state the clue that went with that image. This provides an additional level of repetition and will increase retention of important concepts. If trainees are not English speaking, the description or riddle needs to be repeated in the language of the trainees. When the game takes place in this way, trainees need to think about the class content before selecting the appropriate square on the board. Before a trainee identifies the correct image on a game board, the trainee must first think of the correct answer. It's important for trainers to allow adequate time for trainees to think about and identify the correct answer. As described in Chapter 21, this retrieval practice is a great way to increase retention of the material.

A sample Safety Lotería game for a safety training class on personal protective equipment (PPE) is shown in Figure 24.8, and the corresponding clue sheet is shown in Figure 24.9.

Figure 24.8 ✦ Sample Safety Lotería game for PPE (Source: Tapp 2019)

Hazard Hunt

Hazard Hunt is a game involving a small group working together to identify hazards in a supplied photo or drawing. The photo or drawing should include at least six hazards; the hazards should not all be obvious but ideally should be related to class content. This is also a great game for learning general safety training tips on such topics as hazard recognition or hierarchy of controls. As with most safety training games and activities, it is recommended that a class of trainees be divided into small groups and asked to identify the hazards in the photo. The importance of using small groups or teams is discussed in Chapter 15 on teamwork. Each team should be given approximately 10 minutes

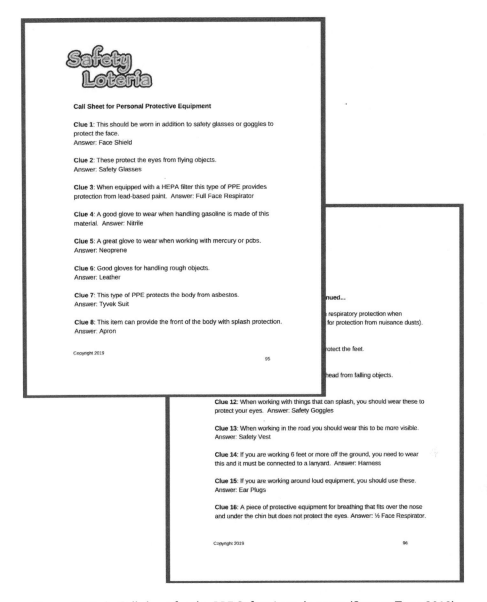

Figure 24.9 ✦ Call sheet for the PPE Safety Lotería game (Source: Tapp 2019)

to work together on identifying the hazards. Then each group should be asked to report how many hazards they identified in the picture. Various groups undoubtedly will have identified a different number of hazards. Trainers should start with the groups with the biggest lists, asking them to describe what they found. If team members name something that another team did not include, lively discussion will probably follow, which is one purpose of this exercise. Similar to the Safety Lotería activity, trainees will need to retrieve and rely on past knowledge to participate but will also need to discuss their thoughts with others in order to complete the game. This activity is great for learning from other participants, reinforcing class content, and recalling knowledge gained in other safety training classes, which will lead to increased retention.

Safety Sequence

Safety Sequence, as described in Chapter 19, is a good activity to use with training topics that include a series of steps or a safety procedure, such as lockout-tagout or confined space entry. Safety Sequence accompanied by illustrations can be a great learning tool, especially for trainees with limited reading ability. To organize a safety sequence activity with images, you will need to find a simple illustration or photo of each step in the procedure (one taken internally is fine if the picture quality is good and clearly shows the step). For a simple exercise on confined space entry, images might illustrate the following steps:

1. Review the permit.
2. Lock out the equipment.
3. Establish a method of communication.
4. Take an initial air sample.
5. Place ventilation inside the tank.
6. Set up a tripod/rescue equipment.
7. Put on a harness and connect to the tripod.
8. Enter the tank and check for hazards.
9. Complete the work or repairs.
10. Monitor air throughout the entry and record results every 30 minutes.
11. Climb up the ladder and out of the tank.
12. Complete the entry process and sign off on the permit.

Once these steps are written out and images have been selected, copies should be made of each illustration. It's helpful if each step is printed out on its own full-size piece of paper. The instructions for Safety Sequence, with or without images, are the same and are described in Chapter 19. Teams of trainees are each given an identical set of the safety sequence cards (shuffled so they are out of order). If possible, one card representing one step is given to each trainee on the team. The trainees are told that this is a race to see which team is the quickest to line up the steps in the correct order. Figure 24.10 illustrates the steps for a confined space entry procedure.

This activity can be used at the beginning of a safety training class or after the material has been covered. If trainees attempt this activity without any prior knowledge of the procedure, they will most likely struggle when they attempt to determine the correct sequence. However, this initial frustration has a benefit, as discussed in Chapter 14 on productive failure. If trainees are told, after their initial attempt, that the activity will be practiced again at the end, they will pay more attention during class since they will be motivated to do better on their second try.

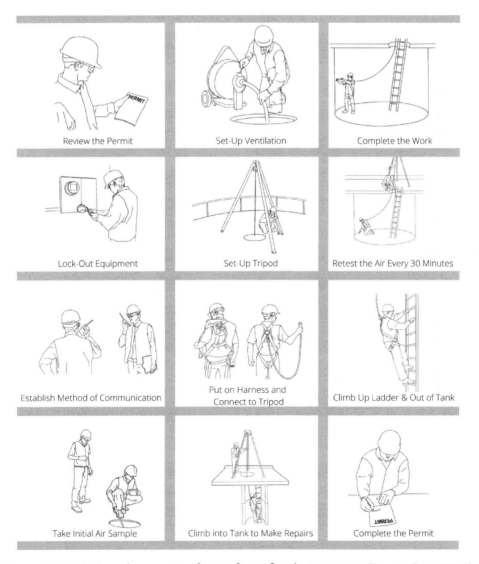

Figure 24.10 ✦ Sample sequence for a safe confined space entry (Source: Tapp 2015)

When one team believes it has the cards in the correct sequence, the activity should stop. That team should be asked to read out its answers—that is, the correct sequence. The trainer should ask the other teams if they have the same order or if they disagree. The class should work together, with the trainer's guidance, to put the steps in the correct order as one final review of the material. When creating safety sequence images, it is advantageous to include a small amount of descriptive text next to each image.

Pictogram Partners

Pictogram Partners is a game that not only takes advantage of the benefits of images in safety training but also the benefits of memorization that can come from drawing. To play Pictogram Partners, a trainer should explain to the class what a pictogram is and then ask teams of class members to draw a pictogram representing a topic related to the training class. Trainees can randomly pick an image related to the topic, or alternatively, a trainer can prepare small slips of paper with a word or phrase related to the class written on each paper. The trainees can then randomly select one of them. After 10 minutes, the trainer should ask each team to present its individual pictogram to the class without announcing what the pictogram represents. Each team should guess the topic, and the trainer should keep a record of the answers. The team that correctly identified the pictograms most frequently is the winner. This activity can also be used with pairs. In this case, each member of the pair shows his or her image to the partner at the end of the allotted time to see if he or she can identify it.

This activity not only provides some humor to the class, but it's also an effective way for trainees to remember content. When a trainees try to draw something from memory, they have to retrieve past knowledge and think about how the object is designed. If trainees in a class on confined space entry try to draw a harness or tripod, they will need a good understanding of how those things work, and working through the details in their mind will aid retention.

Pin the Pain

Pin the Pain is another image-based activity that works well with any topic related to chemical hazards, or any topic that covers injury and illness prevention for specific body parts. To play Pin the Pain, trainers can create a simple line drawing or go online to find a simple body outline that is not copyright

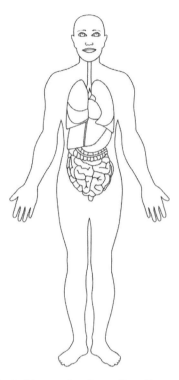

Figure 24.11 ✦ Human body outline (Source: Tapp 2018)

protected. The trainer should make a copy of the image for trainees, or even better, print it out poster size. A sample body outline is shown in Figure 24.11.

After presenting the training class content, each team should be given a copy of the body outline and a pack of small colored stickers or markers, along with either a safety data sheet for a product used at the facility or an empty container representing that product. Based on the information presented in the training class and the information in front of them, trainees should be told to identify where injury or illness could occur as a result of improperly working with the chemical(s) they have received information on. For example, if a trainer were presenting a class on the safe handling of hydroflouric acid, it would be expected that each group pin the pain on the eyes, skin, heart, nose, and lungs, for example. After each team has had the chance to pin the pain, the teams should be asked to present their body outlines and explain why they pinned the areas they did. A variation of this activity could be played with each team receiving a particular workplace task instead of a chemical. Various workplace tasks could be written on index cards and randomly assigned to teams. The trainees would be instructed to go through the same process. A twist that can be added to make the activity more challenging is to ask teams to draw the necessary PPE on the body outline after the body parts that have potential for injury or illness have been identified. Depending on the length of the class and the experience of the trainees, the drawing assignment for Pin-the-Pain can provide a great, extended version of this safety training activity.

Make Your Mark

Make Your Mark is an activity that takes advantage of visual representation of data. To use this activity, trainers should ask trainees to rank how dangerous or how safe an activity or condition seems to them. Several pieces of flip-chart paper should be hung around the room and trainees given a supply of small stickers. The trainer should select several different conditions or hazards, write one on each flip-chart paper, and distribute an equal number of stickers (approximately ten) to each trainee. After everything is set up, trainees should be asked to get up and place some of their stickers on each page. The number of stickers they place on each page should correlate to how unsafe they feel the stated situation is. They can choose to place none, all ten, or just a few on each page. After all trainees have completed the exercise, the trainer will be able to see which condition they believe is the most dangerous and which they believe poses the least risk. This will lead to class discussion and possibly debate. It also provides a visual aid that shows trainees how unsafe or safe something is perceived to be as a whole. While they might have thought an action was relatively risk free, they could begin to look at it differently if the majority of other trainees marked it as high risk. Instead of simply asking trainees this question and listening to their answers, the trainees will be creating their own visual aid.

When using images in safety training materials and in interactive activities, keep the following in mind:

1. People learn better from words and pictures than from words alone. People gain a deeper understanding of material when they can engage in active learning (Clark and Mayer 2016). When material is represented in both words and pictures, trainees are encouraged to make connections between the image and the text, making the experience more meaningful and assuring the material will be committed to long-term memory.

2. Use color graphics instead of black and white graphics whenever possible.
   One study that looked at the differences between color graphics and black and white graphics determined that the use of color graphics promotes achievement, particularly when learning concepts (Kleinman and Dwyer 1999).
3. Include a small amount of text along with images.
   One study involving learners with low levels of prior experience compared learning that used multimedia summaries to learning that used only a text summary. When the group was tested, results showed that when a summary is comprised of a sequence of annotated illustrations depicting the steps in a process with a 600-word text summary the knowledge retention and transfer was greater than when the summary was only presented verbally. It is also important to note that a small amount of text along with the multimedia presentation is more effective than the presentation with a large amount of text (Stokes 2002). The Picture Superiority Effect says that terms studied as pictures are better remembered than terms studied as words, even when test items are presented as words (Defeyter et al. 2009). Images and associated text should be included when possible in safety training materials, although it is not necessary to include the images when testing learners' knowledge of the same material.
4. Do not use images haphazardly.
   Although many studies have shown the benefits of using visuals in training programs, visuals should not be used haphazardly. Images serve to add underlying meaning to the content or encourage the trainee to think or reflect upon something. Images should not be used merely to inject excitement or entertainment, and if they are also unrelated to the training material, they may even interfere with the trainees' ability to learn (Sherry 1995).
5. Consider having trainees create their own illustrations.
   Studies have shown that drawing to-be-learned information enhanced memory and was a reliable, replicable means of boosting performance (Wammes et al. 2016). In many of the activities described in this book, it's suggested that trainers add appropriate images to clarify key safety points. Specific images may be difficult to find and may need to be created by graphic designers. An alternative is to ask trainees to create these images for use in safety training activities. The Pictogram Partners

activity discussed earlier is one way to increase trainees' learning and retention through drawing.

Image-based safety training is an essential learning ingredient for individuals with poor reading and writing skills. Along with information, it provides much needed clarification for this group. Using images in safety training not only ensures that trainees will pay attention but that the information will be remembered for a longer period of time. If safety training content is not retained, trainees will not be able to apply what they learned on the job, which is the ultimate goal of safety training efforts.

Review and Retention Activity

Safety Lotería is an image-based activity described in this chapter.

Safety Lotería is not intended to be played alone, but for the purpose of showing how this activity can be used to increase retention through repetition, a sample lotería card (Figure 24.12) focusing on image-based safety is provided, as well as a clue sheet. To use this activity as a review, look at the clues and then find the image that represents the best answer to each clue on the lotería card. When found, cross it off. In a classroom lotería game, clues would continue to be read until one of the participants has crossed off all squares across, down, or on the diagonal. As a solo review activity, answer all the clues so that every image on the lotería card is crossed off.

Safety Lotería Clue Sheet

1. An example of a good image, because it is highly recognizable
2. This type of image is unnecessary and increases the cognitive load
3. An example of a cliché image
4. An example of a "How" illustration
5. Visual communication aids that bring together information in a new and interesting way
6. An activity that requires studying an image and identifying hazards
7. A small amount of this along with an image can increase comprehension
8. An example of an image that can be used in the Pictogram Partners activity

Figure 24.12 ✦ Image-based Safety Lotería card

9. A training activity that works well with safety procedures involving a particular set of steps that must be done in a particular order
10. A large, image-based activity that can be used to identify chemical exposure
11. An activity for the visual representation of data
12. This type of illustration is good for showing "How Much"
13. This can enhance memory and boost performance
14. This represents the percent of U.S. employees who are functionally illiterate
15. Humans, first and foremost, process information this way
16. Image-based bingo

References

Bureau of Labor Statistics. 2019. "Hispanic Share of the Labor Force Projected to Be 20.9 Percent by 2028." October 2, 2019. www.bls.gov/opub/ted/2019/hispanic-share-of-the-labor-force-projected-to-be-20-point-9-percent-by-2028.htm.

Chambers, R. 2002. *Participatory Workshops: A Sourcebook of 21 Sets of Ideas and Activities*. London; Washington: Earthscan.

Clark, R. C., and R. E. Mayer. 2016. *E-Learning and the Science of Instruction: Proven Guidelines for Consumers and Designers of Multimedia Learning*. 4th ed. Hoboken, NJ: John Wiley & Sons, Inc.

Clark, R. C., and C. Lyons. 2010. *Graphics for Learning: Proven Guidelines for Planning, Designing, and Evaluating Visuals in Training Materials*. 2d ed. San Francisco, CA: John Wiley & Sons, Inc.

Defeyter, M. A., R. Russo, and P. M. McPartlin. 2009. "The Picture Superiority Effect in Recognition Memory: A Developmental Study Using the Response Signal Procedure." *Cognitive Development*, Vol. 24, Issue 3, July–September:265–273. doi: 10.1016/j.cogdev.2009.05.002.

Diamond, S. 2013. *The Visual Marketing Revolution: 26 Rules to Help Social Media Marketers Connect the Dots*. Indianapolis, IN: Que Pub.

Dirksen, J. 2016. *Design for How People Learn*. Berkeley, CA: New Riders.

Dooling, K. 2020. *ACIP Phased Allocation of COVID-19 Vaccines*. ACIP COVID-19 Vaccines Work Group. Centers for Disease Control. Accessed Dec. 22, 2020. https://www.cdc.gov/vaccines/acip/meetings/downloads/slides-2020-12/COVID-02-Dooling.pdf.

Einstein, M. 2019. "Some Amazing Statistics about Online Data Creation and Growth Rates—Information Overload Research Group." April 17, 2019. https://iorgforum.org/case-study/some-amazing-statistics-about-online-data-creation-and-growth-rates.

Evans, J. E., and W. M. Lindsay. 2008. *Managing for Quality and Performance Excellence*. Mason, OH: Thomson/South-Western.

Hodgdon, L. A. 2015. *Visual Strategies for Improving Communication: Practical Supports for Autism Spectrum Disorders*. Troy, MI: Quirkroberts Publishing.

Kleinman, E. B., and F. M. Dwyer. 1999. "Analysis of computerized visual skills: Relationships to intellectual skills and achievement." *International Journal of Instructional Media*, 26(1):53–69.

Lankow, J., J. Ritchie, and R. Crooks. 2012. *Infographics: The Power of Visual Storytelling*. Hoboken, NJ: John Wiley & Sons.

Lefever, L. 2013. *The Art of Explanation: Making Your Ideas, Products, and Services Easier to Understand*. Hoboken, NJ: John Wiley & Sons.

Nash, J. 2005. "Protecting a Multilingual Work Force." Accessed May 1, 2020. https://www.ehstoday.com/safety/article/21911580/protecting-a-multilingual-work-force.

National Center for Education Statistics. 2019. "Adult Literacy in the United States." United States Department of Education: NCES. July 2019. https://nces.ed.gov/datapoints/2019179.asp.

Nightingale, Florence. 1858. *Notes on Matters Affecting the Health, Efficiency, and Hospital Administration of the British Army. Founded Chiefly on the Experience of the Late War. Presented by Request to the Secretary of State for War*. London: Harrison and Sons.

Roam, D. 2010. *The Back of the Napkin (Expanded Edition): Solving Problems and Selling Ideas with Pictures*. New York: Portfolio.

Sherry, L. 1995. "Issues in Distance Learning." *International Journal of Educational Telecommunications*, 1(4):337–365. Charlottesville, VA: Association for the Advancement of Computing in Education (AACE).

Siegler, M. G., and E. Schmidt. 2010. "Every 2 Days We Create As Much Information As We Did Up To 2003." August 4, 2010. https://techcrunch.com/2010/08/04/schmidt-data/.

Stokes, S., 2002. "Visual literacy in teaching and learning: a literature perspective." *Electronic Journal for the Integration of Technology in Education*, 1:10–19.

Szudy, E. 1994. "The Right to Understand: Linking Literacy to Health and Safety Training." University of California, Berkeley, Labor Occupational Health Program (LOHP).

Tapp, L. 2015. *Safety Sequence: Putting Your Safety Training in Order*. Madison, NJ: Ennismore Publishing.

Tapp, L. 2018. *Activities for OSHA Outreach Trainers*. Madison, NJ: Ennismore Publishing.

Tapp, L. 2019. *Safety Lotería*. Madison, NJ: Ennismore Publishing.

Thalheimer, W. 2004. "Bells, whistles, neon, and purple prose: When interesting words, sounds, and visuals hurt learning and performance—a review of the seductive-augmentation research." Retrieved January 10, 2020. http://www.work-learning.com/seductive_augmentations.htm.

Wammes, J. D., M. E. Meade, and M. A. Fernandes. 2016. "The Drawing Effect: Evidence for Reliable and Robust Memory Benefits in Free Recall." *Quarterly Journal of Experimental Psychology*, 69(9):1752–76. https://doi.org/10.1080/17470218.2015.1094494.

Ware, C. 2020. *Information Visualization: Perception for Design*. 4th edition. Morgan Kaufmann Series in Interactive Technologies. United States: Elsevier Science and Technology.

Chapter 25
Self-Learning and Retention Techniques for the Reader

Safety and health professionals who maintain a reputable certification are required to continue with their learning after a certification is achieved. The idea of being a continuous learner is familiar and expected by professionals holding certification in a variety of fields—not just safety. Although this book is focused on providing safety professionals ways to help others remember and transfer information back to their day-to-day responsibilities, it is important that safety professionals themselves take the time not only to learn new skills that can be applied to occupational safety training but also to plan how this new information will be remembered long after they finish reading this book. Putting plans in place for applying this new knowledge when designing and delivering safety training in the future is an important part of getting the most from this book. The ability to teach oneself new subjects and skills remains essential (Young 2019).

Many of the suggested techniques for increasing retention of training materials discussed in this book can be used by readers to increase their own retention of the ideas and methods presented here. Safety professionals can consider the following suggestions as ways to continue learning more about training and retention as well as to increase the transfer of the material in this book back to their own training class design and delivery.

Microlearning

Microlearning is an effective way for safety professionals to learn new training skills and reinforce what they have already learned. *Microlearning*, as discussed in Chapter 12, refers to learning in small, focused chunks. It can be a great idea for safety professionals who may be too busy to spend an extended length of time away from work. Instead of taking a class that is a day or more in length to learn a lot about a particular subject, microlearning modules can be studied and digested when there are short windows of opportunity. Most people can easily accomplish 5 or 10 minutes a day of focused learning. With a little effort, safety professionals can create their own daily microlearning programs.

One example of a possible form of microlearning is a podcast. There are many podcasts available on safety, adult learning, and workplace training. Some podcasts are relatively short, 15 minutes or so, and others are closer to an hour. The key is to identify those that provide the most value and information about topics a trainer wants to learn more about and then subscribe to the podcast so notifications are received about new recordings as they are released. Many podcasts also include show notes that can be used to further increase learning. Podcasts allow learners to listen while doing something else. A good podcast will be brief enough for listeners to digest an entire topic in one sitting yet be interesting enough to hold their interest.

In *Ultralearning* by Scott Young, the author offers various strategies for acquiring skills and knowledge that are both self-directed and intense. A few of the ideas in *Ultralearning* are closely related to the ideas for getting safety training to stick and can also directly benefit readers of this book. These techniques include directness, retrieval, feedback, retention, experimentation, and more. Concrete suggestions and examples for a few of Young's ideas are provided below.

Directness

Directness refers to learning by doing the thing you want to get good at. "Directness is the idea of learning being tied closely to the situation or context you want to use it in" (Young 2019). The safety trainer should jump right in and try to implement the training skills discussed in this book as soon as possible. By immediately trying out the new ideas and skills, safety professionals can use the directness method. Learning this way is hard. It's more frustrating and challenging than reading a book about the topic or listening to a webinar. A trainer can do this by tackling a project directly related to the new skills that are being learned.

Safety professionals can start a new project even when they are not completely knowledgeable about a technique or method. If they are interested in learning how to create games to be used in training classes, they should just design a game and ask people to try playing it. They could spend a lot of time reading many books on game design, taking courses, and even possibly attaining a gamification certification, but there is great value in simply getting into a project and sweating over it. Very quickly the trainer will see what works and what doesn't work. The newly created game may not be the best safety training activity out there, and efforts may fail the first several times, but by producing something concrete, a lot will be learned in the process.

Retrieval Techniques

Retrieval techniques, discussed in Chapter 11, work just as well for safety professionals hoping to learn and retain new information as they do for trainees. Retrieval techniques are closely related to the testing effect. A core principle of the testing effect is that it's better to work harder to recall information than simply to review it. A beneficial way to use the testing effect is to test knowledge before the test taker feels ready. Safety professionals can use this to their own advantage as well. Testing oneself may be a way to assess knowledge mastery, but it is also a way to create it. Even before viewing the content or beginning to read, it can be good for learning and retention to create a mini-quiz for self-testing. After looking at a chapter heading, safety professionals can ask themselves what major ideas might be presented in the chapter. This simple step will help them remember and retain the information better.

Another way to practice retrieval is to create a mind map. A safety trainer can start by drawing a mind map with the center circle representing safety training retention. Next, lines could be drawn out from the center circle to show key points, and then subcircles can be added to back up each of those points. How well a learner does on this form of self-testing would be a good indicator of how well the material has been learned. An exercise such as this is very effective in learning and retaining new material. A starter mind map based on Part 1 (Chapters 1–7) of this book is shown in Figure 25.1, but the reader should not look at it before attempting to draw his or her own mind map. Additionally, to get the most benefit from a mind map exercise, notes and highlights throughout the book, or any other notes taken, should not be accessed—the map should be created purely from memory.

Imagine the reader has taken notes throughout this book in an effort to learn the ideas so they could be applied to safety training classes as necessary.

After finishing the book, if the reader closed it and tried to write down everything he or she could remember, this would be more advantageous for learning and retention than if the reader skimmed back over the pages and reviewed the highlighted items and notes. The idea and benefits of a braindump are discussed in Chapter 11. By trying to write freely everything one remembers about a particular topic, the information is being retrieved from long-term memory, and new connections are being made that will prompt that information to be retrieved in the future.

Some of the ideas in this book can only be rehearsed when there is a group of trainees. It can be difficult to practice safety training techniques if there is no live setting, but it is still possible to benefit from a simulated experience. In *Ultralearning*, Scott Young states that "It's important to note that what matters for transfer is not every possible feature of the learning environment, such as what room you're in or what clothes you're wearing while you learn. Rather, it's the cognitive features—situations where you need to make decisions about what to do and cue knowledge you've stored in your head. This suggests that when direct practice is impossible, a simulation of the environment will work to the degree to which it remains faithful to the cognitive elements of the task in question" (Young 2019). The benefits of simulations for trainees are discussed in Chapter 9, "Make it Real," and these benefits also apply to safety professionals striving to become better trainers.

For safety training, this means that any environment where a training class can be simulated and the techniques described tested, the practice will have a beneficial effect, even if this practice does not occur in front of a real safety training class filled with trainees looking to gain specific knowledge. Offering a brief virtual safety training class for free to a volunteer group would provide an environment where new skills could be practiced. Groups such as local church organizations, Habitat for Humanity build groups, and scouting troops can be great practice organizations. These obviously will not include the same types of trainees with the same demographics that would exist in the workplace, but the learning situation would be very similar to that presented by actual trainees.

Make It Public

Another suggestion made in *Ultralearning* by Scott Young is to decide in advance that a project will be viewed publicly. This will create a different mindset directed toward improving performance rather than just checking off a box showing completion. If a training session is videotaped and posted online for the world to see, the presenter will probably take a more positive approach to learning the skills and concepts that will be on display before everyone.

Feedback

Feedback is important for anyone trying to learn new skills or knowledge. Failing a test provides one kind of feedback. Being unable to complete a concept map successfully as discussed earlier is another form of feedback. Trying out a new idea in front of a group of trainees and having a negative response from those trainees is another type of feedback. Asking trainees to evaluate the programs put into place is another kind of feedback, and sometimes, this is uncomfortable as well. Failure as a form of feedback is not fun, and something most people strive to avoid. It's easy to skip asking trainees for their feedback after trying something new in a training class, but asking for the feedback and taking action on it is an important part of self-improvement.

As uncomfortable as it may be, scientific studies on the acquisition of expertise have shown that deliberate practice with immediate feedback is an essential ingredient in reaching expert levels of performance (Ericsson et al. 1993).

Without feedback, progress will be halted. For example, if a safety professional wants to be a better safety trainer, deliberately practicing the necessary skills is not enough. Without feedback, which may be painful, the safety trainer is not going to improve. The famous mantra "practice makes perfect" is also not true. A better statement is "perfect practice makes perfect," and the only way to know what *perfect* practice is, is through feedback. Doing things outside one's comfort zone is a great way to learn.

Experimentation

Experimentation is another of the methods proposed by Young. The ideas in this book, including experimentation, are based on many scientific studies conducted over many years by a diverse group of academics and practitioners around the world. All of this accumulated knowledge is a great starting point, but it does not mean that's all there is. Safety professionals can take the ideas and concepts in this book and experiment by adding what personally works and what works for a specific workforce. Safety professionals can try something that is quite different from what trainees are used to. Even if an idea for a training activity from this book raised eyebrows because some thought the technique or activity would never work with a particular group of trainees, a safety professional should take a chance and try it. The worse thing that could happen is that a lesson is learned about what not to do the next time. Doing something different can help trainees improve, and when they realize that something is different, that will increase retention.

There are several ways a safety trainer can experiment in order to learn from and apply new information. One is to use the idea of *copy then create*. To copy something, it first has to be understood, and this often involves deconstructing it. By doing this, the learner will not only become familiar with it but will more truly understand it, which will make it easier to create something new.

Another way to experiment is to add self-imposed limits or constraints. For example, a trainer could try to create and/or deliver a safety training topic in 15 minutes instead of 1 hour or attempt to create a set of safety training class slides with images only and no text. By forcing oneself to work with defined parameters, new ideas, methods, and solutions may become apparent. Safety trainers can experiment and see what works best for the trainees that rely on them to provide the most effective safety training materials and experiences. If trainers have an experimental mindset and get out of their comfort zone, great things can result. Experimentation will also prove or disprove what a safety professional may be thinking. A safety professional that thinks, "This would never work here," might be right, but even more likely might be pleasantly surprised.

Review and Retention Activity

The TABB activity is described in Chapter 7 on facilitation and motivation.

On a clean piece of paper, make four columns and write the letters T, A, B, and B across the top of the page (one letter per column). These letters stand for Takeaways, Actions, Barriers, and Benefits. Write the appropriate responses under each of the columns, and then have a colleague review the TABB sheet. This can firm up future plans to implement what has been learned as well as identify

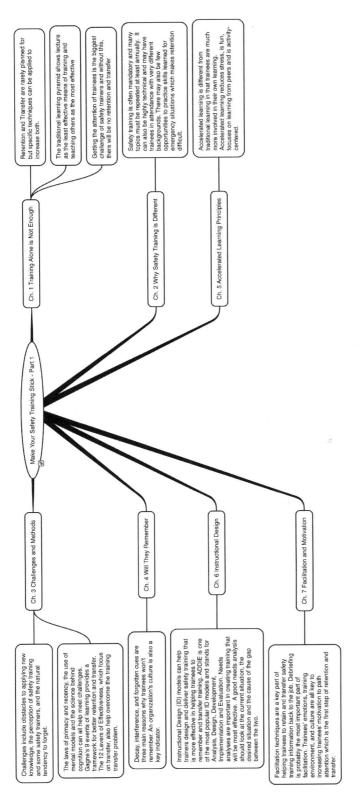

Figure 25.1 ✦ Starter mind map for chapters 1–7

strategies and resources that can be utilized to overcome barriers that may make it difficult to implement ideas in this book. The completed TABB sheet can also be saved for later review as a means of reinforcing content.

References

Ericsson, K. Anders, R. T. Krampe, and C. Tesch-Römer. 1993. "The Role of Deliberate Practice in the Acquisition of Expert Performance." *Psychological Review*, 100(3):363–406. doi: 10.1037/0033-295x.100.3.363.

Young, Scott H. 2019. *Ultralearning: Master Hard Skills, Outsmart the Competition, and Accelerate Your Career*. New York City: Harper Business.

Index

A

Accelerated learning, 4, 69–78, 84, 85, 220, 226, 234, , 236, 267–268, 280
    activity-centered, 74–77, 95
    defined, 69
    increases transfer, 70
    involves mind and body, 70–72, 85
    principles, 69–78, 95
    provides visual content, 74–75, 77
    social learning, 73, 102, 158, 217, 315
    stresses having fun, 72–73
    versus traditional learning, 69–71

Accepted Practices For E-learning in Safety, Health and Environmental Training (ANSI/ASSE Z490.2-2019), 20, Section 4.1, 329

ACTION conversation model, 96–97
Adaptive expertise, 142–143
Adaptive performance, 143
Adaptive thinking, 141
ADDIE (Analyze, Design, Develop, Implement, Evaluate), 80–82
    method of instructional design, 80
    poster activity, 93
Advanced organizers, 122–123
AEDs, *see* Automated external defibrillators
Aerial lift hazard recognition simulator, 139
A great safety training sort activity, 265
Aldrich, Clark, 191
Alexa, 129, 232
Allocation of initial Covid-19 vaccine, 338
Amazon, 232
American Express study, 122, 129
American National Standards Institute (ANSI), 20–21, 45
    Accepted Practices For E-learning in Safety, Health and Environmental Training (ANSI/ASSP Z490.2-2019), 20, 329
        Section 4.1, 329

    Criteria For Accepted Practices In Safety, Health and Environmental Training (ANSI/ASSE Z490.1), 20–21, 101
American Society of Safety Professionals (ASSP), *see* American National Standards Institute
Amygdala, 101
Analogies, 76, 99–100
Andragogy, 91–93
ANSI, *see* American National Standards Institute
Apple Inc., 232
AR, *see* Augmented reality
A sequencing activity for Gagné's Nine Events of Learning, 273
ASSP, *see* American Society of Safety Professionals
Association for Talent Development (ATD), 17, 153, 189, 194
Asynchronous online learning, 314, 316, 327
ATD, *see* Association for Talent Development
Atlas complex, 234
Augmented reality (AR), 135, 139–140
    AR markers, 140, 190
Automated external defibrillators (AEDs), 129, 131
Avatars, 136, 264, 315
Average attention span, 181
A–Z Race activity, 237, 301–303, 309–310

B

Baron, Sherry, M.D., 343
Bartle, Richard, 238
Beyond Transfer of Training: Engaging Systems to Improve Performance (Mary L. Broad), 60
BLS, *see* Bureau of Labor Statistics
Braindump, 99, 172–173, 289

Bureau of Labor Statistics (BLS), 344
Business Preparedness for Pandemic Influenza Second National Summit, *see*, Center for Infectious Disease Research and Policy

C

Call sheet for the PPE Safety Lotería game, 347
Center for Infectious Disease Research and Policy, 148
    Business Preparedness for Pandemic Influenza Second National Summit, 148
Chatbots, 89, 128, 129, 231–232
Checklist for choosing the best training game, 254
Checklists, 188, 254
Choosing activities for training, 245–254
    appropriateness, 245–246
    cultural differences, 232, 247, 254, 329
        power distance, 247
    environment, 246–247
    humor and fun, 249
    know the audience, 246
    locus of control, 247–248
    matching game mechanics to trainee motivations, 250
    physical requirements, 246
Chunking, 5, 13, 75, 84, 86, 182, 184, 191–194. *See also*: Microlearning
    dividing up content, 191–192
    suggestions for use, 194
Clickers, 202, 292–294
Cognition, 50–51. *See also*: Knowledge *and* Learning, cognitive load theory
    defined, 50
Communication skills, 18, 21, 25, 96, 138
Conceptual knowledge, 188
Confined space entry, 165, 188, 210–211, 348–349
Crane operator testing and certification, 86, 138
Criteria For Accepted Practices In Safety, Health And Environmental Training (ANSI/ASSP Z490.1), 20–21
Criterion reference testing, 86
Culture, 5, 24–25, 27–28, 232, 247, 254. *See also*: Organization

D

Data injects, 149
DeBoer, Jill, 148
Debriefing, 5, 12, 96–99, 155, 231, 262–263, 270–272, 294
    activities, 98–99, 294
        One Big Thing, 55, 98
        1-2-3, 98
        Red Light/Green Light, 98
        TABB Exercise, 98–99
    Hazard Hunt debrief session, 262–263
    Lone Ranger debrief session, 277
    postexercise, 137
Declarative knowledge, 6, 50–51, 188
Deep learning, 5–6
Desirable difficulty, 172, 174–175
Deterrents to remembering, 57–58. *See also*: Memory formation
    decay, 57–58
    interference, 58
    forgotten cues, 58
Diamond, Stephanie, 334
    The Visual Marketing Revolution, 334
Digital assistant, 315
    avatar, 315
Directness in self-learning, 360
Dopamine, 101
Dunning-Kruger effect, 62
Dweck, Carol, 247
    Mindset, 247

E

Ebbinghaus effect, 57
Ebbinghaus forgetting curve, 45–46, 57, 159
Ebbinghaus, Herman, 45–46
Einstein, Albert, 230
e-learning, *see* Online learning
Electrical safety comparison photos, 261
Electronic performance support systems (EPSSs), 128
Embedded tutorials, 128
Emotional intelligence, 136

Entertainment Software Rating Board study, 230
EPSSs, *see* Electronic performance support systems
Error-based activities, 257–264
    amusing activities, 259–260
        TV show *The Office*, 260
    ask experts, 257–258
    comparison photos, 260, 261
    e-learning courses, 260
    Hazard Hunt, 262–263
        debriefing session, 262–263
        photos, 262
    images and illustrations, 260
    safety sort, 260, 264–265
    serious error-based games, 263–264
        in construction, 263–264
        in public safety, 264
    What Happens Next?, 258
Error-based examples, 257
Evaluations, 3, 5, 63–66, 90, 236, 295. *See also*: Safety training, evaluations
    ADDIE, 81, 82
    Kirkpatrick model, 63–65
Experiential learning activities, 89, 135–136, 235
Extrinsic motivation, 105–106
Extrinsic rewards, 105

F

FACE, *see* Fatality assessment and control evaluation
Facebook, 147
Facilitation, 79, 95–101, 220
    analogies, 100
    debriefing, 96–97
    experiencing emotions, 100–101
    metaphors, 99–100
    of games, 230–231
    of training activities, 234
    retrieval, 99
Facilitator, 95
Fail to Learn, 214
Fall protection harness safety sequence, 269
Fatality assessment and control evaluation (FACE) reports, 147
Feedback cards, 292–294
Feynman, Richard, 62, 99
Feynman Technique, 62–63, 66–67, 224
Field trip, 76
Finkel, Donald, 234
Fire safety, 131–132, 211
    error-exposure training, 212
    fire extinguisher P.A.S.S. poster, 160–161
    fire extinguisher use, 26, 61, 267, 323
    Fire Safety Committee, 132
First-aid training, 60–61, 137, 172–174
Flash cards, 239–240, 287–288
Flipped classroom, 118–119
Florence Nightingale, 342
    Florence Nightingale map, 342
Forgetting, 45–46, 57–58, 131, 155–156, 162, 165
    decrease, 62, 154, 159
Free recall activities, 172–173, 289–292, 330

G

Gagné, Robert, 51–53, 82, 109
    Nine Events of Learning, 51–53, 272–273
Games, 47–48, 75–76, 84, 89, 91, 104, 136–137, 160, 209, 213, 223, 229–239, 245, 248
    accelerated learning, 74
    access with QR codes, 324
    as evaluations, 236, 295
    bendy rules, 237
        A–Z Race, 237–238
    bingo, 75, 290–292, 294–296
    choosing, 246, 248
    competitive, 219, 230, 250
    creating, 361
    crossword puzzles, 75, 110
    debriefing, 231
    defined, 229
    determining types of trainees, 238–239, 246
    developing personas, 250–253
    effectiveness, 233
    end-of-day, 285
    facilitating, 230–231, 234

Games (cont.)
    failure opportunities, 209, 236–238.
        See also: Productive failure
    fun as part of, 234–235, 249
    image-based, 344–355
    immediate feedback, 236, 237
    increase retention, 229–230, 253
    Jeopardy, 287
    learner personas, 239, 250–253
        defined, 250
        Mike the Mechanic, 251–252
        Pauline the Packer, 252
    mechanics of, 250, 251
    modifying, 250
    online, 232–233, 235, 326
        OSHA game-based training tool for hazard control, 235
    role-playing, 245
    serious, 137, 223, 235, 263–264
        aviation industry, 235
    teamwork, 217, 223, 234
    trial run, 233–234
    types of players, 238–239
        achievers, 239
        explorers, 238
        killers, 239
        socializers, 238
    versatility, 232–233, 250
    visual aids, 245
Gamification, 102, 140, 185, 190–191, 213, 229–232, 238. *See also*: Games
    defined, 229
    forced engagement, 185
    game mechanics, 250, 251
    improves engagement, 230
    productive failure, 213, 236–238
    storytelling, 232
    structural, 190–191
    using technology, 231–232
        chatbots, 231–232
    versatility, 232
Gamification flash cards, page 1, 240
Gamification flash cards, page 2, 240
GHS, *see* Global Hazard Classification System

Glasser, William, MD, 249
    Choice Theory: A New Psychology of Choice Freedom, 249
Global Hazard Classification System (GHS), 186, 187, 279, 286
Google, 147, 333

H

Habitat for Humanity, 362
Handouts, 74, 91, 193
Hazard Hunt, 99, 221, 223, 262–263, 319, 346–348
Hazardous Waste Operations and Emergency Response (HAZWOPER), 20, 23, 143
Helper therapy principle, 224, 227
Hierarchy of controls, 306, 346
Hippocampus, 101, 202
Hispanics in the U.S. labor force, 24, 344
Human body outline, 351
Human visual processing, 334–335

I

Illiteracy, 268, 333, 343, 344, 355
    U.S. government study, 343
Illustration of desktop simulator, 138
Image-based communication, 333
Image-based Safety Lotería card, 355
Image-based safety training, 75, 140, 147, 268, 292, 329, 333–355. *See also*: Visual aids
    considerations for use, 352–354
    for foreign-born workers, 343–344
    infographics, 342–343
    reinforces learning, 335–336
    sample activities/games, 344–352
        Hazard Hunt, 346–348
        Make Your Mark, 352
        Pictogram Partners, 350
        Pin the Pain, 350–352
        Safety Lotería, 292, 344–347, 354–355
        Safety Sequence, 348–350
    six types of problems and associated visuals, 336–341
        how, 337, 341

how much, 336–337, 338
when, 337, 339
where, 337, 341
who and what, 336, 338
why, 337, 341
Immersion, 11–12
Infographics, 133, 157, 194–195, 298–301, 321–322, 342–343
defined, 321
Information dump, 219
Information overload, 13, 48. *See also*: Overlearning
Information Overload Resource Group, 333
Injury and illness rates compared to fume hood use, 341
Injury data, 8–9, 89, 147, 341
Inspection reports, 9, 89, 278
Instagram, 333
Instructional design, 6, 7, 13, 53, 59, 79–93, 214, 248, 253
ADDIE system (Analyze, Design, Develop, Implement, Evaluate), 80–82, 93
pilot testing, 81
confidence ratings, 214
creating safety training programs, 87–88
main theories, 83–87
behaviorism, 85–86
cognitivism, 84–85
constructivism, 83–84
SAM (Successive Approximation Model), 80, 82
Interaction, 69, 111, 187, 212, 218, 229, 316, 318, 326–328. *See also*: Social interaction
online, 326–328
Interactive training activities, *see* Safety training, interactive activities
Interleaving, *see* Learning, interleaving
Internal document libraries, 128
International Data Corporation, 139
Worldwide Semiannual Augmented and Virtual Reality Spending Guide, 139
Interpersonal skills training, 17

Intrinsic motivation, 105–107
Intrinsic rewards, 105

J
Jeopardy Flashcard Activity, 287
Job aids, 53, 89, 91, 128–129

K
Kahn, Philippe, 335
Kahoot, 294
Knowledge, 3–4, 10, 26, 27, 41, 50–51, 54, 60–61, 64, 188. *See also*: Learning
conceptual, 188
construction, 83
declarative, 6, 50–51, 188
gaps, 62
procedural, 50–51
transfer, 41, 54, 60
Knowles, Malcolm, 91
theory of andragogy, 91–93

L
Language,
barriers, 343–344
differences, 24–25, 232, 247, 334
specialized vocabulary, 334
Leadership training, 17, 96
Learning, 223. *See also*: Accelerated learning *and* Memory formation
accommodation, 83
active, 75, 76, 95, 245, 246, 352
adult, 50, 52, 82, 91–92, 101, 104, 235, 360
assimilation, 83, 84
blended, 89–90, 122, 176, 313
cognitive load, 189, 192, 335
reducing cognitive load, 193–194
cognitive load theory, 192–194
extraneous load, 193, 335
germane load, 193
intrinsic load, 192
cooperative, 218, 222–225
curiosity aids retention, 102, 110, 202–203
distributed practice, 194

Learning (*cont.*)
- emotional component, 4–5, 11, 58, 71, 73, 101–102, 149, 199, 206, 249, 263, 264
- experiential, 89, 135–136, 235
- Feynman Technique, 62–63, 66–67, 224
- hands-on, 10, 76, 89, 268
- interference, 13, 57–58
- interleaving, 153–154, 162–166, 182, 194
  - defined, 154, 162
  - mixing learnng activities, 163
  - trainee test questions, 165–166
  - versus blocking, 163–164
- methods, 8–10, 52, 73, 75–77, 122–123, 315
- overlearning, 61–62
- predicting results, 146–147, 199–202
  - accident/incident case studies, 141, 147, 212–213, 258–259
  - Pause–Predict–Ponder, 200
  - using technology, 202
  - What Happens Next?, 146–147, 200
- recall, 5, 52, 91, 137, 160, 164, 171, 174, 185, 192, 201, 203, 224, 280, 294, 309, 343, 348
  - free, 172, 288–289, 330
  - immediate, 156
  - tests, 173, 175, 361
- repetition, 66, 118, 153–155, 157, 158, 162, 186–187, 194, 230, 270, 283, 285–286, 328, 334. *See also*: Repetition and retrieval activities
  - defined, 154
  - spaced, 161, 174, 283, 286
- research findings, 10, 45–46, 50, 51–54, 57–58, 61, 69, 71, 91–93, 99–101, 103, 105–107, 137, 144–147, 154, 156, 162–165, 172, 174, 176, 178, 181, 200, 202, 204–205, 209, 211–213, 214, 235, 249, 314, 315, 316, 326, 334
- retrieval practice, 58, 93, 99, 153–154, 159–161, 162, 171–178, 212, 275, 285–286
  - activities, 176–178. *See also*: Repetition and retrieval activities
  - analysis of case studies or lessons learned, 160
  - covert, 178, 185
  - defined, 154
  - desirable difficulty, 172, 174–175
  - distributed, 162
  - failure, 162, 209–214
  - first-aid training, 172–174
  - follow-up material, 160
  - forward testing effect, 204–205
  - pre- and postevaluations, 160
  - pre- and posttests, 160, 173
  - quizzes, 159, 171, 172, 289–290, 297
  - Safety Lotería, 177–178, 292
  - safety posters, 160–161
  - self-test, 159, 172, 175
  - skill practice, 160
  - spacing out, 160, 174, 286
  - testing effect, 154, 157, 203
  - tests, 171, 173, 175, 178, 203
  - Training Tutor, 177, 225
  - written agenda, 178
- skills evaluation, 204
- soft skills, 259
- spacing, 45, 62, 153–159, 160, 162, 164, 166, 174, 328
  - defined, 154
- stressful, 72, 101, 249
- styles, 11, 73
- surprise, 209–210
- theories, 82–87
  - behaviorism, 85–87
  - cognitivism, 84–85, 87, 235
  - constructivism, 82–84, 87, 235
- vicarious, 121–122
- visual processing, 334–335

Learning management platform, 314
Learning Methods and Retention Pyramid, 9–10, 224

Lefever, L., 335
    The Art of Explanation: Making Your Ideas, Products, and Services Easier to Understand, 335
Leitner, Sebastian, 286
    Leitner box system, 286, 328
Letter to Self activity, 132
Levers of Transfer Effectiveness, 53–54
Lewin, Kurt, 129–130
    Lewin's Force Field Analysis, 129–130
LightSurf Technologies, 335
LinkedIn, 147
Lockout-tagout (LOTO) procedure, 6, 75, 140, 163, 267, 268, 324, 348
Locus of control, 247–248
    internal, 247–248
    external, 248
Lone Ranger, 277
Long-term memory, 3, 5, 12, 46–48, 50, 52, 82, 85, 95, 141, 155, 160, 161, 164, 171, 176, 184, 185, 193, 199, 235, 288, 309, 315, 352, 362
LOTO, *see* Lockout-tagout
Lozanov, Georgi, 69
    theory of suggestology, 69

M

Make Your Mark, 352
Management
    advised of training objectives, 121
    perception barriers, 42, 43
    responsibilities, 7, 43, 54
    training, 24, 96, 277
    training support, 28, 41, 57, 59, 107, 110, 122, 125, 127–128, 130, 189
Marienau, C., 95
Maslow's Hierarchy of Needs Theory, 105
Match Game, 278–279
Memory formation, 4–5, 45–48, 101, 143, 153, 171, 203, 209. *See also*: Learning *and* Long-term memory *and* Short-term memory
    consolidation, 161
    debriefing, 6, 96–99, 137, 155
        activities, 98–99
    postexercise, 137
    deterrents, 57–58
    downtime, 47, 48
    primacy effect, 5, 46–48
    primacy–recency curve, 47
    recency effect, 5, 46–48
    spacing effect, 45, 155–159
    stages, 4–5
Mental models, 5, 48–50, 103, 155, 209
Mentimeter website, 306
Metaphors and Analogies, 76, 99–100
Microlearning, 48, 62, 75, 132, 140, 155, 161, 181–191, 192, 194–195, 328, 359–360
    combined with interleaving, 182
    defined, 183, 359
    delivery platforms, 188
    designing, 187–188
    gamification, 185, 190–191
    hands-on activities, 189–190, 251
    implementation, 189–190
    management support, 189
    not a good fit, 183, 188
    three main elements, 184
    three types of engagement, 185, 326–328
    simulations, 189, 191
        short sim, 191
    six types, 185–187
        pensive, 185
        performance-based, 186
        persuasive, 186
        postinstruction, 186, 190
        practice-based, 186
        primary, 186–187
Microlearning infographic, 195
Microsoft study on attention span, 181
Mind maps, 78, 307–309, 365
    bloodborne pathogens, 308–309
    creating, 78, 361
    for chapters 1–7, 365
Mobile phone apps, 202
Monk, Stephen, 234
Moore, Kristine, 148
Most Frequent Violations as a safety training activity, 301

Most Frequent Violations as a sample infographic, 300
Motivation to learn, 44, 92–93, 95, 103–105
Motivation to pay attention, 109–111
Motivation to transfer, 53, 59, 103, 106–107
Motor cortex, 72
Movie Reviewer, 289–290
Murre and Dros research, 45

N

National Center for Educational Statistics (NCES), 343
National Commission for Certified Crane Operators (NCCCO) study, 138
National Institute of Occupational Safety and Health (NIOSH), 139, 343
    aerial lift hazard recognition simulator, 138, 139
NCCCO, *see* National Commission for Certified Crane Operators
NCES, *see* National Center for Educational Statistics
Needs analysis, 61, 88–91
    procedure, 88
Nine Events of Learning, 51–53, 272–273

O

Occupational Safety and Health Act of 1970, 19
Occupational Safety and Health Administration (OSHA), 19–20, 24–25
    bloodborne pathogens standard (1910.1030), 19, 23
    education and materials for Spanish speakers, 344
    electrical safety standard (1910.332), 12–13
    "Fatal Facts" reports, 141, 147, 258, 259
    HAZWOPER standard (29 CFR 1910.120), 20, 23, 143
    langauge barriers and workplace fatalities, 344
    Occupational Noise Exposure (1910.95), 23
    online, game-based training tool for hazard control, 235
    Respiratory Protection training standard (1910.134), 23–24
    "Training Requirements in OSHA Standards," 19
    training standards, 23–24, 28–37, 64, 74, 76, 193
        specific chemicals, 23
One Big Thing, 55, 98
1-2-3, 98
Online learning, 313–330, *See also*: Safety training, delivery method
    action plan for training transfer, 320–321
    asynchronous, 314, 316, 327
    audio and visual aids, 329
    defined, 313
    disadvantages of, 316, 323–324
    discussion boards, 327
    distractions, 314, 317
    email and texting, 320–321, 327
    instructor feedback, 327–328
        instructional videos, 327
        modeling learning behavior, 328
        one-on-one virtual meetings, 327
    interaction, 326–328
    interactive activities, 318–326
        Drag and Drop, 325
        free recall, 330
        Hazard Hunt, 319
        infographics, 321–322
        preclass, 317–318, 320, 322–323
        Seek and Find, 325–326
    live streaming, 325
    microlearning, 328
    needs assessment, 328–329
    new models, 316–319
        computer confidence, 317–318
        reliable technology, 317
        synchronized media, 317
    passive, 328
    QR codes, 324–325
    repetition, 328
    research, 316, 326, 327, 328
    sharing results, 320
    social interaction, 315, 318–320
        breakout rooms, 315, 319

chats, 294, 315, 318, 327
colaboration platforms, 320, 325
polling, 315
strategies, 326–328
spaced practice, 328
survey tool, 321
teams, 319–322, 325–328. *See also*: Teams *and* Teamwork
testing, 314–315, 328
videos, 323
Organization, 28, 42–43, 54
climate factors, 44, 59, 107–108
goals, 4, 7, 59, 61, 88, 89, 117–118, 124–125, 253
learning culture, 5, 7, 42, 57, 59–63, 107–108
six supporting factors, 60–61
microlearning, 185, 189–190
safety culture, 107
safety training impact, 65, 107–108, 124
wiki page, 323
OSHA, *see* Occupational Safety and Health Administration
OSHA FatalFact No. 14–2016, 259
OSHA Fatal Facts No. 15–2017, Warehouse Fall from Pallet Elevated by Forklift, 142
Overlearning, 61–62

P

Pause–Predict–Ponder, 200
Personal protective equipment (PPE), 278–279, 304, 305, 345, 352
Pictogram Partners, 350
Picture superiority effect, 353
Pinterest, 252, 333
Pin the Pain, 350
Piskurich, George M., 246
Rapid Instructional Design, 246
Plan, Do, Check, Act, 340
Podcast, 157, 190, 360
Positive affective state, 71–72
Posttraining, *See also*: Safety training, postclass communication
interference, 42–43
interventions, 25, 125–126, 128–129
Power distance, 247

PowerPoint slides, 74, 110, 159, 334
PPE, *see* Personal protective equipment
Practice opportunities, 5, 25–26, 47–48, 52, 53, 61–62, 85, 86, 104, 121, 128, 135, 155, 160, 190.
Primacy–recency curve, 47
Probable cause sorting activity, 281
Productive failure, 26, 83, 84, 136, 209–214, 236–238, 263–264, 363
benefits, 210–211
confidence ratings, 213–214, 237
error-exposure training, 212
evaluation results, 214
in gamification, 213
instant feedback, 209
stories, 212–213
tests, 211–212, 214
Programmed learning, *see* Skinner, B. F.
Provence, Scott, 214, 236
Fail to Learn, 214, 236
Pushing vs. pulling infographic, 298
Pushing vs. pulling infographic as a fill-in-the-blank activity, 299
Pygmalion Effect, 131–132

Q

QR codes, 110, 129, 190, 324–325
Questions 176–177
Quiz Creator, 227, 306–307

R

Red Light/Green Light, 98
Reflection, 99
Reinforcement, 20, 25, 41, 46, 48, 85, 93, 96, 126–133, 160, 166, 202, 270, 279, 283, 290, 303, 309, 325
action planning, 96–97
ACTION conversation model, 96–97
lack of, 42–43
microlearning, 90, 161, 186, 188, 194
on-the-job performance support, 128–129
job aids, 128–129
electronic performance support systems (EPSSs), 128

Repetition and retrieval activities, 283–296
    Braindump, 289
    flash cards, 286–287
        Jeopardy Flashcard Activity, 287
        Safety Flash, 287–288
    Movie Reviewer, 289–290
    Safety Bingo, 290–292, 294–296
    Snowball Fight/Ask in the Airplane, 284–285
Repetition and retrieval activity—Safety Bingo, 295
Repetition, spacing, retrieval practice, and interleaving crossword puzzle, 168
    Answer key, 169
Retention techniques for online learning, see Online learning
Retrieval, 93, 99, 160, 162, 171–174, 178, 203–205. See also: Learning, retrieval practice and Repetition and retrieval activities
    cues, 58
    tests, 203–205
Return on investment (ROI), 8, 65, 80, 90, 166, 253
Roam, Dan, 336
    six basic drawing types, 336–341
    The Back of the Napkin, 347
Role-playing, 148, 245

S

Safe drum handling illustration, 123
Safe housekeeping procedures, 43, 64–66
Safe lifting techniques, 18, 65, 86, 100, 186, 323, 339
Safety Bingo, 290–292, 294–296, 344
Safety Bingo sample for hand safety, 290
Safety Consultant for a Minute, 83, 226
Safety Flash, 287–288
Safety Lotería, 177, 292, 344–347, 354–355
Safety management system, 28
Safety Sort activities, 275–281
Safety training, 3, 8, 10, 13, 17–37, 229, 232, 236, 237, 250–251, 260, 286, 303–304, 305, 324, 327, 329, 333, 335, 359. See also: Training

accelerated, 70–77
activities, see Safety training, interactive activities
adaptive performance, 143
case studies, 91, 99, 102, 140, 141, 143–144, 147, 150, 157, 159, 199, 212–213, 258–259. See also: Stories
chemical hazards, 7, 25, 158, 164, 257, 279, 334, 350–352
confined space entry, 165, 188, 210–211, 348–350
customized for the audience, 49–50
delivery method, 10, 88–91
    active, 10, 72, 230, 245, 328
    blocking, 163–165
    face-to-face classes, 89, 118, 181–182, 313, 315, 316
    hands-on, 10, 17, 72, 120, 135, 159, 189, 251
    lecture, 10, 17, 27, 45, 91, 96, 98, 111, 157, 334
    mixed, 89–90, 313
    on-demand, 181–182
    online, 17, 89, 118, 124, 176, 181–182, 214, 313–330
    on the job, 17, 89
    passive, 10, 27, 72, 328
    self-study or self-directed, 17, 89, 91, 118–119
design, 3, 7, 19, 27, 44, 48–49, 50–51, 53, 54, 65–66, 72, 73, 117, 120, 125, 129, 136, 149, 181, 248, 316, 329. See also: Instructional design
    ADDIE, 81
    workplace terminology, 125
developing stories, 144–147. See also: Stories
Dunning-Kruger effect, 62
effectiveness, 3, 10, 26–28, 41, 54, 82, 205
environment, 21, 41, 42, 54, 71–72, 77, 101–102, 226, 237, 246, 247, 249, 314, 317
error-exposure, 143–144, 212–213
    firefighters, 212

evaluations, 5, 21, 63–66, 85, 90, 119, 175–176, 205
    ADDIE, 82
    end-of-class, 60, 95, 124, 165
    formative, 124
    games as, 236, 295
    Kirkpatrick model, 63–65
    postclass, 124, 160
    preclass, 110, 160, 237
    sequencing activities, 270
    summative, 124
    tabletop exercises, 148
    toolbox training, 225
    workplace observations, 60, 64–65
exercises, 5, 74, 84. *See also*: Safety training, tabletop exercises
    information-accessing, 74
    problem-posing, 74, 77, 84
for diverse audiences, 24–25
games, *see* Games
influencers, 121
insufficient, 3
interactive activities, 10–11, 12, 47–48, 71–72, 77, 81, 84, 89, 96, 102–103, 106, 110, 141, 149, 160, 177, 209, 223, 225. *See also*: Choosing activities for training *and* Online learning, interactive activities
    appropriate use, 245
    A–Z Race, 237, 301–303, 309–310
    Braindump, 99, 172–173, 289
    error-based, *see* Error-based activities
    debriefing, *see* Debriefing activities
    Feynman Technique, 62–63, 66–67
    flash-card activities, 171, 239–240, 286–288
    free recall, 172–173, 289–292, 330
    Hazard Hunt, 99, 221, 223, 262–263, 319, 346–348
    Most Frequent Violations, 301
    Movie Reviewer, 289–290
    Pause–Predict–Ponder, 200
    postclass, 90
    preclass, 90, 118–119, 320
    Safety Bingo, 290–292, 294–296, 344
    Safety Consultant for a Minute, 83, 226
    Safety Lotería, 177, 292, 344–347, 354–355
    sequencing, *see* Sequencing activities
    sorting, *see* Sorting activities
    summarizing, *see* summarizing activities
    TABB Exercise, 98–99, 132, 364, 366
    What Happens Next?, 146–147, 200, 258
lessons learned, 140, 141–142, 143, 212. *See also*: Stories
mandatory and compliance, 12, 17, 19–22, 103, 104, 159, 225, 313
needs analysis, 61, 88–91
off-the-shelf, 25, 65, 87–88, 125, 183
on-the-job performance support, 128–129
    job aids, 53, 89, 91, 128–129
    electronic performance support systems (EPSSs), 128
overtraining, 61–62
participatory, 10, 81, 230
pilot testing, 81, 121
postclass communication, 25, 42, 124–133, 149, 160, 187, 190, 285
    5-minute refreshers, 125–126
    infographics, 133
    reinforcement, 20, 41, 93, 126–133
    summative evaluation, 124
    workplace posters, 93, 105, 129, 132, 157

Safety training (cont.)
    preclass communication, 27, 62, 90, 102, 110, 117–123, 285, 317–318, 320
        advanced organizers, 122–123
        flipped classrooms, 118–119
        objectives, 120–121
    predicting outcomes, 199–202
    presentation strategies, 153–166
    realistic, 6, 20, 26, 44, 135–149, 191, 214, 325. *See also*: Simulations
        augmented reality (AR), 135, 139–140
        experiential learning activities, 89, 135–136, 235
        virtual reality (VR), 135, 137–139
    refresher courses, 22–23, 27, 172, 174, 176, 186, 205, 225, 232, 233
    retention, *see* Training, retention
    role models, 121–122, 328
    scrap 7–8, 18
    site-specific, 25
    skills vs. knowledge, 51
    spacing, 154, 155–159, 160, 162, 164, 166, 174, 182, 286, 287
    standards, 12–13, 19–21, 23–24, 28–37, 45, 64, 101, 143, 329
    tabletop exercises, 26, 89, 135, 148–149, 219
    teamwork, 217–227
    technical, 25, 183
    tests, 53, 64, 85, 91, 314–315, 328, 363. *See also*: Learning, retrieval practice
        end-of-class, 186, 236
        informal quizzes, 160, 161, 214
        posttests, 91, 160, 232
        pretests, 91, 157, 160, 165, 205, 214
        self-test, 159, 175
    tiny course, 187
    transfer, *see* Training, transfer
    videos, 200, 205, 245–246, 251, 323
        asking questions, 205
        preinstruction, 317–318
    visual aids, 245, 329, 333–336, 342–344, 352
    workplace terminology, 125
Safety training programs, 3, 11, 21–22, 51, 66, 81–82, 87, 131, 149, 155, 159, 161, 226, 231, 238, 248, 253, 336, 341
    externally created materials, 87–88
Sales representative accident occurrence by time of day, 339
SAM (Successive Approximation Model), 80, 82
Sample emergency evacuation plan, 340
Sample mind map for a bloodborne pathogen training class, 308
Sample photo for the What Happens Next activity, 258
Sample Safety Bingo call sheet for hand safety, 291
Sample Safety Lotería game for PPE, 346
Sample safety-sort card set for scaffolding training class, 276
Sample sequence for a safe confined space entry, 350
Scaffolding Sort, 276
Schmidt, Eric, 333
Scrap learning, 7–8
Screencasts, 327
Search engine providers, 147
Seek and find activities, 325–326
Self-determination theory, 105–107
Self-instructional packages, 118–119
Self-learning and retention techniques for safety professionals, 359–366
    directness, 360–361
    experimentation, 363–364
        add self-imposed limits or constraints, 364
        copy then create, 364
    getting feedback, 363
    microlearning, 359–360
        podcasts, 360
    post the training sessions online, 363
    retrieval techniques, 361–362
        creating a mind map, 361
        offering a virtual safety training class, 362
        practicing braindump, 362

self-testing, 361
training class simulation, 362
starter mind map, 361, 365
testing effect, 361
Sequencing activities, 267–273
confined space entry, 348–349
creating, 268–270
debriefing, 270–271
sample questions, 272
defined, 267
donning a fall protectoin harness, 268–270, 271
Fall protection harness safety sequence, 269
modifying, 271–272
Nine Events of Learning, 272–273
Safety Sequence, 221–222, 348–350
using teams, 267, 268, 271
adding competition, 270
Sherlock (Safety) Holmes, 309
Shopping for Safety, 303–304
Short-term memory, 5, 46–48, 95, 164, 192
Simulations, 26, 89, 91, 135–138, 148, 189, 362
avatars, 136
games, 136–137
postexercise debrief, 137
short sims, 191
Skinner, B. F., 85
programmed learning, 85
building skills, 86
identification, 86
memorization, 86
Smile sheets, 63–64
Snowball Fight/Ask in the Airplane, 284–285
Social interaction, 187, 234, 235, 318
Sorting activities, 275–281
Safety Sort, 275–276
Lone Ranger, 277
Probable Cause, 279–281
While You Were Out, 277–278
Match Game, 278–279
Starter mind map forchapters 1–7, 365
Steps for safe lifting, 339
Stories, 12, 20, 62–63, 76–77, 85, 100–101, 102, 132, 140–142, 143, 144–147, 212–213, 230, 232, 258, 297, 300–301, 309
defined, 141
story-based interventions, 144
tips for developing, 144
Subject matter expert (SME), 79, 81, 90, 103, 121, 124, 126, 188, 257, 318
Suggestology, 69
Summarizing activities, 48, 237, 297–310
A–Z Race, 237, 301–303, 309–310
infographics, 298–301
Florence Nightingale map, 342
Pushing vs. pulling, 298–299
Most Frequent Violations, 300–301
mind maps, 78, 307–309, 365
bloodborne pathogens, 308–309
for chapters 1–7, 365
Quiz Creator, 306–307
Sherlock (Safety) Holmes, 309
Shopping for Safety, 303–304
Summary Group Grids, 305–306
hierarchy of controls, 306
personal protective equipment, 305
Ten-Cent Summary, 304–305
Timeline, 307
Word Cloud, 306
Mentimeter, 306
WordArt, 306
Word It Out, 306
Summary Group Grids, 305–306
Supervisor
as role model, 108, 122
communications with, 22, 90, 120–121, 130
enforcing training, 106
interviews, 89
observing trainees, 50
refresher sessions, 126
responsibilities, 7, 54, 59, 97
support for training, 107–108, 110, 118, 122, 127–130
surveys, 8, 321

Supervisor (*cont.*)
 training, 17, 96–97, 128, 136–137, 150, 189, 277
 training evaluation, 82, 204
Surface learning, 5
Sweller, John, 192
System safety, 79

T

TABB Exercise, 98–99, 132, 364, 366
Tabletop exercises, 26, 89, 135, 148–149, 219
 after-action reports, 149
 designing, 149
 developing scripts and data injects, 149
 mini-tabletop exercise, 149
Taylor, K., 95
Team(s), 62, 63, 71, 75, 76, 218–222. *See also*: Teamwork
 defined, 218
 designing tabletop exercises, 148
 developing summary quizzes, 297
 disruptive behavior within, 221–222
  active uninvolvement, 221–222
  dominating, 222
  passive uninvolvement, 221–222
  working independently, 222
 forming, 218–221, 234
  adequate space and resources, 220
  member selection, 219–220
  size, 218–219
 games, 150, 232
Teamwork, 217–227, 234, 250, 251. *See also*: Team(s)
 benefits, 217–218, 223–225
 breaking up information dump, 219
 collaboration, 73, 223
 connectedness, 223–224
 creating quizzes, 77, 289–290, 297, 306–307
 defined, 218
 interactive activities, 73, 77, 95, 102, 110, 146, 201–202, 217–219, 220, 223, 225, 246–247, 267–272, 275–280, 286–309, 319–326
  A–Z Race, 237–238, 300–303
  Feynman Technique, 63
  flash-card activities, 286–288
  Hazard Hunt, 262–263, 346–347
  infographics, 299–300
  Mind Map, 307–309
  Movie Reviewer, 289–290
  online learning integration, 319–326
  Pictogram Partners, 350
  Pin the Pain, 350–352
  Quiz Creator, 227, 306–307
  Safety Consultant for a Minute, 226
  Safety Sequence, 348–350
  sequencing activities, 267–272
  Shopping for Safety, 303–304
  sorting activities, 275–280
  Summary Group Grids, 305–306
  Ten-Cent Summary, 304–305
  Timeline, 307
  Training Tutor, 177, 225
  What Happens Next?, 258
  Word Cloud, 306
 positive interdependence, 222–223
 research findings, 218, 222, 223
 teaching others, 224
  helper therapy principle, 224, 226
 toolbox training, 225
 virtual, 220–221, 319–322, 325–328
Ten-Cent Summary, 304–305
Testing effect, 154, 157, 203
The Art and Science of Training (E. Biech), 191–192
The Back of the Napkin, 347
The NPD Group, 229–230
Timeline, 307
Toolbox talks or huddles, 125–126. *See also*: Teamwork, toolbox training
Trainee
 attention, 4–5, 11–13, 51–52, 64, 85,

100–101, 103–105, 109–111, 135, 141, 209–210, 226, 229, 230, 249, 322, 330, 334, 354
- at beginning of class, 109–110, 144, 322
- emotional significance, 4–5, 11–12, 100–101, 143, 149, 201
- link to existing memory, 5, 160

capabilities, 60–61
confidence, 213–214
engagement, 3, 185, 230, 248, 318–328
interviews, 8, 89
motivation, 44, 92–93, 95, 103–105
- lack of, 3, 329
- posttraining, 117
- pretraining, 117
- principles, 104

participation, 12, 104
peer support, 108–109, 223–224
perception barriers, 42–43
pressure from coworkers, 42, 43
recognition, 54, 86
responsibilities, 7, 83, 91, 97, 236
surveys, 8, 118

Trainer
- as facilitator, 83, 95, 104, 111, 200, 220, 230–231, 234
- credibility, 45
- modeling learning behavior, 122, 328
- perception barriers, 42
- questions to ask, 61–63, 87–88
- responsibilities, 7, 12, 43, 53, 124, 214
- subject matter expertise, 21, 47

Training, *see also*: Safety training
- aids, 140, 146, 188, 254
  - checklists, 188, 254
  - videos, 188
- assessment, 53, 63–66. *See also*: Safety training, tests
- content, 52
- culture improvement, 60–63
- defined, 3
- design, 53, 65–66, 181, 248
- feedback, 52, 60, 85, 86, 143, 154, 161, 172, 327–328

- natural group, 109
- objectives, 52, 54, 86, 90, 120–121
- retention, 53, 64–66, 72, 74, 84, 99, 111, 118, 153–155, 158, 162–163, 165, 181, 185, 194, 199–204, 229–230, 253, 263, 270, 272, 330, 334, 335, 359–366. *See also*: Online learning
  - adding difficulty, 272
  - defined, 3
  - emotional involvement and personal connections, 263, 264
  - lack of, 17–18
  - measuring, 7–10, 204
- six supporting factors, 60–61
- transfer, 53, 59–60, 64–66, 70, 98, 111, 141, 144, 165, 181, 209, 272, 313, 315, 316–321, 324, 330, 362
  - barriers, 42–43, 54
  - defined, 4
  - delivery factors, 44–45, 65, 248
  - design factors, 44, 46, 248
  - effectiveness, 53–54
  - error-based examples, 257
  - far, 6, 44
  - learner characteristics, 44, 247–248
  - measuring, 7–9, 21–22, 27, 204
  - near, 6, 43–44
  - new models for online training, 316–319
  - organizational climate factors, 44, 59, 63, 107–108, 248
  - peer support, 108–109, 223–224
  - problem, 41–42
  - removing constraints, 129–131

Training Magazine, 313
Training room, 72, 77, 110
Training Tutor, 177, 225
Transtheoretical model (TTM), 119, 124
TV show *The Office*, 260
Twitter, 147
Types of repetition and their effectiveness, 156

U

Ultralearning, 360
U.S. Department of Labor, 334

V

Virtual reality (VR), 135, 137–139
    defined, 137
    headsets, 26, 137
    mobile, in aviation industry, 235
Virtual training, 313, 314. *See also*: Online learning
Visual aids, 245, 329, 333–336, 342–344, 352. *See also*: Image-based safety training
    custom made, 336
    increased comprehension, 335
    promote retention, 335
Visualization, 5, 77, 334–335
    preattentive attributes, 335

W

Waehrer and Miller research, 18
Weber, Emma, 96–97. *See also*: ACTION conversation model
Webinar, 313
Weinbauer-Heidel, Ina, 53–54, 105
    What Makes Training Really Work: 12 Levers of Transfer Effectiveness, 105
What Happens Next?, 146–147, 200, 258
While You Were Out, 277–278
Wiki page, 323
WordArt website, 306
Word Clouds, 202, 306
Word It Out website, 306
Workplace observations, 60, 64–65, 77
WorkSafe BC hazard alerts, 141

Y

Young, Scott, 360, 362, 363
    Ultralearning, 360, 362
YouTube, 186, 251

Z

Zoom, 294, 314
    chat box, 294